The Conundrum of Mas(

CW00341219

Popular culture is awash with discussions about the difficulties associated with being a man. Television talk shows, media articles and government press releases discuss not simply the problem of men, but they have more recently focused on the problems of being a man.

The Conundrum of Masculinity challenges highly advertised beliefs that men are in crisis and struggling to hold onto traditional masculine habits whilst the world around them changes. Indeed, whilst there is a range of valuable contributions to the field that examine how men live out their lives in different contexts, there are few accounts that examine in detail the building blocks of masculinity or how men are really 'put together'. Thus, this innovative and timely volume seeks to provide a systematic exploration of the different aspects of masculinity—in particular hegemony, homosociality, homophobia and heteronormativity.

An original approach to the field of Masculinity Studies, this book ultimately presents a critical synthesis that brings together disparate approaches to provide a clear and concise discussion to address the true nature of masculinity. *The Conundrum of Masculinity* will appeal to undergraduate and postgraduate students interested in fields such as Gender Studies, Masculinity Studies and Sociology.

Chris Haywood is a Senior Lecturer and Director of Research in Media and Cultural Studies at Newcastle University, UK.

Thomas Johansson is Professor of Pedagogy with specialization in Child and Youth Studies at Gothenburg University, Sweden.

Nils Hammarén is an Associate Professor of Child and Youth Studies in the Department of Education, Communication and Learning at the University of Gothenburg, Sweden.

Marcus Herz is a Senior Lecturer and Researcher in Social Work at Malmö University, Sweden.

Andreas Ottemo is a Senior Lecturer at the Department of Education and Special Education, University of Gothenburg, Sweden.

Routledge Research in Gender and Society

For a full list of titles in this series, please visit www.routledge.com

The Conundrum of Masculinity

Hegemony, Homosociality, Homophobia and Heteronormativity

Chris Haywood, Thomas Johansson, Nils Hammarén, Marcus Herz and Andreas Ottemo

Routledge
Taylor & Francis Group

LONDON AND NEW YORK

First published 2018 by Routledge

2 Park Square, Milton Park, Abingdon, Oxfordshire OX14 4RN
52 Vanderbilt Avenue, New York, NY 10017

Routledge is an imprint of the Taylor & Francis Group, an informa business

First issued in paperback 2019

British Library Cataloguing-in-Publication Data
A catalogue record for this book is available from the British Library

Library of Congress Cataloging-in-Publication Data
A catalog record for this book has been requested

ISBN: 978-1-138-67469-1 (hbk)
ISBN: 978-0-367-87344-8 (pbk)

Typeset in Times New Roman
by Apex CoVantage, LLC

Contents

Acknowledgements

We would like to thank our colleagues in the *Masculinities in the Margins* network: Anette Hellman, Anette Hoel, Anne Dorte Christensen, Björn Haglund, Elin Kvande, Firouz Gaini, Jens Christian Nielsen, Jeppe Fuglsang Larsen, Jesper Andreasson, Mairtin Mac an Ghaill, Morten Kyed, Niels Ulrik Sørensen, Peter Håkansson, Philip Lalander, Sune Qvotrup Jensen, Xiadong Lin and Ylva Odenbring. Thank you for valuable viewpoints on many of the thoughts presented in this book and for stimulating discussions on contemporary masculinities more broadly. The present book is in many senses also closely associated with and inspired by the work with Marginalized Masculinities (Routledge, forthcoming, 2017). Thank you to Jonathan Allen and Frank Karioris for their insightful engagement with discussions on masculinity. Also thanks to Liviu Popoviciu, Catherine Walsh, Gareth Longstaff and Jhitsayarat Siripai for listening to ongoing reflection on this book. Preparing this manuscript, we also benefited from the comments received on two of the chapters (4 and 6) on the Gender and Education Biennial Conference, 2013, Compelling Diversities, Educational Intersections: Policy, Practice, Parity. Alongside this Chapter 6 benefitted from discussions at the American Men's Studies Association 2016. Chapter 7 was helped by useful discussion with colleagues in the Sociology Department at the University of Aalborg and American Men's Studies Association, 2017.

1 Introduction

Mapping the Conundrum

Introduction

Popular culture is awash with discussions about the difficulties associated with being a man. Television talk shows, magazines, editorials and government press releases discuss not simply the problems of men but also more recently the problems of *being* a man. Some media commentators have suggested that men are in crisis and are struggling to hold onto traditional modes of being a man whilst the world around them changes. Some argue that men are losing ground, with girls now achieving higher grades than boys at every stage in school, mothers establishing greater rights over their children, and claims that women in their twenties (for the first time ever) are being given a higher hourly paid wage than men. Men, it is argued, are being left behind. Not only is it claimed that women are gaining the upper hand; it seems that men are also becoming the 'new' victims in society. For example, men's eating disorders are rising faster than those found in women, men are overwhelmingly the victims of physical violence, and men are three times more likely than women to commit suicide (Braswell and Kushner, 2012).

Therefore, it is argued that men are not simply being left behind; they are also becoming weaker and more vulnerable. Not only has the media focused the spotlight on men's difficulties, but it has also begun questioning the very essence of what makes a man. The 'metrosexual', the 'menaissance man' and the 'post-sensitive man' have emerged as new gender motifs to describe new ways of being a man. Alongside this, the increasing media-led fascination with trans-gendered, intersexual and queer lives has intensified one of the most-pressing gender conundrums in contemporary society: What does it mean to be a man? In response to these media-led narratives, this book helps the reader navigate through these popular confusions and contradictions to address and explore this question. In short, the book provides a theoretically robust, empirically grounded engagement with men and masculinity to unpack the conundrum of masculinity.

It is suggested that concerns about men and masculinity, often sensationally called 'crises of masculinity', have occurred across history and have taken many forms but appear to take shape when societies undergo rapid social and economic transformations. For example, in the late nineteenth-century United States, there was much concern about men losing their masculinity as they migrated from rural to urban spaces. The rise of industrialisation and urbanisation, it was argued, meant that men were no longer in touch with their true selves. As Bailey (2007, p. 48) points out:

> The word 'masculinity' which did not enter the English language until the middle of the eighteenth century, referred to the privilege awarded to men in matters of inheritance. Manhood and 'manliness' were the terms used in the sixteenth century to connote those qualities essential to civility, which was identified teleologically as the definitive characteristic of the adult man.

Crises at the time oscillated between men being too civil and losing their basic masculine drives. In contrast, men were also seen as being too 'basic' and lacking self-control and rational action. More recently, Atkinson (2008, p. 451) has pointed out that commentators on masculinity and change

> contend that with the symbolic fracturing of family, economic, political, educational, sport-leisure, technological-scientific and media power bases, masculinity codes have been challenged within most social settings. As such, men no longer possess exclusive ownership over the social roles once held as bastions for establishing and performing hegemony.

What is interesting is that such change is read through gender, and, in the context of late modernity, we have seen gender emerging as a key cultural flashpoint. The dynamic of a flashpoint is that it operates in disparate ways at the same time. What this means is that whilst highlighting the normativity of gender relations, a cultural flashpoint simultaneously fractures and problematises taken-for-granted assumptions (Mac an Ghaill and Haywood, 2007). It is suggested that these cultural flashpoints become ways to understand the conundrums that surround men and masculinity as they shine a light on the cultural expectations that underpin gender relations.

Although commentators tend to focus on an apparent collapse triggered by women's political rights, by liberation from reproduction and by parity within the workplace (if not achieved), concern is also raised about the ways men themselves are changing. If the division between men and women is being challenged by women, it is also being challenged by men in new forms of body projects. For example, Frank (2014) discusses the emergence of 'manscaping' where men are beginning to self-fashion themselves by manipulating their bodies. One of the areas that Frank discusses is that of trimming or removal of hair. She suggests that this is a feminine practice that is highly transgressive for men and masculinity.

However, given that the exclusive resources through which men make masculinity are being reduced or removed, it is suggested that men are exploring new ways in which to recover their loss of male power. Thus, the body has become a device through which men can re-articulate their masculine status. A different response to the crisis of masculinity might be to reconstruct the body in a way that evidences itself as masculine. As social and cultural markers of masculinity become blurred through transformations in areas such as work, family, and politics, men are seeking alternative ways to establish ontological certainty of their identities. Therefore as resources of masculinity become less accessible, men are drawing upon a range of different resources through which to make their identities. Whereas the crisis of masculinity has been premised on the lack of access to traditional masculine resources, it is suggested that there has been a discernible shift in the resources from that of production to that of consumption. Alexander (2003, p. 535) suggests that as social structures are transforming, 'consumption becomes more important than production.'

A similar argument exists around the phenomenon of 'laddism'. As a contemporary form of masculinity, 'laddism' in the UK has been seen as a backlash response to Feminism and has been viewed as a 'reclamation of patriarchal masculinities' (Rizos, 2012, p. 40). It is not entirely clear how 'laddism' became identified as a new trope of masculinity, but commentators agree that in many ways it was a response to the predominance of the new Feminist-friendly and equality-committed representations of men from the 1980s (Carrington, 1998; Gill, 2003). The emergence of the 'New Lads' has often been linked to the rise of the men's magazines *Loaded* and *FHM*; the 'New Lads' have been described as unreconstructed men who recognise the values of equality but would align themselves to practices that were antithetical to those values, such as objectification of women's bodies. Unlike traditional masculine practices that involved homophobia, misogyny, and racism, it is suggested that 'lads' appreciate and recognise the harm of such practices and representations and therefore attempt to reposition themselves to consume the fantasies, without activating the politics. Or as Benwell (2003, p. 152) suggests, 'laddism' is a 'cheeky knowingness and self-reflexiveness (commonly glossed as irony), which enables it to simultaneously affirm and deny its values. . . . It allows a writer to articulate an anti-Feminist sentiment, whilst explicitly distancing himself from it, thus disclaiming responsibility from or even authentic authorship of it.' One of the strategies to regain power has been to adopt a marginal position in which white heterosexual men draw upon their victim status in order to re-articulate their power and control. In many ways, for Brayton (2007), men can hold onto their victim status and their articulation of masculine traits at the same time. Thus, through the victimisation and shaming of men to reach idealised (hegemonic) versions of masculinity, those idealisations remain intact: 'An ironic white masculinity is produced, one that is self-marginalizing and therefore implausibly victimized' (p. 69). However, an example of the conundrum of masculinity surrounds how young women are also involved in 'laddish' behaviours. Dobson (2014) highlights, in her work on young women's social media, how they are representing themselves in ways that would be deemed traditionally unfeminine. Dobson argues that women are subverting the traditional binaries that underpin masculinity and femininity, and thus introduces a notion of gendered flexibility. It is suggested that masculinity is characterised by its flexibility, which can be taken on by men, women, transgender and intersex individuals. This constitutes a further element of the conundrum—masculinity is not something that is always performed by men; it is also something that men do not have to do. The fluidity of the concept of masculinity, the idea that it is both present and immediately absent and thus is in constant need to re-make and establish itself, is a particular tension embedded in men's lived experience.

Although there are a number of texts in the field that provide excellent overviews of the study of men and masculinity, currently what is missing is a systematic exploration of the different aspects of masculinity. In other words, there are a range of valuable contributions to the field that examine how men live out their lives in different contexts. However, there are few accounts that examine in detail the building blocks of masculinity or how men are 'put together'. This book unpacks the conundrum of masculinity by engaging with how masculinity is made up. It achieves this in two unique ways.

First, the book offers a comprehensive, up-to-date renewal of the key concepts that underpin approaches to masculinity. The book explores four different concepts that can help to explore what we understand as men and masculinity: hegemony, homosociality, homophobia and heteronormativity. The book explores these concepts in order to lay bare what makes masculinity. Thus, the book places at its centre a more complex analysis of power that allows an inter-relation between the social, cultural and inter-personal. It does this by locating masculinity as part of structures of inequality such as class, 'race'/ethnicity, age, and sexuality, whilst at the same time acknowledging the fluidity and the malleability of gender. It is within this tension between the structural and cultural, and how it is lived out within both men's emotional histories and their future aspirations, that we unpack men's behaviours and what masculinity means.

Second, this renewal of the key concepts signals a shift towards an understanding of masculinity as a process that moves from a focus on individuals and/or local contexts towards an understanding of the relationships that connect individuals and contexts. It has been suggested that these connections are often characterised by the dependence on, or the collapse of, differences between other men and women. For example, it is often argued that heterosexual masculinity is established through an 'Othering' of that deemed less authentically masculine such as gay-identifying men. At the same time, there is an emerging approach that argues sexual difference is becoming less important and that men are now accommodating homosexuality as part of their masculinities. In these accounts, it is sameness with other men and women which forms the basis of men's identities. In response, the book suggests that in order to understand the nature of men's behaviours and identities, we need to understand sameness and difference as fluid, fragmented and passing (dis)connections that are contextually contingent. This shifts the focus of the book towards the processual nature of masculinity, to explore their practices and the meanings attached to those practices rather than simply trying to locate men within gendered dualities.

The Conundrum of Masculinity takes an original approach to masculinity by attempting a critical synthesis that brings together a number of different concepts, providing a clear and concise discussion to address the question of what masculinity is. Central to the study of masculinity are tensions between the changes and fluidity of masculinity and static positions of power. It is important that this complex and multifaceted area of study is clearly unpacked and systematically examined.

Aims of the Book

Theoretically, this book builds upon the differing approaches outlined above, to explore the problematic, negotiated, and contested nature of masculinity and the range of ways that it is understood at individual, organisational, cultural and societal levels. It has a number of interrelated aims in providing up-to-date accounts of research and writing on men and masculinity across a number of different social and cultural arenas. The aims are developed in the context of making explicit an extended evaluation of how we understand and unpack the conundrum of masculinity.

1. It explores the popular cultural juxtapositions between older and more traditional masculinities that are often characterised by anti-Feminism, emotional stoicism and misogyny (Wade and Couglin, 2012), with 'softer' versions of masculinity currently framed through notions of metrosexuality, inclusive masculinities and post-masculinity frameworks. The book will critically explore these different characterisations to address current popular confusions about what masculinity is.
2. The book also aims to produce a synthesis which acknowledges structural differences as accounted for in earlier Feminist writings that focus upon patriarchal relations, while incorporating insights from more recent reflection on representation, identity and cultural difference with reference to men's contemporary social experiences. Tracing a shift from earlier mono-causal models of power to more inclusive forms of power, the book explores the interplay and intersection between different social divisions and cultural differences—including sexuality, class, ethnicity and generation.
3. The book provides an understanding of masculinity that recognises the importance of wider social and cultural transformations that are characteristic of late modernity. The book uses four key concepts that are used to engage with masculinity, namely, hegemony, homosociality, homophobia and heteronormativity. Such concepts operate as devices to explore how men and masculinity can be understood historically and transnationally within different social, cultural and economic contexts.

Chapter Synopsis

Chapter 1 introduces the reader to the importance of exploring masculinity, drawing from several examples from popular culture to underline the contradictory and confusing stories being told about men. It highlights the importance of a book that not only provides a way of making sense of men and masculinity but also connects theory up to specific practices. The chapter then provides a brief overview of the aims of the book and its rationale. It then situates the study of masculinity within the political context of social policy and academia. The chapter finally provides a short summary of the subsequent chapters and their key themes and contexts.

In Chapter 2, a brief historical overview of the different approaches that have underpinned Masculinity Studies establishes the various models that have been employed to capture the nature of men's lives. Importantly, the chapter engages with the notion of 'cultural epistemology', the evidential framework that is used to explain men's attitudes and behaviours. One of the themes to emerge from this discussion is to recognise how masculine subjectivities are subject to the structural reproduction of gendered inequality, oppression and sexual violence. At the same time, the chapter also highlights how masculinities are also contextually driven. However, rather than simply repeat existing commentary in the field, the chapter opens up the discussion to explore how masculinity is constituted, drawing upon Queer Theory and Trans Studies.

Building on the previous chapter's exploration of the field and the theories and concepts that have been central to it, the four chapters that follow explore in more detail the particularly important concepts of the four 'Hs': hegemonic masculinity, homosociality, homophobia and heteronormativity. In Chapter 3 ('Hegemonic Masculinity: Stability, Change and Transformation'), the challenge of thinking about transformations of hegemonic masculinity, and the moving in-between of stability and change, takes centre stage. Central to the discussion are different ways of conceptualising and theorising power. Traditionally, power and power relations have often been understood as macro-phenomena, underpinning and stabilising such 'immobile' structures as patriarchy. This chapter investigates how different relationships between men and men and between men and women, according to Connell (1995), form an intrinsic part of the patriarchal order, through the notion of hegemonic masculinity. It points out that an important aspect of the concept of hegemony is that it never means total power and control but instead points at a balance of forces and is to be understood as a response to, and consequence of, a continuous and ongoing struggle for power. This chapter submits to the view that hegemony is an important analytical concept when trying to understand the connection between masculinity and power. However, it also pushes the concept of hegemonic masculinity to its limits in suggesting that an analytical decoupling between hegemony and masculinity is warranted. The overarching argument is that such a decoupling could enable masculinity researchers to better grapple with transformations within hegemonic masculinity. It would also enable one to recognise the utopian potentials of change and not only respond to change as reconfigurations of a hegemonic masculinity understood basically as the equivalent of continuing patriarchy. The chapter uses empirical research based upon changing understandings of fatherhood and how fatherhood is being practised by what is sometimes referred to as 'new fathers'. The conceptual and theoretical development proposed builds on Paul Ricoeur's work on ideology and utopia and Laclau and Mouffe's theorising of hegemony. Through this, the chapter aims at opening up new ways of analysing gender, power and masculine subjectivity.

The concept of *homosociality* describes and defines social bonds between persons of the same sex. It is, for example, frequently used in studies on men and masculinities, there defined as a mechanism and social dynamic that explains the maintenance of hegemonic masculinity. A popular use of the concept is found in studies on male friendship, male bonding and fraternity orders. It is also frequently applied to explain how men, through their friendships and intimate collaborations with other men, maintain and defend the gender order and patriarchy (Lipman-Blumen, 1992; Bird, 1996). However, this common and somewhat over-exploited use of the concept—referring to how men, through their relations to other men, uphold patriarchy—tends to simplify and reduce homosociality to an almost descriptive term that is used to show how men bond, build closed teams, and defend their privileges and positions. In contrast to this, Chapter 4 ('Homosociality: Misogyny, Fraternity and New Intimacies') investigates, explores and discusses the concept of homosociality, especially male homosocial relations, in a more multifaceted way. Through a reading of contemporary literature across the world, our aim is to explore and problematise the use of homosociality in studies of gender and masculinity. We will highlight different empirical examples of homosocial relations, in both the available research and popular culture, as well as explore different aspects of homosociality, looking at how these characteristics relate to each other and what implications they might have for gender issues. In this chapter we are especially interested in developing and emphasising the contradictory and ambivalent aspects of the concept, pointing both towards a defence of hegemonic masculinity and towards a silent and slow process that might undermine or reconstruct this power structure, as it appears today.

Chapters 3 to 6 explore the different processes involved in the formation of masculine subjectivities. One characteristic of these processes is a notion of 'Otherness'. In particular, we highlight how heterosexual men tend to construct their identities through the distancing of themselves from what is deemed to be feminine. We have already seen how hegemonic masculinities secure their dominance through the use of homophobia. However, in this next chapter we explore the relationship between masculinity and homophobia in more detail, to examine how it operates to consolidate particular masculine styles and its centrality to gendered power relations, policing what are acceptable and unacceptable attitudes and behaviours. Chapter 5 ('Homophobia, "Otherness" and Inclusivity') begins by exploring the claim that homophobia is made up of two elements. First, it is argued that homophobia is often constituted by a 'fear' or 'hatred' of homosexual acts, behaviours and identities. This also connects to the claim that straight men also fear the prospect of other straight men thinking that they are not straight. The second element of homophobia is that it is premised on interactions with the emotional response to homosexuality, represented in a number of different ways. For example, in the field of social psychology, researchers have explored how homophobia can be internalised. As a result, individuals direct their own fear and loathing of homosexuality in on themselves. Such negative perceptions often result in physical, psychological and emotional damage. At the same time, homophobia has been considered as something that is applied to and used against individuals, groups, cultures, religions or even nations.

However, a closer look at the relationship between masculinity and homophobia reveals a more complex picture. Rather than thinking of masculinity as being formed through relationships of opposition, Anderson (2009) usefully argues that we need to rethink the internal constituents of masculinity itself. This means that masculinity and homophobia can be viewed as conceptually discrete. In other words, heterosexual masculinities can be constituted without relying on homophobia as a constituent factor. However, Bridges (2014) suggests that the reconstruction of masculine subjectivities could be understood as a characteristic of a privilege afforded by groups of white heterosexual men. More specifically, Bridges highlights how men who take on gay aesthetics to distance themselves from a traditional stereotypical masculinity may not necessarily experience a lessening sexual or gendered inequality. This chapter examines these arguments and draws upon interviews with men from a wide range of contexts—including education, leisure and work—to highlight the meanings and experience of using and being subject to homophobia.

In Chapter 6 ('Heteronormativity, Intimacy and the Erotic') we discuss the concept of heteronormativity. Although heteronormativity theoretically focuses on and problematises the dominant position of heterosexuality in society, it sometimes seems to create a certain confusion when applied to an individual's life and choices. One such example is the recently developed notion of the so-called *new homonormativity*. This concept is used and applied as a critique of tendencies among homosexuals to privilege consumption, privacy and domesticity over far-reaching social and cultural change (Duggan, 2003; Rosenfeld, 2009). Although theories of heteronormativity often stay at a societal level or focus on how heterosexual norms tend to affect and to some extent perhaps even control all of us, the concept is sometimes used as fuel for criticising the lives of both homosexual and heterosexual families that do not diverge from what is perceived to be a 'heterosexual way of life'. The aim of the chapter is to analyse and critically examine the *use* of the concept of heteronormativity. Although we find the concept very useful, it also seems important to appropriate and adjust it to some extent in order to analyse, for example, the changes occurring in homosexual families, contemporary gender-equal families or the progressive youth culture. For instance, the more general normalising process in question does not apply to and affect all heterosexuals/homosexuals and married couples in the same way. In this chapter we discuss the following questions: What power structures and forms of relations are commonly investigated and criticised under the heading of heteronormativity? And how could it be possible to both visualise and change repressive heterosexuality without repressing possible changes that might occur among different families?

The penultimate chapter, Chapter 7 ('Post-masculinity: Thinking Over the Limits of Masculinity'), explores the emerging ways in which we are beginning to think about men and masculinity. Research in the field implicitly accepts that, when discussing men, we are automatically involved in the discussion of masculinity. This chapter begins to unpack this claim by questioning whether masculinity can exist without sex or whether gender (sex) can exist without masculinity. As Floyd (2011, p. 46) suggests:

> It is one thing to deconstruct or defamiliarize masculinity in some new way or to insist that, ultimately, there is no such thing as masculinity in the singular but only a dizzying range of masculinities in the plural, as so much scholarship has done so powerfully for so long now. But it seems quite another thing to push the conceptual limits of masculinity studies itself, to try to think an outside to masculinity that does not immediately and predictably reveal itself to be femininity.

In the context of studying men, there is currently a compunction that male subjectivities and practices *have* to be explained by a concept of masculinity. The consequence of resisting the regulatory regime of dyadic gender theory is that a move beyond 'masculinity' as a conceptual and empirical default position is required. One common theme that frames this question is that men's lives might not be understood through particular masculinities and that other social categories and their intersections might be useful ways through which to understand men. As a consequence, male behaviours, attitudes and practices can no longer be simple indicators of masculinity (or even gender). This resonates with Post-structural readings of representation that question the presumption of self-evident and fixed meaning.

The chapter explores a number of popular cultural representations that help 'queer' masculinity to such an extent that we begin to re-evaluate what being a man means. Representations of schooling, comedy and dating provide a number of cultural motifs that expose the limits of masculinity. For example, the status of boyhood highlights the difficulties of equating a masculinity with a male body. Contemporary culture is awash with concerns about boys and boyhood. For example, in the UK, concerns over boys' underachievement in education highlight how culturally precious boys have become. Noble (2006) has argued that boys are coming to be understood as males without masculinity, including a lack of heteronormativity that often constitutes masculinities. Therefore, boys participate in a cultural refusal as part of a broader resistive moment to adult masculinity and its attendant symbolic weight and cultural expectation. It is therefore suggested that social and cultural notions of masculinity are premised on both rejecting and affirming values associated with 'boyness'. The chapter ends with a consideration of the importance of Queer Theory and Trans Theory to explore the possibilities of making sense of subjectivities and practices outside of (institutional) systems of meaning.

In the final chapter ('Conclusion: Conundrums and Concepts') we focus on questions such as: What is the meaning of masculinity? What ideologies have shaped the political debates of the past? What can we learn from minority and cross-cultural masculine subjectivities? What kinds of futures are possible for men and women? In addressing these questions, the concluding chapter brings together the inter-related aspects of *The Conundrum of Masculinity: Hegemony, Homosociality, Homophobia and Heteronormativity*. The main concepts presented throughout the book are drawn together, exploring continuities and discontinuities in the interplay of contemporary social and cultural transformations, with shifting ideologies, discourses and representations of men and masculinity. We hope that this results in a clearer picture of the major ways in which theorists have tried to make sense of the complex relationship between notions of sex, masculinity and sexuality. In turn, we also hope that this results in elucidating some of the crucial questions and tensions that need to be addressed by future research on masculinity at local and global levels.

Conclusion

As indicated above, each of the chapters addresses a number of the key concepts that have been used to explain men and masculinity. These chapters explore the concept and then push the limits of those concepts in a way that results in the revision and reconstruction of the concepts. This book does not reject concepts of hegemony, homophobia, homosociality and heteronormativity; rather, it argues that there is much analytical purchase in using these concepts to examine men and masculinity. But it also suggests how we can gain a greater understanding through a number of adjustments to the internal logics of the concepts. The book also recognises that there may be contexts in which the scope of existing concepts may be limited. A focus on post-masculinity disentangles gender from masculinity to open the possibilities of male subjectivity that may not be explainable by masculinity itself. In short, the chapter pushes masculinity to its edges and considers whether it is the concept of masculinity itself that creates conundrums.

As authors of this book, our primary commitment has been to try to theoretically, conceptually and analytically 'get at' masculinity. Although slippage, tensions and contradictions may appear across the chapters, we engage with theories of masculinity through an inclusive approach. We recognise and agree that at different moments some concepts may be more appropriate than others, and we refrain from advocating an overarching explanatory framework. Instead, we hope that *The Conundrum of Masculinity* is used as a toolbox where different concepts can be employed to explain different aspects of men's lives. As a result, we hope that the book can be used to gain better insights and understandings and, in turn, better explanations for the confusions, the riddles and the conundrums that underpin men and masculinity.

References

Alexander, S. M. (2003). Stylish hard bodies: Branded masculinity in Men's Health magazine. *Sociological Perspectives,* 46(4), 535–554.

Anderson, E. (2009) *Inclusive Masculinity: The Changing Nature of Masculinities.* New York: Routledge.

Atkinson, M. (2008) Exploring male femininity in the 'crisis': Men and cosmetic surgery. *Body & Society,* 14(1), 67–87.

Bailey, A. (2007) *Flaunting: Style and the Subversive Male Body in Renaissance England.* Toronto: University of Toronto Press.

Benwell, B. (2003) Is there anything 'New' about these lads? The textual and visual construction of masculinity in men's magazines. In: Litosseliti, L. and Sunderland, J. eds. *Gender Identity and Discourse Analysis.* Amsterdam: John Benjamin Amsterdam, pp. 149–174.

Bird, S.R. (1996) Welcome to the men's club: Homosociality and the maintenance of hegemonic masculinity. *Gender & Society*, 10(2), 120–132.

Braswell, H. and Kushner, H.I. (2012) Suicide, social integration, and masculinity in the US military. *Social Science and Medicine*, 74, 530–536.

Brayton, S. (2007) MTV's *Jackass*: Transgression, abjection and the economy of white masculinity. *Journal of Gender Studies*, 16(1), 57–72.

Bridges, T. (2014) A very "gay" straight?: Hybrid masculinities, sexual aesthetics, and the changing relationship between masculinity and homophobia. *Gender & Society*, 28(1), 58–82.

Carrington, B. (1998) Sport, masculinity and black cultural resistance. *Journal of Sport and Social Issues*, 22, 275–298.

Connell, R.W. (1995) *Masculinities.* Cambridge: Polity Press.Coughlin, P. and Wade, J.C. (2012) Masculinity ideology, income disparity, and romantic relationship quality among men with higher earning female partners. *Sex Roles*, 67(5), 311–322.

Dobson, A.S. (2014) Laddishness online: The possible significations and significance of 'performative shamelessness' for young women in the post-feminist context. *Cultural Studies*, 28(1), 142–164.

Duggan, L. (2003) *The Twilight of Equality? Neoliberalism, Cultural Politics, and the Attack on Democracy.* New York: Beacon.

Floyd, K. (2011) Masculinity inside/ out: The biopolitical lessons of transgender and inter-sex studies. In: Horlacher, S. ed. *Constructions of Masculinity in British Literature From the Middle Ages to the Present.* New York: Palgrave Macmillan, pp. 33–51.

Frank, E. (2014) Groomers and consumers: The meaning of male body depilation to a modern masculinity body project. *Men and Masculinities*, 17(3), 278–298.

Gill, R. (2003) Power and the production of subjects: A genealogy of the new man and the new lad. In: Benwell, B. ed. *Masculinity and Men's Lifestyle Magazines.* Oxford: Black-well/Sociological Review, pp. 34–56.

Lipman-Blumen, J. (1992) Connective leadership: Female leadership styles in the 21st century workplace. *Sociological Perspectives*, 35(1), 183–203.

Mac an Ghaill, M. and Haywood, C. (2007) *Gender, Culture and Society: Contemporary Femininities and Masculinities.* Basingstoke: Palgrave Macmillan.

Noble, B. (2006) *Sons of the Movement: FtMs Risking Incoherence on a Post-queer Cultural Landscape.* Toronto: Canadian Scholars Press.

Rizos, D. (2012) Lad magazines, raunch culture and the pornification of South African media. *Agenda*, 26(3), 38–49.

Rosenfeld, D. (2009) Heteronormativity and homonormativity as practical and moral resources: The case of Lesbian and Gay Elders. *Gender & Society*, 23(5), 617–638.

2   Approaching Men and Masculinities

Introduction

Towards the end of the twentieth century, a number of gender commentators began to signal a change in the nature of gender relations. It was suggested that men were being disempowered through a number of social, cultural and economic transformations. Traditional work in Western societies was being replaced by increasing service sector employment. Alongside this, the collapse of the traditional heterosexual marriage also fractured older forms of heterosexual masculinities, whose reputation and status were informed by monogamous heterosexual familialism. Furthermore, men's political and civil rights were eroded because of the emergence of Feminist, Lesbian and Gay activists and the broader civil rights movements (Brayton, 2007). Such movements, it has been argued, challenged traditional heterosexual men and their claims to privilege, dominance and the control of others. In response to this lost ground, it is suggested that men have responded to these changes in different ways, primarily through the recuperation of their claims to dominance through a range of different strategies. The notion of crisis has been criticised in that it fails to recognise that such changes only affect certain groups of men, namely working-class men (Jamieson, 2013), and that men remain powerful as existing gendered inequalities remain and high levels of male violence against women continue. Despite this, there is much anxiety about men's roles in the family, failing boys in school, etc., and numerous media commentators, self-help books and therapy books try to establish how we can solve the problem of men.

If popular accounts of men and masculinity offer a range of confusing and contradictory understandings of what it means to be a man, then academic and policy-led research are also marked by contradictions and uncertainty. Established Gender Studies have been suspicious of a Men's Studies or Critical Masculinity Studies approach, and it is only during the last decade that introductory books to the field include men as an area of critical inquiry. Often, studies of men and masculinity are crudely positioned against Women's Studies or even thought of as part of an anti-Feminist project. However, as Michael Kimmel (2002, p. ix) pointed out fifteen years ago: 'Masculinity studies is not necessarily the reactionary defensive rage of the men's rights groups, the mythic cross-cultural nostalgia of mythopoetry, nor even the theologically informed nostalgic yearning for separate spheres of promise keepers.' In fact Kimmel suggested that Masculinity Studies could support and further the political aims of Feminist approaches, something which is very present in contemporary critical studies on men and masculinities.

The difficulty with studies of men and masculinity is that there is no coherent body of work or theoretical approach that can be identified as 'Masculinity Studies' or 'Men's Studies'. Rather, the term has been used to coalesce a wide range of diverse and sometimes contradictory philosophical, disciplinary, political and methodological positions. For example, the study of masculinity can be found in Sex Role theory, film studies, Post-structuralism, Marxism, Queer Theory, historical studies, Symbolic Interactionism, educational theory, literary studies or Feminism (Gottzén and Mellström, 2014). However, the diversity of these approaches provides a wide range of tools with which we can analyse systematically and document coherently the intersection of different forms of power, stratification, desire and subjective identity formation.

Part of the issue when exploring masculinity is trying to understand that which is a familiar part of everyday life—thus: 'What we are struggling with in understanding are not the literal words or sentences, nor some simple logical relationships, but the entrenched concepts, presuppositions, and standards which must be teased to the surface and patiently uncovered' (D'amico, 1989, p. xiii). We understand this struggle as part of a politics of intelligibility that impacts upon and shapes the arrangement of meanings and the formation of knowledge. It is political in a figurative sense, in that ways of thinking and feeling demarcate how masculinity is understood and how it is often manifested in gendered representations. This nominalistic approach to masculinity helps us to understand how assumptions about knowledge are linked in a number of different ways. Thus, in this sense, it is 'the frame of intelligibility that determines the regime of signification and the ensuing "representation" of the real' (Zavarzadeh, 1991, p. 120). Rodriguez (2011) suggests that a politics of intelligibility ensures the opening up and challenging of that which is taken for granted. It is argued here that a politics of intelligibility is intricately connected, is made possible by, and is informed through what we are calling cultural epistemologies. Thus, embedded in intelligibility is the unintelligible, that which does not make sense, that which confuses, and in this way unintelligibility becomes the basis of the conundrum.

The Conundrum: Cultural Epistemologies of Masculinity

The starting point for this book is an explication of contemporary culture's cultural epistemology; we want to explore the theories that enable us but also limit us, in what we are able to know about masculinity. It is important to understand that cultural epistemologies are constituted in specific temporal and spatial moments where 'the shapes of knowledge are ineluctably local, indivisible from their instruments and encasements' (Geertz, 1983, p. 4). It is suggested that current concerns about masculinity are a response to both the changing nature of cultural epistemologies and how the internal logic of an epistemology is manifest in attitudes, experiences, practices and behaviours. Cultural epistemology refers to the diverse range of theories of knowledge that circulate in different historical contexts within particular cultural milieus. Such epistemologies are never fixed but are subject to ongoing transformation, and as such there may be multiple and competing epistemologies operating at one time (Foucault, 1972). As Goetz et al. (2008, p. 517) suggest:

> These beliefs about the world and the nature of knowledge influence attention processes (Masuda and Nisbett, 2001), causal attribution (Choi et al., 1999), the resolution of social contradictions (Peng and Nisbett, 1999), and contradictory self-views.
>
> (Spencer-Rodgers et al., 2004; Chen et al., 2006)

It is argued that conundrums about masculinity arise when there is a clash between cultural epistemologies. Although appearing quite abstract, this can often be seen in very mundane and practical events, for example, around arguments about the best teaching practices for boys. At such instances, there is, for example, a tension on how to understand and best respond to boys underachieving in school. Some claim it is the result of a '*feeling*-centred' school, not customary to boys, while others lean towards an explanation in which boys are socialised into not performing well at school.

At other times, we see knowledge that underpins masculinity fail to explain phenomena. For example, common sense may suggest that masculinity is linked to male bodies and femininity to female bodies. Transgender communities who queer gender roles and their associated symbolic codes challenge not only the linearity of gender in the common sense but also scientific approaches. Crucially, it is not the simple application of these epistemologies to a 'real' phenomenon; rather, it is the application of the epistemology that produces such phenomena. In other words, the frameworks that we use to understand masculinity in themselves become performative of masculinity itself (Butler, 2004).

It is argued that understandings of men and masculinity are not simply about the meaning system out of which our knowledge unfolds, but rather that such meaning systems contain a number of iterative regularities. These regularities refer to the epistemic arrangements of the epoch and how these arrangements are lived out at global, national and local levels. The argument follows that history has enabled the possibilities for the concept of masculinity to emerge and construct culturally located truths about men and masculinity. Therefore, such truths about men and masculinity are not something that are objectively measurable, but rather they are created through the very cultural epistemologies that make them available. This position is indebted to Foucault's perspective: 'Everybody both acts and thinks. The way people act or react is linked to a way of thinking, and of course thinking is related to tradition' (Foucault in Martin, 1988, p. 14). The possibilities of knowing according to Foucault are historically located processes of intelligibility that are constituted by the temporally focussed episteme:

> By episteme we mean (. . .) the total set of relations that unite, at a given period, the discursive practices that give rise to epistemological figures, sciences, and possibly formalised systems. (. . .) [T]he episteme is not a form

of knowledge or type of rationality which, crossing the boundaries of the most varied sciences, manifests the sovereign unity of a subject, a spirit, or a period; it is the totality of relations which can be discovered, for a given period, between the sciences when one analyses them at the level of discursive regularities.

(Foucault, 1972, p. 191)

The episteme is the temporally located ordering of things where understandings comply with a particular knowledge. This historical reading of the constitution of thinking posits that the rules of knowing are historically situated and thus impact upon the possibilities of social and cultural thought. Thus, ways of knowing are constituted by specific regulations that correspond to a particular episteme. In this way the episteme provides the template that manipulates what we are able to know and how we are able to know it. As a result, the episteme designates and deploys the possible semiologies and potential semantic relationships between object and representation.

The complexity that surrounds masculinity is often a consequence of the multiple ways in which it is used to explain and understand men's and women's attitudes and behaviours. The study of men is nothing new—as men are routinely placed at the centre of social, economic, and cultural worlds, and by understanding how men think and behave, we have a window into those social worlds. However, men as a gendered phenomenon often goes unnoticed as discussions *about* men tend not to recognise men *as* men. A recent example of this can be found in media reports of shootings taking place in schools across the world. Although the majority of such crimes are undertaken by young men, the gendered nature of these crimes remains invisible and unspoken. Klein and Chancer (2000) highlight that the main narratives surrounding such crimes focus on gun control, exposure to violent media and family backgrounds.

In contrast, crimes committed by women are reducible to not only social deviancy but also their femininities. As such, the institutional and cultural production of men's gendered meanings, emotions and practices often goes unnoticed and often results in hidden and insidious articulations of power. The issue here is that the (in)visibility of men and the socially constructed nature of masculinity reduce men's emotions, meanings and practices to being unproblematic and self-evident. Confusion emerges when that which is deemed self-evident within a broader cultural epistemology no longer makes sense. In response, physical and social scientists alike, social commentators, and the popular media draw upon a number of evidential frameworks to explain men's practices.

Physiology, Evolution and the Return of the 'Real Man'

One of the most pervasive understandings of being male is that it is often reducible to notions of biology, physiology and, more recently, genetics. More specifically, masculinity has been understood as a consequence of a number of underlying biological processes. This means that bodies, practices and attitudes become, in some way, ontologically connected to the biological infrastructure of a sexually dimorphic type of maleness. An interesting example of this can be found in Jia et al.'s (2014) research on men's faces and financial misreporting. In this research, the authors claim that the facial structure (facial width to height ratio, or fWHR) is associated with a number of different (masculine) behaviours such as 'egocentrism, risk seeking, and a desire to maintain social status' (n.p.). Although the authors remain cautious about the relationship between physiology and individual behaviours, they do however suggest that face shape is influenced by neo-natal distribution of testosterone. Although the exact mechanisms of this distribution are not known, the face has emerged as an important biological indicator of masculinity. Therefore, it is argued that the face in this research is able to be used as a cipher for masculinity and that this can help to understand financial misreporting.

In Jia et al.'s study, the face and masculinity become synonymous, meaning that the face *is* masculinity. Using pictures of 1,136 CEOs from companies in 2009, they measured the fWHR. They found that misreporting of financial accounts is 98% higher for men with an above-media fWHR. Thus, men who have more masculinity are more likely to commit financial misreporting. Other work has suggested that levels of fighting success can be gauged from looking at the face, such as that of Tsujimura and Banissy (2013), who measured the baseball performance and fWHR in Japanese professional baseball players. They found that fWHR had a significant impact on run performance. As a result, fWHR tends to reference levels of testosterone, and these are linked to more masculine behaviours such as aggression, dominance, competitiveness and sexual competence. Others, however, have questioned the validity of the fWHR and instead suggested that a more accurate indicator of masculinity is to look at body size (Deaner et al., 2012; Kramer, 2015). Rather than body size, others have suggested that finger length is indicative of levels of masculinity. It has been suggested that when a man's ring finger is longer than his index finger this is a consequence of exposure to pre-natal testosterone or androgens. Bailey and Hurd (2005), for example, found that more difference between the lengths of the fingers indicated more aggressive traits within men.

Alongside this, there is the assumption that higher 'levels of masculinity' result in a particular form of sexual orientation. For men, the lack of exposure to pre-natal testosterones or androgens results in increased homosexual tendencies. For example, Lippa (2006) researched a sample of over 2,000 men and found that the men had lower 2D:4D finger ratios than women; 2D and 4D refer to the second digit (index finger) and the fourth digit (often referred to as the ring finger). Furthermore, men who identified as heterosexual had a lower ratio than those men who self-identified as homosexual. Writing in *Nature*, Williams et al. (2000) reported that women who have been exposed to more pre-natal androgens, and exhibit a particular finger-length ratio, are more likely to be homosexual. Here it appears that there are links between the higher levels of testosterone or androgens and a greater desire for women. Therefore, masculinity in contemporary research appears to operate simultaneously as a code for levels of heterosexuality. Therefore, from this perspective, those who are closer to maleness contain higher levels of masculinity with the attendant biologically driven desire for women. This then feeds into cultural representations of camp and effeminate men being less likely to be attracted to females. On the same continuum, women with high levels of masculinity are themselves prone to desire female bodies, while women who have lower levels of masculinity are more likely to be attracted to male bodies.

This approach to men and masculinity pervades a number of cultural epistemologies and it is essential for a politics of (un)intelligibility. For example, when men transgress legal and moral laws, the unintelligible becomes explained by this physiological approach. There are, though, other implications of this approach. For example, by locating masculinity as tangible, we can physically measure it. This means that the levels of masculinity can be identified as a quantitative feature, and some can have more or less masculinity than others. Although in the studies above, this can also be a key element of psychological approaches to explaining men's behaviours. Underpinning this approach is an ontology of foundationalism: a philosophical position that insists that masculinity can exist outside of history. In this sense, masculinity should speak on its own terms irrespective of who the audience is. Alongside this, masculinity is deemed to be a natural trait in males and one that society can distort and pervert. Thus, men need to stay in touch with their real selves.

Sex Role Theory: Too Much or Not Enough Masculinity?

Through socialisation, Sex Role theorists argue, males and females are conditioned into appropriate roles of behaviour. Polarised norms and expectations between genders are central to such definitions of masculinity. According to Pleck (1981), living up to a gender role is more problematic for boys because of the weight of social expectations that males experience. In particular, expectations of strength, power and sexual competence form the basis of male roles. Boys, he argues, are likely to experience failure because of the contradiction between the ideal 'role' and the lived experience. However, unlike cultural epistemologies that are based upon physiology, Sex Role theories suggest a certain 'plasticity' of gender. For example, Bluck's (2012) work indicates how attitudes and behaviours can change based on how the body is perceived. Primarily underpinned by socialisation theory, in Sex Role Theory, males and females learn appropriate ways of being masculine and feminine.

Embedded in this way of looking at gender is the centrality of difference. Men and women, irrespective of biological difference, are socialised into gender-specific roles. These attributes and traits are often understood as part of the stereotypes that society imposes on men and women. Thus, men and women become shaped by the expectations and stereotypes that are ascribed to them based on their sex. As a result, this social designation controls and assigns normative gendered behaviours, where women are often allocated child-rearing and caregiving roles, whilst men are channelled into more 'provider' and 'protector' roles. These roles therefore cultivate particular ways of thinking, feeling and behaving in that they shape social relations. As such men are often posited with varying amounts of masculine traits. Psychologists have developed a number of methods to measure and document masculinity, including the Brannon Masculinity Scale (Brannon and Juni, 1984), the Gender Role Conflict Scale (O'Neil et al., 1986) and the Masculine Gender Role Stress Scale (Eisler et al., 1988). Such tests tend to operate by measuring the levels of masculinity that have been socialised into people; the amount of masculinity that someone has can be measured. As with the physiological approach above, objective measures of masculinity can be developed and applied by establishing an index of gender norms that are socially located.

One early approach to sex roles is understood as the Gender Role Strain Paradigm, which refers to the ways that men internalise cultural expectations of masculine roles (Pleck, 1981; Pleck and Thompson, 1986). Another social role approach is discussed by Levant et al. (1992), who draw upon the Male Role Norms Inventory (MRNI), which uses 57 items with a number of sub-scales that was designed to measure traditional masculine ideology. This was later revised in 2010 to a 39-item scale that covered areas such as avoidance of femininity, negativity toward sexual minorities, self-reliance through mechanical skills, toughness, dominance, importance of sex, and restrictive emotionality. These involve statements such as 'A man should prefer watching action movies to reading romantic novels' (avoidance of femininity) or 'A man should always be the boss' (dominance). Responses to the scale are recorded on a 7-point Likert scale where 1 = strongly disagrees and 7 = strongly agrees. Thus, higher scores can detail the levels at which men are more likely to ascribe to traditional masculine ideologies. This approach can then be applied to research around why men are involved, for example, in self-destructive behaviours. For example, Uy et al. (2014) suggest that traditional masculine ideologies are connected with health-damaging alcohol drinking patterns. They recruited 109 men with a history of alcohol use and measured their masculinities using the MRNI-R. The measure uses a Likert scale to rate self-perceived levels of masculinity. They found that those men who declared greater affiliation with traditional masculine ideologies were more likely to consume more alcohol. Furthermore, such ideologies were related to the frequency of alcohol consumption and thus lent themselves to increased health risks.

From a sex role perspective, men become containers for the depositing of correct masculinity. This means that social and psychological problems emerge if men have been socialised into either too much masculinity or not enough masculinity. Examples of this can be found across the world. Masculinity as a 'natural' indicator of maleness can also be seen in an educational context. The media annually reports on how, in relation to girls, boys are performing less well in certain subjects, such as English. The response to this has been to reconsider how schools are producing this underachievement by looking at how they teach boys. In some accounts, there is a natural state of 'boyness', and, according to physiological and psychological accounts, young males are pre-disposed to 'boyish' behaviours. In a recent YouTube video, Hoff Sommers (2015, 4.42m) states, 'Boys need to work off their energy. They need to be free to play the games that they enjoy. As our schools become more feeling centred, more competition free, more sedentary, they move further away from the needs of boys.' Therefore, from this approach, it is the natural disposition of boys to not concentrate and to be loud and boisterous.

It thus follows that once institutional support has been aligned to boys' identities and involved in supporting and cultivating their 'boyness', then social roles and physical dispositions are harmonious. In recent school shootings in the United States, one of the main narratives has been around the young men being exposed to violent video games, films and influences. In other words, they are exposed to the wrong kinds of masculine influences at unacceptable levels. Interestingly, some Sex Role theorists suggest that there is an experiential space outside of the sex role. This means that young men, for example, are structured and forced into societal roles and as a consequence experience suffering, as they find it difficult to live up to or match social expectations of what it means to be a real man. This, it is argued, can result in a cultural dissonance between the experiences of the individual and society's gendered expectations.

Returning to how men's and boys' practices are often understood, those that deviate from the norm are explained through notions of poor socialisation. An example of this is Pollack's (1999) 'boy code', which is based upon the difference between a boyhood that is happy, content, and free, and the imposition of the social role of manhood that carries the weight of the social expectations of a particular kind of masculinity. Therefore, standing outside of the social role is a 'vulnerable self' where boys' 'genuine' self-expression becomes disciplined by society's masculinity norms that are based on stoicism, toughness and individual isolation. This is named by Pollack as 'gender straightjacketing' and causes boys to negotiate between their own emotional needs and the expectations of society. When boys fail to manage the divide and their emotional voice become silenced, this often results in issues of violence, suicide and depression. It is the social pressure of living up to a particular role of being a boy, and the shame associated with failure, that causes physical and emotional damage to boys and those around them. As boys self-silence, in order to meet the gender norms of society, they suspend their ability to communicate and their ability to open up their feelings. The notion of shame is an important dynamic in their negotiation of masculinity. The implication of this is that boys' emotional voice becomes silenced as a means of ensuring access to socially ascribed masculinity. Of significance is Pollack's (2006) claim that there is a gendering, a way of being a boy, that can exist outside of masculinity. In other words, there is a gendered space which boys occupy prior to entry into masculinity. Pollack's position is based upon interviews with 200 boys between the ages of 12 and 18. Of these, 175 were recruited for extensive quantitative tests and were also involved in a further two-hour interview. He suggests that the rationale behind the sampling is to access everyday boys. From this research, Pollack argues: 'At the heart of boys' fears is their concern over masculinity' (p. 193). However, boys are also locked in a tension between the esteem and status that traditional masculinity is deemed to provide, on the one hand, and the emergence of successful girls on the other, which is producing confusion about how to become a 'real' man.

The criticisms of Sex Role Theory are well rehearsed, but it is important that we raise a number of them here. Baxter (2003) provides an excellent summary of the different criticisms levelled at Sex Role Theory. First, it is suggested that there is a permanency with sex roles, in that the structures that are imposed on boys remain unchanging. As boys are socialised, the expectations and pressures of those roles endure. Thus, the possibility that there are multiple and contradictory gendered expectations remains underexplored. Second, there is an ambiguity between the role as a descriptor and the role as explanatory. Therefore, when identifying the nature of masculinity, we are at the same time explaining. There is also a circularity of the argument where the gender role becomes the mechanism with which to understand men, and where men become central to the understanding of the gender role. The response is that we are unable to think about gender without the reassertion of sex. However, one of the progressive elements of Sex Role Theory is that it allows for the fluidity of males taking on femininity and females being understood as masculine. This has interesting connections with Queer Theory, Trans Theory and Post-Feminism. If social roles become problematic, then the shift towards a more fluid understanding of men and masculinity involves the disconnection of masculinity from physiology. This means that masculinity has become a social and cultural configuration that is overlaid onto a body. A different way of thinking about the overlay of cultural configurations onto the body is by connecting it to notions of power such as domination, control and subordination through the concept of patriarchy.

Power, Inequality and the Production of Masculinities

From the 1980s to the 1990s, studies of men and masculinity demonstrated a shift from understanding men and women through fixed categories of biological difference, towards an understanding of gender relations based on local contexts. In short, such studies began to question the basis of masculinity not simply by challenging the epistemological assumptions that underpinned it but also by questioning the institutional and cultural practices that authorised them (Traister, 2000). Thus, accounts of men positioned within dialectical relationships with women began to move towards understanding men and masculinity through institutionally and culturally specific social relationships. These texts argued for the need to rethink categorical theories that suggest that gender/sexual relations are shaped by a single overarching factor. More specifically, studies of men and masculinity began to disaggregate overinflated concepts, such as patriarchy, maintaining that these relations are multidimensional and differentially experienced. This shift was captured by a move from understanding men's attitudes and behaviours through a 'masculinity', and it instead began to recognise that men were engaging in different *masculinities*.

Pivotal to the new emphasis on masculinities was the work of Raewyn Connell. Her research began to suggest a more complex understanding of masculinity and how it is experienced by men and women in a variety of different ways. For Connell, masculinity becomes articulated through a series of relationships, and in order to explain the nature of these relationships she moves from a concept of masculinity to masculinities. One of the issues that Connell attempts to explain is how seemingly 'normal' everyday men support and contribute to structured inequalities between men and women. One of the ways this is done is by adopting a more plural framing of masculinity that results in a re-distribution of power, which is no longer contained by a logic of the powerful/powerless couplet. This means that men become subject to the power of other men and repressive regimes of masculinity. Instead of using a Hegelian dialectic that frames gendered difference, Connell (1987) uses Gramsci's concept of hegemony. More specifically, Connell understands masculinities as shaped by specific social contexts, and as a result some masculinities become more influential than others. As some masculinities occupy privileged positions, other masculinities are subordinated and marginalised. In different contexts, it is argued that some men will occupy more powerful positions than others and that they achieve this through winning the consent of other men and women in order to do so.

Connell's (1989) earlier work operationalised the concept of hegemonic masculinity in the context of schooling. Her focus on '*Cool Guys, Swots and Wimps*' signalled that different ways of being a young man are placed within a hierarchy of social power. Thus, the 'Cool Boys' from labouring classes with low academic ability are viewed as the 'trouble-makers' and take part in resisting school authority structures. In this context, masculinities are organised in relation to hierarchies of the institutional knowledge of the school, so academic knowledge becomes the most legitimate and institutionally sanctioned knowledge. With the 'Cool Boys' working against this institutional sanctioning through forms of resistance, other boys align themselves to the school. As a result, some boys become hegemonic, whist others become marginalised. Those men who are marginalised are often those men who used hegemonic masculinity to sustain its power. For example, men occupying hegemonic masculinity will often 'other' different groups of men—such as gay men, black men or disabled men—to sustain the legitimacy and normalisation of their own masculinity. Michael Kimmel's work on the constitution of masculinity suggests that masculine subjectivities are constituted through the rejection of that which is culturally deemed as feminine. An example of this is how men objectify heterosexuality in order to validate their identities as masculine. As a result, masculine identities are structured through a heterosexuality that creates its stability through the rejection of that which is feminine (read as homosexual) and 'that the reigning definition of masculinity is a defensive effort to prevent being emasculated' (Kimmel, 2007, p. 80). It should be added that rather than displace a Feminist politics, Connell's hegemony of masculinity creates the possibilities for a more comprehensive understanding of patriarchy. Aboim (2010) points out that although hegemonic masculinity is underpinned by men's domination of women, it also serves to oppress men who may be from a lower class, identified through particular racial or ethnic categories or through sexuality. In short, hegemonic masculinity sustains 'a gender order that segregates men in accordance with how far removed they are from the hegemonic norm: white, heterosexual, professionally successful' (p. 3). Thus, the involvement of some men in the hegemony and the subordination of others is due to the patriarchal privilege that is accrued by being in power or being complicit in such powerful positions. Analysing men as a politically gendered category removes it from its normative location as transparent, neutral and disembodied. This is part of a more general trend in culturally based theories whereby the ascendant social categories in established binaries (for example, men, heterosexuals, whites and the able-bodied) are becoming the new objects of critical appraisal. There is much empirical and conceptual work to be done in exploring the gendering of men.

According to Connell (1995, p. 77), hegemonic masculinity refers to 'the configuration of gender practice which embodies the currently accepted answer to the problem of the legitimacy of patriarchy' and which results in the dominant position of men and the subordination of women. The concept is often used to analyse a historically changing and mobile power structure and a hierarchical relation between different groups of men and women. Hegemonic masculinity is constructed in relation to subordinated and marginalised masculinities as well as in relation to femininities. However, hegemony does not imply total power and domination, but instead it is focussed on a balance of forces and an ongoing struggle for power. When historical conditions and social patterns in society change, the hegemonic position can also be confronted and questioned, meaning that hegemony is never absolute or fixed. The concept thus points to possible changes in and transformations of masculinity. Yet Connell uses the term *complicity* to theorise how men relate to power and to the hegemonic structures of masculinity. According to Connell, most men have a complicated, dependant and ambivalent relation to power. In Connell's definition of hegemonic masculinity, patriarchy is changing, albeit slowly, but it is still quite a stable power structure. The organisation of gender on a larger scale is centred on a single fact: 'the global dominance of men over women' (Connell, 1987, p. 183).

The theory of hegemonic masculinity has had a great impact on Gender Studies; it has become a key concept and could be interpreted as more dynamic and flexible than, for example, the notion of patriarchy. However, a number of scholars have stressed a criticism of the concept (Whitehead, 2002; Beasley, 2008; Anderson, 2009). For example, Hearn (2004) points out some critical problems with the concept of hegemonic masculinity, especially the lack of a discussion of resistance and the problems of adapting it to analyses of specific and local masculinities. He argues for the study of multiple forms of hegemony in the gender order and for a concept that focuses on both stable and changing structures and gender identities. In a similar way, Beasley (2008) criticises the monolithic and unchanging use of the concept, calling for a subtler and more usable concept that will allow analysis of particular forms of masculinity, men and masculinities at different levels of abstraction. There are similarities here to the way that we critique and try to develop the concept in the next chapter.

The Queering of Masculinity

The final approaches that this chapter explores are those which make visible the tensions between gendered attitudes, affects and behaviours, and masculinity. This section takes its point of departure from Weston's (2002) approach that highlights a moment prior to the ascription of gender categories to bodies where existing frames of recognition are no longer useful. It is suggested by Mirsky (1996) that studies of masculinities tend to treat men's lives as co-extensive with masculinity. The consequence of this is that the institutional and cultural authorising of men's practices can be understood only through the concept of masculinity. This prompts a number of epistemological questions that include: Is the focus on enquiry for gender theorists the study of masculinity or men? Can we study men without recourse to gender? Can masculinity exist without gender? One common theme that frames these questions is that

> men's lives might not be contained through particular masculinities; that there may be areas or moments in men's lives where by explaining those moments though masculinity might be irrelevant: such possibilities are not comprehended in a men's studies approach which, against its stated intentions, theorizes masculinity as a necessary attribute of human males.
>
> (p. 30)

Mirsky usefully suggests that if men's practices can be understood or explained only through the concept of masculinity, then the concept loses its analytical traction. According to Mirsky, masculinity is constituted in two key ways. First, masculinity is often defined in opposition to women, and, second, men are positioned as being in a more dominant position than women. This approach appears similar to early Pro-Feminist men's projects where gender interventions involve a political strategy that requires a radical rejection of their masculinity, which was seen as essentially tied up with a relationship of power. In this way, approaches to the study of men need to think about not simply identifying the range of masculinities but moments where masculinity is resisted and the implications of this. One way to think about this is through the notion of *post-masculinity* (Haywood and Mac an Ghaill, 2012).

The debate as to how the internal dynamics configure masculinity continues to have a major impact on the development of Masculinity Studies in European contexts. However, another direction of analysis that has had less influence is a more radical, challenging approach to understanding masculinity. This approach calls into question the epistemological foundations of Masculinity Studies by examining fixed notions of male and female and the ascription of binary gender categories of masculinity and femininity. This approach is usually associated with Queer Theory. Queer theorists have productively explored the destabilisation of biological categorisations of sex. One of the aims of studies of men and masculinities has been to denaturalise sex, gender, and desire and to emphasise the active cultural production of masculinities. This aim has also been facilitated by work with a wide range of sexual minorities including lesbians, gay men, bisexuals, transsexuals and transgendered groups.

At the same time, there continues to be a range of popular ascriptions that link sexual choice and gender with an assumed association between homosexuality and femininity, and between lesbianism and masculinity. This association serves to deny the validity of same-sex desire, while producing heterosexuality as conceptually inescapable (Pringle, 1992). Early work by Richardson (1996, p. 4) suggested: 'Historically, lesbians have been portrayed as virtual men trapped in the space of women's bodies: "mannish" in appearance and masculine in their thoughts, feelings and desires, rendering their existence compatible with the logic of gender and heteronormativity.' Emerging decentred female and male gay subjectivities provide concrete evidence that femininity and masculinity are not something one is born with or an inherent possession but rather an active process of achievement, performance and enactment (Weeks, 1977; Plummer, 1981). In short, Gay and Lesbian scholars and activists have been some of the most dynamic contributors to recent sexual theorising in destabilising sociological and common-sense connections between men/women and masculinity/femininity within the broader structure of gender relations. However, one of the productive contributions of Gay and Lesbian movements has been to deconstruct these connections.

Early gender theorists usefully questioned the social construction of the biological categories of male and female (Laqueur, 1990; Gatens, 1996; Fausto-Sperling, 2000) and highlighted that 'either sex is privileged as a biological attribute upon which a gender ideology is imposed, or sex is denied as merely the ideological mystification that obscures cultural facts about gender' (Elam, 2000, p. 267). One of the ways to demonstrate the social construction of biology has been through the queering of gender/sex categories. For example, Halberstam (1998) in her discussion of female masculinities suggested that female bodies are able to take on and live out particular masculinities, just as male bodies are able to take on femininities. In other words, the study of masculinity from Halberstam's approach is not directly focussed on the biological category of men. Hence, female masculinities become a means of understanding how bodies are tied to particular social and cultural codes of maleness. In many ways masculinity becomes dis-embodied and operates precisely because the material evidence (biology, chromosomes, genetics, hormones) in which masculinity has been traditionally fixed becomes unanchored.

Hird (2000, p. 353) situates the relationship between sex and gender as political in the sense that 'the authenticity of gender resides not on, or in the body,' but by a 'particular system of knowledge, power and truth.' This suggests that the relationship between sex and gender is held together by particular ways of conceptualising the body. As a result, biological sex is a historical construct and is thus materialised through its application to the body. Hence, masculinity in this approach is not something that is associated with culturally defined bodies but can also operate across a range of bodies. Importantly, a Critical Masculinity Studies have the potential to turn in on itself and question the viability of what makes masculinity and whether a masculinity is, or should be, associated with culturally coded maleness.

One of the implications of the understanding of the discursive formation of biology is an emerging question of the epistemological status of the 'real' body. More specifically, genital difference becomes framed as a discursive regime that enables coherent stable biologies that do not exist. This prompts the possibility, as Judith Butler (2004) pointed out, of an inversion where the coherency of biological sex exists primarily through the discursive re-iteration of gender. Thus, gender is performative in the sense that it provides the conceptual possibilities of biological sex to exist. Performance is used not in a theatrical sense but rather as a form of citation. This means that the actual citing of gender produces the possibility of biological sex. In this way, the citational operates as a material presence that secures and establishes the existence of gender. As a result, the idea of the social construction of masculinity, as opposed to the biology of man, become destabilised.

In a Foucauldian analysis, biological maleness becomes understood as a social historical framing of ideas where 'western ideology takes biology as the cause, and behaviour and social statuses as the effects, and then proceeds to construct biological dichotomies to justify the "naturalness" of gendered behaviours and gendered social status' (Lorber, 1993, p. 568). In this way, biology operates as ideology that constructs maleness. In other words, the designation of bodies exists as a context in which discourses of maleness and femaleness are written. This gender binary presupposes the nature of male and female through an appeal to 'biology as ideology'. As Floyd (2011, p. 45) remarks:

> Is gender a 'destination'? Is this a useful way of putting it? Is gender a location? A place? A space? Is the line separating masculinity from femininity a border one can cross like a wall or a fence? What about the region between these two territories, which transgender and intersex studies have begun to map for us? The metaphors brought to bear in the effort to identify differently gendered bodies, in the struggle to find language that can push the limits of available vocabularies, can themselves be revealing.

One of the ways in which a post-masculinity position might align itself with Queer or Trans Theory is by thinking about a theory of gender that is not dependent upon masculinity *and* femininity identities. For example, Butler (2004) explains how gender can be understood as a regulatory concept that operates to link masculine and feminine attributes to culturally designated bodies. In her account of gender, masculinity and femininity do not necessarily have to be reducible to gender, and gender does not have to be reducible to masculinity or femininity. The result of this is that a conceptual space can exist between masculinity and femininity on one hand and gender on the other: 'To keep the term gender apart from both masculinity and femininity is to safeguard a theoretical perspective by which one might offer an account of how the binary of masculine and feminine comes to exhaust the semantic field of gender' (p. 42).

It is interesting to consider what might emerge from this conceptual space once the semantic possibilities of gender have been exhausted. According to Butler, this entails thinking about the ways that gender has become proliferated, where gender operates beyond the binaries of the feminine and the masculine. For Butler, the conceptual de-linking of masculinity from gender is a productive possibility. As a consequence, male behaviours, attitudes and practices can no longer be simple indicators of masculinity (or even gender). This resonates with Post-structural readings of representation that question the presumption of self-evident and fixed meaning. In the context of studying men, there is currently a compunction that male subjectivities and practices *have* to be explained by a concept of masculinity. The consequence of resisting the regulatory regime of dyadic gender theory is that a move beyond 'masculinity' as a conceptual and empirical default position is required.

Queer theorists enable an understanding of how the regulatory basis of a dyadic notion of gender as masculinity and femininity requires a conceptual frame whereby subjectivities and practices have to be incorporated within that system. In short, there can be no space outside of masculinity where men's subjectivities and practices can be explained. This is the basis of one of Noble's (2006) critiques of female masculinities, where the ascription of female masculinities leads to the re-inscription of an existing gendered signification, albeit via new representational strategies. More specifically, Noble argues, '[B]y gender I mean the sets of cultural meanings and technologies that, in the case of masculinity, have allowed power, an imaginary construction of the male body, and masculinity to all function as synonyms for each other' (p. 33). She goes on to argue that masculinity and the male body are not reducible to each other, but each is articulated through the other. One of the difficulties of this approach is that it is hard to provide empirical examples. However, Noble achieves this by focusing on understanding the relationship between men, boys and masculinity. She highlights how contemporary culture is now fascinated with the notion of the boy—from Hollywood films through to music and boy bands.

In the UK, concerns over boys' underachievement in education highlights how culturally precious boys have become. The appeal, according to Noble, is that boys have become understood in opposition to men. The appeal of boys, if we agree with Noble, is that it both promises a phallic power and escapes the heteronormativity that often constitutes masculinities. Therefore, boys are required to participate in a cultural refusal as part of a broader resistive moment to the adult masculinity and its attendant symbolic weight and cultural expectation. It is therefore suggested that social and cultural notions of masculinity are premised on the rejection of boyhood, and boyhood becomes a 'productive failure' of manhood (Noble, 2006). An example of this can be found in recent media reports on boys and sexual activities with their female teachers. One of the patterns found in media accounts is that female teacher and boy pupil sexual relations are not simplistically reported as sexual abuse. Rather, boys' sexual activity is at one moment explained through their status as children, whilst at another moment it becomes configured through epithets of adult heteronormative masculinity. One headline that is used repeatedly when reporting on female teachers and male pupils is that of the 'Miss Kiss'. By positioning teacher and pupil behaviours through this language, the sexual activity shifts from that of attack and abuse to one of childlike playground activities. For example, a report on a teacher who was convicted of 'kissing a 15-year old boy in a school cupboard' highlights that the judge warned the teacher about her 'immature and romantic nonsense' (*The Guardian* 26.11.05). Other reports refer to 'teen romps', 'groping', 'flirting', 'snogging' and

'Miss sacked over kisses', occurring in a range of UK news reports since 2000. The language reflects boys' under-developed sexual competency and inexperience. But rather than position the boys as innocent, they occupy a space of an active sexuality.

Although news reports draw upon a 'too young' discourse as a means of contextualising their moral and legal concern, sexual practices that are 'falling outside the heterosexualist continuum are effectively rendered unintelligible by mainstream narratives, including (and especially) those focussed on boyhood and emergent masculinity' (Quint, 2005, p. 42). Thus, what appears as the sexual practices of men has to be re-signified. From this perspective, desire can only legally and morally exist within the possibilities of the category of childhood, and, at that point, it is re-coded as an ineffectual and immature childhood desire. However, these sexual practices stand outside of the childhood discourse but cannot be contained within an adult masculinity. As a result, the gender of boys cannot be cohered through the concept of masculinity or childhood. As of yet we have not developed our gendered theory sufficiently to accommodate this gendered liminality.

Transgender Masculinities

Gardiner (2013) brings our attention to masculinity theorists who tend to frame the constitution of masculinity through psychological structures. She suggests that writers such as Michael Kimmel, Raewyn Connell and Carrie Pascoe draw upon Freudian notions of personality formation that require the distancing and objectification of the feminine in order to constitute masculine identities. Transgender Studies, and their awareness of the normalisation of biology, provide a new context for the study of men and masculinity. One of the reasons for this is that Masculinity Studies tend to locate discussion based on male identity gendered intelligibilities. Transgender research disrupts the often neat segregation of culturally ascribed categories of male and female, and such studies highlight the social and cultural deployment of gender dimorphism by state institutions.

Masculinity Studies have nervously recognised and acknowledged transgender and intersexuality, not simply because of the (dis)location of men, but because of the challenge to the intelligibility of gender. If gender begins to operate outside of dimorphic frames of understanding, then the epistemological traction achieved by naming social relations as masculinity (and femininity) becomes limited. Medical surgeries that, on the one hand, curtail and seek to partition bodies within male/female binaries begin, on the other, 'to make available all kinds of embodied subject positions that seem to inhabit an outside of the very distinction between male and female, the way in which human beings are now able to inhabit some space that seems irreducible to received gender vocabularies—precisely because of this rapidly changing technology' (Floyd, 2011, p. 41). This has implications for how we understand the conundrum of masculinity, as the cultural epistemology that requires mimesis between male bodies and masculine attitudes and behaviours is potentially and productively disrupted by transgender subjectivities.

Part of the cultural difficulty with masculinity, and embedded within this conundrum, is a positivist understanding of gender and in particular masculinity. Thus, when men take part in culturally coded feminine behaviours, masculinity is questioned or contested. More specifically, physiology, biology and genetics operate though an epistemology of maleness. An interesting example of how this might work can be found in Iranian society, often viewed by Northern Hemisphere countries as a hotbed of radical religious conservativism, which has state-backed programmes for gender re-assignment. For example, Bluck (2012) discusses the legalisation of gender re-assignment in Iran. As Ayatollah Khomeini came to power, he issued a Fatwa that allowed Iranian citizens to have gender re-assignment. However, the consequence of the change, Bluck argues, is that it re-imposes the expectation of a traditional gendered role. This process, therefore, is supported by a view of the world in which male and female are clearly designated and discernible.

Again, intersex—where the markers of 'sex' such as genitalia, sex organs and chromosomes do not correspond with the social or cultural norms (Preeves, 2003)— is often understood in relations to a dimorphic physiological basis ofgender. A recent revision by the General Medical Council has promoted the term Disorder of Sexual Development (DSD). Davis (2015) usefully points out that medical institutions have the power to name sex status even though diagnosis itself is a cultural narrative. Although Davis notes that there is much discussion within the intersex community around the use of intersex and DSD, the process of diagnosis as a social concern rather than as a medical concern remains in place. Therefore, the mimesis between physical state and social norm is stabilised by using social role as an empirical and conceptual concern.

In Trans men and women experiences, it is important not to conflate MTF (male to female) with FTM (female to male) experiences. As Herman-Jeglinska et al. (2002) suggest, there may be different ascriptions and identifications to masculinity between FTM and MTF. Furthermore, they argue that FTM experiences may be more aligned to cis-gender experiences. It is, however, important to recognise that transgender may be experienced in different ways. Hansbury (2005) uses the notion of the Trans-masculine community, and this refers to those individuals who were assigned female at birth but identify more with masculinity. Importantly, Hansbury argues that within the Trans-masculine community, there are those who feel more comfortable with the gender dyad of male and female, and then there is another group who find the gender dyadic as limited. Aware of the limitations of typology, Hansbury suggests that within the Trans-masculine community there are three key groups that, on a continuum, are more essentialist to more constructionist: Woodworkers, Transmen and Genderqueers. Hansbury (p. 245) suggests that there is

> an unscientific, somewhat linear fashion, from (perhaps) the more male-identified to the more non-binary, these labels include, but are not limited to, Man, MTM, FTM, Transsexual Man, Man of Transsexual Experience, New Man, Transman, Transfag, Transqueer, GenderQueer, Guy, Boi, Trans-Butch,

Tomboy, Boy-Chick, Gender Outlaw, Drag King, Passing Woman, Bearded Female, Two-Spirit, Ungendered, Gender Trash, Questioning, Just Curious. And these identities are not always 'self-identical'; one transmasculine person's FTM may be another's Gender Trash.

In terms of the three positions, Hansbury suggests that the 'Woodworkers' are those men who blend into the woodwork and are embedded within existing social and cultural gender structures. Their gendered position remains undisclosed publicly, and as Hansbury suggests such men may call themselves MTM—men who have always been men but with a history of a female body. The embodiment of a male body was part of an integration into becoming, as Hansbury would suggest, unremarkable men who closely adhere to the cultural rules of masculinity. Hansbury sensitively recognises this group without judging them. The second group that Hansbury discusses is Transmen. This group of men are those who acknowledge the process of their gendered identities. They are a group where the prefix refers to change without ever arriving at a final destination:

> Both the Woodworker and the Transman present themselves to the world as men, but the Transman may be more likely to allow some segment of that world to know about his trans-sexuality and his female past—and not only to know about it, but to celebrate it to a certain extent.
>
> (p. 255)

The final classification by Hansbury is the Genderqueers: 'This group challenges categorizations and position themselves as not white and male' (p. 258). Within this group there are those who do not take up the process of passing and thus endure suspicion within the Trans-masculine community and open discrimination outside of it. This group within the Trans-community do not accept gendered categories and labels. In many ways, they are in a middle ground between Trans and Transphobic communities.

> More and more, Genderqueers are seeking a comfortable place in the middle, outside any and all boxes. Many eschew gender-specific pronouns, or, conversely, they embrace ambiguity. Some of the labels this group uses are: androgyne, gendermutt, ungendered, and polygendered.
>
> (p. 258)

What Hansbury's work enables us to look at are the ways in which being male and practicing masculinity can be undertaken differently. The Trans-community questions and challenges the underlying ontology of maleness on which social and cultural norms either emerge from or can be written and practiced on. Such work contests the nature of 'sex' and suggests that we need to understand that the importance of being authentically male is not a process reducible to the Trans-community but rather something that all cis-gender men have to negotiate. The resulting question here is that if the ontology of male is removed, then what is left?

The importance of exploring Hansbury's work in some depth is that it begins to challenge the biological basis of masculinity. It becomes illustrative of the way in which we can deconstruct notions of 'maleness'. Reis (2013) reminds us of the fragility of biology and how the biological category of maleness is made through socially and culturally loaded interpretations of the body. Reis argues that it is social anxieties about the body that impact upon the decisions that surgeons make when viewing babies: 'Intersex, also known as disorders of sex development or DSD, is a congenital incongruence between internal reproductive anatomy, chromosomes, hormones, and genitals' (2013, p. 138). Reis argues that there is often a 'normalising' process when a baby is born to ensure a congruence between the external aesthetics of the genitals and the internal anatomy. Often, it is a reconstruction of the external genitalia to make the baby look like the assigned sex.

One of the ways in which we can begin to think outside of gender is by using Weston's (2002) concept of the 'unsexed'. She uses this idea to open up a space of gendered ambiguity. This ambiguity occurs at times when gender becomes undefined. She uses examples of transgender or queer experiences where sex remains unknown and it is difficult to assign male/female sex. This moment, she argues, is not about the emergence of another gender type, for example, a 'third sex' or intersex; it is a moment that disrupts the gender categorisation based upon masculinity and femininity: 'Unsexed refers to that passing glimmer of an instant just before an acceleration into meaning gives way to what is commonly called "gender" ' (p. 33). Thus, the disruption of gender norms is a temporal disruption—an interval of meaning—where difference itself becomes displaced. It is precisely through researching moments of gendered ambiguity that we are enabled to think outside of masculinity and femininity. In other words:

> By attending to fleeting moments when gender zeros out and bodies become unsexed, the discussion can go beyond the business of identifying the referent or exposing the nonexistence of the referent, whether you want to locate gender's referentiality in the genes, or in the domain of history and culture, or nowhere at all. Zero allows for movement in and out of gender-soaked categories, a movement that depends upon the possibility of gender's short-lived dissolution. By holding open the 'place' of unsexed before giving way to a gendered classification, zero is the sign that makes that subtle movement apparent.
>
> (Weston and Helmreich, 2006, p. 117)

As Weston points out, it is the moment between the first glance and the second glance, before whatever gender category is being used, that we need to explore in more detail. It is suggested that the process of gender transitivity can be found in everyday situations. This is not the same as performativity where repetition congeals to form ontologies; the unsexed is the moment within the spaces of its repetition. As Queer Theory and Transgender Studies begin to break down and challenge the binary structures of gender and masculinity, they enable us 'to imagine, to try to think, an outside to the very distinction between masculinity and femininity, to aid the development of categories, concepts, and knowledges adequate to such an outside' (Floyd, 2011, p. 46).

Conclusion

This chapter has highlighted the ways in which men and masculinity have already been approached. More specifically, it has set out different theoretical approaches as cultural epistemologies—inherited theoretical and common-sense strategies to establish knowledges about men and masculinity. In many ways, the chapter presents a potted history of approaches, moving from more physiological approaches to more Cultural Studies approaches. However, this would be misleading as each of the approaches mentioned in this chapter is currently used by social, political and popular commentators to explain men and masculinity. Such approaches are often in a competitive relationship, vying to be the authoritative voice of intelligibility. Such a relationship is integral to the mapping out of how men and masculinity are constructed and of the nature of the resulting conundrums that surround them.

Furthermore, the book suggests that it is these approaches and their underpinning intellectual scaffolding that circulates through approaches to gender that create the conundrums that we witness in contemporary society. As such, the authors of this book suggest that there are a range of conundrums that circulate round what is understood as men. In the following chapters, we revisit a number of the main concepts embedded in the theoretical approaches to masculinity, elaborating on them in order to explore how they can be used to unpack and understand it. We use concepts as a means to unlock insights into how the conundrum (or, more accurately, how conundrums) of masculinity are constructed.

References

Aboim, S. (2010) *Plural Masculinities: The Remaking of the Self in Private Life*. Aldershot: Ashgate.

Anderson, E. (2009) *Inclusive Masculinity: The Changing Nature of Masculinities*. New York: Routledge.

Bailey, A.A. and Hurd, P.L. (2005) Finger length ratio (2D: 4D) correlates with physical aggression in men but not in women. *Biological Psychology*, 68(3), 215–222.

Baxter, J. (2003) *Positioning Gender in Discourse: A Feminist Methodology*. Basingstoke: Springer.

Beasley, C. (2008) Rethinking hegemonic masculinity in a globalizing world. *Men and Masculinities*, 11(1), 86–103.

Bluck, S. (2012) Transsexual in Iran: A Fatwa for freedom? In LGBT transnational identity and the media. In: C. Pullen, ed. *LGBT Transnational Identity and the Media*. Basingstoke: Palgrave Macmillan, pp. 59–66.

Brannon, R. and Juni, S. (1984) A scale for measuring attitudes about masculinity. *Psychological Documents*, 14 (Doc. #2612). New York: NYU Scholars, pp. 6–7.

Brayton, S. (2007) MTV's *Jackass*: Transgression, abjection and the economy of white masculinity. *Journal of Gender Studies*, 16(1), 57–72.

Butler, J. (2004) *Undoing Gender*. Oxfordshire: Routledge.

Chen, S., English, T. and Peng, K. (2006) Self-verification and contextualized self-views. *Personality and Social Psychology Bulletin*, 32, 930–942.

Choi, I., Nisbett, R.E. and Norenzayan, A. (1999) Causal attribution across cultures: Variation and universality. *Psychological Bulletin*, 125, 47–63.

Connell, R.W. (1987) *Gender and Power*. Cambridge: Cambridge University Press.

Connell, R.W. (1989) Cool guys, swots and wimps: The inter-play of masculinity and education. *Oxford Review of Education*, 15(3), 291–303.

Connell, R.W. (1995) *Masculinities*. Cambridge: Polity Press.

D'Amico, R. (1989) *Historicism and Knowledge*. New York: Routledge.

Davis, G. (2015) *Contesting Intersex: The Dubious Diagnosis*. New York: New York University Press.

Deaner, R.O., Goetz, S.M., Shattuck, K. and Schnotala, T. (2012) Body weight, not facial width-to-height ratio, predicts aggression in pro hockey players. *Journal of Research in Personality*, 46(2), 235–238.

Eisler, R.M., Skidmore, J.R. and Ward, C.H. (1988) Masculine gender-role stress: Predictor of anger, anxiety, and health-risk behaviors. *Journal of Personality Assessment*, 52(1), 133–141.

Elam, D. (1994) *Feminism and Deconstruction*. London: Routledge.

Elam, D. (2000) Gender or sex? In: Tripp, A. ed. *Gender*. Basingstoke: Palgrave Macmillan, pp. 168–181.

Fausto-Sterling, A. (2000) Sexing the Body: Gender Politics and the Construction of Sexuality. New York: Basic Books.

Floyd, K. (2011) Masculinity inside out: The biopolitical lessons of transgender and intersex studies: In: Horlacher, S. ed. *Constructions of Masculinity in British Literature From the Middle Ages to the Present*. New York: Palgrave Macmillan, pp. 33–51.

Foucault, M. (1972) *The Archaeology of Knowledge and the Discourse on Language*. London: Pantheon Books.

Gardiner, J.K. (2013) *Masculinity Studies and Feminist Theory: New Directions*. New York: Columbia University Press.

Gatens, M. (1996) *Imaginary Bodies: Ethics, Power and Corporeality*. London: Routledge.

Geertz, C. (1983) *Local Knowledge*. San Francisco: Basic Books.

Goetz, J.L., Spencer-Rodgers, J. and Peng, K. (2008) Dialectical emotions: How cultural epistemologies influence the experience and regulation of emotional complexity. In: Sorrentino, R. and Yamguchi, S. eds. *Handbook of Motivation and Cognition Across Cultures*. Amsterdam: Academic Press, pp. 517–539.

Gottzén, L. and Mellström, U. (2014) Changing and globalising masculinity studies. *NORMA: International Journal for Masculinity Studies*, 9(1), 1–4.

Halberstam, J. (1998) *Female Masculinity*. Durham, NC: Duke University Press.

Hansbury, G. (2005) The middle men: An introduction to the transmasculine identities. *Studies in Gender and Sexuality*, 6(3), 241–264.

Haywood, C. and Mac an Ghaill, M. (2012) 'What's next for masculinity?' Reflexive directions for theory and research on masculinity and education. *Gender and Education*, 24(6), 577–592.

Hearn, J. (2004) From hegemonic masculinity to the hegemony of men. *Feminist Theory*, 5(1), 49–72.

Herman-Jeglińska, A., Grabowska, A., & Dulko, S. (2002) Masculinity, femininity, and transsexualism. *Archives of Sexual Behavior,* 31(6), 527–534.

Hird, M.J. (2000) Gender's nature: Intersexuality, transsexualism and the 'sex'/'gender' Binary. *Feminist Theory*, 1(3), 347–364.

Jamieson, L. (2013) Personal relationships, intimacy and the self in a mediated and global digital age. In: Orton-Johnson, K. and Prior, N. eds. *Digital Sociology: Critical Perspectives*. Basingstoke: Palgrave Macmillan, pp. 13–28.

Jia, Y., Laurence, V.L. and Yachang, Z. (2014) Masculinity, testosterone, and financial misreporting. *Journal of Accounting Research*, 52(5), 1195–1246.

Kimmel, M. (2002) Foreword. In: Gardiner, J.K. ed. *Masculinity Studies and Feminist Theory: New Directions*. New York: Columbia University Press, pp. ix–xi.

Kimmel, M. (2007) Masculinity as homophobia: Fear, shame, and silence in the construction of gender identity. In: Cook, N. ed. *Gender Relations in Global Perspective: Essential Readings*. Ontario: Canadian Scholars Press, pp. 73–83.

Klein, J. and Chancer, L. (2000) Masculinity matters: The role of gender in high-profile school violence cases. In: Spina, S. ed. *Smoke and Mirrors: The Hidden Context of Violence in Schools and Society*. New York: Rowman and Littlefield, pp. 129–162.

Kramer, R.S.S. (2015) Facial width-to-height ratio in a large sample of commonwealth games athletes. *Evolutionary Psychology*, 13(1), 197–209.

Laqueur, T. (1990) *Making Sex: Body and Gender From the Greeks to Freud*. Cambridge, MA: Harvard University Press.

Levant, R. F. Hirsch, L. S., Celentano, E. and Cozza, T. M. (1992) The male role: An investigation of contemporary norms. *Journal of Mental Health Counselling*, 14(3), 325–337.

Lippa, R.A. (2006) Finger lengths, 2D: 4D ratios, and their relation to gender-related personality traits and the Big Five. *Biological Psychology*, 71(1), 116–121.

Lorber, J. (1993) Believing is seeing: Biology as ideology. *Gender & Society*, 7, 568–581.

Martin, R. (1988) Truth, power, self: An interview with Michel Foucault. In: Martin, L.H., Gutman, M. and Hutton, P.H. eds. *Technologies of the Self: A Seminar With Michel Foucault*. London: Tavistock, pp. 9–16.

Masuda, T. and Nisbett, R.E. (2001) Attending holistically versus analytically: Comparing the context sensitivity of Japanese and Americans. *Journal of Personality and Social Psychology*, 81, 922–934.

Mirsky, S. (1996) Three arguments for the elimination of masculinity. In: Krondorfer, B. ed. *Men's Bodies, Men's Gods: Male Identities in a (Post-) Christian Culture*. New York: New York University Press, pp. 27–43.

Noble, B. (2006) *Sons of the Movement: FtMs Risking Incoherence on a Post-Queer Cultural Landscape*. Toronto: Canadian Scholars Press.

O'Neil, J.M., Helms, B.J., Gable, R.K., David, L. and Wrightsman, L.S. (1986) Gender-role conflict scale: College men's fear of femininity. *Sex Roles*, 14(5–6), 335–350.

Peng, K. and Nisbett, R.E. (1999). Culture, dialectics, and reasoning about contradiction. *American Psychologist*, 54, 741–754.

Phillips, D.A. (2005) Reproducing normative and marginalized masculinities: Adolescent male popularity and the outcast. *Nursing Inquiry*, 12(3), 219–230.

Pleck, J.H. (1981) *The Myth of Masculinity*. Cambridge, MA: MIT Press.

Pleck, J.H. and Thompson, E.H. (1986) The structure of male role norms. *American Behavioural Scientist*, 29(5), 531–534.

Plummer, K. (ed.) (1981) *The Making of the Modern Homosexual*. London: Hutchinson.

Pollack, W.S. (1999) *Real Boys: Rescuing Our Sons From the Myths of Boyhood*. New York: Henry Holt & Company.

Pollack, W.S. (2006) The "war" for boys: Hearing "real boys'" voices, healing their pain. *Professional Psychology: Research and Practice*, 37(2), 190–195.

Preeves, S.E. (2003) *Intersex and Identity: The Contested Self*. New Brunswick: Rutgers University Press.

Pringle, R. (1992) Absolute sex? Unpacking the sexuality/gender relationship. In: Connell, R.W. and Dowsett, G.W. eds. *Rethinking Sex: Social Theory and Sexuality Research.* Melbourne: Melbourne University Press, pp. 76–101.

Quint, C. (2005) Boys won't be boys: Cross-gender masquerade and queer agency in *Ma Vie en rose*. In: Pomerance, M. and Gateward, F. eds. *Where the Boys Are: Cinemas of Masculinity and Youth*. Detroit: Wayne State University Press, pp. 41–60.

Reis, E. (2013) Intersex surgeries, circumcision, and the making of "normal". In: Denniston, G.C., Hodges, F.M. and Milos, M.F. eds. *Genital Cutting: Protecting Children From Medical, Cultural, and Religious Infringements*. The Netherlands: Springer, pp. 137–147.

Richardson, D. (ed.) (1996) *Theorising Heterosexuality*. Buckingham: Open University Press.

Rodríguez, R. T. (2011) Intelligible/unintelligible: A two-pronged proposition for queer studies. *American Literary History,* 23(1), 174–180.

Sommers, C.H. (2015) www.youtube.com/watch?v=OFpYj0E-yb4 (accessed 9th November, 2016).

Spencer-Rodgers, J., Peng, K., Wang, L. and Hou, Y. (2004) Dialectical self-esteem and East—West differences in psychological well-being. *Personality and Social Psychology Bulletin*, 30, 1416–1432.

Traister, B. (2000) Academic Viagra: The rise of American masculinity studies. *American Quarterly*, 52(2), 274–304.

Tsujimura, H. and Banissy, M.J. (2013) Human face structure correlates with professional baseball performance: Insights from professional Japanese baseball players. *Biology Letters*, 9(3), 1–4.

Uy, P. J., Massoth, N. A., & Gottdiener, W. H. (2014) Rethinking male drinking: Traditional masculine ideologies, gender-role conflict, and drinking motives. *Psychology of Men & Masculinity,* 15(2), 121.

Weeks, J. (1977) *Coming Out: Homosexual Politics in Britain From the Nineteenth Century to the Present*. London: Quartet.

Weston, K. (2002) *Gender in Real Time: Power and Transience in a Visual Age*. London: Routledge.

Weston, K., & Helmreich, S. (2006) Kath Weston's Gender in Real Time: Power and Transience in a Visual Age. *Body & Society,* 12(3), 103–121.

Whitehead, S. (2002) *Men and Masculinities*. Cambridge: Polity Press.

Williams, T.J., Pepitone, M.E., Christensen, S.E., Cooke, B.M., Huberman, A.D., Breedlove, N.J., Breedlove, T.J., Jordan, C.L. and Breedlove, S.M. (2000) Finger-length ratios and sexual orientation. *Nature*, 404(6777), 455–456.

Zavarzadeh, M. (1991) "Argument" and the politics of laughter. *Rethinking Marxism*, 4(1), 120–131.

3   Hegemonic Masculinity
Stability, Change and Transformation

Introduction

In the spring of 2008, 20 Swedish men were interviewed about their experiences of staying at home for at least six months with their infants (Johansson and Klinth, 2008, Johansson, 2011a, b). Most of these men had a middle-class background, working in highly paid professions with flexible work hours, but there were also some exceptions. The decision to stay at home and split parental leave did not seem to be a great issue in these men's lives. When asked to talk about how they rationalised their decision to share parental care, they seemed puzzled and answered that *'there was never any doubt*: staying at home was not optional.' In many cases, money was not regarded as a problem and was not even considered an issue. Many of the couples had similar occupational levels and wages, so regardless of who stayed at home, family finances would not be greatly affected. Although the interviewees were aware that money could be an issue for many people, they instead put forward other motivations and factors that had influenced them. Staying at home with small children and a better quality of life were more important than financial concerns.

While there were similarities among the factors that motivated men's decisions, there were also differences between the men, for example, regarding their attitudes towards feminism, debates on gender equality, and debates on the state's involvement in decisions concerning family life. On the one hand, we have men who expressed negative attitudes towards what they saw as feminism and who regarded the state's impact on family life as a threat. On the other hand, we have men who praised the Swedish state for trying to create gender-equal families and who represented quite a radical way of looking at gender and identity. Those who worked in technical or economic sectors, thus earning quite a good wage, seemed generally to have more negative attitudes towards 'Feminism' and state involvement, whereas the attitudes of architects, researchers and care professionals seemed to be more positive.

The explanation for why certain men choose to spend a considerable amount of time with their small children is not easy to pinpoint or empirically reduce to one or two causal factors. Here, we must consider a complex combination of factors, such as social class, status, values, political views, economic restructuring and so on. But while it is difficult to pinpoint which exact aspects of a 'caring father' discourse some men are 'gripped by' (Glynos and Howarth, 2008), we can nevertheless bring to the fore that changes in parenting and parental leave practices represent changes also in the configuration of gender relations. Assuming an understanding of patriarchy as based on men's separation from and subjugation of women, we can also suggest that this serves as evidence of the 'unfixed' nature of patriarchy. When middle-class men begin talking in terms of life values, children, care and human capital, where does this leave us? If we agree that the presence of fathers staying at home with their children and engaging in the practices of nurturing and caring can be seen as signs of men engaging in practices traditionally deemed feminine, how should we conceive of such a change? How can we theorise a situation where masculinity seems less caught up in keeping a distance from what has traditionally been coded as feminine?

In this chapter, we will argue that the answers to questions like these are intimately caught up with how one understands the notion of *hegemonic masculinity*. We will also argue that how one understands hegemonic masculinity is intimately connected to how one thinks about and theorises stability and change. Recognising that some degree of fluidity and the possibility of change is a key aspect of any gender order is, of course, a central starting point to most Feminist theorising. For many Feminist researchers, it could even be described as the very reason for engaging in masculinity research at all. Yet, how one responds theoretically when change can be empirically discerned varies. On the one hand, it might be argued that there are all too many reasons to be quite sceptical, and sometimes perhaps even cynical, when it comes to claims that masculinity is changing and that the 'new man' who is less homophobic, less misogynous and less concerned about distancing himself from femininity is emerging. Following Demetriou (2001), we could argue that changes like these represent merely a reconfiguration of hegemony that might not be progressive at all. Hence, we should be wary that hybridisation and the articulation of new elements with hegemonic masculinity might only make hegemonic masculinity '*appear* less oppressive and more egalitarian' (Demetriou, 2001, p. 355, emphasis added). We should not be fooled by appearance and should instead notice that hegemonic masculinity

> changes in a very *deceptive* and unrecognizable way. It changes through negotiation, appropriation, and translation, through the transformation of what appears counter-hegemonic and progressive into an instrument of backwardness and patriarchal reproduction. [. . .] To understand hegemonic masculinity as hybridity is therefore to avoid falling into the trap of believing that patriarchy has disappeared simply because heterosexual men have worn earrings or because Sylvester Stallone has worn a new masquerade.
>
> (Demetriou, 2001, p. 355, emphasis in original)

Again, such scepticism might be warranted when thinking about the development of a 'new fatherhood' as a sign of shifts in patriarchy. In the public debate, it is sometimes argued that paternal leave should be considered a merit and something that you can put on your CV. It is argued that going on parental leave is a perfect opportunity to refine your emotional intelligence (Johansson, 2011a, b), develop your empathic abilities and further your leadership skills. Echoing such sentiments, we find texts explaining '[h]ow 6 months paternity leave made me a better entrepreneur' (Jakobsson, 2015), where we can learn from one Swedish entrepreneur that going on paternal leave is a way to learn how to prioritise and 'empower other people' through delegating responsibilities.

Here, one might indeed argue that what we are witnessing through the emergence of a 'new fatherhood' discourse is not so much a lessening of patriarchal power as an adaptation of hegemonic masculinity to changes in the economy and neoliberal restructuring. With Demetriou, we could argue that what we see is not progressive change at all but rather the appropriation of skills previously coded as feminine into hegemonic masculinity, which ultimately strengthens patriarchy through reconciling it with changes induced through economic restructuring. Such an analysis is not, however, the only possible conclusion to draw from changes like these. For example, it stands in sharp contrast to the way Eric Anderson (2009), whose work we will return to shortly, looks at contemporary changes in masculinity. For Anderson, changes like this instead represent a weakening of hegemonic masculinity and signify the arrival of a more progressive form of 'inclusive masculinity'.

It is around this conundrum—this tension around how to understand reconfigurations of masculinity in between stability and change—that this chapter revolves. At the centre is the notion of hegemonic masculinity and what analytical purchase this concept might have when it comes to understanding changing masculinity. It may be that we are currently observing a shift from a hard-core hegemonic masculinity—which is often described in terms of control, discipline, power, material values and so on (Connell, 1995)—to a more sensitive, caring, present and gender-equal masculinity and gender position. Although this is, of course, a slow and unevenly distributed transition, showing great variation across social strata and different countries, such a potential shift encourages us to adapt our conceptual framework and come up with new ideas about how we should analyse and theorise gender, power and masculinity. To some degree, we will argue in this chapter, the notion of hegemonic masculinity can stand in the way of such theoretical development. But, as we will also argue, transformations such as those described above can still be interpreted and dealt with in a revised and reformulated framework of hegemonic masculinity.

In this chapter, we will engage in such a reformulation and reframing. We will do so through a theoretical exploration of the concept of hegemonic masculinity, performed through an engagement with a few carefully selected theoreticians and studies. The main principle behind selecting these theoreticians/studies is the fact that they focus on hegemony and/or related concepts. Methodologically, the work will be performed in four steps: (a) As a starting point, we will work through Connell's conceptual framework, at the same time pointing out certain weaknesses in her theory. (b) Thereafter, we will revisit the critique directed at the concept and theoretical position outlined by Connell. (c) This will be followed by two sections presenting some possible ways of elaborating the concept. We will use Paul Ricoeur's theory of ideology and utopia to reflect upon the relation between the concepts of ideology and hegemony. This theoretical excursion will be used in order to look more thoroughly at the concept of hegemony and at alternative ways of elaborating upon this concept. Here we will use Laclau and Mouffe's theory of hegemony as a tool to explore more dynamic ways of conceptualising power and power relations, (d) which will lead to a more general discussion on how we can formulate a possible new theoretical framework, and what this means in relation to empirical research on fatherhood, for instance. Concluding the chapter, we will also discuss how the gap between the different positions outlined above (represented by Demetriou and Anderson) can to some degree be redressed through a discourse of the theoretical understanding of hegemony.

Ultimately, the ambition of this chapter is to develop the concept of hegemonic masculinity in such a way that it becomes useful for thinking about both stability and potentially progressive change. We suggest that this is important both for masculinity theory more broadly and specifically in relation to fatherhood research, where a theoretical model that emphasises and develops the dynamic qualities of Connell's theory of hegemonic masculinity is needed. We contend that this can be achieved by exploring a network of different masculine positions and by carefully investigating the often-contradictory aspects of hegemonic masculinity. In our view, Connell leans too much on the conceptual pair of hegemony-complicity, which leads to an underestimation of actual changes in gender patterns. The critique of traditional male hegemony—in which Feminist movements and oppositional masculinity have played a significant role—might now slowly be pointing towards the development of new patterns of power in everyday life but also to new possibilities for subverting gender and creating multiple gender positions. At the same time, it is important not to underestimate a more nostalgic and conservative masculine position that defends patriarchy and fights to protect men's privileges and power positions in society.

Hegemonic Masculinity

In the previous chapter, we touched upon some important aspects of how the notion of hegemonic masculinity can be understood. In order to elucidate some of the difficulties and challenges connected to the use of this concept, let us return for a moment to the way in which it was first established and introduced into the field. This is important because some of the problems that we will address, and to some degree try to transcend in this chapter, are present already in Connell's early definition of the concept, found in the ground-breaking 1995 study *Masculinities*. In this book on the transformation of masculinity, Connell defined hegemonic masculinity as follows:

> Hegemonic masculinity can be defined as the configuration of gender practice which embodies the currently accepted answer to the problem of the legitimacy of patriarchy, which guarantees (or is taken to guarantee) the dominant position of men and the subordination of women.

(Connell, 1995, p. 77)

This means that when historical conditions and relational gender patterns in society change, the hegemonic position can also be challenged and questioned. Consequently, hegemonic masculinity should be recognised as a historically changing configuration of relations between different groups of men and women. As can be seen, the concept is explicitly open for recognising change. Rather than specifying some ahistorical or universal content of masculinity, it points instead to a particular function in the gender order, namely to secure patriarchy. How this is done can vary, and the form of masculinity that is hegemonic at any given point in time hence varies and can be understood as the result of the struggle for hegemony. In this, the concept of hegemonic masculinity has been an alternative way of approaching and analysing gender relations, transgressing some of the limitations of more static theories of patriarchy that tend to portray gender relations in a structurally deterministic way (Nicholson, 1990; Haywood and Mac an Ghaill, 2003). However, the important question of whether this conceptual turn in fact leads to a more dynamic theory of the relation between structure, agency and change remains disputed. Connell herself has recently pointed out, 'The relation between hegemony and masculinity needs reassessment' (2016, p. 303). Even if Connell here argues that it is mainly Postcolonial critique and an intervention from the global South that motivates such reassessment, some of the problems she points to are very similar to the ones we discuss here. For instance, she aligns with Ratele (2013) in raising the question of whether '"traditional" masculinity automatically means patriarchal dominance' (Connell, 2016, p. 304) and recognises that notions of hegemonic masculinity risk becoming ahistorical when formulated in a way in which 'the reproduction of a hierarchical system is assumed' (p. 305). So, even if our argument in this chapter is based on other empirical material as the base for a mostly theoretical intervention, we find that further investigation into the concept is warranted, based on both Connell's own contemporary work and the critique against the concept formulated by others.

Connell had originally begun using the concept of hegemonic masculinity in the 1980s. The idea was that introducing this concept would facilitate a discussion on historical changes in patriarchy (Hearn, 2004). In doing this, she is following a long tradition of Marxian theory influenced by Italian Marxian Antonio Gramsci. Whereas Gramsci used the concept to analyse changes in Italian politics and focussed on struggles for hegemony between different political actors, Connell adapted the concept in a discussion of historical changes in the gender order. In *Gender & Power* (1987), Connell explains the way she uses this concept as follows:

> Ascendency of one group of men over another achieved at the point of the gun, or by threat of unemployment, is not hegemony. Ascendency which is embedded in religious doctrine and practice, mass media content, wage structures, the design of housing, welfare/taxation policies and so forth is.
>
> (p. 184)

Hegemonic masculinity is constituted and formed primarily in relation to three other masculine 'types' or rather modes of relating to the hegemonic position that will be discussed more closely below: namely, the complicit, subordinated and marginalised masculinities. Central to its construction is also its relation to women and femininity. The interplay between different masculinities is, according to Connell, an intrinsic part of the patriarchal order. A connected and important aspect of the concept of hegemony is that it is never fully established or stabilised. It does not suggest absolute power, autonomy or control but can instead be understood as a pragmatic response that neutralises challenges and balances out opposing forces temporarily. In an attempt to gain hegemony, it is possible to use different strategies and to be prepared to mix traits, attitudes and values into a blend of aspects and cultural patterns that form hegemonic masculinity.

This blending also underpins the fact that hegemonic masculinity is never entirely harmonious or even identical with itself. It relies on its 'outside' and could be considered impossible for any man or group of men to perfectly embody. It is here that Connell's notion of *complicity* becomes important. Connell uses the concept to discuss how men relate to power and to the hegemonic structures of masculinity. Even if actual men can never fully practice and embody hegemonic masculinity, Connell argues that many men have a kind of relation to hegemony that might be ambivalent but that is still, to some degree, rewarding in its relation to power. This contributes then also to the relative stability of patriarchy as a power structure that changes only slowly. Further contributing to this stability, Connell argues, is that 'a single structural fact—the global dominance of men over women'—permeates social life on all levels, from 'the level of the whole society [. . .] to the patterns of face-to-face relationship within institutions' (Connell, 1987, p. 183).

In *Masculinities* (1995), Connell elaborates on the concept of hegemony and especially on the relation between different masculinities. She also introduces a more complex discussion on the interplay between gender, race and class. Hegemony is still tightly connected to patriarchy and is described as a strategy to legitimise a particular gender order and a constellation of cultural ideals, institutional power, and politics. But the hegemonic position is always contestable and changeable. The power structure put forward is dynamic but also fairly stable and durable. This structure also builds on a hierarchical system of different gender relations and positions. In relation to the *hegemonic* position, these aforementioned positions are described either as being *subordinated* (for example, gay masculinity or 'feminine men') in terms of *complicity*—which means that the majority of men gain from the hegemonic patterns and benefit from the patriarchal dividend—or as being *marginalised*. Connell emphasises that these should not be considered 'fixed character types but configurations of practice generated in particular situations in a changing structure of relationships' (1995, p. 81). In her book, Connell also extends the discussion of possible relations to other structures such as class and race, and she introduces other configurations of masculinity such as protest masculinity. The book then builds on this short exposé on the concept of hegemony and the proposed relationship between hegemony, domination/ subordination and complicity, combined with a discussion of how marginalised masculinities intersect with these gender patterns, thus forming complex patterns of subordination and domination.

Since the publication of *Masculinities* in 1995, there has been intense academic discussion centred on the notion of hegemonic masculinity, and a number of articles have discussed, critiqued and tried to develop the theory of hegemony and masculinities put forward and developed by Connell. We will turn to this literature in the next section. Before continuing, we will discuss some of the impressions we have gained by reading Connell. First, the idea of hegemony is, strangely enough, underdeveloped. It is merely described as a strategy, based on cultural and symbolic expressions, that is used to maintain a stable gender order. Second, the different positions or relations described entail either control, power, and domination or loss of control, powerlessness, and subordination. The only relation/position that allows us to think beyond this polarised relational drama is complicity. However, this position does not allow for much resistance or change, because it is first and foremost described as underpinning hegemony. This impression is in line with Buschmeyer and Lengersdorf's (2016, p. 194) argument that Connell seems to be mainly concerned with the hierarchically structured binary categories of hegemonic versus subordinated masculinity, while the ' "other" categories of complicit and marginalised masculinity do not seem to fit into the hierarchical order she proposes and remain imprecise and underdeveloped.' Finally, our main impression from reading Connell is that she stays firmly within structuralism and that the difference between former theories of patriarchy and this theory of hegemonic masculinity is subtle and sometimes difficult to discern. There is of course a certain dynamism introduced in suggesting that the concrete manifestations of hegemonic masculinity can (and will) change, but, in our reading, Connell never transcends the structuralist notion that any such manifestation will ultimately work to secure patriarchy. So, while it is probably possible to interpret her theory of hegemonic masculinity as an attempt to move beyond theories of patriarchy and structuralism, we will nevertheless argue in this chapter that Connell stays firmly within structuralism. We will further argue that this connects to the conundrum of thinking about hegemony in relation to change and that it might be one of the reasons why qualitative shifts in hegemonic masculinity sometimes becomes hard to recognise and perhaps even encourage when warranted. Ultimately, our ambition is therefore to help renew the concept to better be able to account for both stability and change in contemporary hegemonic masculinity.

Modifications, Reformulations and Critique

Some of the problems pointed at above—connected to the latent structuralism and a tendency to recognise all change in hegemonic masculinity as reconfigurations aspiring to secure stability/patriarchy—have led masculinity researchers to either try to reconfigure the concept (Connell and Messerschmidt, 2005; Demetriou, 2001), challenge it (e.g. Anderson, 2009) or try to avoid it all together (e.g. Berggren, 2012). We have already touched upon this criticism in the previous chapter, but let us here be a bit more specific.

Jeff Hearn (2004) carefully evaluates and discusses the concept of hegemonic masculinity and its place in the research on men and masculinity. The main purpose of his article is to develop a critical framework usable in the studies on men. However, in his discussion, the concept of hegemony has a central position. Hearn presents an overview of the development of the concept from its Marxian beginnings up to Connell's elaboration. He argues for the study of multiple and differentiated forms of patriarchy and for a notion of hegemony that can be used to focus on both stable and changing structures as well as on fixed and flexible forms of gender identities. He also argues for more careful, detailed and empirically oriented studies of men and men's practices, not least to be able to better account for and recognise resistance, something he argues that Connell's notion of hegemony overlooks.

To some degree these aspects of Hearn's critique are in line with how Christine Beasley (2008a, b) critiques the monolithic and uniform use of the concept to refer to transnational business masculinity. She proposes a distinction between supra- and sub-hegemonic masculinities, in order to analyse men and masculinities at different levels of abstraction. In a reply, Messerschmidt (2008) claims that Connell actually deals with and has already solved these issues, pointing to a chapter published in the *Handbook of Studies on Men & Masculinities* (2005), where Connell writes extensively on the relation between local, regional and global masculinities.

More radically, Anderson can be seen as trying to empirically rebut the whole concept. We will engage more closely with Anderson's work here, both because it has caused some heated discussion among masculinity researchers (see e.g. Bridges, 2014; O'Neill, 2015) and because it is useful as a pedagogic device in representing a position far distanced from more structurally deterministic understandings of masculinity. Anderson's book *Inclusive Masculinity* (2009) can also be seen as representing a growing body of literature on gender, Queer Theory and masculinity. Anderson's thesis is that we are today witnessing a considerable change in masculinity. A lessening of homophobia gradually leads to a widening of the range of masculine identities and positions possible to embody and perform. Anderson (2008) nurtures quite an optimistic view on gender and changes in gender structures. However, he is fully aware that these changes are uneven and that in many masculine contexts and milieus masculinity is still defined as the opposite of femininity and homosexuality. At the same time, he is obviously describing and putting forward a scenario where masculinity is gradually becoming more inclusive and permissive and where there is less use for the concept of hegemony:

> Connell's model is unable to capture the proliferation of men's femininity and parity among masculinities that occurs in these settings. Results from this research show that heterosexual men exhibiting various forms of inclusive masculinity are not complicit to or subordinated by any singular version of masculinity. These men are not looking up to another form of hegemonic masculinity, or desiring to be associated with any one dominant archetype.
>
> (Anderson, 2009, p. 154)

As discussed in the beginning of this chapter, it is certainly possible to read changes such as these as a reconfiguration of, rather than a radical rupture in, hegemonic masculinity (see e.g. Demetriou, 2001). What we want to point at, however, is how the theoretical development and the critique of structuralism within gender theory and in particular Queer Theory has led to a questioning of certain categories, definitions, and ways of approaching and interpreting power and power relations (see also Halberstam, 1998). These theoretical advancements and descriptions of gender, families and identities are in many ways utopian, even though they also point at certain movements and changes in contemporary masculinities. It might also be, however, as some commentators suggest (O'Neill, 2015) that such flexibility and utopic visioning come at the price of losing track of gendered power relations.

Nevertheless, it seems from our reading of the discussion of hegemonic masculinity that most of the discussions have been centred around the issue of how to make the concept more usable in specific and local studies on masculinity and men's practices (Beasley, 2008a, b; Hearn et.al., 2012). Most of the critical voices accept the main premises and definitions of the concept but are calling for elaboration of different aspects of it. All in all, the concept has become part of a wider framework of Gender Studies and become a member of the category of accepted, and perhaps to some extent overused, concepts. However, when we accept and use this concept, we also place ourselves in a position where we tend to analyse the stability, fixity and ideological apparatus that keep the existing gender order intact and in place. This leaves little room for studies on change, on transformations and on contradictions. But the alternative route, as exemplified by the concept and discussion of inclusive masculinity, in the worst case leaves us without a theory of power.

In the following sections, we will introduce some ideas about how to develop the concept of hegemonic masculinity and will formulate ideas and develop conceptual tools that help us construct a more dynamic theory of gender, change and identity. We will use as our inspiration our readings of two central texts that contribute to the discussion on ideology, utopia and hegemony. In the first section, we will follow in the footpaths of Ricoeur and introduce his distinction between ideology and utopia in order to sharpen the focus on the dynamics between stability versus change and to explore the possibilities of opening up the concept of hegemony, and thus constructing a more dynamic theory of gender and society in transformation. The section following thereafter will investigate the possibility of connecting to and using Laclau and Mouffe's notion of hegemony in order to develop the theory of hegemonic masculinity.

The Dialectic between Ideology and Utopia

In his seminal work, *Lectures on Ideology and Utopia* (1986), Paul Ricoeur follows and discusses the concept of ideology from Marx via Mannheim, continuing to more recent applications of the concept. The greater part of this work is devoted to Marxian works on ideology, but a large section also presents and brings forward a discussion on utopia, and the dialectic between ideology and utopia. Even though the discussion Ricoeur builds on is, of course, more closely connected to class and capitalism rather than gender and patriarchy, we contend that there are also important theoretical insights that can be borrowed from Ricoeur when discussing gender and masculinity. More precisely, we suggest that this work can provide useful theoretical tools for thinking about and recognising shifts in hegemonic masculinity, as represented for instance by changes in contemporary fatherhood.

The concept of ideology is a close relative of hegemony, which was developed within Marxian and neo-Marxian analysis of the cultural level and its importance for maintaining social order (Hall, 1997). Although there are certain key differences between the concepts of ideology and hegemony—such as different intellectual roots in Marxian theory and different approaches to culture—there are also similarities. Whereas ideology is often defined as an integrative mechanism, securing the status quo, hegemony points more towards transition and substantial changes in societal and structural conditions (Howarth, 2000, p. 88ff). Perhaps it would be relevant to say at this point that the concept of hegemony presents a more dynamic and flexible way of approaching the same problems and questions formerly treated under the heading of ideology. We find his way of developing and expanding the concept useful, also when looking at hegemony.

Ricoeur distinguishes between three aspects or levels of ideology. First, it serves to *legitimate* the existing order. Second, it works to *distort* information and to present the existing order as an ideal order. Finally, it has an *integrative* function. When this function becomes frozen, ideology turns into an *ideological* and more rigid system of thought, desperately defending the existing order. According to Ricoeur, human social life is always intrinsically symbolic and therefore possible to distort. In his careful dissection of ideology, Ricoeur contributes to a more elaborate analysis of the concept. These elaborations are also useful when looking more closely at the concept of hegemony, as they suggest that careful analysis of how hegemony is constructed through distortions (e.g. media images presenting acceptable and normative definitions of gender, family and identity) and of its integrative function (i.e. creating an impression not only that the existing order is the best order but that it has to be defended and kept; otherwise, chaos and disorder will follow) may be fruitful. Hegemony points to a dynamic struggle between different groups of individuals and collectives, leading to a temporarily but quite stable and legitimised gender order. Note that this order, according to Connell and her followers, is by definition a patriarchy, which leads us back to the concept of ideology.

The twin concepts of ideology and hegemony are very useful when analysing how a traditional or a 'new' gender order is defended, maintained, stabilised and presented. But if we wish to analyse change and cultural transformations, we also need a vision and perhaps a utopia. Contrary to a commonsensical notion of utopia as an unrealistic and futuristic vision, utopia should not, according to Ricoeur, be thought of as merely a dream or an unrealisable concept. According to Ricoeur, the relation between ideology and utopia can be described as follows:

> A utopia is then always in the process of being realized. Ideology, in contrast, does not have the problem of being realized, because it is the legitimation of what is.
>
> (1986, p. 273)

Ricoeur considers that ideology is connected to dominant groups and their self-representations and presentations of their self, whereas utopia is plausible, fictional and connected to ascending groups. The key idea here is that utopia is not unrealisable but instead a reasonable vision of what can be achieved through struggle for change.

Connecting Ricoeur's distinction between ideology and utopia back to our reading of the discussion on hegemonic masculinity, we would argue that this literature has first and foremost focused on how the present gender order is being preserved and defended, that is, the ideological aspects of the gender order. Although the concept of hegemonic masculinity is presented as a dynamic tool for analysing contradictions, changes and transformations of the gender order, attempts at such analyses often end up in descriptions of the existing order. In the end, hegemony equals ideology, that is, a concept that is basically used to describe and analyse how an existing gender order / patriarchy is defended, struggled for and maintained. In doing this, we can use the elaboration of the concept of ideology as introduced by Ricoeur. For instance, Ricoeur's idea that ideology works through distortion connects very well to Demetriou's (2001, p. 355) warning that hegemonic masculinity changes in very 'deceptive' ways. However, if we want to find a way to reconfigure the notion of hegemonic masculinity so as to emphasise its contextual and processual dimension and to push beyond what is already present, to go beyond ideology and find ways of thinking about hegemonic masculinity that can harbour sameness to femininity and be less dependent on the differentiation from and subjugation of women, we should instead pick up on the 'plausible utopian' push in his theorising. One way of doing so (that is, of formulating a more dynamic theory of gender, hegemony and change) is—we would like to argue—to turn to Laclau and Mouffe.

Hegemony in between Stability and Change

If one thinks of changing fatherhood as an empirical example of shifts in hegemonic masculinity that point towards qualitative change rather than mere reconfiguration of patriarchy, the work of Ernesto Laclau and Chantal Mouffe becomes relevant. The notion of hegemony in discussions on hegemonic masculinity is primarily inspired by Gramsci's conceptualisation of hegemony. Oddly enough, Laclau and Mouffe are not mentioned in, for example, Connell's *Masculinities*. Their famous and very influential study *Hegemony and Socialist Strategy* (1985/2001) is not referred to or included in the discussion on hegemonic masculinity referred to above. This work is often considered post-structuralist, which automatically places it in a somewhat strained relation to mainstream sociology. Gramsci is also the starting point for Laclau and Mouffe. These authors are also often referred to as post-Marxists, which should be understood as a label signifying a process of going beyond but also drawing on and re-reading the Marxian tradition. According to these authors, hegemonic struggles are the result of and a response to 'the impossibility of society' (Laclau, 1990, p. 89ff); they are the symptom of the always already dislocated nature of society, of contingency and of the fissures that different groups try to cover over and fill up.

One of the keystones in the post-Marxist understanding of hegemony is the impossibility of an ultimate fixed meaning and hence the impossibility of any fully constituted and completely centred structures. Instead what we are offered is a view of partial fixations, and repeated attempts to arrest the flow of meaning and construct a centre. This also has implications for the definition of the subject. The concept of hegemony was originally used to refer to the partial fixation and stratification of a field of *subject positions*, which are constructed in relation to the open character of every discourse. Subject positions can, however, never be totally fixed and stable. Instead they are moveable and transitional. In later works, Laclau has also elaborated his understanding of subjectivity, suggesting that the subject should be understood as the 'distance between the undecidability of the structure and the moment of decision' (1990, p. 30). We find here a way of thinking about the subject *before* its identification with a subject position, which also draws out a novel way of thinking about agency as rooted neither in something external to the structure nor in something completely internal to it, but rather a potentiality arising from the fact that 'the structure itself is undecidable and cannot be entirely repetitive'.

Another key concept is antagonism. Hegemony is only possible in a field of criss-crossed antagonisms.

Thus, the two conditions of a hegemonic articulation are the presence of antagonistic forces and the instability of the frontiers which separate them. Only the presence of a vast area of floating elements and the possibility of their articulation to opposite camps—which implies a constant redefinition of the latter—is what constitutes the terrain permitting us to define a practice as hegemonic (Laclau, 1990, p. 136).

This also connects to a further aspect of how Laclau and Mouffe theorise hegemony. According to them, the construction of hegemony always involves the working of two logics: a logic of equivalence and a logic of difference. A logic of equivalence operates when identities, groups or elements are made equivalent and appeal for hegemony not through their internal similarities (though there might be such similarities) but rather through a shared oppositional orientation towards a common enemy, competing group or external element (Glynos and Howarth, 2007, p. 143ff). A logic of difference instead operates when hegemony is sought through articulating different elements together emphasising their similarity or compatibility. The terms can be somewhat misleading in that a logic of equivalence points not towards equivalence between the internal elements being articulated but rather their equivalence in opposition to a common Other. A logic of difference instead represents a more inclusive, less confrontative logic in that it tries to include and articulate together different elements or groups through a form of coalition-building emphasising similarity and shared interest. As Glynos and Howarth (2007, p. 144) point at, the two logics always operate at the same time in the construction of hegemony, since any 'inclusive' identity is always established in relation to something external to it. Analytically, one can, however, separate the two in analysing processes of hegemonisation that emphasise one pole more than the other. An example that Glynos and Howarth (2007, p. 144) use to illustrate this is how political struggles against a colonial power can often unite very different groups through a logic of equivalence. One need not share much other than an oppositional stance toward the current regime. Assuming that the struggle is successful and the common enemy is overthrown, we might instead enter a phase where one tries to establish hegemony emphasising a logic of difference, where hegemony is sought through trying to recruit recognisably different groups into the hegemonic project. Laclau and Mouffe (1985/2001, p. 130) discuss the construction of the Welfare State as one such example of a hegemonic project that emphasises a logic of difference. Here, a reliance on including different groups while being 'good for all' is important in legitimising the project. Another example of a situation where a logic of equivalence dominates heavily might be the US response to the terror bombings of 9/11. When Bush declares that you are either with us or against us in 'the war on terrorism', this all but explicitly involves the activation of a logic of equivalence, where terrorism as a common enemy is taken to (hoped to) eradicate all other differences between 'good nations'.

Now, recognising that both of these logics are always at work in the construction of hegemony, we can return to the 'paradox' that opened this chapter, which points at how one can draw very different conclusions regarding the meaning of such elements as 'care' and 'sensitivity' previously coded as feminine, articulated *into* hegemonic masculinity. On the one hand, we have writers such as Demetriou (2001) and O'Neill (2015) who suggest that what we see is merely a reconfiguration of hegemonic masculinity that obscures the male subjugation of women. On the other hand, we have Anderson and inclusive masculinity theorists who seem to suggest that we have somehow arrived in a situation 'beyond hegemony', where plural masculinities exist without being hierarchically ordered relative to each other or to women. If we, for the argument, accept that it is a correct observation that masculinity at the current point in time does not rely so heavily on expressions of misogyny or distancing from femininity as it once did, we can now, drawing on a discourse of the theoretical understanding of hegemony to some degree, reconcile both of these positions. What these two positions represent can be seen, then, as merely a difference of emphasis in relation to what logic is given precedence. Demetriou and O'Neill seem to emphasise the working of a logic of equivalence where it can be accepted that, yes, new elements (such as 'care' or 'intimacy') are articulated with masculinity but that the overarching logic to be wary about is the operation of a logic of equivalence that depends on women as Other in establishing its hegemony. In the case of inclusive masculinity theory, we can instead recognise an emphasis on a logic of difference, in that new elements are articulated with heterosexual masculinity in a way that is less reliant upon an oppositional relation to femininity. Recognising with Laclau and Mouffe (1985/2001) that both of these logics are always in operation in the establishment of hegemony, we are inclined to agree with critics of inclusive masculinity theory that what we see here is not an upheaval of hegemonic masculinity but rather a reconfiguration that in its adaptation to new societal conditions articulates new (previously 'unmanly') elements within masculinity. This does not mean, however, that we need to be as pessimistic as Demetriou and O'Neill and suggest that what we see is a preservation of the status quo and merely an 'obscuring' of the real oppressive relation always present between men and women.

What it does suggest, however, is that there might be good reason to try to connect aspects of Ricoeur's thinking on utopia with Laclau and Mouffe's theorising of hegemony. We believe there is room for such Ricoeurian optimism in Laclau and Mouffe's theorising of hegemony for several reasons. Compared to more structurally deterministic understandings of hegemony, we find that Laclau and Mouffe draw out the discussion of hegemony and hegemonic struggles through formulating a more open field of discourses, language games, and antagonisms, which leads to a more dynamic view on hegemonic articulations and struggles. Within this view, hegemony is never fully achieved. It is always in motion and a constitutive part of 'the political', and, because it is ontologically conditioned by an ever-present contingency, we will never be able to go 'beyond hegemony'. However, this should not be read as a dystopic vision suggesting that we will never be 'free'. Rather, it can be seen as a call to struggle against repressive structures by trying to redefine and rearticulate the current hegemony and in so doing construct a new and more desirable (temporary) order. Laclau and Mouffe have also written extensively on how to imagine a more just and democratic society, embodied in a vision of what they call radical democracy (1985/2001; see also, e.g., Mouffe, 2000). Our point here, however, is not to discuss the details of how they imagine this radical democratic order but more to point out the simple fact that they do. That is, they, like Gramsci, approach hegemony not as something one should try to get rid of but rather as something to struggle for. In Ricoeur's sense, they can hence be seen as utopian in that they try to conceive of better and more democratic ways of hegemonising the social.

Transferred to the discussion on hegemonic masculinity, the concept of hegemony should be used to analyse antagonisms, transitional subject positions and the ongoing struggle to create hegemonic formations. This means, for example, that one should avoid using the concept as a merely classificatory tool, or using it to analyse stable positions or relations. Applying a post-Marxian concept of hegemony means that we are primarily interested in changes, transitions and articulations of new and potentially radical strategies for changing the gender order.

Connecting Hegemony and Utopia

Following this line of reasoning, it is our view that a dynamic and fruitful concept of hegemony for masculinity theory can be found in the relation between hegemony and utopia. Ricoeur helps us to understand that ideology primarily serves to stabilise and maintain a certain order, for example, the gender order or patriarchy. Through his discussion of the dialectic between ideology and utopia, and his particular way of reading and understanding utopia as a realisable social and cultural condition, he also helps us look for a conceptualisation that will enable us to analyse hegemonic re-articulations and transformations. In this regard, his notion of utopia can be connected to Laclau and Mouffe's ambition of trying to hegemonise the social in terms of radical democracy.

In our reading, Laclau and Mouffe point forward towards a possible theoretical framework when they stress the unstable equilibrium of hegemony, and the possibilities of transitioning towards a more democratic society. In this view, radical democracy can be achieved through a struggle to establish new and alternative chains of equivalents and significations. Social change is primarily based not on renouncing and destroying a certain order but instead on re-writing and re-defining this order. According to Laclau and Mouffe, the liberal-democratic ideology, for example, can be expanded and deepened into a project of radical and plural democracy. The *unfixity* of the liberal discourse permits a number of possible articulations and re-definitions, which will accentuate and enhance the democratic moment. Discussions of hegemonic masculinity often end up in an analysis of how the contemporary gender order is upheld and fixed. When change can be discerned, instead of reading this as giving rise to potential ruptures to be exploited, what is recognised are often the aspects that do not change, that still remain stable and that should be seen as 'deceptive' reconfigurations of hegemonic masculinity rather than real change. Although the ambition has been to create a dynamic concept and theoretical tool, these types of analysis have often resulted in categorisations and quite demobilising descriptions of the oppressive and never-changing gender order. We are not suggesting that we should replace these kinds of analysis with more optimistic and probably naïve conceptualisations of society, gender and identity. However, by using Laclau and Mouffe's approach to hegemony, we can begin to analyse how the relation between ideology and utopia is developing in contemporary times. If we accept that the social is open for redefinitions and change, which in turn leads to a plural space of different possible subject positions, we will also have tools that allow us to analyse how hegemonic re-articulations lead not only to a status quo—that is, a reinforcement of the given order—but also to the formation of a new and perhaps also more desirable order.

The crucial limitation of many discussions of hegemonic masculinity is the tendency to predetermine the agents of change and to automatically treat changes in masculinity as signs of a strengthening of patriarchy and not possible movements towards a new hegemony that contains the seeds of utopian visions of how the relation between men and men and between men and women can be performed (Kimmel et al., 2005). One then often ends up in somewhat cynical analyses that suggest that all we ever see is surface change rather than efforts to identify and deepen potentially progressive ruptures in hegemonic masculinity and hence take part in rearticulating the concept.

Hegemony, Masculinity, Femininity: Breaking the Structuralist Triad

We contend that one reason for this might be that one is so caught up in Connell's structuralist understanding of hegemonic masculinity as the legitimising response to challenges to patriarchy that any other form of hegemonic masculinity becomes inconceivable. To avoid this we would suggest instead a re-articulation of the concept that enables us to envision other forms of hegemonic masculinity, for instance, in response to shifts in contemporary fatherhood. For such a re-articulation of hegemony to be desirable, however, we must of course break with Connell's structuralist notion of hegemonic masculinity as always being defined in opposition to 'emphasised femininity'. This is a term chosen deliberately to fix femininity—even in theory—as always subjugated to masculinity (Connell and Messerschmidt, 2005, p. 848). If we follow Demetriou (2001), however, we can analytically try to separate the aspects of hegemony that correspond to *internal* hierarchies between men from the *external* relation of hegemonic masculinity to women. As Demetriou suggests, it is unfortunate that Connell does not discuss explicitly the relation between these different dimensions of hegemony (which corresponds to the possibility of differing emphasis between the logics of difference and the logics of equivalence in the construction of hegemony, as discussed above). While Demetriou argues that these two are interconnected and represent 'arguably inseparable functions of hegemonic masculinity' (2001, p. 341), we agree with Demetriou that a separation between these two logics might be analytically fruitful. This is because if we break the unclear and taken-for-granted connection between internal and external hegemony, it becomes possible to argue that what hegemonic masculinity represents is not a discourse that ultimately *always* works to subjugate women/femininity (cf. Moller, 2007, p. 268ff). What we have to break with then is also the notion that all forms of hegemony are equally bad and that the ultimate goal of emancipatory struggle must be to do away with hegemony. As Laclau (1990, p. 33) argues:

> A harmonious society is impossible because power is the condition for society to be possible. [. . .] Even in the most radical and democratic projects, social transformation thus means building a new power, not radically eliminating it. Destroying the hierarchies on which sexual or racial discrimination is based will, at some point, always require the construction of other exclusions for collective identities to be able to emerge.

Following Laclau and Mouffe, we hence accept the notion that: 'there is no "beyond hegemony" ' (Mouffe, 2005, p. 118). Yet suggesting this must not be interpreted as foreclosing on the possibility of thinking beyond patriarchy. Rather, the notion that there is no 'beyond hegemony' must be qualified so that it cannot be taken as a suggestion that masculinity will always be hegemonic in relation to femininity. What we need to do, then, is to try to disentangle the notion of hegemony from its taken-for-granted connection to some specific form of masculinity.

Part of the problem here, we would like to suggest, is that the term 'hegemonic masculinity' tends to conflate what we can understand as the ontic category of masculinity with the ontological notion of hegemony. When discourse theorists assert that there is no 'beyond hegemony', this is because indeterminacy, contingency and the struggle for hegemony are part of one's social ontology. As Howarth (2000, p. 112) explains:

> [I]it should be stressed [. . .] that Laclau and Mouffe's discursive approach is not concerned with the nature of specific types of object, practice, institutions, or even concrete discourses. In Heidegger's terms, they are not conducting an ontical analysis of particular sorts of entities, but are concerned with the necessary presuppositions of any inquiry into the nature of objects and social relations (Mulhall, 1996, p. 4). In short, they are concerned with ontological questions.

What Howarth points out in this quote, drawing on Heidegger's distinction between the ontic and the ontological, is that there is a difference between engaging with ontological questions such as what makes society (im)possible or how hegemony operates and engaging with empirical analysis of 'particular sorts of entities' at the ontical level (see also Dreyfus, 1991, p. 19f; Howarth, 2004; Marchart, 2007; Mulhall, 1996). Masculinity, conceived in Connell's terminology as a particular configuration of gender practice, should in our view be seen as such a 'particular sort of entity' and hence as an 'empirical phenomena at the ontical level' (Glynos and Howarth 2007, p. 30). Hegemony, on the other hand, is an ontological concept deeply intertwined with what makes society (im)possible (Laclau, 1990, p. 33). Suggesting, as Mouffe, that there is no 'beyond hegemony' must hence be seen as a proposition at the ontological level.

The confusion to be avoided, then, is to conflate these two and to read the proposition that there is no beyond hegemony as suggesting that there is no beyond hegemonic masculinity—or, perhaps more to the point, that there is no way of going beyond a situation in which masculinity is privileged over femininity. As Laclau and Mouffe have argued, it is important to keep these levels apart and not to 'specify the content of these elements [e.g. masculinity] at the ontological level, as this would predetermine their character at the ontical level in ways reminiscent of Marxist theory' (Howarth, 2000, p. 118). Translating this to the context of the present chapter, we can hence argue that just as it is unfortunate for Marxian theory to theoretically presuppose that the working class will be the agent of revolutionary change, it is unfortunate for a theory of gender to presuppose that we will always find a configuration of masculinity hegemonic when conducting research on the ontical level. Thus, from a discourse theoretical perspective, we can conclude that one should not confuse the ontological proposition that hegemony will always exist (because society is 'impossible', since a structure can never be fully closed) with the 'content oriented' ontic category of masculinity. The concept of hegemonic masculinity can, then, be seen as a somewhat unfortunate mixture of ontic and ontological concepts, and we think that this can explain some of the difficulties associated with thinking beyond patriarchy through the notion of hegemonic masculinity.

This is also where we think there might be a productive point of convergence between Ricoeur's notion of utopia and Laclau and Mouffe's notion of radical democracy. Combining Ricoeur with Laclau and Mouffe encourages us to start thinking about how one can imagine less injurious forms of hegemonic masculinity. This can help us avoid getting caught up in what Wendy Brown (1993), with reference to Nietzsche, calls '*ressentiment*', focusing all our analytical energy on the injuries suffered from hegemonic masculinity.The object of such a project would then be not to try to leap 'beyond hegemony' but rather to start sketching a new masculine imaginary that might not have to rely so heavily on being defined as opposed to and privileged over femininity.

Part of such a struggle, we believe, would be to start articulating elements that have been historically associated with femininity with masculinity as well. To use the words of Laclau and Mouffe already quoted above, this would be a matter of putting 'the instability of the frontiers' that separate masculinity from femininity to good use. It would be a matter of destabilising the frontier by extending chains of equivalence across it. And this, we would like to argue, is precisely what we see happening in relation to the new fatherhood discourse. Articulating child care and life quality beyond the work sphere with masculinity might not ultimately lead to a complete upheaval of masculinity. But it might be part of a reconfiguration of hegemonic masculinity that might not a priori have to be understood as privileged in relation to femininity but rather take a more negotiating position in relation to norms of femininity. This is of course utopian, but only in Ricoeur's sense—as something that is possible to imagine and realise—rather than utopian as in a complete flight from the political and beyond all hegemony.

Conclusion

The new cultural patterns in fatherhood, and the specific processes which have taken place within certain families, can be taken as evidence of substantial changes in contemporary masculinity/fatherhood. These changes leave imprints on values/ ethics, lifestyles, issues of career and life planning, and, most importantly, the constant ongoing construction of masculinity/identity. We have, of course, not yet achieved the kind of inclusive masculinity Anderson describes and puts forward, but, based on the introductory example of men staying at home with their infants, we can discern traces of such changes. This is also just one of many examples of changes in the gender landscape. Ultimately, then, whether we should understand this new fatherhood discourse as just an update and adaptation of hegemonic masculinity to new societal circumstances, or as a more radical break with earlier notions of hegemonic masculinity, is to some degree an analytical choice. What we would like to suggest, however, is that even if we look at this discourse as (merely) a reconfiguration of hegemonic masculinity, it may still represent a desirable move. Using a Post-structuralist notion of hegemony, we can imagine that a gradual reconfiguration of hegemony could be a goal worth struggling for.

Hegemonic masculinity is an important concept in gender research and critical studies on men and masculinity. Larger parts of the discussion and revision of the concept are taking place within a structural framework, and the concept is mostly used to analyse how patriarchy is maintained, safe-guarded and upheld by men. Based on our reading of Ricoeur, we have argued that hegemony is often read through the lenses of the concept of ideology. In order to set things in motion, Ricoeur introduces the conceptual pair of ideology and utopia. This distinction clarifies certain things, but it is in itself too rigid and polar. Laclau and Mouffe formulate a theory of hegemony that allows us to, on the one hand, introduce more options and agency into the theory of hegemony and, on the other, to read and understand re-articulations of hegemony as part of the struggle for gender equality and a more just society. Once evacuated of the power to always ultimately subjugate women or femininity, struggles for reconfiguring hegemonic masculinity can be read as containing and pointing towards utopia and a to hope for changes towards a more gender-equal and less patriarchal society. According to Laclau and Mouffe, there will always be antagonisms and struggles for power, but this does not necessarily mean that all hegemonic projects are equally as bad.

The case study on Scandinavian fatherhood that introduced this chapter can be read as an example of a slow but gradual process towards a more gender-neutral and equal parenthood. This study points towards variation, complexity and possible developments in hegemonic masculinity. It is possible to use this case as an example of a re-configuration of hegemony, containing the seeds and the hope of a transformation of intimacy and close relations, in line with the ideals of gender equity and equal rights. Again, looking at the bigger picture, we of course acknowledge that we are merely observing partial changes in hegemony. These changes are also closely connected to the middle class, and we need to analyse more closely—using intersectional analyses—how these transformations affect more general gender relations in society. However, if what we are witnessing now in certain countries and contexts can be analysed as a significant change in hegemonic masculinity, then this historical process can also be read and understood as a key transformation of, and a partial disruption of, patriarchy. If we accept this, then it becomes necessary to identify and analyse the evolvement of subject positions and articulations that enable us to renew and create a more gender-equal order in society. This change would probably still be possible to understand as part of changes in the formation of a specific type of hegemonic masculinity, but it could also lead us to other ways of approaching hegemony.

Following a similar line of reasoning, let us finally also return to the gap regarding how to theorise a possible shift in hegemonic masculinity initiated by the transitions in fatherhood which opened the chapter. As we have argued throughout this chapter, a recognition that there is no 'beyond hegemony' should not lead to the passivating conclusion that any one hegemony is as bad as the other. So, while Anderson and inclusive masculinity theorists seem to forget about gendered power relations and misrecognise the working of a logic of difference in constructions of hegemonic masculinity for the end of hegemony, we are inclined to suggest that there still might be something progressive with such a reconfiguration of hegemonic masculinity—not because it takes us beyond hegemony, but rather that it might represent a shift in hegemonic masculinity towards less reliance on misogyny and an associated fear of femininity among men. Extrapolating such a development, we might even begin to envision a version of masculinity that is not caught up in a gender binaristic system where its hegemony is established through the subjugation of women as the Other. This would then represent nothing as revolutionary as Anderson and inclusive masculinity theorists suggest, but, in its being conceivable, we can still with Ricoeur (1986) understand it as utopian.

References

Anderson, E. (2008) Inclusive masculinity in a fraternal setting. *Men and Masculinities*, 10(5), 604–620.

Anderson, E. (2009) *Inclusive Masculinities: The Changing Nature of Masculinity*. London: Routledge.

Beasley, C. (2008a) Rethinking hegemonic masculinity in a globalizing world. *Men and Masculinities*, 11(1), 86–103.

Beasley, C. (2008b) Reply to Messerschmidt and to Howson. *Men and Masculinities*, 11(1), 114–115.

Berggren, K. (2012) 'No homo': Straight inoculations and the queering of masculinity in Swedish hip hop. *NORMA—Nordic Journal for Masculinity Studies*, 7(1), 50–66.

Bridges, T. (2014) A very "gay" straight?: Hybrid masculinities, sexual aesthetics, and the changing relationship between masculinity and homophobia. *Gender & Society*, 28(1), 58–82.

Brown, W. (1993) Wounded attachments. *Political Theory*, 21(3), 390–410.

Buschmeyer, A. and Lengersdorf, D. (2016) The differentiation of masculinity as a challenge for the concept of hegemonic masculinity. *NORMA—Nordic Journal for Masculinity Studies*, 11(3), 190–207.

Connell, R.W. (1987) *Gender & Power*. Cambridge: Polity Press.

Connell, R.W. (1995) *Masculinities*. Cambridge: Polity Press.

Connell, R.W. (2005) Globalization, imperialism, and masculinities. In: Kimmel, M.S., Hearn, J. and Connell, R.W. eds. *Handbook of Studies on Men & Masculinities*. London: Sage, pp. 71–89.

Connell, R.W. (2016) Masculinities in global perspective: hegemony, contestation, and changing structures of power. *Theory and Society*, 45(4), 303–318.

Connell, R.W. and Messerschmidt, J. (2005) Hegemonic masculinity: Rethinking the concept. *Gender & Society*, 19(6), 829–859.

Demetriou, D.Z. (2001) Connell's concept of hegemonic masculinity: A critique. *Theory and Society*, 30(3), 337–361.

Dreyfus, H.L. (1991) *Being-in-the-World*. Cambridge, MA: MIT Press.

Glynos, J. and Howarth, D. (2007) *Logics of Critical Explanation in Social and Political Theory*. London: Routledge.

Glynos, J. and Howarth, D. (2008) Structure, agency and power in political analysis: Beyond contextualised self-interpretations. *Political Studies Review*, 6(2), 155–169.

Halberstam, J. (1998) *Female Masculinity*. Durham, NC: Duke University Press.

Hall, S. (1997) *Representation: Cultural Representations and Signifying Practices*. London: Sage.

Haywood, C. and Mac an Ghaill, M. (2003) *Men and Masculinities*. Buckingham: Open University Press.

Hearn, J. (2004) From hegemonic masculinity to the hegemony of men. *Feminist Theory*, 5(1), 49–72.

Hearn, J., Nordberg, M., Andersson, K., Balkmar, D., Gottzén, L., Klinth, R., Pringle, K. and Sandberg, L. (2012) Hegemonic masculinity and beyond: 40 years of research in Sweden. *Men and Masculinities*, 15(1), 31–55.

Howarth, D. (2000) *Discourse*. Buckingham: Open University Press.

Howarth, D. (2004) Towards a Heideggerian social science: Heidegger, Kisiel and Weiner on the limits of anthropological discourse. *Anthropological Theory*, 4(2), 229–247.

Jakobsson, H. (2015) How 6 months paternity leave made me a better entrepreneur. *Entrepreneur* [Available 2016–09–21] www.entrepreneur.com/article/249430

Johansson, T. (2011a) Fatherhood in transition: Paternity leave and changing masculinities. *Journal of Family Communication*, 11(3), 165–180.

Johansson, T. (2011b) The construction of the new father: How middle-class men become present fathers. *International Review of Modern Sociology*, 37(1), 111–126.

Johansson, T. and Klinth, R. (2008) Caring fathers: The ideology of gender equality and masculine positions. *Men and Masculinities*, 11(1), 42–62.

Kimmel, M.S., Hearn, J. and Connell, R.W. (eds.) (2005) *Handbook of Studies on Men and Masculinities*. London: Sage.

Laclau, E. (1990) *New Reflections on the Revolution of our Time*. London: Verso.

Laclau, E. and Mouffe, C. (1985/2001) *Hegemony and Socialist Strategy: Towards a Radical* Democratic *Politics*. 2nd ed. London: Verso.

Marchart, O. (2007) *Post-Foundational Political Thought: Political Difference in Nancy, Lefort, Badiou, Laclau. Edinburgh*: Edinburgh University Press.

Messerschmidt, J.W. (2008) And now, the rest of the story: A commentary on Christine Beasley's rethinking hegemonic masculinity in a globalizing world. *Men and Masculinities*, 11(1), 104–108.

Moller, M. (2007) Exploiting patterns: A critique of hegemonic masculinity. *Journal of Gender Studies*, 16(3), 263–276.

Mouffe, C. (2000) *The Democratic Paradox*. London: Verso.

Mouffe, C. (2005) *On the Political*. London: Routledge.

Mulhall, S. (1996) *Heidegger and Being and Time*. London: Routledge.

Nicholson, L.J. (1990) *Feminism/Postmodernism*. New York: Routledge.

O'Neill, R. (2015) Whither critical masculinity studies? Notes on inclusive masculinity theory, postfeminism, and sexual politics. *Men and Masculinities*, 18(1), 100–120.

Ratele, K. (2013). Masculinities without tradition. *Politikon*, 40(1), 133–156.

Ricoeur, P. (1986) *Lectures on Ideology and Utopia*. New York: Columbia University Press.

4 Homosociality
Misogyny, Fraternity and New Intimacies

Introduction

The concept of *homosociality* describes and defines social bonds between persons of the same sex. It is, for example, frequently used in studies on men and masculinities, there defined as a mechanism and social dynamic that explains the maintenance of a hegemonic masculinity. A popular use of the concept is found in studies on male friendship, male bonding and fraternity orders. It is also frequently applied to explain how men, through their friendships and intimate collaborations with other men, maintain and defend the gender order and patriarchy (Lipman-Blumen, 1976; Bird, 1996). However, this common and somewhat overexploited use of the concept, referring to how men uphold patriarchy through their relations to other men, tends to simplify and reduce homosociality to an almost descriptive term that is used to show how men bond, build closed teams and defend their privileges and positions. In this chapter, we aim to explore, unpack and re-define the concept of homosociality, especially male homosocial relations. Our ambition is to make this concept available for understanding how men look upon intimate relationships, in terms of power, friendship and transformation. Through a reading of contemporary and significant Anglo-Saxon and European literature, in particularly Cultural Studies, that uses the concept to analyse different textual and social phenomena, our ambition is to explore and problematise the use of homosociality in studies of gender and masculinity. We will highlight different empirical examples of homosocial relations, in both the research and popular culture, and we will explore different aspects of homosociality, looking at how these characteristics relate to each other and what implications they might have for men's relationships, for relationships between gay men and for female homosociality.

This chapter is especially interested in developing and emphasising the contradictory and ambivalent aspects of homosociality, pointing both towards the defence of hegemonic masculinity and towards a silent and slow process that might undermine or reconstruct this power structure, as it appears today in many Western countries. In our view, the concept of homosociality is often defined as a mechanism and social dynamic that explains the maintenance of hegemonic masculinity, situating gender relations within a reasonably stable power structure. Connecting to the ongoing discussion of reformulations and redefinitions of hegemonic masculinity, we want to explore how homosocial processes contribute to the gradual deconstruction and reconstruction of gendered power structures (Buschmeyer and Lengensdorf, 2016). A central theme in this book is the gradual transformation of what we mean by hegemony, especially in relation to masculinity. One way of looking upon this relation is to bring the attention to the gradual loosening of the earlier somewhat tighter connection between hegemony and masculinity. However, another thought on this would be to discuss a thorough transformation of what hegemonic masculinity means today and to turn the attention to how power is restructured and taking new gendered shapes and forms.

A complex, refined and dynamic view on homosociality is found in Eve Kosofsky Sedgwick's classic study *Between Men* (1985). Instead of using the concept merely as a tool to analyse social bonds and power relations between men, Sedgwick discusses the relation between different types of desire and intimate relationships between men:

> To draw the 'homosocial' back into the orbit of 'desire', of the potentially erotic, then, is to hypothesize the potential unbrokenness of a continuum between homosocial and homosexual—a continuum whose visibility, for men, in our society, is radically disrupted.
>
> (Sedgwick, 1985, pp. 1–2)

Through her analysis of the complex relationship between homosociality, homosexuality, and homophobia, Sedgwick develops an interesting and useful theory of gender and masculinity. Her main thesis is that a continuous relation is radically disrupted and gradually turned into a discontinuous relation of male homosocial and homosexual bonds, whereas there is a much more continuous relation between female homosocial and homosexual bonds:

> For instance, the diacritical opposition between the 'homosocial' and the 'homosexual' seems to be much less thorough and dichotomous for women, in our society, than for men. [. . .] The apparent simplicity—the unity—of the continuum between 'women loving women' and 'women promoting the interests of women', extending over the erotic, social, familial, economic, and political realms, would not be so striking if it were not in strong contrast to the arrangement among males.
>
> (Sedgwick, 1985, pp. 2–3)

The discontinuity between male homosociality and homosexuality results in male homosocial relationships being a form of 'male bonding', which is characterised by homosocial desire and intimacy, as well as a homosexual panic. 'Homosocial desire' refers to men turning their attention to other men, and 'homosexual panic' refers to the fear of this attention gliding over into homosexual desire. In an attempt to emphasise heterosexuality, fear or hatred of homosexuals and misogynist language are developed.

The sexual harassment of young men by other young men can be seen as a technique not only to consolidate heterosexuality but to be a premise for homosociality. It is important to see such harassment as a dynamic process in which power operates across a number of intersections. An example of this can be found in a study by Mac an Ghaill (2000), which focused on how groups of men attending a training course used different kinds of heterosexuality both to make connections with their peers and to objectify them. There was a group of what were called 'Fashionable Heterosexuals', and this was a group of 18- to 19-year-old men on an apprenticeship for the automobile industry. In their peer culture, they prioritised their competence of being attractive to females by way of writing imagined female desire onto their bodies through fashionable clothes. In this group, Richard, Gareth and Jeremy use James, as a 'Sexual Outsider', to develop their sense of homosociality:

Richard: Oi Gayboy what you sitting here for?
James: Why not?
Gareth: Look we can't have long haired people sitting with us.
James: So?
Jeremy: O.K. long greasy hair.
Gareth: Why can't you get your hair cut? Why don't you have short hair and be a bit fashionable?
James: Why should I? You lot are mad. You only follow what's fashion, like with your clothes and with your hair and your music.
Gareth: Look I have always listened to Oasis and Blur ever since they came out. See you do it all the time, why can't you take a joke?
James: I can take a joke, but you go on about it all the time.
Jeremy: That's because you get wound up all the time. Why can't you just laugh along with us, and we wouldn't take the piss so much.
James: Well, I don't want to. I don't give a damn what you think either, you're all the same, you can't be different. Don't you care what others think?
Richard: Look, I think you're out of order, I don't give a shit about what you think and I ain't gonna change how and what I do. If you can't handle it then just fuck off. What you gonna do when you are on the track and older men take the piss out of you? You are gonna die.
Gareth: You don't even drink and then you go and listen to some heavy metal band, Pantera or whatever, you just don't add up.
James: Yeah, but you have to don't you? You have to.

(Mac an Ghaill, 2000, pp. 206–207)

From this conversation, it is possible to see that James is feminised through his youth cultural style. What becomes evident in reading the extract above is the way in which the 'Fashionable Heterosexuals' display a desire to incorporate James into their own subculture. The antagonism displayed by the 'Fashionable Heterosexuals' is that they are unable to get James to join in with them. This means that they are attempting to teach James how to behave; it is a process of sanctioning unacceptable behaviour with a view of how James will be viewed by older men that he may work with in the future. In this way, the homophobic abuse that James is experiencing could also be seen as an attempt to protect his future vulnerability in the workplace. It is interesting that the boys would always touch his hair, play with it and often plead with him to get it cut. Homosociality in this sense runs across a number of conduits of power, as a means both to objectify that which is 'Other' and to desire the 'Other'. For the 'Fashionable Heterosexuals', James was provocative, but he was desirably provocative.

In many ways, Sedgwick has set the agenda for future studies on homosociality. At least three different types of readings and interpretations of the concept have evolved. *First*, as pointed out above, the concept is often used to analyse how men, through their relationships and social bonds with other men, construct power blocs and protect male territory and privilege. *Second*, there is a whole body of literature that pursues queer readings of homosociality and explores the underlying continuum of desires and relations. *Finally*, there is a growing body of literature on female homosociality that presents a somewhat different picture of the phenomenon in question. This literature connects in part to Sedgwick's arguments, but there are also some significant developments, for example the questioning of Sedgwick's thesis on the asymmetry between male and female homosociality. There are, obviously, no absolute boundaries between using these three different approaches to homosociality, but discussing them separately makes it easier to analyse different aspects of the concept. In the next three sections, we will, therefore, dig deeper into each of these three different areas of the concept of homosociality. The next step, then, will be to develop further ways to approach this conceptual landscape and especially ways to connect this discussion to the book's overall ambition to develop gender and masculinity theory.

Hegemonic Masculinity and Homosociality

> We must recognise, then, a continuum of homoerotic experience among working-class men in a number of social settings. At the same time we must acknowledge that this experience is silenced, that the public language of the peer group and the workplace is heterosexual. Moreover, it is often seriously homophobic. 'Poofters' are an object of derision, sometimes hatred.
>
> (Connell, 2000, p. 109)

There is a massive body of literature on the homosocial ordering of men's relations and on all the different strategies men use to maintain the conventional gender order and to uphold male privileges (Mac an Ghaill, 1994; Bird, 1996; Messner, 2001; Flood, 2008). In this category of research, we have a number of classic studies, for example Paul Willis' study *Learning to Labour* (1977) about a group of working-class boys ('the lads') who, in their informal group, make not behaving well, i.e. not behaving according to middle-class ideology, the honourable thing to do. In his classic study of how young men are socialised into masculinity, British scholar Paul Willis shows how contempt for the Other helps to keep the group together. The teenage working-class boys under study revolt against the middle-class school culture. This revolt involves not only a struggle against the predominant culture at the school but also development of a fragile feeling of superiority. We have chosen an excerpt from Willis' book that mirrors these young men's construction of boundaries in relation to the Other.

PW: [. .] Why not be like the ear'oles, why not try and get CSEs?
—   They don't get any fun, do they?
Derek: Cos they'm prats like, one kid he's got on his report now, he's got five
             A's and one B.
—   Who's that?
Derek: Birchall.
Spanksy: I mean, what will they remember of their school life? What will they
             have to look back on? Sitting in a classroom, sweating their bollocks
             off, you know, while we've been. . . . I mean look at the things we can
             look back on, fighting the Pakis, fighting on the Jas [i.e. Jamaicans].
             Some of the things we've done on teachers, it'll be a laff when we look
             back on it.

                                                                    (Willis, 1977, p. 14)

From this excerpt, we see, in a condensed form, just how the young men are trying to construct a convincing identity. The geeks and the teachers are used to symbolise the middle-class school culture. Through jokes, sarcasm, and mischief, the boys transform the legitimate school culture into something non-desirable and reprehensible. Group solidarity and male identity are created at the cost of respect for teachers, geeks, immigrants and women. Nothing is allowed to threaten this male fellowship. The greatest threat to this form of intimacy is constituted by the young men's increasingly frequent dealings with the opposite sex. Girls can never be full-fledged members of these groups of young men. They are viewed as occasional guests and, as such, are also granted only peripheral positions in the gang. In Máirtín Mac an Ghaill's classical study of school youth, this pattern emerges with considerable clarity. The following is an excerpt from one of his many group discussions with teenage boys:

Noel: On the first instinct you're interested in looks, then other things later
             on, like having a laugh. You're with your girl and you think she's like
             a pot of gold. Like my mates are jealous of me with my girlfriend and
             she keeps on at me about them. Sometimes it's difficult to keep every-
             one happy.
Stephen: When you're trying to pick a girl up, then yes, if you're out with your
             mates, you would spend more time with her to chat her up. But if she's
             a more regular girlfriend and you're out with her and your mates come
             in, yes you would spend more time with them and she would go into
             the background.

M.M.:   Why is that?

Wayne: It's just normal. Girls are important but a particular girl isn't going to be around long is she? You always come back to your mates in the end, don't you?

M.M.:   What do young women think?

William: Some accept it. Others are unreasonable and go off moaning, which just shows you we're better off without her.

M.M.:   Don't you think it's fair they act like that?

Stephen: Most girls know the score, the others will only give you trouble, believe me.

(Mac An Ghaill, 1994, p. 105)

Although far from all sex-mixed group constellations are of this nature, the pattern does recur in several different investigations of boys' and youth gangs. Girls who protest against this male dominance are viewed as deviant and problematic. For the young men that Mac an Ghaill studied, girls only complicated their otherwise rather simple shared existence. Their male fellowship was idealised and presented as an oasis of trust and mutual friendship.

Another example of an angle on these male-to-male relations can be found in Michael Flood's (2008) article on how bonds between young men also shape their relations with women and form their sexual attitudes and behaviour. In his interviews with young men aged 18 to 26 at a military university, there were many examples of how friendship between men builds on and involves fantasies and experiences of having sex with women, as well as sharing memories of collective sexual harassments and sexual encounters. Women become a kind of currency men use to improve their ranking on the masculine social scale. According to Flood, homosociality organises men's sociosexual relations in a couple of ways. For some young men, male-male social bonds take priority over male-female relations, and friendly and non-sexual relationships with women are dangerously feminising. Sexual activity is an important path to masculine and heterosexual status, and other men are the imagined or real audience for one's sexual activities. Heterosexual sex itself can be the medium through which male bonding is endorsed.

Furthermore, men's sexual storytelling and bragging is moulded by homosocial masculine cultures. According to Flood, homosociality refers first and foremost to nonsexual and same-sex bonds, involving quite high degrees of homophobia. However, it is also possible to read and understand this externalised homophobia as a sign of underlying homoerotic desires. Flood (2008, p. 355) concludes:

Male-male relations organize and give meaning to the social and sexual involvements of young heterosexual men in powerful ways. Homosocial bonds are policed against the feminizing and homosexualizing influences of excessive heterosociality, achieving sex with women is a means to status among men, sex with women is a direct medium of male bonding, and men's narratives of their sexual and gender relations are offered to male audiences in storytelling cultures generated in part by homosociality.

Another much-discussed issue in relation to homosociality is the proposed lack of intimacy in men's friendship relations. Homosociality is often seen as being based on and formed through competition and exclusion. Recent research has put forward another and more complex image of masculinity and friendship. In an article exploring the 'stag night', the premarital ritual whereby a man who is soon to be married and his friends celebrate the coming wedding, there is evidence for certain changes in men's relationships. Thomas Thurnell-Read (2012) conducted participant observations with eight separate stag-tour groups. The observations confirmed a picture of male participants actively working to maintain and develop their friendship bonds. These groups of men were striving for group cohesion, togetherness, and intimacy rather than interpersonal competition and the creation of male hierarchies. Even though this phenomenon can be seen as a part of hegemonic masculinity, there are also traces of changes and re-definitions of masculinity. In contrast to Willis' study, for example, the focus here is on the creation of a more sensitive and intimate masculinity.

Although there is a growing body of literature that brings forward more nuanced images of masculinity, thus stretching and extending the concept of homosociality in order to investigate potential changes in or redefinitions of hegemonic masculinity (Anderson, 2008, 2009), there is also an extensive body of work that reproduces the image of homosociality as a mechanism that supports and reinforces rather stereotypic images of masculinity (Bird, 1996; Kiesling, 2005; Gilmartin, 2007; Snyder, 2007). We are not arguing that these authors are unaware of the complexity of the concept, but their findings and conclusions clearly promote the notion that homosociality evidently is a part and extension of hegemonic masculinity.

It is easy to find examples supporting a one-dimensional image of homosocial relations among men. Throughout this chapter, we will, however, locate and discuss examples pointing towards a more elastic way of approaching and defining homosocial relations. Our ambition is to open an imaginative space for thinking differently on homosocial relations, and thus we want to contribute to a re-definition of the concept.

Homoeroticism and Homosociality

In November 1994, the *metrosexual* male was identified and described by the cultural critic Mark Simpson (Coad, 2008). This market segment consisted of young, urban, white, middle-class men—consumers and young, narcissistic men preoccupied with looks, style and image. In the 1990s, these men and this phenomenon indicated a crisis in masculinity, a closer relation between homo and hetero men, and a general movement towards a new masculinity. Coad (2008, p. 197) writes:

> Metrosexual males may look prettier and more beautiful than their nonmetrosexual brothers, but metrosexuality is the motor behind more decisive changes in the realm of sexual politics; it influences how heterosexual males interact with homosexual males and it is in the process of replacing traditional categories of sexual orientation.

However, the views on and interpretations of this phenomenon vary. Shugart (2008) argues that metrosexual masculinity defines and casts homosociality as a kind of universal male solidarity. Instead of pointing towards a new masculinity, and a more sensitive and inclusive masculinity, metrosexuality reorganised homosociality in order to define homosexual men as different from both women and heterosexual men. According to Shugart (2008), the main result of this movement is a highly commercialised masculinity and a strengthening of the normative masculinity. To understand and position the whole discussion of a new masculinity, and the potential erasure of the boundaries between heterosexuality and homosexuality, we have to return to Sedgwick. Her definition of homosociality is characterised by a triangular structure, in which men have bonds with other men and in which women serve as the conduits through which these bonds are expressed. However, this triangle may portray as rivalry what is actually an attraction between men. The argument and the idea that there is an underlying continuum between different kinds of male homosocial desires draw out a potential arena for research on the fragile boundaries and lines between different masculinities and heterosexuality/homosexuality.

In his influential study on homosexuality and modernity, Henning Bech's (1997) ideas fit into this way of approaching homosociality. He identifies something he calls *absent homosexuality*. He writes:

> The mode of being of absent homosexuality can only be comprehended in its relation to the other pole in the modern form of male-male eroticism, i.e. the homosexuals, in its simultaneous connection to and demarcation from them.
>
> (p. 84)

He describes absent homosexuality as a ghost-like character, present but absent, desired and denied, known and unknown. Using examples from the cinema, Bech uncovers the hidden narratives of homosexual desire. In *Dead Poets Society* (1989) a new teacher upsets the school's rigid discipline and routines, transforming poetry classes into an adventure. Together with their teacher, the students form the 'Dead Poets Society', instilling American ideals such as individualism, self-exploration, bravery and courage. The teacher's style of teaching is somewhat different from all the other teachers at the school, here illustrated by a famous quotation:

> 'O Captain, my Captain.' Who knows where that comes from? Anybody? Not a clue? It's from a poem by Walt Whitman about Mr. Abraham Lincoln. Now in this class you can either call me Mr. Keating, or if you're slightly more daring, 'O Captain, my Captain.'
>
> (From the film *Dead Poets Society*, 1989)

The romantic exploration of poetry, masculinity and dreams ends, however, in a disaster. One of the boys decides to follow his dreams of becoming an actor, but, when his father finds out, he tries to send his son to the military academy. The boy commits suicide, and the teacher and leader of Dead Poets Society becomes the scapegoat. Consequently, he is dismissed. The film ends with the pupils standing on their desk, saluting their 'Captain'. Analysing the condensed homosocial relationship between the Captain and the boys, Bech points out that any time a suspicion might crop up that there are homosexual feelings involved in this relationship, large efforts are made to dismiss it. Analysing the film, Bech suggests that the numerous and exaggerated attempts to counteract suspicions of homosexual desires can be read as evidence of absent homosexuality. Bech concludes: 'Homosexuality can and must be shown for everyone as that which everyone might perhaps like to experience; that is, if it can remain unarticulated and one ends up revolted or disgusted' (Bech, 1997, p. 58).

This idea of an absent homosexuality that structures society and men's life-styles and desires has certain similarities with Judith Butler's idea of melancholia and identity. In *The Psychic Life of Power* (1997), Butler starts from Freud's theory of melancholia and uses this description of clinical depression as an inspiration for analysing the construction of a heterosexual order. According to Butler, heterosexuality naturalises itself by insisting on the 'Otherness' of homosexuality. Then the heterosexual identity is based and sculptured on a melancholic incorporation of the love that it disavows. According to Butler, the man who 'insists upon the coherence of his heterosexuality will claim that he never loved another man, and hence never lost another man' (p. 139). The idea of a homoerotic continuum has inspired several cultural analyses. What is often found is a blurred boundary and distinction between homosociality and homoeroticism. There is a complex and dynamic relation between, for example, the legitimate culture and the underground print culture. Janes (2012) studied a leading British educational magazine for children (1962–1982) and found queer subtexts and a manifold of expressions of homoerotic desire in these magazines. Janes argues that it is not surprising to find a homoerotic space in writings produced by men for boys. The interplay between homophobia and close homosocial and homoerotic bonds between men created in fiction—but also, for example, in schools and in the military—can be seen as evidence for the thesis of a continuum of desires.

Cultural analysis shows how fragile and anxiety-ridden the indistinctness that marks homosociality is, and it points towards the continuous boundary work being done to uphold and defend the heterosexual order (Brady, 2012). Thus, even though we have an underlying stream of homosocial desire, there are also constant attempts to suppress and rein in these streams in the heterosexual and normative order. J. Jack Halberstam (2002) describes one such cultural mechanism in the neo-homosocial triangles. In these triangles, a new constellation of one heterosexual man and one overtly gay man in the position as a rival for the woman's affections replaces the ordinary constellation of two men and a woman. By studying films such as *As Good as It Gets* (1997) and *Chasing Amy* (1997), Halberstam dissects and analyses how the straight homophobic man enters into a learning process and learns how to accept a fully human and more gender-equal model of manhood. However, this narrative usually ends up in a reinforcement of the heterosexual order, although with some new nuances:

> At the end of *As Good*, Jack Nicholson gets the girl, the girl's son gets better, the girl gets laid, the black guy gets lost, the gay man gets his dog back, and

that's as good as it gets. It can get much better, I would contend, but only when we find productive ways as feminists to theorize minority forms of masculinity.

(p. 363)

Although the idea and theory of a continuum of homosocial desires and erotic expressions has greatly influenced thinking in the field of gender and queer analysis, it seems there is no easy escape from the patriarchal system and hegemonic masculinity. The subversive forces point towards breaches and leakages in the gender system, but in the end there is a strong tendency to subordinate and neutralise resistance and utopian forms of thinking about gender and sexuality.

Female Homosociality and the Gender Continuum

The suggested continuum between female friendship, Feminist solidarity and same-sex desire has great support in the literature. But there is also a growing critique of this way of approaching female homosociality. Sedgwick put forward a thesis on the asymmetry between male and female homosociality. She argues that male homosociality is first and foremost fashioned through the exchange of women and the consolidation of men's power within society, whereas for women this sharp cleavage between homosociality and homosexuality is not that distinct, clear or stable. According to Binhammer (2006), this is a somewhat idyllic and perhaps even naive image of women's relationships. She argues that women in many ways circulate in and are permeated by the same capitalist economy and system as men are. Women's bonds are created not outside the dominant sexual economy but as a part of it. Women's relations are, therefore, not by definition and automatically a challenge to hegemonic masculinity.

In an interesting article, Henriette Gunkel (2009) discusses and analyses the 'mummy-baby' relationship in the South African schools. Briefly, this is a culturally specific form of female same-sex intimacy, although similar forms are found in, for example, British boarding schools. An older girl at the school helps the newcomers, the younger girls, and provides them with emotional support. Sometimes this relation develops into sexual encounters and relationships. Although this is taking place in a highly policed and homophobic environment, this particular form of relationship seems to exist alongside the sexuality apparatus and to be accepted. The point here is that homosociality needs to be theorised and understood in different ways depending on the national and socio-cultural context.

In contrast to this study of accepted, but highly policed, sexual relations between women, Christine Griffin (2000) argues that all young women in the West have to deal with the accusation of being a lesbian. This accusation also affects all women, albeit in different ways and with different effects. Griffin calls for research that is open to aspects of female friendship that are coloured and permeated by desire, fantasies and a passion for same-sex relationships. This type of friendship is immediately drawn into the naturalised model of compulsory heterosexual relationships and the pressure of 'getting a man'. According to Hammarén (2008), concepts of love and intimacy are feminised. In his study on identity

constructions among young men in multicultural suburbs, female intimate relationships are understood as expressions of friendship and heterosexuality. Young
women who kiss, hold hands with, and hug each other are considered not lesbians
but rather women involved in normalised feminine heterosexual behaviour. Lesbians are, therefore, made invisible and are ignored. According to a heteronormative order and the male gaze, women's intimate relations are understood as
friendship or a sexual display aimed at heterosexual men.

There is clearly a lack of research exploring female friendships as something
other than desexualised relations. Therefore, sexual minority women's relations
are not explored and researched (Arseneau and Fassinger, 2006). There is also a
paucity of literature on friendships between black and white women, for example
(Granger, 2002), or of cross-racial friendships in general. There is obviously a
need to study and problematise the idea of a continuous relation between female
homosocial and homosexual bonds and friendships (see for example Marcus,
2007). The whole idea of a sharp contrast between how this works in a male versus female spectrum of desire and relations seems to be the result of a predominantly polarised view on gender and identity (Johansson, 2007).

Towards a Theory of Homosociality

The three different focuses on homosociality are, of course, partly overlapping.
In the literature, this concept is mainly used as a tool to understand and dissect
male friendships and men's collective attempts to uphold and maintain power
and hegemony. The most common use of the concept is inspired by Sedgwick's
approach and the whole discussion and idea of a homoerotic continuum. Most
authors also stress and focus on the radical disruption of this continuum and the
consequences of this disruption for homophobia and for a fragile but power-
seeking masculinity. Bird (1996), for example, argues that homosociality maintains
hegemonic masculinity and patriarchy, acting to institutionally and interpersonally
segregate men and women and to suppress non-hegemonic masculinities. Bird
claims that when there is an understanding among heterosexual men in homosocial relations that masculinity means being emotionally detached and involves
perceiving women as sexual objects, they perpetuate a system that subordinates
femininity and non-hegemonic masculinities. She argues that non-hegemonic
masculinities do not succeed in influencing the gender order significantly because
their expression is either transferred to heterosocial settings or suppressed completely. However, this common use of the concept—which refers to how men,
through their relations to other men, uphold and maintain patriarchy, in terms
of emotional detachment, competitiveness, homophobia and sexual objectification of women—tends to reduce homosociality exclusively to a heteronormative,
androcentric and hierarchical term, used to show how heterosexual men bond and
defend their privileges and positions. In contrast, female homosociality is often
described as something completely different—more in terms of a closer relation
between sociality and sexuality. As we have discussed, this way of framing and
analysing homosociality is in need of reinterpretation. Is it not possible to discuss,

for example, male homosocial relationships in terms of intimacy, gender equality, and non-homophobia, without disregarding the possible advances of maleness?

We will now introduce the distinction between *vertical/hierarchical homo-sociality* and *horizontal homosociality*. Hierarchical homosociality is similar to and has already been described as a means of strengthening power—of creating close homosocial bonds in order to maintain and defend hegemony. Although this description is primarily used to talk about men's friendships and the exchange of means and valuable cultural and social capital, it is also possible to frame and investigate women's relations using this concept. But we will not argue that this concept and the idea of a vertical and hierarchical homosociality are totally gender neutral. Horizontal homosociality is similar to what was earlier described as female homosociality. This concept is used to point towards relations between, for example, men—relations that are based on emotional closeness, intimacy and a non-profitable form of friendship. There are, clearly, no absolute boundaries between these two approaches to homosociality. Aspects of hierarchical homosociality in horizontal relations and vice versa might be present, but making a distinction between them and discussing them separately makes it easier to analyse different aspects of the concept and highlight different implications. As discussions of vertical homosociality are more common in the literature, we will now turn our attention towards horizontal homosociality.

In popular culture, the concepts of 'bromance' (which combines the words 'brother' and 'romance') and 'womance' (combining 'woman' and 'romance') have been introduced, discussed and debated. Dave Carnie is credited with coining the terms as editor of the skateboard magazine *Big Brother* in the 1990s to refer to relationships that develop between skaters who spent a great deal of time together (DeAngelis, 2014). Bromance and womance refer to close and intimate non-sexual homosocial relationships between two (or more) men or women. Womance is similar to the above-mentioned concept of female homosociality; bromance, however, differs from traditional understandings of male homosocial relations and does not necessarily fit within the construct of masculinity found in some masculinity theories focusing on competition and hierarchies. Bromance emphasises love, exclusive friendship and intimacy that are not premised on competition and the often-described 'shoulder-to-shoulder' friendship, e.g. watching football, playing golf or training for a marathon together. Bromances provide a space for intimate male friendship (Chen, 2012), even though studies also show that male friendships might include utilitarian aspects, desire, rivalry and self-interest pointing towards a less idealised picture contrary to bromance (Bray, 2003).

The concept is barely discussed by academic scholars but returns regularly in the media, portrayed in movies, on TV, in gossip magazines and in more or less obscure blogs and websites. A number of celebrities have engaged in close bromances—for example, Ben Affleck and Matt Damon, and George Clooney and Brad Pitt. Fictional bromances on television have also become more commonplace, and shows and dramas such as *Boy Meets World* (1993–2000), *Boston Legal* (2004–2008), *Scrubs* (2001–2010) and *The Big Bang Theory* (2007–) have had lead characters with bromantic relationships including long-lasting friendships and love. The same applies to different boy bands such as One Direction or to films such as *The King's Speech* (2010). According to Chen (2012), bromances comprise three general constitutive elements: They are restricted to men, they are asexual, and they are locations for intimacy, love and affection between men. They are also described as a complicated love and affection shared by *straight* males. The 'bro' aspect of bromance may perhaps emphasise heteronormativity, as well as homophobia, indicating that it is not gay because it's between men. The focus on heterosexual men, however, seems to differ. Bromances or homosocial relations between gay men or between a straight man and a gay man are quite rare but do exist (Nardi, 2001). Bromances imply intimacy that slips between the boundaries of sexual and non-sexual relationships:

> Bromances notably provide a space for male intimacy, in sharp contrast to the general types of friendship that society permits men to have. They recognize intimacy without sex, in contrast with general conceptions of intimacy.
>
> (Chen, 2012, pp. 248–249)

Today we can witness men as having close and intimate relationships with their friends, not least as represented in media and films. Increasingly men's friendships are portrayed like a kind of love relation—guys who hang out all the time talking about everything and who like to hug each other. Bromance is commonly described as a non-sexual love affair between men, which has been made possible through the undermining of a traditional gender order. These kinds of relations are similar to what we call horizontal homosociality, also described earlier as female homosociality.

Examples of *womances* in popular culture seem to be more exceptional, although the film *Thelma and Louise* (1991) is sometimes said to be one. The terms bromance and womance are often used to refer to two heterosexual partners, although there have been celebrity male gay-straight bromances (also called homomances or hobromances). We are not suggesting that bromances and womances are similar. The popular concept of bromance, unlike the concept of womance, is perhaps a reflection of the different values assigned to male and female friendships. Additionally, for example, *Thelma and Louise* is about fighting misogyny and male abuse; many bromances are about how men make highly enjoyable friendships and focus on each other. Consequently, there would seem to be an underlying power relation between the concepts.

Intersected Power Relations

In constructions of homosocial relations, some differences between people are marked, and some may be obscured. For example, the assertion of gender may overlook sexualities, age, 'race' or local differences. Often the literature on homosociality has a quite one-dimensional focus. Theories of the intersections between sexuality, class, ethnicity, age and gender are seldom used to elaborate critical perspectives on these issues (Mohanty, 1998; Collins, 1998; McCall, 2005; Tayler et al., 2010). These social and cultural categories influence the individual at the same time, constituting flexible and often complex processes of belonging and power relations. According to this view, power relations and social positions are by necessity connected to a plurality of categories. An intersectional framework acknowledges the multi-dimensionality of societal factors, identities and power (as opposed to focusing on class or gender individually). It also attempts to capture how social factors influence one another. For example, being male, heterosexual, middle class and of the majority ethnic population can be considered as occupying a hegemonic position, in contrast to being a female, working-class lesbian (Connell, 1995). However, these positions are very much contextual and situated, resulting in complex and sometimes ambiguous social relations. Consequently, an intersectional approach involves locating individuals within these dynamics and examining how people become subjected to a plurality of changing variables.

Oware (2011), doing research on homosociality and black masculinity in rap music, claims (like several other scholars) that hip-hop and especially 'gangsta rap' music reflects a stereotypical black masculine aesthetic. Yet, unpacking the idea of hegemonic black masculinity, Oware claims that there are also progressive ways that male rappers express themselves towards friends and loved ones. He also argues that sexism, homophobia and hyper-masculinity represented in rap music should be understood in relation to societal stereotypes and market forces. Since white teenagers are the largest consumers of the music and large corporations have overtaken small independent music labels targeted towards minority populations, many black hip-hop artists are limited in the sort of topics that they can discuss for fear of not selling records. Oware argues that radical or empowering rap would not sell records. Rather, rappers who sell stereotypical images of black males appeal to consumer society:

> In this constrained and limited environment, there exists a symbiotic relationship between record companies and rap artists whereby, from the label's perspective, only certain types of lyrics or imagery are believed profitable, thus the demand for that kind of music. Understanding this demand, artists offer songs that mainly consist of misogyny, violence, and homophobia. Therefore, there exists an over-representation of the thug or pimp motif in rap music targeted towards record labels who want the next multiplatinum selling artist and an audience that eagerly wants to consume such imagery.
>
> (Oware, 2011, p. 32)

Accordingly, stereotypical black male behaviour represented in rap music must be understood in relation to market forces and a racialised society. Specifically discussing homosocial relations among black male rappers, Oware points out that since prior research on hip-hop has documented the harmful aspects of black masculinity, the potentially empowering, vulnerable, emotional and caring homosocial interactions between black male rappers he found in his research have been overlooked. He also underscores that the often present concept of boys-behaving-badly in previous research on homosociality among males may be a consequence of the fact that those who have been interviewed are predominantly white males, i.e. individuals 'closest' to the dominant form of white masculinity. Because many black males are marginalised in American society, they face a different relationship to hegemonic masculinity. Highlighting power relations related to 'race' and masculinity, Oware concludes that his findings of positive and progressive homosocial relationships call for a rethinking and re-evaluation of conventional understandings of black masculinity: '[B]lack masculinity, in general, must be understood to parallel *and* transgress hegemonic masculinity' (Oware, 2011, p. 33).

Homosocial relations are often described in relation to white men, heterosexuality, and shared activities, such as games, playing musical instruments, watching movies, sports activities and drinking (Messner, 2001). However, relating to intersectionality, homosociality does not necessarily imply, for example, either heterosexuality or homosexuality, and these relations might also entail emotional sharing. While the concept of homosociality (and bromance) has often been applied to relations between straight men, mixed gay-straight or gay-gay non-sexual relationships between men *or* women could just as well be defined as homosocial (Nardi, 2001). Bromances are said to maintain the heteronormative hierarchies, as only heterosexuals can have a bromance (Chen, 2012). This particular boundary reflects the phenomenon of 'straight panic' in which individuals experience anxiety about how others perceive their sexuality, and thus they feel a need to confirm their heterosexuality. However, because men in bromances are often identified in society as heterosexuals, they can have intimate friendships, without risk of being misperceived as gay. At the same time, bromances are a source of subordination, encouraging men to stay within rigid boundaries of sexuality norms. Bromances are also described as restraining the pool of intimate friends men can have—gay men are excluded, and consequently the culture reinforces homophobia and the subordination of the Gay community (Chen, 2012).

Yet friendships between gay men and the development of networks and neighbourhoods legitimise alternative forms of masculinity, thereby challenging hegemonic masculinities. In his study on the politics of friendship in the Gay social movement, Nardi (2001) claims that gay friendships have the potential to produce communities, reinforce gay identity and effect socio-political change on a larger scale. The Gay community helps members to find meaning and dignity in a society that is trying to impose a hegemonic male order. The friendships of gay men serve to create a sense of belonging and thus help sustain a sense of 'gay identity'. Obviously, gay men would not automatically pose a challenge to the male hegemony. They do not necessarily resist notions that, for example, men are superior to and should dominate women. However, they may undermine traditional aspects of hegemonic masculinity in that heteronormativity is questioned and homosexuality is made visible (Mills, 2001). Even though Chen (2012) characterises bromances as maintaining heteronormativity, she concludes her article by claiming that bromances are a starting point for deconstructing homophobia and represent a queering of heterosexual male friendship. Consequently, they open up space for men to experience intimacy outside the heterosexual pairings, which may also lead to a dismantling of compulsory heterosexuality. Furthermore, and contrary to Chen, situating bromances in mixed gay-straight or gay-gay non-sexual relationships might deconstruct homophobia and contest heterosexist norms even more (Rumens, 2011).

For Karioris (2016) homosociality refers to a way of discussing the relationships that men have with other men. Critical Masculinity Studies scholars often position homosociality in an opposition to homosexuality. This means that hegemonic masculinity relies on a sharing of homophobic abuse in order to sustain unequal circuits of power. Karioris suggests that we can begin to unpack different kinds of homosocialities such as collaborative and conflictual. In essence, Karioris is disconnecting the relationship between particular kinds of masculinities and male practices, and homosociality. On one hand, the conflictual underpins violent relationships; men are more likely to experience violence from other men than women. On the other, there is a sense of collaborative homosociality, articulated not simply through homophobic relations but through intimacies and friendships. Alongside this, it should also be mentioned that this is neither a situation of one nor another but that different kinds of relationships between men can exist at the same time. From this position,

> [r]ather than see, to come back to Sedgwick's use of the triangle, a simple connectivity between 'rival' and 'friend', it is important to understand the way that while friends can be rivals with each other (possibly falling under the category of 'frenemy') there are always those with whom one falls in direct (open or otherwise) conflict with and whose relationship is founded on this animosity. Even in the term frenemy one sees—for whatever reason—a necessity for friendliness, suggesting that there are those for whom there is not this need. Through the suggestion of collaborative homosociality and conflictual homosociality it does not mean to abstract or simplify the messy relations between men—as some of the above thinkers seek to do through their usage of homosociality—but to negotiate the ways that men may find themselves at the crossroads of a variety of relations that, while certainly never straightforward, encourage and encompass interconnected homosocialities.
>
> (Karioris, 2016, p. 74)

The result is that we need to begin to see homosocialities as relationships not simply cohered through identity categories. In many ways, this way of understanding homosocialities for Karioris is about the development and learning of particular ways of doing masculinity. It also provides a more holistic understanding of relationships between men. One of the features of the above work is that it provides a way of navigating how we conceptualise homosociality, and there appears much scope to expand it from a limited notion of 'patriarchal masculinity'. One of the consequences of this study is that the power dynamic that underpins homosociality needs to be reconfigured. As a starting point for that reconfiguration, this chapter returns to engaging with hegemonic masculinity and how a differently conceptualised notion of homosociality can impact how we begin to reconfigure hegemonic masculinity.

Reconstructing Hegemonic Masculinity and Homosociality

Although there have been some efforts to transcend and redefine the concept of homosociality, pointing towards potential changes in and redefinitions of hegemonic masculinity (Anderson, 2008, Thurnell-Read, 2012), the concept of homosociality is often, as previously mentioned, defined as a mechanism and social dynamic that explains the maintenance of hegemonic masculinity (Gilmartin, 2007; Snyder, 2007). There is a clear and growing body of literature that brings to the fore more nuanced images of masculinity, thus stretching and extending the concept of homosociality in order to investigate possible reconstructions of hegemonic masculinity (Anderson, 2008, 2009). The overall picture from the research, however, promotes the notion that homosociality is clearly a part and extension of hegemony, thus serving to always reconstruct and safeguard male interests and power.

However, changes in masculinity—for example, the construction of horizontal homosociality, in which emotional closeness, intimacy and a non-profitable form of friendship are developed—are not necessarily a sign of a strengthening of patriarchy, as many discussions on hegemonic masculinity suggest. The same applies to bromances, which has a description that sometimes differs from traditional understandings of male homosocial relations and does not always fit within the construct of masculinity found in some masculinity theories focusing on competition and hierarchies. In accordance with a Post-structuralist reading, our proposal is that we do not predetermine the agents of change. Instead, analysts should remain open to the possibility of discovering potential movements towards a redefined hegemony that contains the seeds of utopian visions of the gender order (Kimmel et al., 2005). Even Connell (1995) suggests that it is not necessary to offer a general descriptor of hegemonic masculinity, but instead posits that a hegemonic form of masculinity is the form that is most desired in a particular *context* (see Chapter 3). Consequently, different contexts can inhabit different hegemonic ideals. We are not suggesting that, for example, metrosexuality or bromances are shifts in 'un-acceptable' forms of masculine performances. The idea that male friendships defined by homophobia and distance seem to loosen up, resulting in close and intimate friendship relations, can still be interpreted in an accepted but still reformulated framework of hegemonic masculinity, though perhaps a more desirable one.

As argued in the previous chapter on hegemony, it does not follow from Laclau and Mouffe's (1985/2001) suggestion that there is no beyond hegemony, that there is no beyond patriarchy, and that masculinity will always be hegemonic in relation to femininity. As further argued, for a re-articulation of hegemony to be desirable, we must however break with Connell's notion that hegemonic masculinity is always defined as being opposed to and privileged over femininity (Connell and Messerschmidt, 2005). To some degree, the discussion in this chapter has contributed to such a break. We have both implicitly tried to raise the question of whether all hegemonies are equally bad and more explicitly tried to discern how different masculinities correspond to (and underpin) the different ways of articulating hegemonic masculinity. One way of reading this chapter is also to understand it as pointing towards how elements historically related to women are articulated within masculinity as well. To some degree, we suggest that this is what is happening when male performances and friendships become closely associated with intimacy, love and affection (Johansson and Klinth, 2008). Of course, we acknowledge that articulating intimacy and emotional closeness with masculinity may not lead to a complete disruption of masculinity. It might, however, point to a potential reconfiguration of hegemonic masculinity that is not a priori and necessarily privileged in relation to femininity.

Conclusions

The concept of homosociality may uphold and maintain homogeneous gender categorisations, focusing on single-sex groups and often referring to hierarchical gender relations in which (often white) men strengthen certain hegemonic gender ideals. However, applying a Post-structuralist understanding of the concept helps us to problematise a common structuralist understanding of the relation between hegemonic masculinity and homosociality. Moreover, by making a distinction between the vertical and horizontal practice of homosociality, we can develop a more dynamic view on homosociality. Taking a vertical/horizontal view on homosociality emphasises its relation to a structuralist hegemonic gender order, i.e. to what degree homosocial relations uphold and maintain 'traditional' hegemonic male and female social positions. A Post-structuralist reading of hegemony makes it possible to interpret potential re-articulations of hegemony as part of a struggle for gender equality and a more just society. Perhaps the development and conceptualisation of bromances and horizontal homosociality point towards variation and transition and, consequently, a reconfiguration of hegemony including tendencies towards an eventual transformation of intimacy, gender and power relations. However, we acknowledge that we are only touching on potential and partial redefinitions of hegemony, also those often closely connected to the middle class, and thus we need to analyse the gender order more thoroughly by taking an intersectional approach to examining how these performances may affect more general gender relations in society.

In addition, there is a clear need to study and problematise the idea of a continuous relation between female homosocial and homosexual bonds and friendships. The whole idea of there being a sharp contrast between how this works in a male versus a female spectrum of desire and relations seems to be the result of a polarised view on gender and identity, not least related to the notion that hegemonic masculinity is defined as opposed to and privileged over femininity. It is likely that the more polarised the gender order and the more heteronormative that the sexual codes are, the more traditional forms of homosociality one expects to find in society. As this order slowly changes and loosens up, thus re-articulating hegemony, homosociality may take other forms, and friendships may relate not only to same-sex relations but also to heterosocial forms of friendship and intimate non-sexual relations (Rumens, 2011, 2012). For example, in the absence of societal policing of gender and sexual orientation, men would be able to have friendships with other men regardless of sexual orientation (Chen, 2012). Sexual orientation would not be the basic principle for friendship. Rigid boundaries between friendships and romantic relationships would not be necessary, and the potential for fluidity in relationships would increase:

> Men would not need to categorize people in terms of 'friend' or 'potential lover', but would instead have a singular category of relationship in which they could both provide and receive intimacy and care. This proposition would also undermine sexual fluidity as a woman-specific construct, and permit men to experience more fluidity in both relationship forms and sexual relationship partners.
>
> (Chen, 2012, p. 262)

Adding age/generation to this analysis, some Swedish studies have shown that recent generations of men raised by feminist mothers and fathers in the 1970s and afterward are more emotionally open and more expressive (Johansson, 2007). There is also less concern among contemporary young men about the notion of being identified as gay, and thus they are more comfortable with exploring deeper friendships with other men (Johansson, 2007). Finally, relating to Chen and her vision presented above, situating homosociality in an intersectional framework develops, emphasises and makes visible the inconsistent and ambiguous aspects of homosociality, focusing not only, as in the case of Chen, on straight men but also on women and different sexual positions, 'races' and generations. Using this approach further allows us to point toward a defence of a post-structural framing of hegemonic masculinity by referring to vertical/hierarchical homosociality, and toward a potential and slow process of rearticulating hegemony by referring to horizontal homosociality. This does not mean that we adhere to a post-Feminist celebration of change and a post-hegemonic world. Rather than lifting forward, for example, inclusive masculinity as a new theoretical foundation of critical studies in men and masculinities, we are trying to balance between vertical and horizontal transformations of gender relations and sexualities (O'Neill, 2015).

References

Anderson, E. (2008) Inclusive masculinity in a fraternal setting. *Men and Masculinities*, 10(5), 604–620.

Anderson, E. (2009) *Inclusive Masculinities: The Changing Nature of Masculinity*. London: Routledge.

Arseneau, J.R. and Fassinger, R.E. (2006) Challenge and promise. *Journal of Bisexuality*, 6(3), 69–90.

Bech, H. (1997) *When Men Meet: Homosexuality and Modernity*. Cambridge: Polity Press.

Binhammer, K. (2006) Female homosociality and the exchange of men: Mary Robinson's Walsingham. *Women's Studies*, 35(3), 221–240.

Bird, S.R. (1996) Welcome to the men's club: Homosociality and the maintenance of bonding, and male friendship. *Men and Masculinities*, 15(3), 249–270.

Brady, A. (2012) *The Transgendered Kiwi: Homosocial Desire and 'New Zealand identity'*. Buckingham/Philadelphia: Open University Press.

Bray, A. (2003) *The Friend*. Chicago, IL: The University of Chicago Press.

Buschmeyer, A. and Lengersdorf, D. (2016) The differentiation of masculinity as a challenge for the concept of hegemonic masculinity. *NORMA*, 11(3), 1–18.

Butler, J. (1997) *The Psychic Life of Power*. Stanford: Stanford University Press.

Chen, E.J. (2012) Caught in a bad bromance. *Texas Journal of Women and the Law*, 21(2), 241–266.

Coad, D. (2008) *The Metrosexual: Gender, Sexuality, and Sport*. New York: SUNY Press.

Collins, P.H. (1998) It's all in the family: Intersections of gender, race and nation. *Hypatia*, 13(3), 62–82.

Connell, R.W. (1995) *Masculinities*. Cambridge: Polity Press.

Connell, R.W. (2000) *The Men and the Boys*. Cambridge: Polity Press.

Connell, R.W. and Messerschmidt, J. (2005) Hegemonic masculinity: Rethinking the concept. *Gender & Society*, 19(6), 829–859.

DeAngelis, M. (ed.) (2014) *Reading the Bromance: Homosocial Relationships in Film and Television*. Detroit: Wayne State University Press.

Flood, M. (2008) Men, sex, and homosociality. How bonds between men shape their sexual relations with women. *Men and Masculinities*, 10(3), 339–359.

Gilmartin, S.K. (2007) Crafting heterosexual masculine identities on campus. *Men and Masculinities*, 9(4), 530–539.

Granger, D. (2002) Friendship between black and white women. *American Behavioural Scientist*, 45(8), 1208–1213.

Griffin, C. (2000) Absence that matter: Constructions of sexuality in studies of young women's friendship. *Feminism & Psychology*, 10(2), 227–245.

Gunkel, H. (2009) "What's identity got to do with it?" Rethinking intimacy and homosociality in contemporary South Africa. *NORMA: Nordic Journal of Feminist and Gender Research*, 17(3), 206–221.

Halberstam, J. (2002) The good, the bad and the ugly: Men, women and masculinity. In: Gardiner, J.K. ed. *Masculinity Studies and Feminist Theory: New Directions*. New York: Columbia University Press, pp. 344–367.

Hammarén, N. (2008) *Förorten i huvudet: Unga män om kön och sexualitet i det nya Sverige*. Stockholm: Atlas.

Haywood, C. and Mac an Ghaill, M. (1997)'A man in the making': Sexual masculinities within changing training cultures. *The Sociological Review*, 45(4), 576–590.

Janes, D. (2012) Homosociality and homoeroticism in the leading British educational magazine for children, Look and Learn (1962–1982). *Continuum*, 26(6), 897–910.

Johansson, T. (2007) *The Transformation of Sexuality: Gender and Identity in Contemporary Youth Culture*. Hampshire: Ashgate.

Johansson, T. and Klinth, R. (2008) Caring fathers: The ideology of gender equality and masculine positions. *Men and Masculinities*, 11(1), 42–62.

Karioris, F.G. (2016) Between class and friendship: Homosociality in an all-male residence hall in the US. Unpublished PhD Thesis.

Kiesling, S.F. (2005) Homosocial desire in men's talk: Balancing and re-creating cultural discourses of masculinity. *Language & Society*, 34(5), 695–726.

Kimmel, M.S., Hearn, J. and Connell, R.W. (ed.) (2005) *Handbook of Studies of Men & Masculinities*. London: Sage.

Laclau, E. and Mouffe, C. (1985/2001) *Hegemony and Socialist Strategy*. 2nd ed. London: Verso.

Lipman-Blumen, J. (1976) Toward a homosocial theory of sex roles: An explanation of the sex segregation of social institutions. *Signs: Journal of Women in Culture and Society*, *1*(3, Part 2), 15–31.

Mac an Ghaill, M. (1994) *The Making of Men: Masculinities, Sexualities and Schooling*. Buckingham, UK: Open University Press.

Mac an Ghaill, M. (2000). Rethinking (male) gendered sexualities: what about the British heteros? *The Journal of Men's Studies*, 8(2), 195–212.

Marcus, S. (2007) *Between Women: Friendship, Desire, and Marriage in Victorian England*. Princeton/Woodstock: Princeton University Press.

McCall, L. (2005) The complexity of intersectionality. *Signs: Journal of Women in Culture and Society*, 30(3), 1771–1800.

Messner, M. (2001) Friendship, intimacy and sexuality. In: Whitehead, S.M. and Barrett, F.J. eds. *The Masculinities Reader*. Cambridge: Polity Press, pp. 253–265.

Mills, M. (2001) *Challenging Violence in Schools: An Issue of Masculinities*. Buckingham/ Philadelphia: Open University Press.

Mohanty, C.T. (1998) Under western eyes: Feminist scholarship and colonial discourses. *Feminist Review*, 30, 61–88.

Nardi, P.M. (2001) "A vicarious sense of belonging": The politics of friendship and gay social movements, communities and neighbourhoods. In: Whitehead, S.M. and Barrett, F.J. eds. *The Masculinities Reader*. Cambridge: Polity Press, pp. 288–306.

O'Neill, R. (2015) Whither critical masculinity studies? Notes on inclusive masculinity theory, postfeminism, and sexual politics. *Men and Masculinities*, 18(1), 100–120.

Oware, M. (2011) Brotherly love: Homosociality and black masculinity in Gangsta rap music. *Journal of African American Studies*, 15(1), 22–39.

Rumens, N. (2011) *Queer Company: The Role and Meaning of Friendship in Gay Men's Work Lives*. Farnham: Ashgate.

Rumens, N. (2012) Queering cross-sex friendships: An analysis of gay and bisexual men's workplace friendships with heterosexual women. *Human Relations,* 65(8), 955–978.

Sedgewick, E.K. (1985) *Between Men: English Literature and Homosocial Desire*. New York: Columbia University Press.

Shugart, H. (2008) Managing masculinities: The metrosexual moment. *Communication and Critical/Cultural Studies*, 5(3), 280–300.

Snyder, M. (2007) Crises of masculinity: Homosocial desire and homosexual panic in the critical Cold War narratives of Mailer and Coover. *Critique: Studies in Contemporary Fiction,* 48(3), 250–277.

Tayler, Y., Hines, S., & Casey, M. E. (eds.). (2010) *Theorizing Intersectionality and Sexuality*. London: Palgrave MacMillan.

Thurnell-Read, T. (2012) What happens on tour: The premarital stag tour, homosocial bonding, and male friendship. *Men and Masculinities*, 15(3), 249–270.

Willis, P. (1977) *Learning to Labour: How Working Class Kids Gets Working Class Jobs*. London: Saxon House.

5 Homophobia, 'Otherness' and Inclusivity

Introduction

The term 'homophobia' was first coined in 1972 by the American psychologist, writer and activist George Weinberg, in his book *Society and the Healthy Homosexual*. Weinberg argued that people harbouring prejudices and hate towards gays and lesbians were in fact suffering from a form of psychological disturbance and irrational thoughts (Kantor, 1998). He also became an important voice in the struggle to have homosexuality removed as a diagnostic category in *The Diagnostic and Statistical Manual of Mental Disorders* (DSM). This approach to homophobia, as an emotional disorder, has lingered on, and many of the present connotations to the concept are in one way or another tied into our understanding of this phenomenon. According to Kantor (1998), for example, most homophobes tend to be *dereistic*—that is, they are living in a mental world characterised by idiosyncratic thinking, myth and a lack of congruence between their own atavistic thinking and the social reality. Kantor (1998, 2009) even divides homophobes into different diagnostic categories, such as phobic, paranoid and obsessive. Consequently, he sees homophobes as pathological individuals. This is also reflected in his suggestion on how to solve this 'problem':

> While gays and lesbians can merely convince or cover homophobes into no longer hating them, they can sometimes help pass laws that keep homophobes from acting on their hatred. Education and psychoanalysis are the best ways to change a homophobes mind. But legislation is the fastest way to change a homophobe's behaviour.
>
> (Kantor, 1998, p. 205)

At the same time, the term *homophobia* has become a part of the terminology used in anti-discriminatory work in general, and in schools in particular. For example, there is also a critique against the psychiatric definition and use of this term. This critique often leans on how homophobia, as a concept, is considered to internalise the historical pathologisation of homosexuality in itself (cf. Foucault, 1990). As a consequence of this discussion, instead of looking at the phenomenon at large as a personal or individual problem, there are attempts to analyse homophobia as a set of social, cultural, collective and systematic forms of oppression (Griffin, 1998; Plummer, 1999; Mason, 2002). In line with this work, there have been several attempts to find alternative words for this phenomenon, such as *heterosexism,homonegativity* (Wickberg, 2000), or *gay hatred* and *hate crimes* (Herdt and van de Meer, 2003). But the term homophobia is still very much used in everyday life as well as in research, showing that this has become an important tool when targeting certain types of behaviour and prejudices.

In this chapter we will try to reposition the discussion on homophobia from the psychiatric field of understanding towards a more sociological explanation of this phenomenon. The duality between individual and structural explanations creates tension when understanding homophobia, and it is consequently intertwined with masculinity as a conundrum, i.e. how men are 'put together' and masculinity is made up. However, by locating masculinity and homophobia as part of structures of inequality such as class, 'race'/ethnicity, age and sexuality, whilst at the same time stressing the fluidity and fragmentation of gender, it becomes possible to understand the relationships that connect individuals, homophobic tendencies and contexts. In doing this, we can focus on individual as well as societal and cultural aspects without reducing the discussion to simplistic pathologisation and individualism. We will situate homophobia and investigate some central areas and empirical fields, such as male peer groups, education, sport and different national contexts where we tend to find expressions of this form of intolerance. We will also approach the connection that is often made between the construction of masculinity, homophobic sentiments and different strategies to regulate sexual boundaries and sustain heterosexuality. Initially, we will discuss diverse understandings of homophobia in relation to different national contexts and then turn our attention to how the demarcation line between manliness and unmanliness is tied into studies on homophobia. Thereafter, we will discuss the problematic relation between visibility—coming out as a homosexual in public—and violence. However, we will also draw on some studies showing the instability of heterosexuality and how there are tendencies to a decreasing homophobia in society. Finally, we will return to the question of how to define, use and integrate the concept of homophobia in critical studies on men and masculinity.

Situating Homophobia and Masculinity

When homophobia is being discussed, it often tends to be done through certain discourses on gender, sexuality and identity. These often very Western-influenced views are, however, being contested, especially from an African point of view but also in discussions on how different forms of homophobia and different degrees of homophobia should be understood in comparison between different countries or regions. Take, for instance, the notion of how men, in order to 'become' masculine, also need to pursue a compulsory heterosexuality and thus need to not behave in ways considered gay (Kimmel, 2003). Although this is often seen among young male peer groups in Western countries, as noted above, it is not always the case either globally or historically. This connection between that of being a man, being heterosexual, and thus not being homosexual that is often taken for granted presupposes a static position(ing) between heterosexual men and homosexual men in terms of identity. Kimmel (2003) claims, for instance, that maintaining an appearance of heterosexuality is an organising principle of masculinity. Homophobia then almost becomes part of one's own heterosexual and masculine identity-formation. To be able to put these static positions into motion and show why homophobia rather needs to be situated, we will need to examine both how homophobia is manifesting itself and how it is being fought in different contexts. Awondo et al. (2012) build on what is often described as an increase of homophobia in Africa and its alleged differences from the more 'open' and 'libertarian' West. What is interesting in their comparison between four African countries (Senegal, Uganda, Cameroon and South Africa) are not primarily the differences in their views on homosexuality per se but rather how it is considered as being a threat.

To simplify it, then, there are three apparent threats being used to foment homophobia that differ between some of the countries. First of all, there is a view of homosexuality in which it is considered as a form of subjection or weakness. This view is probably the most similar to dominant ways of describing homophobia in Western countries. Men engaging in or being suspects of engaging in 'homosexual activities' are seen as lesser men and thus being a danger to the country. Secondly, there is a view of homosexuality as being a part of witchcraft and occult practises, these men being considered almost ultra-masculine and thus not weak but still a threat to the nation. The third view is how homosexuality has been connected to the imperialistic West and to people of power, thus homophobic attitudes, laws and persecution being used to oppose power (Awondo et al., 2012).

The West has influenced and affected homophobic tendencies and laws in Africa through the more apparent colonialism but also through what might be more unapparent post-colonial activism. Such post-colonial gay and lesbian activism, however, often implies a discourse of a 'global gay identity' (Awondo et al., 2012; Massad, 2007). These interventions, because they have tended to focus on the universality of homosexual versus the heterosexual, rather than helping, have led to even greater difficulties for people who do not agree with that epistemology (Massad, 2007). This shows the importance of putting a concept of homophobia into motion and to situate it locally in order to understand how it is enacted as well as how to best counteract it. In this section the notion of the 'homophobic Africa' has been deconstructed and the West has received somewhat of a static Othering; however, this of course is not the point. Similar movements can be seen, for instance, in Europe and the United States as well. Latvia is one country that stands out when it comes to attitudes towards homosexuality in a European context. What is interesting is that Latvia even differs in relation to the other Baltic countries, which have gone through similar historical changes, but this does not explain the homophobic attitudes. Mole (2011) claims that it instead has to do with a nationalistic discourse on the 'Latvian people' and their continuing existence. Similar relationships between nationalism and homophobia are also viewable among other nationalist movements in Europe (Graff, 2010).

Other important factors to aid understanding of homophobia globally are, for instance, religion and economy. Sometimes they both interact. Peterson (2011) shows how Christian organisations in the United States use neoliberal discourses of self-governance and marketisation to exclude gay and lesbian families. These organisations also play a key role in understanding homophobia in some African countries (Awondo et al., 2012), in which homophobic tendencies often are fuelled by certain Christian and Islamic organisations. To be able to both analyse as well as put effort into eradicating homophobia, it is necessary to see beyond the rather static taken-for-granted relationship between sexuality, masculinity, and identity and instead to view its place, time and context. If not, homophobia only risks being invisibilised and further fuelled.

Unmanliness and Gender Melancholia

> Homophobia is a mobile polymorphous prejudice that incorporates a range of meanings, many of which are nonsexual. This makes it difficult to assign a satisfactory name to homophobia. Boys learn about homophobia before they understand adult sexuality and sexual identity. This ordering effectively 'dehomosexualizes' homophobia, but increases its development and social importance because the prominent prehomosexual phase set the scene for forthcoming sexual maturation: homophobia underwrites a boy's emerging understanding of adult sexuality and shapes his sexual identity because it comes first.
>
> (Plummer, 1999, p. 305)

There are numerous words used to label weak and unmanly boys and men. Derogatory words such a 'poofter', 'sissy', 'wuss' and 'nancy' are used to draw a sharp line between 'real' men and other men. Consequently, these words are used to mark undesirable otherness. Plummer (1999) shows in his interview study of young Australian men that they fear being defined as a 'poofter', for example. Other insulting words such as 'dickhead' or 'wanker' are preferred, because they do not share the very distinct stigmatising effect of the homophobic labels. According to Plummer, homophobia commences and peaks in early adulthood, and thereafter it starts to partly dissipate. *The homophobic passage* plays a key role in the formation of masculinity, and it has a formative effect stretching from childhood until early adulthood (Plummer, 1999).

Some studies stress that this passage positions boys both as heterosexual and as 'being' boys. Young male peer groups particularly tend to use homophobic language as a way of positioning themselves against others (Hall and La France, 2012; Birkett and Espelage, 2015). An interesting result from that particular study shows how boys who had themselves been called homophobic names later tended to call others homophobic names (Birkett and Espelage, 2015). Furthermore, boys taking part in bullying also tend to use homophobic name-calling to a greater extent than other boys. Although there are reasons for scepticism towards studies trying to measure gender identity, the fact that people tend to enhance their heterosexual identity when being labelled homophobically is, in relation to other studies, somewhat interesting—that is, the way in which people being called homophobic names to a greater extent try to enhance their own heterosexual identity (Carnaghi et al., 2011).

A common view is that the formation and fashioning of the masculine self also places severe limitations—in terms of the restricted freedom to explore and develop different abilities and traits—upon the boy and the young man (Butler, 1997b; Plummer, 1999; Mills, 2001). Being a homophobe comes with a price. One of the young men in Plummer's (1999, p. 165) study reflects upon the destiny of the homophobes:

S: . . . that's really funny to think that all of those that were on the top are now social outcasts, almost. . . in my class you know, I'd say that the top twenty-five are all unemployed.

D: Is that top twenty-five academically or. . .

S: No. . . powerful. They're all tattooed and they're all drug fucked (laughs). But they're the ones that literally, 'held the standard.' They're the ones that controlled whatever people thought about male power. And now they're social outcasts. (A1)

The restricted freedom to explore and construct masculinities not reduced to a 'traditional' heteronormative and homophobic position is also showed in Hammarén's (2008) study about young men living in multi-ethnic suburbs in Sweden and their constructions of gender and sexuality. Some of the heterosexual young men expressed the pressure they felt from their peers to construct a 'correct' and heterosexual masculinity. Samir reflects on his friends' reactions after he had a date with a girl:

S: It is always like this. They ask: 'What happened, what happened, tell us.' I respond: 'No, nothing.' And then: 'Didn't you fuck her?' 'No, I didn't.' And then: 'Are you faggot, didn't you fuck her, are you faggot? Ha ha ha.'

In this quote, the friends of Samir implicitly question his manhood. They are looking for evidence that proves his possible masculinity. If he doesn't, however, stage a proper masculinity—being straight, sleeping with girls etc.—he risks being positioned as abnormal and consequently 'not-man-enough'. As Connell (1996) and Mills (2001) show, heteronormative and homophobic practices and discourses oppress not only homosexual guys but also straight guys, positioned as something else than straight.

The homophobic passage is often described as a long-term process affecting boys and young men and their 'victims' in a destructive manner, fashioning a male self that is responding to certain masculine ideals, such as being controlled, aggressive, dominant and rational. If we look closer at this process, it seems that the effects vary a lot between different boys and men, however. The quotation from Plummer above shows how the young men embracing hyper-masculinity and violence are later on positioned as social outcasts and losers, whereas the 'ear'oles' (that is, the more academically successful children and 'lads') are now on the top (cf. Willis, 1977). This way of approaching homophobia and homosexuality is further developed, as earlier mentioned, by Judith Butler in *The Psychic Life of Power* (1997b). According to Butler, heterosexuality naturalises itself by stressing the radical otherness of homosexuality. Butler argues that this leads to an identity based on the refusal to avow an attachment and on the refusal to grieve the loss of any potential relation. In this sense, masculinity and femininity are formed and shaped by loss, denial and *ungrievable love* (cf. Adam, 1998; Redman, 2000). Furthermore, this makes it possible to talk about a culture of *gender melancholia*. A linguistically related, but not identical, concept is 'melancholic masculinity' (Kenway et al., 2006). This configuration of masculinity is experienced by those men who remain bounded to 'traditional' notions of masculinity and heavy industrial work, which they don't have access to. Consequently, this type of grief is related to the conflict between employment as central to the definition of masculinity and the impending risk of being unemployed in a new and post-industrial society.

Policing Sexual Boundaries

Another example of the interplay between straightness, heterosexuality, homosexuality and homophobia can be found in earlier research on a group of young boys in a Further Education College (6. This study explored a group of young men who had recently been made redundant from a car manufacturing factory. The industry was in decline, and young people on apprenticeships were the first to be made redundant. As part of their redundancy package, they were offered training at a local college. Their options were a course in Car Manufacturing (from which they had been made redundant) or Sports Therapy. A group of six young men enrolled in the course who self-defined as working-class, heterosexual males: James, Faraday, Gary, Paul, Stuart and Keith. With the exception of Keith, who was African/Caribbean, the trainees were white and aged between 16 and 24. The college at the time was subject to economic upheaval and had to make savings. As Sports Therapy and Beauty Therapy courses both offered massage, the college decided to merge that component of the course. Therefore, the young men not only learned about sports massage; they also were learning about full body, often termed Swedish, massage. Initially there was much resistance to the massage as the young men resisted the idea of undressing and touching each other's bodies. They saw this as a homosexual practice, and it was only when they began to discursively position the body through a medical model that they were able to progress with their assessments.

What emerges within the course is these young men's negotiation of the management of each other's bodies. The use of a medical model of the body, such as how to maximise tissue enlargement on biceps and triceps, gave the young men legitimacy to touch each other without the threat of being labelled. As the young men became more skilled, they began to offer an open clinic for staff and students to deal with sports injuries. Although they had very few clients, the sense of professionalism further depersonalised their relationships with bodies. That was until the end of the course when a young female dancer visited the clinic, on a Wednesday afternoon, for a massage. The young woman was confident and was not intimidated by the male presence:

James: What do you want?
Christie: A full massage.
James: I have to do the tops of your legs, right up here?
Christie: I don't care.
James: Right if you get undressed.
Christie: Are you gonna go out?
James: Yes, when you get undressed.
Christie: Do you want me to take my knickers off?
James: You don't have to take them off if you don't want to.
             Christie finishes getting undressed and calls them all back in and opens the curtains.
James: Do you want courtesy towels?
Christie: No, it's only my tits in it? You've seen it all before, so why bother?

In this hyper-heterosexual context, it would be assumed that this scenario would have been highly desirable. Indeed, whilst James massages Christie, the other males are laughing and joking and wishing that they were in James' place. But after the massage, a different dynamic began to take shape:

Paul: Here is the pervert.
Stuart: Jailbait. You ought to get off with her no problems.
James: Listen to you, I don't want to get off with her, they'd be real problems wouldn't there Chris?
Chris: I don't think it would be a marriage made in heaven.
James: See I told you. Who would you rather do, a man or a young girl? I know which I would prefer.
Stuart: A raw nerve I suspect. When are you going to give her a pearl necklace?
Paul: Listen when are you going to shag her?
James: You are all just fucking sick.
Stuart: It isn't us touching up 15-year-old jailbait is it? But you can tell her to bring her friend next time.

These young men were using particular sexual discourses to police James' behaviour with particular heterosexual discourses being used against heterosexual practices. As the conversation progressed, the arguments became heated, and being a 'pervert' elided into being a 'nonce' and subsequently 'a fucking queer'. The male/female massage had problematised what had been a de-sexualised and de-gendered collective understanding of the practice. In this case, heterosexual practice became re-coded as a different form of sexuality and ultimately resulted in homophobic discourses. As such, heterosexual practice in this case becomes the material through which homophobic abuse can occur. Therefore, it is important to recognise the complex dynamics that surround how we understand homophobia.

Relating to heterosexualised policing, Messner (2001), in his study on 30 male athletes between 21 and 48 years of age, finds out that the need to prove one's manhood and non-homosexuality through sexual conquests of women is experienced as a burden by many young heterosexual males, resulting in a 'sexual schizophrenia'. That is, their minds lead them towards sexual conquest, while their hearts pull them toward intimacy and emotional feelings. Messner writes that the need to prove manhood through heterosexualisation could be especially oppressive for gay men. One of the interviewees in the study, Mike T., who threw himself into sport rather than into dancing (because he was afraid that people might find out that he was gay), gives the following account (Messner, 2001, pp. 260–261):

> I hated high school. I mean, I just didn't know who I was. I think I had quite a bit of negative self-esteem at that time, because I really felt different. I mean, I didn't drink, I didn't like to screw around, and this was what all my friends did, so I felt compelled to go along with this stuff, and all the time hating it. I dated some women, some that I loved because they were just really fine people—[but] physically, there was not a great deal of passion. For *males*, there was a passion. [But] homophobia was rampant, especially in athletics. You see, I think a lot of athletes go into athletics for the same reason I did. They need to prove their maleness. And I did, I readily admit it. I felt I've got to hide this thing—because I know what they were thinking: If I were gay, they would see me as less than a man, or *not a man*. So I'm going to *be a man*, because *that's what I am*.

Messner concludes that though Mike T's secret knowledge of his own sexuality makes this process a more conscious one, his construction of masculinity as heterosexual is not that different from his non-gay teammates' constructions: 'Whether gay or heterosexual, the denial and denigration of gayness and femininity (in oneself and in others) were important to these young men's construction of masculine identities and status in their male peer group' (Messner, 2001, p. 261). Consequently, the pressure to be seen as 'real man' kept most of the young men in conformity (at least 'on stage' and not always willingly) with homophobic and sexist locker room talk.

Even though the approaches to understanding homophobia put forward in this and the previous section differ somewhat, they tend to add up to the same conclusion—that is, that masculinity is largely shaped by processes connected to homophobia and homo-hatred. These mechanisms cast their shadow over male intimacy, dividing gender and identity into a homosexual/heterosexual dichotomy. Even though this explanation seems to have certain validity, it also tends to reduce masculinity and gender into long-term consequences and effects of homophobia. It seems farfetched to claim that masculinity is simply based upon a rock-hard foundation of homophobia and hatred, and, even though there seems to be some kind of relation between repressed homosexuality and masculinity, causality is probably not that linear and straightforward. We will return to this point later on in the chapter.

In the next section we will turn our attention towards the social arena and look closer at how people who identify as LGBT (lesbian, gay, bi, transgender) and people labelled as 'Others' and 'gender-different' deal with the violence and prejudices that abound in the public sphere.

Visibility and Violence

Violence against LGBT people is a central issue in discussions on homophobia. Although there are social and cultural changes towards a more liberal and open attitude towards LGBT people in many countries, risks of violence and abuse are still unreasonably high. Mason (2002) argues that homophobia-related sentiments are strongly related to cultural anxieties about gender identity in transformation. Homophobia-related violence can be seen as a more or less localised practice used to monitor and minimise visible manifestations of certain spectra of human sexuality. In some countries this violence is monitored by the state and even regulated in the law; in other countries prejudices, norms and widespread attitudes serve to regulate sexuality.

Violence and harassment are directed not only towards LGBT people but also towards the people associated with them. A study on youth with LGB (lesbian, gay, and bisexual) parents showed that these young people experienced harassment and sexual stigma (Kuvalank et al., 2014). Three types of responses were identified: fearful, defiant and detached. Fear often resulted in avoidance and attempts to become invisible. This is a common strategy used also among many LGBT people, drawing safety maps and calculating risks when moving around in public (Mason, 2002). Others fought back, confronted people and struggled with sexual stigma. A third strategy consisted in ignoring sexual stigma and trying to detach and not worry about homophobia. This study shows how violence and harassments partially and momentarily contribute to constructing identities, even though they never determine how these identities will be lived and reinvented in everyday life.

External violence is, of course, effective in manipulating people's behaviour, in the worst cases making them invisible and silent. Many lesbians in sport, for example, choose to remain invisible and silent; this is simply a survival strategy (Griffin, 1998). However, the existence of homo-negative attitudes and prejudices towards LGBT people is widespread, and there is a considerable risk that negative images and prejudices are transformed into *internalised homophobia* (Malyon, 1982; Herek, 1998; Coyle and Kitzinger, 2002). This concept has mainly been used in order to talk about how pejorative social attitudes are internalised, leading to an impaired identity. However, this simplified and psychological way of using the concept has met critique. Instead, a more contextualised and relational understanding of the concept has emerged. The phenomenon of internalised homophobia is grounded in a collective experience, and it is fertilised in social and political contexts and in the pathologisation of LGBT people in society. This implicates us all in these processes:

> Most of us have had a lifetime's exposure to these stereotypes; they are part of the socio-linguistic air we breathe, the attitudinal fog in which we are immersed. As members of the social community that communicates these attitudes, we not only receive these meanings but also participate in their transmission. Even without attention to the matter, each of us becomes an agent through whom cultural beliefs are spoken into the social sphere.
>
> (Russell and Bohan, 2006, p. 350)

As a result, these processes of homophobia have been suggested to influence violent crimes, not only those aimed at gay men and lesbian women per se. For instance, a study on what is called 'random school shootings' (that is, young people bringing weapons into schools and opening fire) in the United States shows a connection between homophobic bullying and perceived threats to their manhood (Kimmel and Mahler, 2003). Similar themes have been discussed on violence and killings during psychosis, where psychotic and more or less bizarre and homophobic perceptions of society and self-influence these individuals to carry out violent crimes on others as well as to experience suicidal tendencies (Murphy, 2006). Linking to the collectivisation of homophobia—the heteronormative order claiming that men should desire women in order to be considered normal— also regulates gender relations. For example, many heterosexual men experience oppression related to their specific representation of masculinity. Indeed, these men identify themselves as heterosexuals but are positioned as something else (Connell, 1996; Mills, 2001).

Although affecting everybody, violent homophobia, of course, first and foremost affects people themselves identified as LGBT. Violence and hostility towards the LGBT community from heterosexuals are common. Statistics in Sweden show for example that young LGBT people are overrepresented in terms of exposure to violence, threats and hate-crimes. In addition, the perpetrator is rarely known to the victim (Brottsförebyggande rådet, 2014). Similar results are shown in the UK and the United States, and are even found to escalate in the United States (Hunter, 2012; Rivers and Ryan, 2003). Making disclosures of your own sexuality could be especially sensitive, having often led to social marginalisation and negative responses as well as violence and threats. Although in many countries there has been an ongoing LGBT-liberation, this is not always viable among, for instance, young people still in school or among older people. LGBT people still struggle with possible disclosures, often very aware of the risk of being targeted and marginalised.

As previously mentioned, an argument has been made for a connection between the oppression of women and the oppression of LGBT people, in terms of violence being an expression of eradicating what is considered as femininity among men (Herdt and van der Meer, 2003). There are, however, studies indicating that violent acts against gay men (known as 'gay-bashing') can be understood as a performance of certain notions of masculinity. The growing visibility of homosexuality in contemporary society is a key feature to understanding this performance of masculinity through violence. The visibility of homosexuality, together with a fear of becoming desired by gay men, seems to trigger the violence used to (re-)acquire a macho and masculine status for these young men (van der Meer, 2003). The violence thus in itself becomes a part of the performance of masculinity. These different approaches to homophobia spotlight the importance of situating homophobia; the same kinds of acts could have different backgrounds and thus need to be approached differently.

Inclusive Masculinity

> When homosexuality is regarded as normal, good, and equal to heterosexuality, homophobia will more likely diminish.
>
> (Innala, 1995, p. 41)

In *Inclusive Masculinity* (2009), Anderson's thesis is that we are today witnessing a considerable change in masculinity. The lessening of homophobia gradually leads to a widening of the range of masculine identities and positions that are possible to embody and perform. Anderson nurtures an optimistic view on gender and changes in gender structures. However, he is at the same time fully aware that these changes are uneven and that, in many masculine contexts and milieus, masculinity is still defined as the opposite of femininity and homosexuality. However, this said, he is obviously describing and putting forward a scenario in which masculinity is gradually becoming more inclusive and permissive (Anderson, 2008, 2009):

> In a culture of diminished homohysteria, boys and men will be free to express emotional intimacy and physical expressions of that relationship with one another. Accordingly, this culture permits an ever greater expansion of acceptable heteromasculine behaviours, which results in a further blurring of masculine and feminine behaviours and terrains. The differences between masculinity and femininity, men and women, gay and straight, will be harder to distinguish, and masculinity will no longer serve as the primary method of stratifying men.
>
> (Anderson, 2009, p. 97)

An ethnographic study on heterosexual boys in a sixth-form class in the South of England showed that the boys were able to associate with gay students, to be emotionally close to other boys, as well as to avoid any recourse to a homophobic discourse, without being labelled as LGBT people (McCormack and Anderson, 2010). Male-to-male emotional and physical expressions of intimacy were common and a part of everyday life at this school. The authors interpret their results in line with the theory of *inclusive masculinity* (Anderson, 2009). As earlier mentioned, this theory claims that there is evidence for a decreased level of homophobia in certain parts of society and in certain countries. Furthermore, the authors suggest that global culture produces new spaces and possibilities to transgress and to re-construct gender identities. The rise in feminised masculinity can also be seen as a consequence of the increasing presence of metrosexuality in the media. This approach allows for a more contextualised way of understanding the relation between masculinity and homophobia. Even though boys and men in settings with a high degree of homophobia construct their masculinity in opposition to homosexuality, femininity, and weakness in general, there are other settings where masculinity is defined and constructed in a more fluid and open way.

Anderson and McGuire (2010) discuss men's rugby at a high-ranking academic university in England as one such setting. They show how players, while recognising the presence of homophobia among their coaches, take on a more inclusive approach to their own making of masculinity. Among other things, a lessening of homophobia allows players to be emotionally supportive to fellow players, even in a highly competitive contact sport like rugby. Rather than constructing their masculinity in contrast to femininity or homosexuality through recourse to misogynous or homophobic discourse, the players in Anderson and McGuire's study differentiate themselves in relation to the more orthodox homophobic masculinity found among their coaches. The ambition with Anderson and McGuire's intervention is not to suggest that rugby culture has broadly got rid of its reliance upon homophobia. They note explicitly:

> A deep heterosexualization of these particular men occurs because of their high masculine capital, and this may facilitate their social ability to perform inclusive masculinity in a way that men on lower-achieving rugby teams (or men who come from less privileged racial or classed backgrounds), may not yet be afforded.
>
> (Anderson and McGuire, 2010, p. 258)

What Anderson and McGuire's study does suggest is that even when researching settings that have previously been shown to be imbued with homophobic sentiments, we should not *assume* that performances of masculinity necessarily rely on expressing homophobia or are constructed in opposition to homosexual or subordinated subject positions. However, Bridges (2014) suggests that the reconstruction of masculine subjectivities could be understood as a characteristic of the privilege afforded to groups of white heterosexual men. Similar to Bridges, de Boise (2015) asserts that Anderson (2009) has underdeveloped theoretical arguments and is far too optimistic. De Boise claims that the concept of 'inclusive masculinity is misleading in that what it claims to document, the inclusion of 'Others' into more equal gender practises, is actually the inclusion of some white, gay, men, and boys into hegemonic configurations of power and the hybridization of existing hegemonic practises' (de Boise, 2015, p. 324). The criticism of inclusive masculinity underscores the importance of a contextual and intersectional analysis not necessarily interpreting 'LGBT-friendly' expressions as always progressive, even though they also, in certain societal settings and relations, may be a sign of increasing inclusivity and equality.

Strategies of 'Hetero-protection'

The relationship between masculine capital, heterosexualisation and lessened homohysteria, i.e. cultural fear of being homosexualised (McCormack, 2011), is also present in research conducted by Hammarén (2008) about young men living in multi-ethnic suburbs in Sweden and constructions of gender and sexuality. Indeed, many of these young men constructed their (hetero) sexualities in relation to conceptions of male homosexuality. The power relations that were developed among the young men, for example practices such as excluding individuals who did not fit the norm of masculinity, strengthened the young men's kinship and their efforts to avoid 'homosexualisation' and 'do' male heterosexuality. Consequently, heterosexuality seemed to be a condition for an accepted masculinity, and heteronormativity appeared as a quite strong discourse that upheld borders for possible and impossible identifications and positions for the young men.

However, the heterosexual norm was not clear-cut; many boys expressed ambivalence about their feelings towards LGBT people; at other times, they expressed more tolerant opinions; and on still other occasions, they expressed gender overarching attitudes and positions. Aram reflects on homosexuality, differentiating himself from his older father who was born in Iran:

A: Homosexuality, you know it is much more accepted for me, but perhaps not for my father, being sixty years of age and has lived in Iran for fifty years. It is about generation and age you know.

An especially interesting result in the research conducted by Hammarén is the racialised dimension related to this discussion:

Nils: What do you think about homosexuality?
Barzan: I have been to Gay clubs two or three times. It's actually good looking girls there, lesbian girls you know. A lot of good-looking girls, also girls who don't fancy other girls, but they are there to avoid getting picked up.
N: Are you visiting the club with your friends?
B: Yes, I have been there twice.
N: Why are you visiting Gay clubs?
B: We had nothing to do; we went to the club, lots of good-looking girls. We went there and the doorman said, we were immigrants you know, so the doorman said: 'Don't make any trouble, you know what kind of club this is'. And we answered: 'Yes, we know' and the doorman said: 'Are you completely sure?' The doorman was nice, he asked us ten times if we really wanted to enter, because if someone paw us we could create problems.

N: But, wasn't he prejudiced?

B: Yes, but in a good way, because he knows that immigrants don't like faggots.

N: No, that you don't like faggots?

B: No, and also that we are no faggots, think of someone pawing us, we could freak out.

N: But he couldn't know, maybe you were faggots?

B: Yes, no, but we didn't look like faggots, so the doorman warned us.

                                                    (Hammarén, 2008, p. 250)

In the quote above, Barzan describes that he and his friends are visiting Gay clubs with the intention of meeting good-looking girls. He also says in the interview that the doorman at the Gay club becomes suspicious, because immigrants, according to Barzan, neither like faggots, look like faggots nor act like faggots. Consequently, Barzan positions himself and his friends in relation to a heteronormative discourse and also a recurrent public discourse (reproduced by the doorman) on homophobic migrant young men. In relation to the ethnic polarisation in Swedish society and racialised discourses, the 'migrant young man' is often portrayed as threatening, sexist, traditionally conservative and heterosexual (Hammarén, 2008). In accordance with these representations, many of the young men in Hammarén's study coupled male homosexuality or 'soft' masculinities to a Swedish or Western discourse and expressed that 'immigrants' are seldom gays and can pass as heterosexuals (cf. de Boise, 2015). For some of the young men, as showed in the above quote, the migrant position seemed to function as a masculine capital, situating oneself as hyper-heterosexual and consequently not homosexual. Paradoxically, the heteronormative discourse about 'migrant men' appeared to allow some of the young men to develop an ease in relation to homosexuality and to enable and legitimise closeness and intimacy with peers. The discursive position of the migrant young man hence enabled a kind of 'hetero-protection' and confident heterosexual masculinity, not necessarily generating homohysteria.

Focussing on performing heterosexuality and hetero-protection as a central component in the making of masculinities is also present in Berggren's (2012) study on the production and negotiation of male heterosexuality in Swedish hip-hop. Through a discourse analysis of a broad sample of Swedish rap lyrics produced during the last decades, Berggren explores the use of metaphors, rhetorical negotiations and expressions of homosocial desire in Swedish hip-hop. Even though the symbolic language and the rhetorical expressions are surrounded by a dominant heteronormative discourse, signs of sexual ambiguity and homoerotic desire are also present. One example of this ambiguity:

> I love her but I love my *boys* too,
> but I love my *boys* too, I love my *boooys*! [. . .]
> don't get me wrong, baby, no homo
>
>   (Alexis Weak, 'Mina Boys', 2011, in Berggren, 2012, p. 51)

Berggren suggests that an image of heterosexuality as natural is offered in the rap lyrics that were analysed. A closer look though discloses that this image is also full of contradictions, relating to, for example, homoerotic metaphors, close relations and love between men, partly undermining the heteronormative discourse. However, these fissures require careful supervision in order to be straightened and sustained as credible. Consequently, despite being presented as natural, heterosexuality requires a policing of its boundaries.

Berggren suggests that the concept of straight inoculation—e.g. inserting women into contexts of male homosocial desire or of stating one's straightness, like the expression 'no homo' in the lyrics above—is useful in understanding attempts to maintain heterosexuality in a sexually ambiguous and contested terrain. Straight inoculations 'refer to expressions that function as rhetorical devices and that counter the potential non-heterosexuality implied in discourses and narratives' (Berggren, 2012, p. 57). Berggren underscores that straight inoculations are required when things are ambiguous, aiming to sustain heterosexuality, but 'their very use secretly betrays that this heterosexuality was always already unstable' (p. 59). The use of straight inoculations thus 'vaccinates' male rappers against potential homosexuality and at the same time, paradoxically, allows tenderness and love between men.

What these examples more or less suggest or at least imply, and what Anderson's earlier mentioned work shows more broadly, is that we need not think of masculinity as necessarily being formed through relationships of opposition or lack of intimacy between men. Instead, Anderson's work urges us to rethink the internal constituents of masculinity itself. One important aspect of this is that the way Anderson dis-articulates the often taken-for-granted connection between masculinity and homophobia/homohysteria allows us to see masculinity and homophobia as conceptually discrete. In other words, heterosexual masculinities can be constituted without relying on homophobia and/or homohysteria as a constituent factor. This also enables us to better recognise the discursive function of homophobia (and its opposite) in relation to the production of other categories than masculinity. We have already pointed to some instances where homophobia is articulated primarily as part of nationalistic discourse, rather than masculinity (of course, these two often do not also exclude each other).

The Othering of Homophobia

The relation of homophobia to nationalistic discourse is, however, quite complex. One complicating factor that seems important to recognise—particularly perhaps in relation to Anderson's somewhat utopian and criticised (Bridges, 2014; de Boise, 2015) view that a decoupling of masculinity from homophobia is at hand and by definition progressive—is to relate the decline in homophobia to nationalistic discourse, or, to be more precise, to relate what we can understand as a form of rebuttal of homophobia to nationalism. If we do this, we can recognise that what looks like a rebuttal of homophobia takes on the discursive role of enacting nationalism and racist discourse. As Butler notes:

> In the Netherlands, for instance, new applicants for immigration are asked to look at photos of two men kissing, and asked to report whether those photos are offensive, whether they are understood to express personal liberties, and whether the viewers are willing to live in a democracy that values the rights of gay people to open and free expression. [. . .] Those who are in favour of the new policy claim that acceptance of homosexuality is the same as embracing modernity. We can see in such an instance how modernity is being defined as sexual freedom, and the particular sexual freedom of gay people is understood to exemplify a culturally advanced position as opposed to one that would be deemed pre-modern. It would seem that the Dutch government has made special arrangements for a class of people who are considered presumptively modern. The presumptively modern includes the following groups who are exempted from having to take the test: European Union nationals, asylum-seekers and skilled workers who earn more than €45,000 per year. Also exempt are citizens of the USA, Australia, New Zealand, Canada, Japan and Switzerland, where presumably homophobia is not to be found or where, rather, importing impressive income levels clearly pre-empts concerns over importing homophobia.
>
> (2008, p. 3f)

As Butler points out, the implicit logic of such a practice is of course to suggest that a picture of two men kissing can be seen as liberal and modern and that a rejection of homophobia is part of what it means to be Dutch. What the example makes obvious, then, is that not only can homophobia play a part in the enactment of nationalistic discourse as we have discussed above but the rebuttal of homophobia can take on a similar function. What this also allows us to conclude, in a more theoretical vein, is that while a disconnection of homophobia from masculinity might be conceptually fruitful (in that it allows us to see how homophobia and its opposition work in discourses not explicitly concerned with masculinity), its disconnection as empirically observed cannot by definition be seen as a progressive trend. Instead, homophobia can also be Othered in a way that works in tandem with nationalistic and racist discourse. This analysis further emphasises the need to situate both homophobia and its rebuttal, as we have already argued above.

By Othering homophobia, the above example illustrates the effort to purify a nationalistic discourse from homophobic sentiments. Thus, the homophobic subject is positioned outside of the Netherlands, obscuring actual signs of homophobia inside the country. Interestingly, the practise above uses one Othered category, LGBT people, to identify, control and exclude another Othered category, migrants, thus constructing them as mutually exclusive. Hence, the homophobic subjects are constructed as the pre-modern Other and constitutive outside of a suppositious liberal, yet paradoxically prejudiced and ethnocentric, modernity.

The connection between homophobia and nationalism is also described by Kimmel (2001), in a somewhat different way. Based on American conditions, Kimmel claims that homophobia is not only producing sexism but also racism and nationalism. Kimmel (2001, pp. 280–281) writes:

> At the turn of the 19th century, it was Europeans and children who provided the contrast for American men. The 'true American was vigorous, manly, and direct, not effete and corrupt like the supposed Europeans,' writes Rupert Wilkinson (1986). 'He was plain rather than ornamented, rugged rather than luxury seeking, a liberty loving common man or natural gentleman rather than an aristocratic oppressor or servile minion' (p. 96). The 'real man' of the early 19th century was neither noble nor serf. By the middle of the century, black slaves had replaced the effete nobleman. Slaves were seen as dependent, helpless men, incapable of defending their women and children, and therefore less than manly. Native Americans were cast as foolish and naïve children, so they could be infantilized as the 'Red Children of the Great White Father' and therefore excluded from full manhood.

Kimmel describes how men's fear of being categorised as unmanly generates a male outward behaviour that distresses not only women and homosexual men but also other 'Others'. Through American history, various groups of men have represented 'the sissy' through which the American man has been able to outline the definition of the 'right' masculinity. At the same time, Kimmel describes, this femininisation has a paradoxical and equally brutal negative. Ironically, the same groups of men have at other historical periods been described as oversexualised, violent, rapacious beasts, uncivilised and hypermasculine. Regardless of ascribed feminine or masculine traits, the categorisation of the Other man has always been gendered and constructed as an opposition to the American man. Kimmel describes how different groups of European men (such as Irishmen and Italians) as well as black men, Jews, Native Americans and Asians (the Japanese during the Second World War and the Vietnamese during the Vietnam War) in different historical periods were attributed a status from unmanly, naive, helpless and emotionally controlled to hypermasculine, cruel and sexually violent. Hence, the staging of an appropriate masculinity was made possible only for a minority of men, resulting in a national conditional manhood.

Masculinity, Homophobia and Transformations

Expressions of homophobia, while lamentable, can also be understood as signs that gender-progressive changes are in fact taking place. As suggested above, the growth in homophobic violence can be seen as a response to a growing visibility of homosexuality in contemporary society. We can understand it as violence enacted in response to the destabilisation of gender and sexuality norms. In a way, then, homophobia can also be seen as the expression of a rather 'desperate' need to censor and suppress homosexuality. As Butler has argued, such censoring can never be formulated without also making possible that which it seeks to suppress. She discusses this at length in relation to the by-now abandoned '*Don't ask, don't tell*' policy previously adopted by the US Army. As Butler shows, the word 'homosexual' stands out as 'contagious' in this context, and using it as part of self-definition is prohibited. As Butler notes, however:

> The very regulation in question, must utter the term in order to perform the circumscription of its usage. [. . .] The regulation must conjure one who defines him or herself as a homosexual in order to make plain that no such self-definition is permissible within the military.
>
> The regulation of the term is thus no simple act of censorship or silencing; on the contrary, the regulation redoubles the term it seeks to constrain, and can only effect this constraint through this paradoxical redoubling.
>
> (Butler, 1997a, p. 104)

Given this redoubling, and the unavoidable conjuring of that which one seeks to suppress, one might ask what this homophobic paranoia stands for. Why the desperation?

As Butler shows, the phantasy that structures this policy builds on the assumption that were homosexuality not controlled, it would tear the social fabric that builds community in the military and destroy the possibility for homosocial bonds between men. She writes: 'And if men speak their homosexuality, that speaking threatens to bring into explicitness and, hence, destroy, the homosociality by which the class of men coheres' (Butler, 1997a, p. 121). She discusses how sublimated homosexuality has been positioned as that which makes sociality possible. Hence, prohibiting homosexuality is not about erasing desire but rather about conserving it as a desire that when sublimated enables homosocial bonds between men. In this, Butler both follows and reformulates Freudian thinking on homosexuality.

However, we need not go in this direction in order to understand the discursive function of censoring homosexuality. Instead of looking for potentially repressed homosexuality in each of us, i.e. the 'deeper meaning' of homophobic censorship, we can instead look at this as a 'surface phenomenon'. As Žižek (1997, p. 46) argues, 'sometimes, the most difficult thing is to accept the appearance at its surface value—we imagine multiple phantasmatic scenarios to cover it up with "deeper meanings." ' Following Žižek, we can conclude that no matter what founds homophobia, what gives it strength is that it 'works'. As Žižek notes:

> While fully justified at its own level, the notion of censorship at work in this criticism, with its Foucauldian background of Power which, in the very act of censorship and other forms of exclusion, generates the excess it endeavours to contain and dominate, nonetheless seems to fall short at a crucial point: what it misses is the way in which censorship not only affects the status of the marginal or subversive force that the power discourse endeavours to dominate, but, at an even more radical level, splits from within the power discourse itself. One should ask here a naive, but nonetheless crucial question:

why does the Army so strongly resist publicly accepting gays into its ranks? There is only one possible consistent answer: not because homosexuality poses a threat to the alleged 'phallic and patriarchal' libidinal economy of the Army community, but, on the contrary, because the Army community itself relies on a thwarted/disavowed homosexuality as the key component of the soldiers' male-bonding.

(1997, p. 37)

That is, we need not take part in the homophobic phantasy that the release of homosexual desire would ruin the military (or society more broadly). Instead we can, less speculatively, note that expressing homophobia 'works well' as a homosocial kit, binding men together. In this, Žižek's objection also points back to our previous discussion of how homophobic violence need not be understood as the fearful reaction to possible homosexual desire within the perpetrator himself. Instead, as a 'surface phenomenon', we can note that acting out violence against LGBT people has become culturally established as a way of enacting masculinity. This argument might appear hair-splitting, but the point is that such an analysis again lets us understand masculinity and homophobia as conceptually discrete, something that we have argued for as important throughout this chapter. Rather than being connected out of (psychic) necessity, we can understand homophobic censoring and violence, then, as sometimes connected to the enactment of masculinity, but this link is also contingent. Thinking this connection as contingent, rather than necessary, makes it easier to envision forms of masculinity not dependent on homophobia. Hence, transformation becomes easier to recognise and conceptualise.

Conclusion

This chapter signals a shift towards understanding masculinity and its relation to homophobia as a process that moves from a focus on individuals and psychologising towards an understanding of the relationships that connect between individuals and contexts. It has been suggested that these connections are often characterised by a dependence on differences between other men and women. For example, it is often argued that heterosexual masculinity is established through an 'Othering' of gay men. At the same time, there is an emerging approach that argues sexual difference is becoming less important and that men are now accommodating homosexuality as part of their masculinities. In these accounts it is sameness with other men and women which forms the basis of men's identities. This chapter suggests that in order to understand the nature of men's behaviours and identities, we need to understand sameness and difference as fluid, fragmented and passing (dis)connections that are contextually contingent. This shifts the focus towards the processual nature of masculinities.

One characteristic of the processes involved in the formation of masculine subjectivities is a notion of 'Otherness'. In this book we have highlighted how heterosexual men tend to construct their identities through distancing themselves from what is deemed as feminine. We have already seen how hegemonic masculinities secure their dominance through the use of homophobia. However, in this chapter we have explored the relationship between masculinity and homophobia in more detail, in order to explore how it operates to consolidate particular masculine styles and gendered power relations, policing what are acceptable and unacceptable attitudes and behaviours. However, a closer look at the relationship between masculinity and homophobia reveals a more complex picture. Rather than think of masculinity as being formed solely through relationships of opposition, Anderson (2009) argues that we need to rethink the internal constituents of masculinity itself. This means that masculinity and homophobia can be viewed as conceptually discrete. In other words, heterosexual masculinities can be constituted without relying on homophobia as a constituent factor.

However, as earlier mentioned, de Boise (2015) criticises the concept of *inclusive masculinity* and claims that it is redundant, and what is called 'inclusive' may just be another hegemonic strategy for some powerful men (liberal, heterosexual, white, middle-class) to legitimately maintain power in the wake of Gay rights. Accordingly, the identified unacceptability of homophobic speech or violence may suggest that homophobia and homohysteria are less integral to hegemonic practices but may not disrupt broader inequalities and the institutional privilege of some men. According to de Boise, it is consequently important to frame the discussion on homophobia contextually and underscore that homophobia varies considerably within society and between different societal settings. Even if the perspective of Anderson indeed helps us not to assume that configurations of masculinity necessarily rely on expressing homophobia and opposition to homosexual subject positions, the claims of de Boise open up the importance of an intersectional analysis of homophobia (in relation to class, gender and race/ethnicity) and propose a degree of caution in how to interpret 'gay-friendly' expressions and practices. As our chapter has highlighted, it is most important to understand homophobic sentiments and practices as not just reducible to gender but situated and intertwined with, for example, racialised and nationalistic discourses.

References

Adam, B.D. (1998) Theorizing homophobia. *Sexualities*, 1(4), 387–404.

Anderson, E. (2008) Inclusive masculinity in a fraternal setting. *Men and Masculinities*, 10(5), 604–620.

Anderson, E. (2009) *Inclusive Masculinities: The Changing Nature of Masculinity*. London: Routledge.

Anderson, E. and McGuire, R. (2010) Inclusive masculinity theory and the gendered politics of men's rugby. *Journal of Gender Studies*, 19(3), 249–261.

Awondo, P., Geschiere, P. and Reid, G. (2012) Homophobic Africa? Toward a more nuanced view. *African Studies Review*, 55(3), 145–168.

Berggren, K. (2012) 'No homo': Straight inoculations and the queering of masculinity in Swedish hip hop. *Norma*, 7(1), 50–66.

Birkett, M. and Espelage, D.L. (2015) Homophobic name-calling, peer-groups, and masculinity: The socialization of homophobic behavior in adolescents. *Social Development*, 24(1), 184–205.

Bridges, T. (2014) A very "gay" straight? Hybrid masculinities, sexual aesthetics, and the changing relationship between masculinity and homophobia. *Gender & Society*, 28(1), 58–82.

Brottsförebyggande rådet. (2014) *Hatbrott [Hate crime]*. Stockholm: Brottsförebyggande rådet.

Butler, J. (1997a) *Excitable Speech: A Politics of the Performative*. New York: Routledge.

Butler, J. (1997b) *The Psychic Life of Power*. Stanford: Stanford University Press.

Butler, J. (2008) Sexual politics, torture, and secular time. *The British Journal of Sociology*, 59(1), 1–23.

Carnaghi, A., Maass, A. and Fasoli, F. (2011) Enhancing masculinity by slandering homosexuals: The role of homophobic epithets in heterosexual gender identity. *Personality and Social Psychology Bulletin.*, pp. 1655–1665.

Connell, R. (1996) *Maskuliniteter [Masculinities]*. Göteborg: Daidalos.

Coyle, A. and Kitzinger, C. (eds.) (2002) *Lesbian and Gay Psychology: New Perspectives*. Oxford: Blackwell.

de Boise, S. (2015) "I'm not homophobic, I've got gay friends": Evaluating the validity of inclusive masculinity. *Men and Masculinities*, 18(3), 318–339.

Foucault, M. (1990) *The History of Sexuality: The Will to Knowledge Vol. 1.* Harmondsworth: Penguin.

Graff, A. (2010) Looking at pictures of gay men: Political uses of homophobia in contemporary Poland. *Public Culture*, 22(3), 583–603.

Griffin, P. (1998) S*trong Women, Deep Closets: Lesbians and Homophobia in Sports*. Champaign, IL: Human Kinetics.

Hall, J.A. and La France, B.H. (2012) How context matters: Predicting men's homophobic slang use. *Journal of Language and Social Psychology*, 32(2), 162–180.

Hammarén, N. (2008) *The Suburb in the Head: Young Men's Thoughts on Gender and Sexuality in the New Sweden*. Stockholm: Atlas.

Herdt, G. and Van de Meer, T. (2003) Homophobia and anti-gay violence—Contemporary perspectives: Editorial introduction. *Culture, Health & Sexuality*, 5(2), 99–101.

Herek, G.M. (1998) *Stigma and Sexual Orientation*. Thousand Oaks, CA: Sage.

Hunter, S. (2012) *Coming Out and Disclosures: LGBT Persons Across the Life Span*. New York: Routledge.

Innala, S.M. (1995) *Structure and Development of Homophobia*. Göteborg: Department of Psychology.

Kantor, S.M. (1998) *Homophobia: Descriptions, Developments and Dynamics of Gay Bashing*. London: Praeger.

Kantor, S.M. (2009) *Homophobia: The State of Sexual Bigotry*. Westpoint: Praeger.

Kenway, J., Kraack, A., and Hickey-Moody, A. (2006) *Masculinity Beyond the Metropolis*. Houndmills: Palgrave Macmillan.

Kimmel, M. (2001) Masculinity as homophobia: Fear, shame and silence in the construction of gender identity. In: Whitehead, S.M. and Barrett, F.J. eds. *The Masculinities Reader*. Cambridge: Polity Press, pp. 266–287.

Kimmel, M. (2003) Masculinity as homophobia. In: Kimmel, M. and Ferber, A.L. eds. *Privilege: A Reader*. Boulder: Westview Press, pp. 51–74.

Kimmel, M.S. and Mahler, M. (2003) Adolescent masculinity, homophobia, and violence: Random school shootings, 1982–2001. *American Behavioral Scientist*, 46, 1439–1458.

Kuvalanka, K.A., Leslie, L.A. and Radina, R. (2014) Coping with sexual stigma: Emerging adults with lesbian parents reflect on the impact of heterosexism and homophobia during their adolescence. *Journal of Adolescence Research*, 29(2), 241–270.

Malyon, A. (1982) Psychotherapeutic implications of internalized homophobia. In: Gonsiorek, J.C. ed. *Homosexuality and Psychotherapy: A Handbook of Affirmative Models*. New York: Haworth, pp. 59–69.

Mason, G. (2002) *The Spectacle of Violence: Homophobia, Gender and Knowledge*. London: Routledge.

Massad, J. (2007) *Desiring Arabs*. Chicago: University of Chicago Press.

McCormack, M. (2011) The declining significance of homohysteria for male students in three sixth forms in the south of England. *British Educational Research Journal*, 37(2), 337–353.

McCormack, M. and Anderson, E. (2010) 'It's just not acceptable any more': The erosion of homophobia and the softening of masculinity at an English sixth form. *Sociology*, 44(5), 843–859.

Messner, M. (2001) Friendship, intimacy and sexuality. In: Whitehead, S.M., Barrett, F.J. eds. *The Masculinities Reader*. Cambridge: Polity Press, pp. 253–265.

Mills, M. (2001) *Challenging Violence in Schools: An Issue of Masculinities*. Buckingham/Philadelphia: Open University Press.

Mole, R. (2011) Nationality and sexuality: Homophobic discourse and the "national threat" in contemporary Latvia. *Nations and Nationalism*, 17, 540–560.

Murphy, D. (2006) Homophobia and psychotic crimes of violence. *Journal of Forensic Psychiatry & Psychology*, 17, 131–150.

Peterson, D. (2011) Neoliberal homophobic discourse: Heteronormative human capital and the exclusion of queer citizens. *Journal of Homosexuality*, 58, 742–757.

Plummer, D. (1999) *One of the Boys: Masculinity, Homophobia and Modern Manhood*. New York: Harrington Press.

Pye, D., Haywood, C. and Mac an Ghaill, M. (1996) The training state, de-industrialisation and the production of white working-class trainee identities. *International Studies in Sociology of Education*, 6(2), 133–146.

Redman, P. (2000) 'Tarred with the same brush': 'Homophobia' and the role of the unconscious in school-based cultures of masculinity. *Sexualities*, 3(4), 483–499.

Rivers, I. and Ryan, C. (2003) Lesbian, gay, bisexual and transgender youth: Victimisation and its correlates in the USA and UK. *Culture, Health & Sexuality*, 5(2), 103–119.

Russell, G.M. and Bohan, J.S. (2006) The case of internalized homophobia: Theory and/as practice. *Theory and Psychology*, 16(3), 343–366.

van der Meer, T. (2003) Gay bashing—a rite of passage? *Culture, Health & Sexuality*, 5(2), 153–165.

Wickberg, D. (2000) Homophobia: On the cultural history of an idea. *Critical Inquiry*, 27(1), 42–57.

Wilkinson, R. (1986) *American Tough: The Tough-Guy Tradition and American Character*. New York: Harper & Row.

Willis, P. (1977) *Learning to Labour*. Farnbourough: Saxon House.

Žižek, S. (1997) Multiculturalism, or, the cultural logic of multinational capitalism. *New Left Review*, 225, 28–51.

6 Heteronormativity, Intimacy and the Erotic

Introduction

In this chapter, we will discuss and analyse the concept of heteronormativity and how it connects to masculinity and the studies of masculinities. Heteronormativity is often used as a theoretical concept in Gender Studies and in studies on men and masculinities. Although heteronormativity theoretically focuses on and problematises the dominant position of heterosexuality in society, it sometimes seems to create a certain confusion when applied to individuals' lives and choices. One such example is the recently developed notion of the so-called 'new homonormativity'. This concept is used and applied as a critique of tendencies among, for instance, gay men, to privilege consumption, privacy and domesticity over far-reaching social and cultural change (Duggan, 2003; Rosenfeld, 2009). Although theories of heteronormativity often stay at a societal level or focus on how heterosexual norms tend to affect and to some extent perhaps even control all of us, the concept is sometimes used as fuel for criticising the lives of both homosexual and heterosexual families that do not diverge from what is perceived to be a 'heterosexual way of life'. In terms of masculinity, heteronormativity often tends to imply certain masculine ideals in general and specific forms of masculine power in particular. The concept thus often implies how a specific hegemonic heterosexual masculinity is being positioned against, and even established through, the Othering of gay men or, sometimes, men striving for gender equality. However, with such a static approach, a risk of obscuring differences and resistance among men, as well as other possible power relations, follows.

The aim of this chapter is to examine how heteronormativity is still in many ways a valid concept and also to analyse and critically examine the use of this concept of heteronormativity. When talking about heteronormativity and masculinity, it is impossible not to talk about femininity and women as well as masculinity and men, since these concepts are somewhat interrelated. Thus, this chapter will also relate to femininity and women to be able to fully analyse the concepts of heteronormativity and masculinity.

Although the concept of heteronormativity is very useful, it also seems important to appropriate and adjust it to some extent in order to analyse, for example, the changes occurring in homosexual families, contemporary gender-equal families or progressive youth culture. For instance, the more general normalising process in question does not apply to and affect all straight, gay, and lesbian people and married couples in the same way. The chapter focuses on questions such as: What power structures and forms of relations are intended to be investigated and criticised under the heading of heteronormativity? This is for instance the case when heteronormativity is being promoted through different lifestyles and the violence that sometimes follows in its tracks. Furthermore, how could it be possible to both visualise and change repressive heterosexuality without repressing possible changes that might occur among different families? A challenge for studying and understanding the conundrum of masculinity, and how masculinity is constructed and perceived through the concept of heteronormativity, is both to be able to unpack a possible cultural-hegemonic heterosexuality and to be able to pay attention to—and maybe even support—how men challenge and 'do' masculinity and sexuality differently.

Heteronormativity as a Concept

Since the early 1990s, heteronormativity has become one of the key concepts within gender and queer studies. The term, although introduced by Michael Warner in an article published in 1991 (see Warner, 1991), could be argued to have its roots in the second wave of Feminism. It has, for instance, strong connections to Gayle Rubin's sex/gender system. In the 1970s, Rubin formulated a critical theory of the exchange of women and the sex/gender system. This theory is a critique of Marxian theory and its overriding exclusive focus on the economic system and production. Rubin identifies a system of hierarchical relations between men and women, but she also connects the theory of patriarchy with a more developed line of thought regarding how the suppression of women also leads to the suppression of different sexualities and identities:

> At the most general level, the social organization of sex rests upon gender, obligatory heterosexuality, and the constraint of female sexuality. [. . .] The suppression of the homosexual component of human sexuality, and by corollary, the oppression of gay and lesbians, is therefore a product of the same system.
>
> (Rubin, 1997, p. 40)

Rubin identifies a chain of various forms of oppressions and structurally determined hierarchies. Ultimately, she means that a Feminist revolution would liberate not only women but also 'human personality' from the straightjacket of gender.

The oppression and hierarchies, identified by Rubin, that affect women as well as different sexualities and identities other than heterosexual also imply particular forms of masculine power: masculine power in terms of patriarchy. The critique frames how we, as a society, socially organise family and how heterosexuality favours heterosexual men at the expense of women and other sexualities. Similar critique is further accentuated by researchers such as the above-mentioned

Michael Warner and others like Monique Wittig and Adrienne Rich. Wittig (1997) argues that the oppression of women can be eradicated only through the destruction of heterosexuality as a social system, which produces the doctrine of the polar differences between the sexes. Judith Butler (1990) takes the whole discussion in the direction of post-structuralism, offering a more troubled relation between lesbianism and feminism. The question raised by Butler (1990) is how non-normative sexual practices could eventually call the stability of gender as an entire category into question. Instead of promoting a certain subject, Butler constructs a theory of gender as a performative and regulatory fiction. This reading of sexuality and gender moves us towards a queer understanding of heterosexuality. Butler thus causes us to look more closely at the heterosexual matrix.

The concept of heteronormativity is sometimes used to describe a body of lifestyle norms as well as how people tend to reproduce distinct and complementary genders (man and woman). Like concepts such as hegemonic masculinity and homosociality (see Chapters 3 and 4), heteronormativity works as a tool to analyse *systems* of oppression and contributes to an understanding of how masculinity as well as more general gender structures and hierarchies are constructed in society. But when it is applied directly to everyday life, there is sometimes a tendency to include more and more aspects of gender and lifestyle issues under the heading of heteronormativity. As such, the concept works as a critique not only of systems of masculine and heterosexual power but also of more specific ways of organising masculinity, family, sexuality and lifestyles. On the one hand, it could be argued that the concept of heteronormativity could be used to draw attention to cultural hegemonic aspects of heterosexual masculinity. On the other, it could also be argued that, regardless of how masculinity is constructed or perceived, as long as it is packaged in reminiscences of a heteronormative frame, it reproduces the same masculine ideals and power relations. In our view, this shift in focus could be politically problematic as it could affect the ability of, for example, gay men to organise their families. Furthermore, it could be empirically problematic—that is, unproductive—for empirical analysis about alternative family forms and how they can resist and work against repression. We will return to these challenges, but first we need to discuss how heteronormativity as a concept is spread and promoted in society and how it could affect us as people.

This chapter is divided in two parts, the first focusing on different ways in which heteronormativity affects masculinity through promotion, violence, and the media, as well as globally and in terms of sexuality and intimacy. The second part discusses how the concept in itself could act as something that puts a lid on development, as being a barrier for new or changed ways of creating family and doing masculinity, sexuality and intimacy.

The Promotion of Heteronormativity

One reason the concept of heteronormativity is used to describe certain life choices is because of the active promotion of 'heterosexual choices'. Often this is the case when related to sexual education or school policies aiming at promoting certain life choices above other kinds of 'choices'. Although heterosexuality is most important and is being promoted as the default position, regardless of frequency, heteronormativity is not only promoted as heterosexuality:

> Everyday heterosexuality is not simply about sex, but is perpetuated by the regulation of marriage and family life, divisions of waged and domestic labour, patterns of economic support and dependency.
>
> (Jackson, 1999, p. 26)

These other life 'choices' often tend to be: living monogamously, being married, being middle class and whiteness (cf. McNeill, 2013), as well as implying certain gendered positions. In some cases the act of *promoting* becomes clear, in terms of having a clear and visible sender, such as when schools or literature construct heterosexuality as the primary sexuality. Other cases, however, are more unclear:

- Monogamous lives and marriage—in some states in the United States, the promotion of monogamy and heterosexuality are very much interwoven. In schools, being faithful and not having sexual relations are promoted, that is, in terms of being married before having (hetero-) sex (McNeill, 2013).
- Middle-class sexuality—class shapes our lives in many ways and creates 'boundaries' around what is considered 'appropriate' in terms of gender and sexuality. Beverley Skeggs (1997) is one of many researchers showing the intersection between gender and class, and how this affect views on sexuality. She claims that working-class sexuality is seen as out of place or almost filthy in comparison with the more 'pure' middle-class sexuality.
- White sexuality—heteronormativity not only shapes our view on possible sexual orientations or relations; it also is used to frame and reproduce racialised differences. For instance, as with working-class sexuality, black women have been seen as sexually deviant (Kandaswamy, 2008). Similarly, black men often tend to get sexualised, not in a normative way but rather as sexual deviants (Sánchez Taylor, 2000, 2001; Ward, 2008).
- Gendered positions—heteronormativity frames masculinity in terms of possible and desired positions within family and society. Gay, or 'feminised' men, for instance, are essential for the heterosexual family, in that they are constructed as the unwanted 'Other', sometimes even considered dangerous for society because they might challenge heteronormativity (cf. Jones, 2006; Martino, 2000; Tadele, 2011).

Heteronormativity points at the everyday and mundane ways in which heterosexuality and particular masculine positions are privileged and taken for granted, that is, normalised and naturalised (Myers and Raymond, 2010). As we have seen, these notions (of heterosexuality and masculine positions) are not only tied into conceptions, ideas and acts of sexuality but also viewed as foundational structures to society and culture. In this way, sexuality is rooted in societal structures and connected to central social institutions, such as the family and marriage, as well as in how we perceive and promote desired acts of masculinity.

Heteronormativity as Violence

As a consequence of its promotion as being a life choice, heteronormativity also acts as violence against bodies and people not fitting into the narrow normative life choices. These could be sexual minorities or transsexual people who are vulnerable to violence through their own being. Lloyd (2013) claims that it is the 'binary morphology' in itself that requires the violent materialisation of bodies. Through heteronormativity, heterosexuality and homosexuality are constructed as being binary opposites from each other. This makes it possible to violently act on what Sara Ahmed (2013) calls the regulatory norm; heteronormativity is not only about heterosexuality but also regulatory of masculinity, gender, ethnicity/race and sexuality. Although there are possible similarities between heteronormativity as violence and hate crimes (see Chapter 5), and they sometimes intertwine, it should mainly be read as different kinds of violent mechanisms strengthening heteronormativity.

Violence by heteronormativity is common, and we will provide a few examples of how it can express itself. What often first comes to mind are probably the different hate crimes towards gay and lesbian people—a particular form of which is what often goes under the name 'gay bashing'. However, these kinds of (often) physical and concrete forms of violence are only one type of violence; even acts such as 'corrective surgery' used on intersexed children can be considered to be an act of violence. Lloyd (2013) claims that because of its many expressions, it is important to be aware of these multiple and contradictory ways in which violence is being performed and of how these violent acts actually structure heterosexuality and heterosexual desire.

Hate crimes are crimes aimed at people because of their race, disability, sexuality and more. They are often random (at least when aimed at men), excessive and committed by a group of (white) men (Plumm et al., 2010; van der Meer, 2003). Theo van der Meer (2003) interviewed male perpetrators about gay bashing. Gay bashing is often completely random and performed by a group of men who violently abuse gay men, often in places adjacent to gay meeting points or clubs. What is interesting about van der Meer's study is that the perpetrators use this 'bashing' to assimilate a masculine status; they interpret their action as a service to the community, and one of their own biggest fears is being desired by gay men.

But violence by heteronormativity doesn't have to be this sudden or open. As pointed out by Lloyd (2013), it could also take its form through the 'correction' of intersexed bodies. This surgical and hormonal 'correction' has to do with a normative view on how bodies that don't match with heteronormative assumptions of masculinity and femininity need to be surgically adapted to fit one of these two normative body types. Butler (1990) claims that this urge to 'correct' intersexed 'deviance' comes from a fear of difference and a desire for binaries. Regardless of one's own standpoint, the 'corrections' are seldom surgically needed but rather considered socially or sexually required (Preves, Kaminsky and Hart, 2015).

Another example of violence by heteronormativity is through the *symbolic* use of language. The purpose of using terms like 'faggot', 'gay' or 'queer' as derogatory words is often to repress individuals and groups and at the same time to strengthen one's own position as well as to reduce the perceived risk of the self being presented as gay (Hall and LaFrance, 2012). These kinds of symbolic violence often tend to be forgotten but are used to promote a heterosexual lifestyle as well as to supress a non-heterosexual ditto.

In addition to the more direct and the symbolic form of violence, it is common to add a systemic definition of violence as well (Žižek, 2008). This symbolic form of violence can be illustrated from the UK, where much popular discussion was held in the 1980s, 1990s and 2000s on the state provision of sex education. Discussions about positive representations of gay and lesbian people in children's literature evinced much media and political antipathy. The key concern was that the inclusion of positive representations of gay and lesbian people would damage the moral fabric of the next generation. In this way, children become elided with notions of nationalism, and, as a result, the protection of children is fused with the protection of the nations. The implication of this is that the nation itself is inherently heterosexual, and the positive representation of other sexualities becomes a challenge to the nation. In this account, Englishness becomes read as heterosexual. It is, however, a familial form of heterosexuality that counts as English.

A *systemic* form of violence when talking about heteronormative violence relates to the economic and legislative system. One example is of course legislation on inheritance among non-heterosexual families, another on who is able to marry whom. Such legislation tends to promote certain (heterosexual) lifestyles at the expense of other lifestyles, for instance, gay men not being allowed to get married. Another, maybe more unusual example is the claim that the neo-liberal economic system tends to forget about non-heterosexual lifestyles and thus promotes heterosexual relationships, for instance, through commercials and other kinds of marketing (Peterson, 2011). One such specific kind of promotion is that of televised media, which will be addressed in more detail in the next section.

Televised and Mediated Heteronormativity

One specific and contemporary form of systemic violence is that which is performed through different forms of media. In this section, we will look into the discussion on televised heteronormativity. Television is interesting because it tends to rely upon a rather static and classic form of heteronormativity, as well as being pretty quick to catch up on social change, even in terms of gender and sexuality.

For many years now, reality TV has been dissected by researchers on gender relations and sexuality. Often shows like *Big Brother*, *Survivor* and different kinds of dating shows such as *The Bachelor* or *The Bachelorette* have drawn attention. The reason for this is that they tend to promote a heteronormative masculinity and femininity. The format maintains a myth of being unscripted, which is seldom the whole truth. What these shows often share is how they act through the televised medium as a display for the self by therapising, pathologising and producing certain notions of class, gender and sexual differences. On the one hand, some shows promote certain lifestyles as being considered desirable or as being transformed into being desirable. Examples include shows like the British *What Not to Wear*, which focussed on remodelling women into the 'right' kind of femininity, or the American *Beauty and the Geek*, which transformed geeks and 'unattractive' men into 'hunks'. On the other hand, there are shows exploring lifestyles not considered as being attractive or wanted, such as when displaying the sexual excesses of the working class on vacation in the British show *Sex on the Beach* (Moorti and Ross, 2004).

One reality TV show has, however, stirred some discussion on whether it has changed the view of masculinity and homosexuality or whether it has reproduced a heteronormative narrative. When *Queer Eye for the Straight Guy*, a show about five queer men helping a straight guy get his life together, was still on the air, it was possible to see both of these assays among researchers. Some claimed that the show was contributing to a switch in focus from the heterosexual man to the queer *eye*, while others claimed that gay men still became stereotyped through the show as well as noting that the systematic lack of women contributed to a stereotyped heterosexuality (Moorti and Ross, 2004).

In televised drama it is not as clear as in reality TV. Often there is criticism aimed at drama for being heteronormative and for supporting bias against nonheterosexual individuals and couples as well. To some extent this is of course the case, and it differs among different countries. There has, however, been an interesting shift in how masculinity (and femininity) is being represented in televised drama, especially in terms of sexuality. When Ellen DeGeneres 'came out' as a lesbian on the television show *Ellen* in 1997, the criticism was hard. On one side were the people who found the show 'too gay', and on the other side were those people not finding it 'gay enough', and the show subsequently failed in ratings (Mccarthy, 2015). Ellen did probably come to mean a lot to a lot of people, but she was at the same time criticised for promoting a heteronormative gay life (e.g. the discussion on homonormative below). Although Ellen was by no means considered to be a very outspoken or radical voice for the gay movement, advertisers were concerned, and, even if the episode in which Ellen came out was a success, the show was soon cancelled.

Homosexual characters were not something new at the time when Ellen came out, and other characters and shows have since then continued to shift focus on masculinity and sexuality. Two years after Ellen came out, the British show *Queer as Folk* premiered on Channel 4. It became an international hit as it followed three gay men and their relationships as well as their sexual activities. The show was later re-made for American and Canadian audiences. In the United States, the HBO show *Six Feet Under* (2001–2005), following two brothers having to take over their father's firm after his death, depicted homosexuality, and as the show progressed the homosexual relationship was placed at its centre. In 2015 the writer of *Queer as Folk* returned to Channel 4, producing not one new show but three, all about gay men. *Cucumber* is about middle-aged gay men, *Banana* is a sister series about LGBT youth in Manchester and *Tofu* is a web-based documentary show on sex attitudes.

Contemporary television and media both tend to promote certain lifestyles as well as depict alternatives to these lifestyles. Some of the shows violently push a heteronormative life onto us all, while others are able to challenge it. But as with the discussion about *Queer Eye for the Straight Guy*, it is possible to see a complex and multifaceted response to this development. Some claimed it was a sign of changes taking place; others, that it was more of the same. Equally, the discussion about *Ellen* shows complexity in its responses. As with *Ellen* being considered both 'too gay' and at the same time not 'gay enough', the criticism shows tension towards what could be considered heteronormativity and what could not. The lifestyle in itself (regardless of sexuality) is thus being criticised. This type of criticism is visible and discussed in empirical research as well, a critique we will come back to in the next section.

Global Heteronormativity

> For example, in liberal development discourse, a working class lesbian without children in a country such as Venezuela may appear as 'unproductive' because she does not fulfil a culturally and institutionally prescribed role in national development: She does not contribute to the reproductive imperative of development because she is not a mother; she is not seen as linked to 'the family', which is mostly defined in heteronormative and Eurocentric terms; she is often typically seen as asexual and therefore as not-in-need-of-intervention. She thus remains outside the project of development, through a strategy of invisibilization. The Venezuelan state reproduces this narrative, even in its current 'radical populist' version of 'endogenous development'.
>
> (Lind, 2009, p. 34)

From a global perspective, studies have shown heteronormativity in a wide range of countries and local communities through the use of, for instance, legislation, policies or public reactions to non-heterosexual practices and relationships. It is, however, possible to see it being analysed in a couple of different ways. First, as Lind (2009) points out in the quote above, heteronormativity is treated as an active Eurocentric strategy used by governments and NGOs to reproduce a heteronormative narrative, and thus actively concealing the lives of non-heterosexual peoples. In her study, a 'productive' and 'correct' heterosexual person is seen as being an important part of national development, both by Western NGOs and by local governments, and thus receives support or interventions, while a lesbian without children is not seen as part of the national development and as a result is not given any attention or help.

In Lind's (2009) study it is easy to see how in her case a Western and Eurocentric heteronormative value system is being transformed into local policies and legislations around the world; in other studies this is not always the case. Another common way to approach heteronormativity around the world is more empirical, presenting different cases of ways in which local practices are considered heteronormative within their own context. For instance, Wieringa (2012) shows how heteronormativity marginalises women in Delhi and Jakarta and how it leads to physical, material and subversive violence as well as to them acting and resisting upon these heteronormative notions. Wieringa (2012) claims that heteronormativity in Jakarta and Delhi both affects LGBTQ women and heterosexual divorced women. By doing that, the study makes the heteronormative visible as more than simply being something affecting, for instance, gay men. Many studies undertaking this kind of work tend to slide between considering heteronormativity as a package, marketing a specific heterosexual lifestyle, and considering it to simply be homophobia. Heteronormativity as a form of homophobia is of course partly the case, but sometimes it is difficult to differentiate between the two. One such case is when Jamaica, once named the most homophobic place on earth by *Time Magazine*, is being described in research. Cowell and Saunders (2011) claim that there is a 'settled heteronormative value system' in Jamaica, but arguments for it often fall back on distinctive homophobia in politics and policies, and through the juridical and legislative systems. In comparison with Lind's study above that rather consider heteronormativity as being a complete value system, the Jamaica case becomes rather limitative.

Heteronormativity as a system is often the case when the African continent is analysed and studied. Uganda, with its similarities to Jamaican homophobia, is for instance often being analysed through a system of institutions being used to promote and to preserve patriarchy and subordination (of which homophobia of course is one part). One explanation for this might be the way that non-heteronormative lifestyles in many African countries have been framed by leading elites as being part of a colonial legacy, or 'un-African', and thus able to re-create an African way of life they need to be exterminated. These approaches have resulted in many gay and lesbian people needing to relate to and maybe even respond to allegations of being 'un-African':

> I've done work in the rural areas and I see a chief sitting next to his Mercedes with a cell phone in his hand. Now for me, that could be a perfect picture of what is unAfrican twenty, thirty, even a hundred years ago but now it is part of where we are at developmentally.
>
> (Reygan and Lynette, 2014, p. 718)

The participants in Reygan and Lynette's study testify to an existence of heteronormativity, and notions of deviations from these norms, being interpreted as something 'un-African'. Heteronormativity has become impregnated into the governance of some countries, as a strategy to limit the influence of previous colonial states (cf. Seale, 2009). The concern, when heteronormativity as a concept is used globally, is, first of all, how it tends to cause a slide from acts of homophobia to complete systems of oppression and, second, how this is often connected to colonialism in some form—thus, policing particular kinds of masculinity, or how men act, with distinct colonial norms and values, either as is the case with some leading elites on the African continent, being considered a medicine for colonial inheritance, or as being used to spread Western, Eurocentric ideas about family and sexuality. Nevertheless there seems to be an intricate connection between colonialism and heteronormativity which, as Lind (2009) points towards, urges us all to be careful of who is placed at the centre of our attention and why.

Sexuality, Intimacy and the Erotic

> Not just: how were we fucked by gender, but also: was it possible to fuck without fucking with gender?
>
> (Wiegman, 2006, p. 90)

Although being more than sexuality, heteronormativity has everything to do with sexuality, intimacy, and erotica. The production of sexuality binaries, as previously mentioned, creates for instance sexual boundaries and conceptions on sexuality in a whole. This binary production separates masculinity and femininity and their supposedly inherent sexuality and desires. Masculine sexuality, contrary to feminine sexuality, therefore, tends to be described through the use of a simplistic logic, from the male seduction, via certain steps, and finally ending in a sexual retraction (Lorentzen, 2007). Historically, this logic has created a view on men's sexuality in terms of agency, always being willing, and on men as feeling secure in their sexuality (Herz and Johansson, 2011). But, as Wiegman (2006) points out, is the question whether this heteronormative assumption really is the case in everyday life or whether the sexual acts in themselves challenge us all in terms of gender and sexuality?

One flipside, however, of this heteronormative assumption on male sexuality is that it has not always been considered positive but rather considered as something in need of curbing or limiting. On the one hand is the desirability of being an agent in relation to your sexuality and having an intrinsic ability to enjoy sex; on the other are the dangers connected to not being able to say no to sex. The dualistic construction of gender and sexuality from heteronormative assumptions tends, not the least, to create a situation where male sexuality needs to be balanced between these extremes.

In terms of intimacy, the relationship between heteronormativity and masculinity probably becomes even more complicated. Heteronormativity creates boundaries for intimacy between men and women, since through heterosexual logic it is supposed to be linked to sex. But it also creates boundaries between men and other men. Homosocial relations between men are, with this logic, always a tightrope between masculine and heterosexual friendship and homoerotic acts (Herz and Johansson, 2011). In the episode 'The Outing' of the popular TV show *Seinfeld*, this is evident when the close friendship between two of the main characters George and Jerry is being mistaken for a homosexual relationship.

Jerry: 'Although they maintain separate residences, the comedian and his long-time "companion" seem to be inseparable.' Oh, no! The Associated Press picked up the NYU story. That's going to be in every paper! I've been 'outed'! I wasn't even 'in'!

George: Now everyone's going to think we're gay!
Jerry: Not that there's anything wrong with that.
George: No, not at all . . .

(Charles et al., 1993)

Intimacy among men tends to become somewhat problematic, either as a way to uphold power against others (cf. Seidler, 1992, 2006) or, as with *Seinfeld* above, as an act perceived of as being gay.

Many researchers have pointed at the somewhat surprisingly absent male body in the depiction of sexuality, especially since it pays attention to male pleasure. The male view and the (male) sexual interest in women are instead the main focus (Coward, 1984; Easthope, 2013; Metcalf and Humphries, 1985). A heteronormative erotic view tends to be the (un-erotic) male view aimed towards the eroticised female body. Although power relations between men and women have to some extent changed over time (as have attitudes towards both female and male bodies, as well as attitudes to craving sex, taking the initiative and enjoying sex), bodily depictions have not. The male body is still very robot-like, remaining less expressive, and is intact through the sexual act, while the female body is more expressive, loudly moaning, and is being penetrated. The flipside to this, in terms of masculinity, seems to be a large focus on technique and bodily function among men, especially if we change the focus from the depicted act towards adverts and among men seeking advice and support (Attwood, 2005).

Mühleisen (2006) claims that a focus on the act of penetration has affected the possible analysis of male sexuality. The penetration itself has often been synonymised with oppression, which becomes problematic if penetration does not take place in a heterosexual relationship where the man is the one voluntarily penetrating the woman. When being described or analysed, male sexuality tends to be limited to the position of an offender or into the position of an un-eroticised male robot penetrating his heteronormative object. Although some changes are noticeable, in terms of depicting initiative and craving sex, these changes seldom contradict heteronormative and masculine stereotypes (Taylor, 2005). For men themselves, the relationships between heteronormative assumptions and demands, and sexual desires and acts, are not as simple. As Wiegman (2006) points towards in the quoted introduction to this section, it is probably not even possible to engage in sexuality without, at the same time, challenging gender (although Wiegman uses a different, perhaps more profane, language). Many studies have shown how men and women have similar interests when coming to sex, for instance, in sex education (Allen, 2008) and in pornography (Johansson and Lalander, 2003). Ward (2008) challenges heteronormative assumptions on male sexuality even more in a study on heterosexual men having sex with other men. She shows how men, living as 'heterosexuals', enact whiteness, masculinity and the use of heterosexual archetypes when they are having sex with other men, thus still being positioned as heterosexual. By doing this, Ward (2008) illustrates how sexual practices need to be separated from the way heterosexuality is being conceived culturally and performatively.

To summarise, heteronormativity creates boundaries for what is considered possible or allowed in terms of sexuality, intimacy and erotica. Masculinity tends to be reduced to either something desirable, in terms of agency and power, or something dangerous, in terms of not being possible to prevent from acting. Heterosexual affection from men towards women also creates boundaries for friendship and possible intimacy between men, and between men and women without sexual attraction.

In this section, we have focussed on how heteronormativity can manifest itself in different ways. This is however only one side of it; another side has to do with the concept's close connection to societal and cultural institutions, and how this in turn could affect people's lives and possible choices, even in cases where these lives and choices mean violating the very fundament of heteronormativity, such as is the case with gay families.

Transgressing Heteronormativity

To recap, then, when we use the concept of heteronormativity, we are investigating 'how sexualities are expressed and performed but also how a more extensive societal system of gender is organised, structured and maintained. In other words, heteronormativity not only aims at changing conditions for people identifying as LGBTQ (Lesbian, Gay, Bisexual, Transsexual and Queer) but also targets the whole societal and cultural institution of heterosexuality. Because heterosexuality is also connected to a social and cultural system, we find a far-reaching critique of marriage, nuclear families and the gendering of 'heterosexual lifestyles'. Sometimes this critique is aimed not only at heterosexuality as a social and cultural hegemony but also at people getting married, nuclear families working against oppression and for change, and LGBT families thought to live a 'heterosexual lifestyle'.

Traces of this critique and an almost utopian celebration of queer lifestyles are found in Judith Halberstam's book *In a Queer Time & Place*: *Transgender Bodies, Subcultural Lives*. In an interesting passage, Halberstam develops her thoughts on the possibilities of prolonging youth, and she celebrates resistance to conventional forms of marriage and family life:

> Precisely because many queers refuse and resist the heteronormative imperative of home and family, they also prolong the period of their life devoted to subcultural participation.
>
> (Halberstam, 2005, p. 161)

Halberstam not only introduces a queer critique of the nuclear family and marriage but also indirectly provides possibilities on doing heterosexuality without heteronormativity. Heterosexual practices not relying on 'conventional' forms of marriage and family lives—for instance, through hegemonic ideals of monogamy, nuclear family commitment and childbirth—become a challenge for current ideals that are considered dominant. Another implication is that heteronormativity, by this logic, requires particular forms of masculinity and femininity that are gen-erationally specific.

In her influential book on neoliberal politics, capitalism and social movements, Lisa Duggan explores the connection between neoliberal politics and Gay and Lesbian movement organisations. Duggan observes, for example, an increasing influence of neoliberal views on the Gay movement. This is most notable in her analysis of the Independent Gay Forum (IGF):

> The new neoliberal sexual politics of the IGF might be termed the new homonormativity—it is a politics that does not contest dominant heteronor-mative assumptions and institutions, but upholds and sustains them, while promising the possibility of a demobilized gay constituency and a privatized, depoliticized gay culture anchored in domesticity and consumption.
>
> (Duggan, 2003, p. 50)

In many ways, Duggan brings forward and explores the far-reaching critique of contemporary ways of organising family life, intimacy and sexuality that is inher-ent in the concept of heteronormativity. However, when looking more closely at the arguments put forward by Duggan and, for example, Halberstam, this is appar-ently not only a part of a struggle for a more plural sexuality and sexual politics but perhaps primarily a struggle for another and definitely a more utopian way of organising society. The prospect of a woman being able to live a heterosexual and non-repressive life is rendered almost impossible. Consequently, gay men (and women) aspiring to a lifestyle with marriage, children and family life are some-times seen as almost disloyal to the cause.

Heteronormativity as an Analytical Tool in Empirical Studies

In this section, we will look more closely at different ways in which the concept of heteronormativity analytics is used in empirical studies. Basically, it seems that there are two ways of approaching and using the concept. On the one hand, we have critical studies of the way sexual behaviours that do not fit into the normative sex/gender system are marginalised and made invisible. On the other hand, we have studies focussing on a more extended notion of heteronormativity, where not only sexual behaviour and desires are scrutinised but the critique is also directed at more general issues of lifestyle, family life and forms of life (Ward and Schneider, 2009).

The first way of approaching heteronormativity has to do with the conception of heterosexuality as something 'natural' and unquestioned on different societal levels. The studies in question show how sexuality, on a more individual level, is affected by societal norms and how, in turn, society is organised on the basis of heterosexuality. Heteronormativity is defined as 'a societal hierarchical system that privileges and sanctions individuals based on presumed binaries of gender and sexuality; as a system it defines and enforces beliefs and practices about what is "normal" in everyday life' (Toomey et al., 2012, p. 188). Here, heteronormativ-ity is seen as a system that sanctions as well as condemns people who do not fit in and fail to behave according to an 'acceptable' and 'given' societal value system. It also points at the strong interconnection between sexuality and gender. This approach clarifies how much heteronormativity per se both affects and is affected by our view on gender and sexuality. In the study presented below, heteronormativity is used as an analytical tool to look at bullying among students. The authors' results show the following:

> Consistent with previous research, we found that the forces of heteronormativity continue to be pervasive: harassment due to gender nonconformity was common among the students in this study. [. . .] Our study documented heteronormativity in schools, and provided initial evidence that school policies and programs may challenge this heteronormativity. In particular, we documented differences between schools, and demonstrated that these differences are meaningful for students' perceptions of safety for gender nonconformity, particularly for gender nonconforming male peers. Importantly, these findings suggest that safe school practices that are inclusive of LGBTQ issues have implications for student safety over and above the individual-level effect: schools where greater proportions of students report awareness of safe school strategies are also likely to have less heteronormative climates.
>
> (Toomey et al., 2012, pp. 193/196).

The authors show that heteronormative 'forces' tend to result in students who are not positioned as heterosexuals, or who are considered gender non-conformative, often being harassed and bullied. However, the results also indicate that schools that take an active approach to addressing LGBTQ issues reduce these risks. Heteronormativity is used here as an analytical tool in a context, the school, that often is built on heteronormativity, showing that different schools with different pedagogical approaches may not eradicate, but can at least reduce, the normative influences on young people's behaviours.

In contrast to this perspective and critique, a second more far-reaching approach on heteronormativity also involves individuals' ability or desire to organise their lives. One such example is when a person who defines herself or himself as lesbian or gay decides to start a family with her or his partner and child(ren) and perhaps also get married, consequently adopting a 'heterosexual lifestyle'. Because heterosexuality and ways of organising family life that are associated with heterosexuality are seen as the fundament of a heteronormative society, this way of organising family can potentially be seen as a threat to 'homosexual lifestyles'. Using this more far-reaching definition of heteronormativity, the power structure is also reproduced by gay and lesbian people living as heterosexuals. This way of using heteronormativity could therefore result in unnecessary guilt in and pressure on people living their lives as LGBTQ. It also includes rather static conceptions of both what are considered 'heterosexual lifestyles' and what are considered 'homosexual lifestyles':

> Bård: I don't think people quite understand the explosive force in my [. . .] lifestyle. Apparently it seems to be very normal, and so it is, in many ways safe and bourgeois and all that crap. But at the same time there is a giant gap or a

giant leap between what I thought I would have and what I got. And naturally, for me, living in a context like this safely and openly, with a guy I love and have been together with for several years; two children that I love and see a lot of; the family setting in the neighbourhood, like standing with the other guys talking nonsense over the fence while the kids are playing in the playground, or going to the playground together with another father to pick up two kids who have been fighting—the gap is so wide, and the reality I live in is so different from what I expected, that I don't think people realize the significance of it. And I don't quite realize it myself either. [. . .] Right? When you come to us, you will find a little pedal car standing outside the door. To live in a row of houses with such pedal cars in front is very far from what I envisioned my life would be. And sometimes I have to pinch myself to realize that I have made such a life.

(Folgerø, 2008, p. 143)

Bård, one of the interviewees in this Norwegian study, articulates and empha-sises the 'explosive force' of him living in a 'nuclear' family together with another man. In a sense he describes the development in Norway towards a more inclusive sexual politics, where he now is able to live 'very normally', but at the same time he can be seen as 'disloyal' by some of his homosexual friends. One example of this is highlighted in an editorial in a Norwegian magazine, in which the English writer and gay man Quentin Crisp is discussed:

We often refer to the issues we are dealing with today as 'fights'—we 'fight' for adoptive rights and we 'struggle' to be so integrated that we hardly become visible. But the use of these terms would perhaps not be so easy if we took the time to think about what our predecessors have done. [. . .] At a time and in a community where we are getting more and more similar, where standardizing and homogenizing is the norm, where gays and lesbians lose distinctiveness by insisting on how little different we are from all the heterosexuals that surround us, it would do no harm if we spent some time remembering such a wonderful, original and uncompromising creature as Quentin Crisp. [. . .] The next time you and your friends are giggling over an effeminate man or a powerful butch, keep in mind that the fight they are fighting is considerably more courageous than the 'fight' for adoptive rights and ecclesiastical positions, and we would have been a really colourless and gloomy homo-family without them.

(Folgerø, 2008, p. 144)

The editorial contrasts the construction of a 'real' homosexual identity, for instance in the form of being a butch or an effeminate man, with gays and lesbians fighting for adoptive rights and integration. Note that 'fight' is written in quotation marks when used to describe certain kinds of fights, namely the ones connected to family or children. Another similar example is found in a study of LGBTQ people in Amsterdam:

If marriage and assimilation are the master's tools, what new strategies are needed to dismantle hetero- and homonormativity? Some argue that same-sex marriage can help in ending gender discrimination [. . .], in that it pushes non-normative sexualities into the public sphere. However, LGBT people in Holland have marriage and all other legal rights, and these sexual minorities face pressure to be normal, to blend in, and essentially to become invisible.

(Robinson, 2012, p. 334)

It is clear that although marriage is not treated as exclusively bad, it is treated with suspicion. It is seen here as a tool used by 'the master' to silence the LGBTQ movement. Marriage is seen as something used to pressure people into 'being normal'. This might be traced back to how Rubin (1997) once warned that norms for what should be considered vigorous, mature and moral sexuality could be reproduced even among Feminist, Gay and Lesbian movements. Even the development of 'new' sexual standards might be singular and repressive. Duggan (2003) claims that this is especially important to take into consideration in neoliberal times, and that attention must be paid to how Lesbian and Gay rights traditionally are granted to white, middle-class heterosexuals, often in terms of equal privacy, domesticity, and consumption (Duggan, 2003).

There are, however, three main concerns with this development. First, there is a political one, since there might be a backlash for LGBTQ families living according to homonormative norms, that is, not living as expected, but rather living more or less like what is seen as a 'heterosexual lifestyle'. These families might experience pressure both from a society based on heterosexuality and from groups upholding homonormative assumptions. Secondly, David Grindstaff (2003) makes a valid point that the binary deployment of hetero-homosexuality creates two equations that are separate from each other: male homosexuality = promiscuous = death, and heterosexuality = monogamous (in terms of marriage) = life (in terms of procreation). Although this might not be his main point, the binary created and used both for or against marriage and monogamous relationships, as well as procreation, risks reproducing homosexuality as solely promiscuous and thus excluding other ways of organising one's life. The third concern is an empirical one and has to do with how to analytically differentiate between families that de facto reproduce patriarchal patterns and power asymmetries regarding sexuality, and families that do not. If the nuclear family form (two adults with child[ren]) is automatically considered to reproduce certain societal power asymmetries, it will be impossible to ever organise families in that fashion without being subjected to the criticism of LGBTQ activists. This criticism would then be aimed at homosexual families, feminist families or families working against suppression in some way:

But if queer critique thus turns the tables on heteronormativity by making normativity itself pathological, how, then, can we understand normalization and the political and psychic work of normality itself? Or more to the point, what do we really learn by taking the struggle against normativity as the normative emblem of political good? I was not prepared to encounter these questions,

nor to let my article's failure move me toward this: that making normativity
pathological was to participate in the logic of normalization itself.

(Wiegman, 2006, p. 8)

Wiegman (2006) puts these concerns almost to the extreme when claiming that
we can't make normativity pathological since by doing so we risk participating
in the same logic that creates normalisation. That is, homo- as well as heteronormative assumptions both aim to normalise behaviour, regardless of their point
of departure. Criticising heteronormativity, and thus the risk to pathologise certain behaviours, might lead to the formation of new norms being just as excluding. Sharma (2009) points towards how the binary between heteronormative and
non-heteronormative risks being created, and how this in turn privileges what is
considered non-normative behaviour. Instead, she suggests an approach in which
people's relationships to norms undergo processes of negotiation.

But, there is nevertheless a tension here that has been discussed and analysed in
studies on sexuality and in LGBTQ studies to some extent, that at the same time
make visible the processes Sharma (2009) suggests. For instance, studies made of
photos of same-sex marriage considering them both as a heteronormative reproduction as well as a challenge to such a reproduction (Kimport, 2012). Another
example is Dhaenen's (2012) study on how gay families are portrayed on television through a heteronormative lens, on the one hand, but as having a disruptive
potential, on the other (see the section on mediated heteronormativity above).
What these studies show is the conundrum of masculinity, on one hand, as part of
a possible reproduction of heteronormativity, on the other, as part of a disruptive
act. Together, this tension and the above concerns leave us with the challenge of
developing an analytical tool with which we can make oppression visible, without
at the same time risking oppressing individuals with different family forms.

Ideology, Utopia and Norms

One way to approach this tension between visualising oppression without the risk
to further oppression is to relate the concept of heteronormativity to the discussion
on ideology and utopia (Herz and Johansson, 2015). Norm-critical approaches
and pedagogies focus on the ideological aspects of heteronormativity. This type of
pedagogy targets and tries to deconstruct a specific norm system, and it also tries
to show the possibilities of transgressing this system. In Chapter 3, we discussed
Paul Ricoeur (1986) and how he distinguishes between three aspects of ideology:
first, to legitimise the existing order; second, to distort information and to present
the existing order as an ideal order; and, finally, it has an integrative function.

As with the concept of hegemony, we also would like to suggest a distinction between different utopian approaches to heteronormativity, one a bottom-
up approach and one a top-down. The bottom-up version promotes the same
rights and possibilities for all people, irrespective of sexual preference, and aims
at changing attitudes as well as creating a free and liberated sexual landscape,

allowing for multiple sexualities. The top-down version promotes the necessity of transgressing existing lifestyles and forms of intimacy; it therefore aims much higher than the bottom-up approach. The top-down approach, as we have argued, aims at changing more fundamental structures and institutions in society. So, although activists and people in general can join in on the effort to deconstruct a certain normative sexual and gendered order, the conflicts are apparent regarding the utopian aim of this work and the everyday life pedagogies of norm critique (Herz and Johansson, 2015).

We are aware that these two ways of approaching heteronormativity sometimes overlap and are blended together into a norm-critical approach. The aim of trying to make these approaches overt and visible is to advance a discussion of the analytical limitations of certain ways of framing and theorising heteronormativity. Both the top-down as well as the bottom-up approaches have their limitations.

The bottom-up version tends to underestimate an understanding of how the material and social bases of sexuality have developed historically, and it underplays the importance of analysing social institutions and political systems. It focuses mostly on individuals and their attitudes. The approaches used to change people's lives are also often educational. The problem with the bottom-up approach is that it could lead to a veil of ignorance when it comes to analysing how sexual practices are embedded into social institutions, such as the family and politics. This approach tends to become too idealistic, relying on educational strategies and the possibility of changing attitudes.

The top-down version is firmly grounded in a historical-material analysis of the social and cultural conditions leading to the constitution of an oppressive system. In order to create a more pluralistic society, it is not enough to affect single individuals or groups of individuals; we need to target and change central institutions such as the family, the market and the state. This version is often based on a structural and rather pessimistic view of society, institutions and politics. For instance, in this version of heteronormativity, the nuclear family is by necessity an oppressive societal institution. But this way of conceptualising the family, sexuality and identity also makes it impossible to imagine a transformation of the family that leads to more equal and democratic relations in contemporary families. If nuclear families are, by definition, oppressive social institutions, then people positioned as LGBTQ who choose to live in nuclear families contribute to reinforcing heteronormative structures in society.

Developing Heteronormativity

To avoid the pitfalls of both the top-down and the bottom-up utopian approaches, we suggest the development of a third utopia, one that takes both a bottom-up and a top-down approach. Our position is that society is, of course, in many ways still organised in a heterosexual 'order', but we take exception to a pure top-down approach, because it is important to make visible the many different shapes and forms that this order can take, depending on, for instance, what country, region and local context one lives in. In an influential article, Connell and Messerschmidt

(2005) argue that hegemonic masculinity must be understood and analysed differently depending on the local, regional, national and global variation in how masculinity is enacted, performed and structurally determined. This way of approaching the concept of hegemonic masculinity opens the door to multiple understandings of how masculinity is locally constructed. Along the same lines, heteronormativity can be read and understood in relation to national and local variations in how sexuality and, for example, families are constructed (Herz and Johansson, 2015).

Naturally, heteronormativity is strongly connected to power, which might concern who is considered included or excluded, who is supposed to adjust or not, and sometimes even who has to fear for their lives or not. Thus far everything seems clear, but, when this is applied to people's lives, power asymmetries take on different forms and have different results. This is the case regardless of whether these asymmetries are based on gender, ethnicity, race, class or sexuality. A similar discussion has been pursued concerning inclusion/exclusion based on ethnicity and race (Back et al., 2012; Fangen, 2010) as well as other concepts like homosociality and hegemonic masculinity (see previous chapters). Problems occur because power relations are being played out in different forms, at different times and in different contexts. Rather than considering power in static terms, the focus need to shift towards, paraphrasing Butler's notion, the lived life. Taking a utopian approach to the lived life means shifting our focus to people's agency and social practices and, at the same time, to the structural conditions in which these people act. This means focussing on how specific structural discourses are being used, being alluded to and restricting people in their day-to-day lived lives.

Although we still use the same term—heteronormativity—we have developed a more dynamic, useful and flexible conceptual landscape. To make our position clear, we aim at the following:

1. an analytical approach that allows us to analyse local, regional, national and global changes and transformations of the heteronormative 'orders';
2. enabling an intersectional approach to heteronormativity;
3. making it possible to develop more nuanced, dynamic and progressive analyses of the family; and
4. working to connect and tie together the bottom-up and top-down versions of the concept of heteronormativity.

When using this analytical approach empirically, it means that families and people's everyday lives, agency and social practices need to be the starting point of analysis. By taking this departure, it is, for instance, possible to highlight local differences or even personal differences without losing connections to global or structural phenomena. When empirically approaching a family consisting of a man and a woman located in a working-class area in, for example, Ireland, and a similar family in an upper-class area in New York, their different contexts need to be approached before taking structural or aggregated phenomena into consideration.

By doing this, it is possible to illustrate ongoing changes as well as sluggish heteronormative structures, and maybe most importantly, as a researcher, making it a visible and reflexive approach. We are thus promoting a third utopian way, in which a potential space of reflexivity and political change involves both subjects and structures, gays and lesbians, heterosexuals, Feminists, Gay movements and Feminist men's movements, thus creating alliances between different social movements, the ultimate aim being the end of discrimination, sexual oppression and harassment.

Conclusion

There is an obvious tension between more or less static systems of power—in this case heteronormative power—and ongoing changes in masculinity. This conundrum of masculinity conceals both a possible reproduction of existing heteronormative structures and a possible change in how these structures are being perceived and understood. For instance, the nuclear family might be considered as strengthening heteronormative power, but when being enacted by a gay couple it might also be considered as a challenge to that same power. Another aspect of heteronormativity and masculinities is how it affects relationships both between men and women, and between men and men. The intrinsic concept of sexual relationships between women and men taking place inside a nuclear family creates boundaries for what kinds of relationships are possible. Intimacy between men is thus understood as gay or as a way of upholding power. This is not the same as suggesting that men do not act with intimacy towards each other; they do, and to some extent intimacy among men does seem to be more embraced and visualised. To be able to capture the conundrum of masculinity and still be able to reveal possible heteronormative power, both positions of change and positions of reproduction need to be visualised together. We need to focus both on heteronormativity as a constraining concept and at the same time on changes within and outside of the same concept. If not, we tend to punish family constellations or intimate relationships that challenge heteronormative assumptions doubly, both for being divergent from the norm and for upholding the same norm.

References

Ahmed, S. (2013) *The Cultural Politics of Emotion*. New York: Routledge.

Allen, L. (2008) Poles apart? Gender differences in proposals for sexuality education content. *Gender and Education*, 20(5), 435–450.

Attwood, F. (2005) "Tits and ass and porn and fighting": Male heterosexuality in magazines for men. *International Journal of Cultural Studies*, 8(1), 83–100.

Back, L., Sinha, S. and Bryan, W.C. (2012) New hierarchies of belonging. *European Journal of Cultural Studies*, 15(2), 139–154.

Butler, J. (1990/2008) *Gender Trouble: Feminism and the Subversion of Identity*. New York: Routledge.

Charles, L., Cherones, T. and Sherman, A. (prod.) (1993) *Seinfeld: The Outing* [tv-program] New York: NBC Broadcasting.

Connell, R.W., and Messerschmidt, J. (2005) Hegemonic masculinity: Rethinking the concept. *Gender & Society*, 19, 829–859.

Coward, R. (1984). *Female Desire: Women's Sexuality Today*. London: Paladin Grafton Books.

Cowell, N.M. and Saunders, T.S. (2011) Exploring heteronormativity in the public discourse of Jamaican legislators. *Sexuality & Culture*, 15(4), 315–331.

Dhaenens, F. (2012) Gay male domesticity on the small screen: Queer representations of gay homemaking in six feet under and brothers & sisters. *Popular Communication*, 10(3), 217–230.

Duggan, L. (2003) *The Twilight of Equality? Neoliberalism, Cultural Politics, and the Attack on Democracy*. New York: Beacon.

Easthope, A. (2013) *What a Man's Gotta Do: The Masculine Myth in Popular Culture*. New York: Routledge.

Fangen, K. (2010) Social exclusion and inclusion of young immigrants: Presentation of an analytical framework. *Young*, 18(2), 133–156.

Folgerø, T. (2008) Queer nuclear families? Reproducing and transgressing heteronormativity. *Journal of Homosexuality*, 54, 124–149.

Grindstaff, D. (2003) Queering marriage: An ideographic interrogation of heteronormative subjectivity. *Journal of Homosexuality*, 45(2–4), 257–275.

Halberstam, J. (2005) *In a Queer Time & Place: Transgender Bodies, Subcultural Lives*. New York: New York University Press.

Hall, J. and LaFrance, B. (2012) "That's gay": Sexual prejudice, gender identity, norms, and homophobic communication. *Communication Quarterly*, 60, 35–58.

Herz, M. and Johansson, T. (2011). *Maskuliniteter. Kritik, Tendenser, Trender*. Malmö: Liber.

Herz, M. and Johansson, T. (2015) The normativity of the concept of heteronormativity. *Journal of Homosexuality*, May, 37–41.

Jackson, S. (1999) *Heterosexuality in Question*. London: Sage.

Johansson, T. and Lalander, P. (2003) Ungdom, sexualitet och kön i gränslandet. In: Johansson, T. and Lalander, P. eds. *Sexualitetens omvandlingar: Politisk lesbiskhet, unga kristna och machokulturer*. Göteborg: Daidalos, pp. 9–22.

Jones, A. (2006) Straight as a rule: Heteronormativity, gendercide, and the noncombatant male. *Men and Masculinities*, 8(4), 451–469.

Kandaswamy, P. (2008) State austerity and the racial politics of same-sex marriage in the US. *Sexualities*, 11(6), 706–725.

Kimport, K. (2012) Remaking the white wedding? Same-sex wedding photographs' challenge to symbolic heteronormativity. *Gender & Society*, 26(6), 874–899.

Lind, A. (2009) Governing intimacy, struggling for sexual rights: Challenging heteronormativity in the global development industry. *Development*, 52(1), 34–42.

Lloyd, M. (2013) Heteronormativity and/as violence: The "sexing" of Gwen Araujo. *Hypatia*, 28(4), 818–834.

Lorentzen, J. (2007) Masculinities and the phenomenology of men's orgasms. *Men and Masculinities*, 10(1), 71-84. doi:10.1177/1097184X07299331

Martino, W. (2000) Policing masculinities: Investigating the role of homophobia and heteronormativity in the lives of adolescent school boys. *Journal of Men's Studies*, 8(2), 213–236.

Mccarthy, A. (2015) Making queer television history. *GLQ: A Journal of Lesbian and Gay Studies*, 7(4), 593–620.

McNeill, T. (2013) Sex education and the promotion of heteronormativity. *Sexualities*, 16(7), 826–846.

Metcalf, A. and Humphries, M. (1985) *The Sexuality of Men*. London: Pluto Press.

Moorti, S. and Ross, K. (2004) Reality television. *Feminist Media Studies*, 4(2), 203–231.

Mühleisen, W. (2006) Kjønn og seksualitet. In: Lorentzen, J. and Mühleisen, W. eds. *Kjønnsforskning: En grunnbok*. Oslo: Universitetsforlaget, pp. 256–263.

Myers, K. and Raymond, L. (2010) Elementary school girls and heteronormativity. The Girl Project. *Gender & Society*, 24(2), 167–188.

Peterson, D. (2011) Neoliberal homophobic discourse: Heteronormative human capital and the exclusion of queer citizens. *Journal of Homosexuality*, 58, 742–757.

Plumm, K.M., Terrance, C.A., Henderson, V.R. and Ellingson, H. (2010) Victim blame in a hate crime motivated by sexual orientation. *Journal of Homosexuality*, 57(2), 267–286.

Preves, S.E., Kaminsky A. and Hart, D. (2015) Sexing the intersexed: An analysis of socio-cultural responses to intersexuality. *Signs: Journal of Women in Culture and Society*, 27(2), 523–556.

Reygan, F. and Lynette, A. (2014) Heteronormativity, homophobia and "culture" arguments in KwaZulu-Natal, South Africa. *Sexualities*, 17(5–6), 707–723.

Ricoeur, P. (1986) *Lectures on Ideology and Utopia*. New York: Columbia.

Robinson, B.A. (2012) Is this what equality looks like? *Sexuality Research and Social Policy*, 9(4), 327–336.

Rosenfeld, D. (2009) Heteronormativity and homonormativity as practical and moral resources: The case of lesbian and gay elders. *Gender & Society*, 23(5), 617–638.

Rubin, G. (1997) The traffic in women: Notes on the "political economy" of sex. In: Nicholson, L. ed. *The Second Wave: A Reader in Feminist Theory*. New York: Routledge, pp. 27–62.

Sánchez Taylor, J. (2000) Tourism and 'embodied' commodities: Sex tourism in the Caribbean. In: Clift, S. and Carter, S. eds. *Tourism and Sex: Culture, Commerce and Coercion*. London: Pinter, pp. 41–53.

Sánchez Taylor, J. (2001) Dollars are a girl's best friend? Female tourists' sexual behaviour in the Caribbean. *Sociology*, 35(3), 749–764.

Seale, A. (2009) Heteronormativity and HIV in Sub-Saharan Africa. *Development*, 52(1), 84–90.

Seidler, V. (1992) *Man Enough: Embodying Masculinity*. London: Sage.

Seidler, V. (2006) *Transforming Masculinities: Men, Culture, Bodies, Power, Sex and Love*. London: Routledge.

Sharma, J. (2009) Reflections on the construction of heteronormativity. *Development, Suppl. Sexuality and Development*, 52(1), 52–55.

Skeggs, B. (1997) *Formations of Class and Gender: Becoming Respectable*. London: Sage.

Tadele, G. (2011) Heteronormativity and "troubled" masculinities among men who have sex with men in Addis Ababa. *Culture, Health & Sexuality*, 13(4), 457–469.

Taylor, L.D. (2005) All for him: Articles about sex in American Lad Magazines. *Sex Roles*, 52(3–4), 153–163.

Toomey, R.B., McGuire, J.K. and Russell, S.T. (2012) Heteronormativity, school climates, and perceived safety for gender nonconforming peers. *Journal of Adolescence*, 35, 187–196.

van der Meer, T. (2003) Gay bashing—a rite of passage? *Culture, Health & Sexuality*, 5(2), 153–165.

Ward, J. (2008) Dude-sex: White masculinities and 'authentic' heterosexuality among dudes who have sex with dudes. *Sexualities*, 11(4), 414–434.

Ward, J. and Schneider, B. (2009) The reaches of heteronormativity: An introduction. *Gender & Society*, 23(4), 433–439.

Warner, M. (1991) Introduction: Fear of a queer planet. *Social Text*, 9(4), 3–17.

Wiegman, R. (2006) Interchanges: Heteronormativity and the desire for gender. *Feminist Theory*, 7(1), 89–103.

Wieringa, S. (2012) Passionate aesthetics and symbolic subversion: Heteronormativity in India and Indonesia. *Asian Studies Review*, 36(4), 515–530.

Wittig, M. (1997) One is not born a woman. In: Nicholson, L. ed. *The Second Wave: A Reader in Feminist Theory*. New York: Routledge, pp. 265–271.

Žižek, S. (2008) *Violence: Six Sideways Reflections*. New York: Picador.

7   Post-masculinity

Thinking Over the Limits of Masculinity

Introduction

> It's a warm evening as the sun begins to fall behind the hills. In front, the sand dunes take on a crimson hue, and you can taste the salt in the air from the sea nearby. I had parked up, the texts on my phone had been going crazy, and, with the other cars parked along the way, this was a good time to pull in and text back. I was busy texting back when out of the corner of my eye I could see windows half closed and two men standing round one car. I carried on looking at the texts trying to work out how to explain why I was late. I looked up again. One man was standing, another leaning through the window. I lowered my phone and became more focussed. The silver car had people in the front and back. I looked away, and then immediately looked back. By now the men had swapped over—the other one leaned into the car whilst the other one stood watching. There was movement on the back seat. What was happening? I raised myself off my seat to get a better view of what was happening. The man looking over turned and looked at me, I dropped back down in my seat, and he turned back to carry on.

This was one of the first encounters with dogging that one of the authors came across. It was an intense moment, as it prompted further qualitative research with men on their motivations for and experiences of dogging practices. One of the main themes of the research was to explore how men configured their masculinities as they had sex with men and women at the same time. This chapter draws upon that research in order to develop a number of the themes in the previous chapters. More specifically, the other chapters in this book have used various concepts from Critical Masculinity Studies to understand and explain masculine subjectivities. As such, the conundrums that surround men and masculinity in society have often been explained through notions of hegemony, homosociality, homophobia and heteronormativity: the four 'Hs'. The previous chapters have revised these concepts and expanded them in order to explain such conundrums with greater theoretical precision and empirical accuracy.

In addition to the previous chapters, this one seeks to unravel a number of the conceptual regularities that underpin approaches to masculinity and, in doing so, unpacks the conceptual basis of what we understand as masculinity. If the aim of the other chapters was to use concepts to answer questions about the conundrums that surround masculinity, this chapter develops these points to deconstruct the concept of masculinity itself. This does not mean that the previous concepts should be abandoned; rather, this chapter is complementary to the conceptual chapters. This deconstructive move signals the need to stand outside of our conventional understandings of masculinity and in many ways to take up a position of an alterity where '[d]econstruction may therefore be understood as the desire to keep open a dimension of alterity which can neither be reduced, comprehended, nor, strictly speaking, even thought by philosophy' (Critchley, 1992, pp. 29). As a result, masculine subjectivity is discursively constituted through the conceptual centrality of masculinity. In line with Schwandt (1996), in relation to truth claims, the chapter provides a critical reflection on rejecting the necessity of the regulative norms that underpin the truth claims of masculinity.

Dogging

As indicated above, this chapter uses the case of dogging to re-think the nature of men's subjectivity and question the usefulness of masculinity. Often, 'dogging' is described as a form of cruising for straight people and has its history within the space of the 'lovers' lane'. Dogging appears to be a particularly English phenomenon, although there is evidence that it occurs elsewhere across Europe and the United States. In the UK the 'lovers' lane' was a secluded, usually rural place that people who were dating would drive to in order to escape from their friends and family in order to be intimate. Importantly, it was a space of privacy. However, in the context of dogging, the private becomes a public space as intimacy becomes a public spectacle. As Bell points out (2006, p. 388):

> Typically, a dogging scene involves heterosexual singles and couples driving to secluded locations, and engaging in sexual acts in their cars or in a nearby open space. Other participants at the scene may watch the action, or may ask or be invited to participate.

The reference to 'walking the dog' operates as a form of social camouflage for those on the outside when explaining one's behaviour. Those couples parked up and engaging in sex are often called 'parkers', and those who are watching from the outside are often termed 'doggers', 'peekers' or 'pikers'. However, Dutsch (2014) suggests that etymologically, dogging may be related to the ancient Greek word *kynogamia*, which translates as 'dog marriage'. This, it is argued, refers to the promotion of a particular set of practices by Cynic philosophers who would use their bodies and bodily functions in public in order to highlight their philosophical teachings. However, more recently Bell (2006) suggests this is now a more organised practice that is facilitated by online forums that enable men and women, both individuals and couples, to meet as individuals for sex. Although participants featured in this article do use online resources in order to arrange 'meets', the majority of them tend to visit dogging spots opportunistically on the way home from work or after dropping their children off for football practice.

Others drive to potential sites on the 'off-chance' that there may be some 'action'. In short, the practice of dogging appears to be woven into men's lives as part of a monthly, weekly or, for some, daily routine.

In order to explore the nature of masculine subjectivity with those who go dogging, it is important to recognise that dogging is not an exclusively heterosexual practice, as, more often than not, when arriving at the dogging scene there are only men present. Even when a meet was arranged online, invariably the couple would very rarely turn up. Furthermore, men who go dogging also point out that when women were present they were usually accompanied by another man. Therefore, dogging cannot simply be framed as a heterosexual practice, since it contains an object of desire that is both heterosexual and homosexual. This was demonstrated by the range of sexual activities that fell outside of conventional forms of heterosexuality that included same-sex behaviours such as kissing, mutual masturbation, BDSM, oral sex, rimming, DV, DB and anal sex. Therefore, although the men framed their 'meets' within a heterosexual format, when undertaking dogging they were more likely to meet and have sexual activities with men rather than women. Unsurprisingly, given that the majority of the men interviewed were in a heterosexual relationship, the men publicly identified themselves as heterosexual. All of the men were reluctant to disclose to friends and family any sexual activities that were non-heteronormative. It became evident that whilst the public identity was a projection of a consistency between gender and sexuality (Bertone and Camoleto, 2009), their participation in dogging practices suggested a different kind of relationship between masculinity and sexuality. It is this kind of different relationship that this chapter uses as a device to unpack conventional understandings of masculinity.

From Masculinity to Masculine Subjectivities

One of the features of the discussions about the concepts in previous chapters is that masculine subjectivities are conventionally anchored through the four 'H' concepts. Importantly, such concepts have a number of regularities that position masculinity in a number of ways. As we have previously seen, one of the main themes that underpins the formation of masculine subjectivity is homophobia. Michael Kimmel's (2007) work suggests that masculine subjectivities are constituted through the rejection of that which is culturally deemed as feminine. An example of this is how men objectify heterosexuality in order to validate their identities as masculine. As a result, masculine identities are structured through a heterosexuality that creates its stability through the rejection of that which is feminine (read as homosexual): 'that the reigning definition of masculinity is a defensive effort to prevent being emasculated' (2007, p. 80). Central to this definition of masculinity is an interplay between (homo)sexuality and gender, where homosexuality becomes read as feminine and is thus expelled in the process of forming masculinity.

We have also seen how Anderson (2009) usefully argues that we need to rethink the internal constituent of masculinity itself. He engages with theories of masculinity that suggest that heterosexual masculine subjectivities are constituted through homophobia. Instead, he argues that the constitution of masculinity itself is changing. This means that masculinity and homophobia can be viewed as conceptually discrete. In other words, heterosexual masculinities can be constituted without relying on homophobia as a constituent factor. Therefore, unlike Kimmel's proposal that masculinity is based on homophobia, Anderson argues that at a cultural level, there is less homophobia. This, it is argued, is leading to a more inclusive masculinity that recognises and affirms homosexual 'Otherness' rather than using such Otherness to sustain a masculinity.

More recently, Ward has made a similar point but suggests that rather than same-sex behaviours loosening the connection between masculinity and homophobia, they may actually reinforce it. Ward (2015) suggests that hetero-masculinity can be strengthened by men's participation in homosexual acts and explores the idea of straight men having same-sex relations. She introduces a concept of the 'heteroflexible', in which homosexual identities can also accommodate and reinforce heterosexual identities. Her main claim is that 'homosexual encounters are not in fact discordant with heterosexual masculinity when they are approached through the most recognizable circuits of hetero-masculinity' (p. 189). One of the examples that Ward uses is the process of hazing in the military, where anal endurance and resilience through same sex activities becomes a way of measuring hetero-masculinity. Importantly for Shaw, sex acts are only turned into straight or gay acts through the context in which they take place.

However, central to this work is the underlying assumption that the formation of masculinity involves a symbiotic relationship between masculinity and heterosexuality. In other words, men's sexual behaviours are understood through the intelligibility provided by the concept of heterosexual masculinity. Thus, the existence or the absence of homophobia remains configured through a dependence upon framing masculine subjectivity as premised through a coherent heterosexuality. Thus, there is a dependency upon the coherency of heterosexuality that enables masculinity to stabilise itself. This is interesting because there is the assumption that heterosexuality remains undisturbed by whatever non-heterosexual or feminine practices heterosexuals come in contact with. For example, Frank's discussion of swinging couples highlights how men would make their masculinities through conventional heterosexual identifications and practices. However, Frank also noticed that the context of swinging loosens the implicit imbrication of masculinity and heterosexuality:

> Even short of double penetration, in swinging encounters men are still naked in the presence of other men, watching those men engaging in sexual activity with women, perhaps watching them ejaculate or comment on penis sizes or sexual skills. . . . [S]pectatorship and sexual fantasy is complex in terms of identifications (e.g. Clover, 1993; Williams, 1989) and this is no less true in terms of live spectator/participant situations.
>
> (Frank, 2008, p. 446)

The suggestion here is that the parameters of heterosexual masculinity become widened to include practices that would conventionally trouble claims to heterosexuality, as for example in Cover's (2015) research on the website *Chaturbate* that involves straight-identified men garnering gay men's attention, and involves such men engaging in acts that are associated with gay men such as self-penetration. Cover suggests that although we are unable to disconnect hetero-sexuality from practices, there is scope, he argues, for heterosexual masculinity to be unhinged from the normative discourses that surround identity. The practice of self-penetration, for example, removes the classification of self-penetration as a gay identity activity and re-situates it within a variation of heterosexual masculin-ity. Cover (2015, pp. 14–15) argues that rather than reinforce hetero-masculinities and the notions of dominance and power through patriarchy, the site decon-structs 'innate heterosexualities and homosexualities as distinct sexual orienta-tions, allowing identity to remain but in non-monolithic, heterodoxical forms.' Thus, rather than reinforce hetero-masculinities, Cover argues that new forms of sexual practice enable hetero-homo binaries to be 'challengeable'. It is not, Cover argues, the emergence of newer forms of heterosexual masculinity; rather, it is the reduction of a normativity of masculinity. Therefore, online acts of self-penetration have the potential to produce different structures of masculinity that are not dependent on strict hetero-homo binaries.

It is argued that Critical Masculinity Studies tend to downplay either the rigidity of sexuality or the rigidity of masculinity. There doesn't appear to be a theoretical or conceptual possibility of understanding men's behaviour outside of *either* iden-tity category. In response, we need to think about men's identifications and prac-tices that are not reducible or contained by identity categories. Evidence of this can be found in the interviews with men who participate in dogging practices. As highlighted before, all the men adopted a public heterosexuality but highlighted the limitation of this descriptive category when on the dogging scene. Rather, the erotic charge of the scenario was not through the (dis)identification with a par-ticular hetero-masculinity but through an appeal to 'moments of pleasure'. This means that their subjectivities were not framed as trying to include or expand their hetero-masculinities; rather, their erotic experiences became understood as sexual acts or practices and not objects of desire. For example, when asked what he enjoyed about dogging, John answered by emphasising the sexual activity rather than the gender of the people involved:

John: It is a question of what sex am I going to get. It is purely that. It is purely that. And the mystique and the mystery of somebody that you have never seen before that you might end up with. That is it.

This sexual activity, the pleasure of the activity as it is referred to in these men's accounts, was more about the event or the episode, rather than the continuation of a narrative of sexuality. This was elaborated on in more explicit terms by James, who talks about his experience of being with another woman:

James: There is a layby and you come off the road and it is totally secluded and it is covered by trees. That is the best place. I have only been there once though. I had a girl, from London and I took her down there. And basically we both just bent over like into the boot and they just picked which one of us they wanted to fuck, which is pretty cool. A couple turned up too and we didn't know who was fucking us! There were just fingers, cocks and tongues. But it didn't matter, it was like, just like bursts of pleasure.

The account from James has some parallels with Rebak and Larkins (2010), who undertook interviews with 21 heterosexual men who had sex with men to understand how they managed their heterosexuality. They identify how these men framed their sexual relations through their infrequency, as being recreation or sport, as accidental, or through economic necessity. This suggests that with this group of men a series of distancing strategies are used to maintain their heterosexual identities. This process of compartmentalising the sexual practices took a number of forms. First, there was a depersonalising of the partners. This involved not discussing the partner in intimate terms and refraining from certain activities, for example avoiding kissing or hugging. This reluctance to engage in intimacy and emotional expressiveness, it is argued, resulted in being coded masculine. With the participants who were dogging, the practice did not appear to be negotiated in order to avoid emotional intimacy, but rather to intensify it.

As a consequence, male behaviours, attitudes and practices can no longer be simple indicators of particular models of masculinity (or even gender). Not only are sexual practices disconnected from the sexuality identities ('I may fuck men but that does not make me Gay'), but gendered identifications may also be independent of conventional gendered identities ('I may adopt masculine practices, but this does not confer a masculinity'). In other words, sexual and gender identifications and practices may not be reducible to or contained by masculinity and/or sexuality categories. The suggestion is that there is a potential for a sexual space where the theoretical rubrics of contemporary masculinity theory may not be exhaustive. An interview with Michel Foucault in *Le Bitoux* discussed the anonymity of the body in gay bathhouses and how this could facilitate experiences beyond identity and operate in subversive ways. Foucault et al., (2011) took the point up and suggested:

It is simply regrettable that there are not places like this for heterosexuality. After all, why wouldn't it be something rather marvellous for heterosexuals who wanted to be able to do something like that, in the middle of the day or night, to go to a place equipped with every comfort and every possibility *(laughs)*, all the well-being you could imagine? To encounter bodies that are both present and fleeting? Places where you desubjectivize yourself, that is, you desubjugate yourself in a way that is, I'm not saying the most radical, but in any case in a way that is intense enough so that this moment is, in the end, important.

(p. 399)

Here, Foucault is arguing for an understanding of subjectivity that does not depend upon the object of desire as the defining attribute of sexual identity. In this sense, sexuality can be separated from the erotic, with the erotic being contextually driven. In the context of masculine subjectivity, it is argued that dogging activities provide the space where masculine subjectivity does not depend upon a heterosexuality, hegemony, homosociality or homophobia in order to create itself. This is not to preclude anatomical sensations and prior sexual preferences. Rather, the dynamic for the meaning of the sexual is transfigured through an inter-relationship with certain feelings, thoughts and practices that are

> constituted by the interweaving of many heterogeneous experiences and capacities. These include complex clusters of capabilities, modes of processing, altering and retaining experience, and foci of affect, somatic effects and the transformation of process into various kinds of language, fantasy, delusion, defence, thought and modes of relating to self and others.
>
> (Flax, 1993, pp. 93–94)

Such processes do not stand outside of the social and cultural milieu as pre-meaningful (Lacquer, 1990). Fundamentally, the erotic does not (fully / if not yet) stand outside of or unrelated to the regulatory regime of a masculinity or sexuality. Instead, in the dogging space, sexual practices become *constitutive* of masculine subjectivity rather than *definitional*. Suggesting that we can move beyond masculinity is not to suggest that we can move beyond the cultural resources through which gender relations are configured. Instead, the experience of the erotic is constituted through gendered resources but in new ways.

Restoring, Compensating and (Re-)assembling

One of the explanations for some of the conundrums associated with masculinity is that there is either too much masculinity or not enough; there are very few discussions of men without masculinity, and it appears that in research masculinity should be the frame of reference for understanding men's genders. In other words, it always has to be a constant feature of gendered relationships, meaning that masculinity always has to be present. Importantly, where a masculinity is seen to be lost, damaged, or failed, it has to be replaced. It appears that this can be achieved in only two ways: through either a restorative masculinity or a compensatory masculinity. When discussing the confusing, puzzling mysteries of why men behave in particular ways, these themes of restoration and compensation are often invoked. For example, Boonzaier and De La Rey (2003), in their research on domestic violence, suggest that one of the explanations that has emerged to explain men's behaviours is that of the '*thwarted gender identity*'. This is where men are unable to take up a particular masculine position, and, as a result, they find themselves experiencing an identity crisis. The researchers suggest that embedded in this theory is the idea that when culturally scripted gender roles are no longer available, men experience a crisis because the resources through which their masculinities were articulated are no longer available. This means that men respond to this by 'symbolically reasserting' their masculinity through the use of violence in order to re-establish control and privilege. However, the loss of status may not simply result in violence; it could also manifest itself in depression, shame and anxiety (Sherman, 2009).

It appears that such a response to the loss of masculinity acts as a dynamic to restore masculinity, control and power. An example of this can be found in Kimmel and Mahler's (2003) explanation of school shootings in the United States. They suggest that it is important to consider the broader school context as well as narratives, relationships, interactions and their location within local student and school cultures. They claim that cultural marginalisation is an important dynamic in shaping how young men behave. This is in contrast to more mainstream media narratives that look for the psychological cause of behaviour in the shooter themselves. In the case of the Columbine shootings, a prominent theme in the school culture was the assertion that the shooters, Harris and Klebold, were gay. Kimmel and Mahler point out that 'as an organizing principle of masculinity, homophobia—the terror that others will see one as gay, as a failed man— underlies a significant amount of men's behaviour including their relationships with other men, women and violence. One could say homophobia is the hate that makes men straight' (p. 1446). Embedded in this approach, and as previously discussed in Chapter 5, in a heteronormative context homosexuality becomes a code for masculine failure, and, as a result, such terror impels men to react violently.

In this sense, violence can be understood as an evasive strategy to ensure that those committing murder are not perceived or interpreted as gay. For Consalvo (2003, p. 36), Harris and Klebold rebelled against their subordinate masculinity location. She brings into her argument the 'damaging social hierarchies found in their high school, where jocks and sports culture were regarded as more important and less culpable than other cliques or students.' Larkin (2011) suggests that the demonstration of masculinity becomes the space through which identities become negotiated. Those who do not rise or aspire to an athletic standard of masculinity are perceived as less than men and are then subjected to public humiliation. Violence by school shooters is thus a response to this humiliation. Shooting 'wasn't simply rampage or revenge: but a means to "out masculine their hyper-masculinized victimizers"' (Larkin, 2011, p. 335). Furthermore, as Kimmel argues, violence is about restoring control, and this means that men adopt particular masculinities in order to aspire to restore control. In this way, we need to move away from a notion that violence is restorative of a particular masculinity, or compensatory for an alternative masculinity; rather, it could be argued that it is retaliatory, ensuring that masculinities are made through its response.

One response to such change is through the use of violence and aggression. Tonso (2009) argues that when men's authority is challenged, denied, or taken away, men try to restore control in a way that results in the reclaiming of their masculine status. Central to this claim is the suggestion that men are in the continual process of attempting to secure hierarchies of inequality, in order to maintain control over other men and women. When men lose that control, they respond by attempting to restore it. For example, in school shootings in the United States, young men's experiences of marginalisation and humiliation will be generative of violence. She argues: 'Some young men experienced a sense of humiliation that emerged from perceptions of loss of privilege made evident in schools; and when merged with fantasies of retribution and images of a form of masculinity grounded in violent action their sense of humiliation led some men to open fire in schools' (2009, p. 1278). From a similar position, Klein and Chancer (2000) ask why it is that school shootings have become so frequent at this current historical moment. They respond by arguing that, culturally, men are having to withdraw from traditional notions of masculinity, in order to adapt to new forms of masculinity that are based on tolerance and respect, particularly towards women and gay men. Therefore, those men who are forced to withdraw from 'traditional constructions' of masculinity may use other forms, more extreme practices, in order to compensate for their losses and their inability to live up to culturally appropriate versions of masculinity. Therefore, in schools, boys who feel that their masculinity is being threatened or 'lost' will resort to violent tactics to recuperate their lost identities. Thus, it is suggested that one response to being bullied will be the use of extreme violence to cope with the potential threat and loss of their identities.

It is important to develop this point of the loss of masculinity, as it enables us to grasp the possibility that men's subjectivity may not be configured by a masculinity identity. If the above studies focussed on the restoration of masculinity, then another response might be to compensate with a different masculinity. It is at the point of compensation that we find slippage between masculinity and post-masculinity as comprising gender identities. Through interviews with six white Euro-Americans, Webb and Daniluk (1999) explored men's experiences of infertility. They found that the inability to produce children, often deeded as a biological natural given, produced feelings of anger, frustration, powerlessness and failure. They report on the men's feeling of shock when they realised that they were the cause of infertility. It is interesting that the men began to recreate narratives of parenting that were not based upon genetic hereditary. As Kim (2014, p. 292) suggests:

> Most men's gender practices are intended to approximate hegemonic masculinity, which is constructed in relation to both other men and women. Especially subordinated men (such as men of racial and sexual minorities or with fewer economic resources) sometimes perform what gender scholars have described as *compensatory masculinity*, which entails gendered practices to compensate for their subordination as they try to undermine negative stereotypes associated with themselves by conforming to the hegemonic ideals.

One of the responses of the men to experiencing feelings of inadequacy was to compensate by adopting the style of a jock or by having an extra-marital affair. Others committed time and energy to their careers. In order to manage the situation, Webb and Daniluk suggest that the men had to break the linkage between masculinity and virility. In other words, they had to draw upon different resources through which to make their masculinity. In essence, this meant reconstructing their sense of self-worth and competence and developing a new form of masculine subjectivity.

Despite the assault to their masculinity, infertility represented an opportunity for these men to acknowledge and embrace aspects of their personalities that are more commonly associated with the female gender role. The experience of living with and working through their infertility provided these men with an opportunity to construct lives, marriages and families that were less bound by rigid gender role proscriptions—lives that more fully reflected their complete humanity.

Hanna and Gough (2015) focused on men's experience of infertility and explored a range of research in this area. One of the features of men's experience of fertility is that it is often linked to a sense of 'life crisis'. Hanna and Gough point out that being able to father children is closely connected to norms of manhood, and thus infertility is read as a failure. They pick up on the linkages that have been made culturally between virility and fertility and as part of broader regimes of masculinity. More specifically they argue:

> This attempt to 'prove' manliness is part of what Thompson (2005 cited in Herrera, 2013) refers to as resorting to a parodic representation of exaggerated heteronormativity or hypermasculinity.
>
> (p. 1061)

Importantly, such crises appear not to be about masculinity at all but rather are concerned with how groups of people such as women, gay men and children are approximating the resources and roles that are deemed to be integral to being a man. The crisis is therefore much more about other selves rather than being about men themselves. Crucially, men therefore are dependent on those others and their approximated masculinities to make themselves.

To reiterate, this research on infertility identifies the ways in which men have to reconstruct their sense of identity when dominant masculinities become less available to them. Interestingly, much work on masculinity tends to focus on the construction or the reconstruction, with very little discussion about being in a position within masculinity. In short, masculine subjectivity is brought back to a set of norms or regularities that are demanded by the concept of 'masculinity'. An alternative view of understanding masculinity might be to think about it through a notion of assemblages. Assemblages are understood as a metaphor to capture the ways in which different objects operate as a collage of human and non-human objects. More specifically, as Deleuze and Guatarri (1988, p. 25) put it:

> What is an assemblage? It is a multiplicity which is made up of many heterogeneous terms and which establishes liaisons, relations between them, across ages, sexes and reigns—different natures. This, the assemblage's only unity is that of a co-functioning: it is a symbiosis, a 'sympathy'. It is never filiations which are important, but alliances, alloys; these are not successions, lines of descent, but contagions, epidemics, the wind.

Thus, as Watson (2015, p. 17) suggests, an 'assemblage is a dynamic heterogeneous amalgam made up of whatever components happen to be at hand. The

term assemblage therefore implies singularity as each assemblage is built differently.' In the context of masculinity this means that a range of factors come into
play to configure what is understood as masculinity. The crucial element here is
that those elements that make up a masculinity can change and alter, as components of the assemblage may change according to time and place. This means that
there is never a necessary congruity and coherence to masculinity if understood
through the concept of assemblage. Gottzén (2011) usefully draws out the point
that masculinity as a set of components assembled in terms of a collage could be
en-framed across male and female bodies with both gendered and non-gendered
components. Subjectivities in this way become successive means of stabilising masculine identities as different elements converge and fade to configure a
subjectivity. The key shift here is that structures do not create assemblages but
that structures are determined by assemblages. Gottzén suggests that two other
concepts of Deleuze and Guattari are useful in understanding masculinity—first,
territorialisation and de-territorialisation. These operate to *marcate* and demarcate the borders of the components that circulate in contexts, where '[e]ach new
assemblage creates specific forms of masculinities in relation to other elements
of the assemblage, or in relation or Other assemblages' (Gotzen, 2011, p. 235).
Masculinity is therefore to be regarded not as an identity or position within a hierarchy but as a territorialising process of gender assemblages: attempts to stabilise
multiplicities into coherent 'male' identities, bodies, and practices.

Another way of thinking about assemblages and masculinity is to understand
them through a sense of connections. As a result, '[m]asculinity inheres in the
connections between disparate and sometimes seemingly arbitrary actors and
objects' (Campana, 2015, p. 694). In this way, masculinity is embedded in a range
of components and not through a singular subjectivity. This means that all components of the assemblage are part of a broader performance of masculinity. The
performance for Campana is not in the ongoing iteration of a gendered ontology
but rather through the connectivity of elements that operate to form networks
that are (as a whole) understood as masculinity. The implication of this, as Watson points out, is that there is a multiplicity of masculinities where no two are
alike. In other words, what we mean by masculinity is highly contextually driven.
Therefore, according to Watson, there are multiple models of masculinity that
draw upon religious, scientific and hegemonic models. Hegemonic masculinity
is a model according to Watson that can evolve and change according to the context. He draws upon Demetriou's concept of hegemonic masculinity to develop
the idea. One of the key concepts of Watson's approach is that of 'spare parts'.
In short, aspects of masculinity are drawn upon from a range of sources through
which they are made. This facilitates a more complex and messy configuration of
masculine subjectivities.

Fuller's (2015) discussion of the suburban garage also helps us to understand
how we might begin to understand masculinity as an assemblage. For Fuller the
garage has become part of a mythology, in which the garage has been associated
with working-class youth, but also with start-up entrepreneurial projects, especially around IT. Thus, it offers different kinds of opportunities. For Fuller, such

opportunities should not be seen in relation to the performance of identity, but rather they need to be understood through an anti-substantialist position. As such, an opportunity does not have any substance but rather signifies the possibility of particular action being taken. It is part of an assemblage to 'individuate a pre-personal disposition that is nevertheless embodied by individuals' (p. 133). The assemblage of the garage according to Fuller involves a technical discourse that circulates around the masculine. Importantly, the technical aspects of the engine, for example, are according to Fuller not simply mathematical but also around an emotional intensity triggered by the meaning that is inflected by the engine capacity. Furthermore, the garage is a place that can mobilise masculine bodies into action. One of the features of the garage is the centrality of homosociality and values of respect. However, this respect operates across a number spheres and is not cohered through an overall narrative of masculine subjectivity. For example, Fuller (2015, p. 130) points out:

There are multiple masculine economies of respect and the examples of abject sexual violence ('gang rape') and everyday workplace-based risk taking ('construction sites') described by Bourdieu should not be so quickly collapsed into a single economy of respect premised on warding off the feminine. Masculine respect is an index of value and the character of this respect will be determined largely by the valorising assemblages within which it circulates.

The refusal to allow the collapse of particular masculine values into a singular understanding of gendered behaviour is also part of Clifton Evers' discussion of the interplay between surfing masculinity and sensuality. Again, as with Fuller, the move is away from bodies as being sustained performance, towards masculinity as a singular construct. In many ways, Evers suggests understanding masculinity like a wave 'which is fluid, transformable, and always on the edge of collapse' (2009, p. 894). In this way, bodies become the point of exchange but not reducible to that exchange. As such, Evers argues, 'Masculinity emerges from an assemblage,' and this emergence is understood as that of where the bodily sensations and cultural normativities blur and coagulate—or more specifically:

Gendered discourses are used to sort out, code, over-write, clear up, or get straight what is emerging at any given moment. Our sex and gender are end points, and not starting points. For example, when a body falls from a surfboard it can escape classifications such as masculine/feminine or male/female because it blurs into a 'falling body'. This assemblage blurs as body and seaweed and wave energy and sand and seaweed and fibreglass and sunlight and foam and wetsuit and fear and. . . [g]endered discourses actually have to catch up to work out if it is a 'male' or 'female' body, and 'masculine' or 'feminine' experience.

(Evers, 2009, p. 897)

For Evers, there are moments in the assemblage of masculinity where masculinity is only present in its emergent connections, such as in the case of surfing where the non-human and the human come together to produce the moment of the experience. As surfing conditions change, then the ways in which assemblages are configured change too, resulting an ever-changing fluid living-out of masculinity. At such moments, homosociality between surfers is not through homophobia, which Evers suggests may be on the margins. Rather, it is a sharing of feelings about the surfing experience. Masculinity in this experience is wrapped up within the elements that configure the experiences; the body is part of the elements and not subject to them. Alongside this, discourses of masculinity are often in place to create the insularity and closure that characterises certain forms of manhood.

Re-making the Physical Male

If the above discussion on assemblage helps us to think through masculine subjectivity as a series of connections resulting in an assemblage, there is greater scope for understanding male subjectivity that is not reducible to a model of masculinity. A further attribute of a post-masculinity approach might begin to question the basis of the physical that masculinity appears to be aligned with. In short, concepts such as homosociality are dependent upon male bodies. Masculinity itself has a symbiotic relationship to the body. Masculinity theory tends to hold on to fixed binary notions of sex in order to establish and deploy concepts of masculinity. As such, it is not entirely clear how masculinity operates in the context of intersexuality. More specifically, critical masculinity theorists depend upon biological norms in order to situate their theoretical frameworks. Although much of the work on masculinity theory contests that masculinity is naturally connected to male bodies, very little work on masculinity deconstructs the linkages between the male body and masculinity. One way of understanding this is to try exploring the concept of lesbian masculinity. Love (2016) argues that lesbian masculinities challenge biologically deterministic versions of masculinity, and masculinity itself can be transformed into a specific experience for lesbians. Whilst there is an excellent review of how lesbian masculinity can be disempowering women and re-authorising women with male privilege, the reducibility of masculinity to bodies still remains. In other words, Love's account situates the experiences of masculinity in conjunction with the feminine. Thus, lesbian masculinity is different from men's masculinity because the contextual configurations produce different kinds of normativity.

Wassersug et al. (2012) provide an interesting approach to the study of masculinity by exploring what gender means for men who have been castrated. In their definition, castration refers to those men who have had their testicles removed either chemically or surgically. As they point out, this is different from the Freudian analysis, but they purport that the loss of testicles implicitly means the loss of the erectile function (although this is not always the case—see Wibowo et al., 2012). They point out that men with prostate cancer usually undergo chemical castration, as the production of testosterone is linked to the production of cancer cells. In their work with men undergoing treatment for prostate cancer, Wassersug et al. (2012) suggest a space outside of male and female that may entail an alternative form of gendering, as the impact of chemical castration appears to change how men subsequently experience themselves as men. One of the impacts of this treatment is that men experience themselves as failing to live up to the expectations of a 'normal' sexual masculinity. Their starting point is that men experience a notion of maleness, which is often an internal psychic process that is not reducible to physical function.

Castration, it is suggested, is more than simply a physical removal of the testes, but can also signal the impact of a number of hormonal changes such as the loss of facial hair, a reduction of penis size and the accumulation of breast tissue. As Wassursug et al. (2012, p. 255) point out:

> In other words, castration partially 'feminizes' men beyond the loss of the testicles (Wassersug, 2009a, 2009b). Males castrated after puberty retain facial hair, low-pitched voices, and XY chromosomes; however, while their penises do not shrink to clitoral size nor do they acquire vaginas, their bodies still deviate from the male norm.

The responses of men who are castrated, who as Wassersug suggests are at the boundaries of masculinity, have to reconfigure their sense of masculine selves as new forms of gender identity, or as men who are unable to live up to the normative expectations of masculinity. The impact is that these men come to occupy a liminal space, where they see themselves as not men and not women. According to Wassersug, patients are seen as in between genders and may work to try to pass as heteronormative males. Men who have been castrated can have rewarding and enriching (non)sexual intimacy, but according to Wassersug, some men find it difficult to manage the disjunction between their self-perception and heteronormative expectations. Unlike transgender identifications, where subjectivity is aligned with bodily change, men who have ben castrated find it difficult to identify with their bodily changes. As a result, Wassersug suggests that men could take up the position of eunuch, which itself has had a high profile, and at times has even been revered and respected, in history. However, men tend not to take this up, as in the current social and cultural context it is used pejoratively. However, a eunuch subjectivity could be informed outside of heteronormative models of identities and is not dependent upon sexual object choice. Unlike theoretical discussions of gender variance that emerge from within the heteronormative model, eunuch gender identity is not defined by sexual orientation or sexual object choice. Importantly, the eunuch identity transgresses the binaries of gender and offers an alternative space for identity that is not dependent upon the immediately responsive penis and sexual desire to designate masculinity. The eunuch identity has the potential to stand outside of this, and rather be in a state of gendered dimensionality that can occupy a different kind of gendering.

Reis (2013) reminds us of the fragility of biology and how the biological category of maleness is made through socially and culturally loaded interpretations of the body. Reis argues that it is social anxieties about the body that impact upon the decisions surgeons make when viewing babies: 'Intersex, also known as disorders of sex development or DSD, is a congenital incongruence between internal reproductive anatomy, chromosomes, hormones, and genitals' (2013, p. 138). Reis argues that there is often a 'normalising' process when a baby is born to ensure a congruence between the external aesthetics of the genitals and the internal anatomy. Often, it is a reconstruction of the external genitalia to make the baby look like the assigned sex. An example of this can be found in Brubaker and Johnson (2008), who argue that masculinity is now being made 'more than ever through . . . consumption, sexuality and physical appearance' (p. 131). They suggest that advertising draws upon the crisis in masculinity, or indeed creates it, and then 'sells' the solution to address it. The result is that advertising involves the process of creating new resources of masculinity and the reconfiguration of hegemonic power of men over women, which is illustrated in adverts for penis enhancement. They suggest that adverts operate as a coding system that designates particular forms of masculinity. Drawing upon Bourdieu, Brubaker and Johnson argue that the bodies that are associated with traditional manual labour have become increasingly popular despite the fact that manual labour has declined. They analysed 20 internet adverts and websites for erectile enhancements and identified three key themes: phallo-centrism, a rejection of vanity, and the Othering of women as sexual conquests. It appears that the adverts reconfigure masculinity as something physical, in which penis size becomes a measure of masculinity. Linked to this is a notion of enhancement that rejects associations with vanity. According to Brubaker and Johnson, penis enhancement is not framed through appearance, but rather this occurs as an instrumentality, and enables the men to become more successful in other spheres of their life such as work, family and health. Finally, the theme of Othering, which involves positioning women as passive and subject to men's desire, is achieved by framing sex as something that is done to women. The biggest penis becomes the instrument of control and aggression where sex is a process of 'physical violence and sexual assault'. The importance of this account is that the shift towards the body as a source of masculine power does not necessarily result in the decrease of patriarchal power. As Brubaker and Johnson suggest, the shift to representations of the body is not collapsing the boundaries of men and women's consumerism, but rather the focus on the body operates to reinforce existing forms of patriarchal power.

However, there is an important point here, that the body can be reshaped, and that the physiology that is deemed to underpin masculinity is far more fluid and unstable. One example is found in Atkinson, who explores men and the practice of body modification. Using a crisis of masculinity as a 'conceptual backdrop', he explores why men in Canada undergo body modification. He suggests that in his interviews men are not seeking out extreme forms of modification; rather, they want to blend into the ordinary. This work on the body to become average, Atkinson argues, connects with more traditional themes of Canadian masculinity. In some ways, Atkinson argues, body modification is part of a self-violent regime both in terms of demonstrating the withstanding of pain and at the same time operating as a 'hyperbolically masculine solution to problems of cultural doubt' (2008, p. 78). Furthermore, Atkinson makes a link between body modification and decreasing status at work. The connection of body modification with femininity is offset by a framing of the practice as masculine. It is suggested that surgery enables men to acquire a masculinity that can compete with the changing gendered world around them. Furthermore, whilst men see themselves as victims of a work routine that dehumanises them, cosmetic surgery is marked by their active role in decisions about modification. Atkinson (2008, p. 83) discusses the male-feminine body as 'a body that is at once firm, fit, flexible and fat-free, and open to exploring non-traditional (feminised) forms of bodywork in order to appear as innovatively male.'

Importantly for Atkinson, the claim is that although men are taking on feminine body-work, they are also reinserting traditional masculine narratives of control and dominance. The body modification, therefore, first provides men with a sense of social control, when in other social arenas they perceive that they are losing control. Second, such modifications feed into a self-aggressive nature and the 'risk-taking' associated with masculinity. They also tend to keep the process of modification to themselves, in that discussion of the surgery would fall into a sense of accepting their weakness and limitations. Significant for this chapter is the fluidity through which masculine subjectivity is based. Remaking of the physicality of the body through modification becomes a means through which the original markers of masculinity are becoming reconfigured. It is this reconfiguration, this point of absence of masculinity in order to make it, that enables us to think through the relationship between the body and identity.

Masculinity, Concepts and the Absence of Women

The final theme that underpins this chapter's exploration of post-masculinity is that of an engagement with women. At present, one of the characteristics of current approaches to masculinity is that they have become overly dependent upon understanding relationships between men and men. The focus on this relationship in many contexts has been extremely important and has highlighted, especially in the context of the previous chapters, how the concepts that we have described explain power inequalities. O'Neil's (2015) critique of *inclusive masculinity* theory is suggestive of something far broader across discussions of men and masculinity. She is critical of how sexual politics have been erased from the discussion of masculinity. She argues that 'within this brand of theorizing, sexual political matters are not simply ignored but are instead presented as already settled, or in the process of being settled' (p. 109). More specifically, O'Neil argues that models of inclusive masculinity are premised on a notion of dynamic social change and that inclusive masculinity theory is moving towards a more liberal, tolerant and inclusive society. However, a consequence of this is that sexual politics becomes marginalised. This, as O'Neil points out, is not a critique necessarily of hegemonic masculinity; rather, it is that hegemonic masculinity is based on a prior cultural moment that does not capture the contemporary nature of men's lives. Since hegemonic masculinity was developed as a means of understanding the relationship between men, and men and women, this sense of 'understanding men', for

O'Neil, becomes lost. O'Neil's systematic critique of inclusive masculinity suggests that when revising concepts, we need to be careful about the settlements that have occurred along the way that enable us to do this. It is argued here that whilst O'Neil engages with issues around sexual politics, it could be read that Critical Masculinity Studies have attempted to explore masculinity without reference to women. In addition, this is crucial if we are to understand the conundrums that surround masculinity.

In interviews with long-term unemployed men on an education programme designed to provide them with the skills and support to find another job, the centrality of women's experience to their sense of self was extremely important (Haywood, 2018). During the research, the men spoke about much frustration, pain and self-loathing. For these men there was a distinct feeling of failure. However, men's self-definitions and identifications were not driven by ensuring their reputation with other men; they were driven by the men's relationships with women. The status of these men was predicated on how women would see them, and how their lack of employment would be interpreted. On this programme, reputations were not made through homophobia or the demonstration of heterosexual competence; rather, it was about managing their own interpretations of women's perceptions. This was also not about misogyny and attempting to restore or recuperate traditional ways of being a man through violence. These men talked about the shame that they experienced. In an extreme example, one of the men opted for repeated failure that was driven by his reading of women's perceptions. He was a 30-year-old, and he was married. He had two children under the age of three and had been unemployed for three years. His despair was palpable, and what emerged signalled how gender relations, rather than relationships between men, became detrimental to his success.

Chris: Tell me about the programme. . . how do you feel it is going?
David: No good. I have difficulty reading and writing. I have since school. . . .
Chris: Have you told someone about this?
David: No.
Chris: Why don't you tell someone?
David: I can't can I? I can't tell her [the programme leader] can I? I just feel a failure, I have failed at getting work but I don't want to be seen as failing as a man, do I?
Chris: But that's what they are trained to do. . . .
David: Yes but I go home and my wife sees me failing and then being here she sees me as failing, it might be a bit different if they were a man, they might understand it more, I'd rather not get a job.

This was a critical incident for the research as it brought the issue of women back into understanding masculinity. There is thus a concern that Masculinity Studies have become overly concerned with researching men. In fact, theories of men and masculinity have become a little insular in that they have become disconnected from their original political roots. As indicated in Chapter 1, since the 1980s, Feminists and Men's Studies activists began to see the importance of understanding the oppression of women, not simply from the perspective of women, but from those carrying out the violence. If we were going to understand the processes of patriarchal power, then we needed to understand the dynamics of that power. One way of understanding the conundrum is to return to understanding men and power as located within a gendered relationship, and not simply trying to understand relationships between men.

The key point being made here is that we need to re-assert the notion that gender is relational. In other words, in order to understand the nature of gender relations, we need to recognise the interdependency between masculinity and femininity. We need to hold in focus Raewyn Connell's (1995) claim that 'masculinities do not first exist and then come into contact with femininities. Masculinities and femininities are produced together in the process that constitutes a gender order.' This claim was echoed in 2008, p.142: 'We must remember that gender is relational, that women are as much involved in the formation of masculinities as men are.' Furthermore, where relationships between men and women are discussed, there is a reductionism that suggests that it must take place either through codes of compulsory heterosexuality, in a sense of replacing homophobia, and/or through the practice of antipathy towards, or violence against, women. The work with the unemployed men suggested that their perception of gender was neither of these; instead, it was being understood in relation to the value and significance that these men attached to women's accounts.

To return to the opening discussion of dogging, we can begin to see how men's relationships with women become crucial in how they co-ordinate and manage their subjectivities. There have been a number of commentaries that have suggested that masculinity is underpinned by men's sexual physiology, especially the penis, erection and orgasm. In her study of heterosexual men, Mooney-Sommers (2005) suggests that men detach themselves by using discourses that posit sexual activity as emotionless and physical. As a result, women are reduced to passive objects that are used by men. Furthermore, it is argued that male sexuality is premised on the control and mastery of the 'sex drive' that leads to the securing of masculinity. In the scenario of dogging, there is a shift of emphasis, as it appears that the accomplishment of masculinity is achieved through the centrality of women's pleasure rather than that of their own:

Jay: I like to be there where you put the woman at the centre of the attention, kind of giving her all of the fun that she wants.

Thus, from the men's perspective, participants suggested that their own sexual satisfaction was to deliver on women's wants and needs. It could be argued that by losing themselves in the women's pleasure, men maintain a division between themselves and their bodies. This means that men's bodies achieve a use-value and more importantly a high status use-value that enables them to acquire sexual competence. Although men may use a separation of the self and their body, in this case they expressed a clear sense of the vulnerability of the body. This vulnerability is expressed by Gary:

> Well to be honest, when I had this couple come down, she was speaking online, saying oh you better be ready for us, because for the last time I fought for five hours solid and she was saying well if you can't do this then it is not worth coming. So there was me straightaway thinking fuck, how am I going to handle this? Five hours, she's driving all the fucking way from Glasgow, and this has been building up, speaking for a week, if I shoot me muck in 20 minutes, I'm going to look like a gobshite aren't I? So like I mentioned it to one of my pals, and he gave me this sachet, and it is unbelievable. Kamagra—you get a real tingling feeling and I have used it a few times now, and you can last for hours I mean I could do with some more but it is so good.

The theme of men positioning themselves as objects to be used to facilitate women's pleasure suggests an understanding of themselves as 'tools'. Traditionally, as Murphey (2001) has pointed out, the metaphorical use of tool in sexual practices involves men's pleasure: using women to achieve and accomplish pleasure primarily through men's orgasm. While Murphey's account of the disembodied body resonates with the participants, the key difference is that of positioning women as determining men's competence. Thus, within the dogging scenario, men put themselves in a position of vulnerability that does not simply rely on the functioning of their own bodies but relies on that functioning to be affirmed by women, more specifically, through women's orgasmic response.

Conclusion

In writing about Women's Studies, Brown (1997, p. 122) offers further insight into the problem of masculinity being an object of inquiry:

> There is something about women's studies, though, and perhaps about any field organized by social identity rather than by genre of inquiry, that is especially vulnerable to losing its raison d'être when the coherence or boundedness of its object of study is challenged.

Brown makes an important point as we move towards a post-masculinity understanding of gender; we are in effect challenging the very object of inquiry and how that object is constructed. There is a danger, though, as we develop a move towards a process of de-subjectification in being unable to explain how power operates. For example, in a critique of Foucault's notion of bodies and pleasure Butler suggests (1999, p. 18) that 'works in the service of maintaining a compulsory ignorance, and where the break between the past and the present keeps us from being able to see the trace of the past as it re-emerges in the very contours of an imagined future.' In short, a shift to understanding male gender outside of masculinity removes an analysis of power. Instead, it is suggested here, that returning to Brown's (1997, p. 131) approach, we need to hold onto the historical formations of the subjectivity, whilst at the same time developing 'genealogies of particular modalities of subjection that presume neither coherence in the formations of particular kinds of subjects nor equivalence between different formations.' In other words, critiques of a post-masculinity position might suggest that as we abandon masculinity, we abandon a theory of power relations. In response, it is argued there that in some contexts, we have to move away from models of masculinity in order to acquire a more informed understanding of power relations—maybe an understanding of power relations that is not obscured by an institutional and disciplinary dependence on masculinity.

References

Anderson, E. (2009) *Inclusive Masculinity: The Changing Nature of Masculinities*. New York: Routledge.

Atkinson, M. (2008) Exploring male femininity in the 'crisis': Men and cosmetic surgery. *Body & Society*, 14(1), 67–87.

Bell, D. (2006) Bodies, technologies, spaces: On 'dogging'. *Sexualities*, 9, 387–407.

Bertone, C. and Ferrero-Camoletto, R. (2009) Beyond the sex machine? Sexual practices and masculinity in adult men's heterosexual accounts. *Journal of Gender Studies*, 18(4), 369–386.

Boonzaier, F. and La Rey, C. (2003) "He's a man, and I'm a woman": Cultural constructions of masculinity and femininity in South African women's narratives of violence. *Violence Against Women*, 9(8), 1003–1029.

Brown, W. (1997) The impossibility of women's studies. *Differences: A Journal of Feminist Cultural Studies*, 9(3), 79–101.

Brubaker, S.J. and Johnson, J.A. (2008) 'Pack a more powerful punch' and 'lay the pipe': Erectile enhancement discourse as a body project for masculinity. *Journal of Gender Studies*, 17(2), 131–146.

Butler, J. (1999) Revisiting bodies and pleasures. *Theory Culture and Society*, 16, 11–20.

Campana, J. (2015) Distribution, assemblage, capacity: New keywords for masculinity? *European Review of History: Revue européenne d'histoire*, 22(4), 691–697.

Connell, R.W. (1995) *Masculinities*. Cambridge: Polity Press.

Connell, R.W. (2008) Masculinity construction and sports in boys' education: A framework for thinking about the issue. *Sport, Education and Society*, 13(2), 131–145,

Consalvo, M. (2003) The monsters next door: Media constructions of boys and masculinity. *Feminist Media Studies*, 3(1), 27–45.

Cover, R. (2015) Visual heteromasculinities online: Beyond binaries and sexual normativities in camera chat forums. *Men and Masculinities*, 18, 159–175.

Critchely, S. (1992) *The Ethics of Deconstruction: Derrida and Levinas*. Edinburgh: Edinburgh University Press.

Deleuze, G. and Guattari, F. (1988) *A Thousand Plateaus: Capitalism and Schizophrenia*. London: Bloomsbury.

Dutsch, D. (2014) Kynogamia and cynic sexual ethics. In: Masterson, M., Rabinowitz, N.S. and Robson, J. eds. *Sex in Antiquity: Exploring Gender and Sexuality in the Ancient World*. London: Routledge, pp. 245–259.

Evers, C. (2009) 'The point': Surfing, geography and a sensual life of men and masculinity on the Gold Coast, Australia. *Social & Cultural Geography*, 10(8), 893–908.

Flax, J. (1993) *Disputed Subjects: Essays on Psychoanalysis, Politics and Philosophy*. Routledge: Oxon.

Foucault, M., Morar, N. and Smith, D.W. (2011) The gay science. *Critical Inquiry*, 37(3), 385–403.

Frank, K. (2008) 'Not gay, but not homophobic': Male sexuality and homophobia in the 'lifestyle'. *Sexualities*, 11, 435–454.

Fuller, G. (2015) In the garage: Assemblage, opportunity and techno-aesthetics. *Angelaki*, 20(1), 125–136.

Gottzén, L. (2011) Metaphors of masculinity: Hierarchies and assemblages. In: Biricik, A. and Hearn, J. eds. *GEXcel Work in Progress Report Volume XV: Proceedings GEXcel Theme 9: Gendered Sexualed Transnationalisations, Deconstructing the Dominant: Transforming Men "Centres" and Knowledge/Policy/Practice*. Linkoping: Linkoping University, pp. 229–239.

Hanna, E. and Gough, B. (2015) Experiencing male infertility. *SAGE Open*, 5(4), 1–9.

Haywood, C. and McDermott (2018) *Understanding Men, Masculinity and Disability*. Newcastle: University of Newcastle.

Kearney, R. (1988) *Across the Frontiers: Ireland in the 1990s*. Dublin: Wolfhound Press.

Kim, M. (2014) South Korean rural husbands, compensatory masculinity, and international marriage. *Journal of Korean Studies*, 19(2), 291–325.

Kimmel, M.S. (2007) Masculinity as homophobia: Fear, shame, and silence in the construction of gender identity. In: Cook, N. ed. *Gender Relations in Global Perspective: Essential Readings*. Ontario: Canadian Scholars Press, pp. 73–83.

Kimmel, M.S. and Mahler, M. (2003) Adolescent masculinity, homophobia, and violence random school shootings, 1982–2001. *American Behavioral Scientist*, 46(10), 1439–1458.

Klein, J. and Chancer, L. (2000) Masculinity matters: The role of gender in high-profile school violence cases. In: Spina, S. ed. *Smoke and Mirrors: The Hidden Context of Violence in Schools and Society*. New York: Rowman and Littlefield, pp. 129–162.

Lacquer, T. (1990) *Making Sex: Body and Gender From the Greeks to Freud*. Cambridge, MA: Harvard University Press.

Larkin, R.W. (2011) Masculinity, school shooters, and the control of violence. *Control of Violence*, 3, 315–344.

Love, B.E. (2016) Lesbians, masculinities, and privilege: The privileging of gender and the gendering of sexuality. *Dissenting Voices*, 5(1), Article 4, 1–24.

Mooney-Somers, J. (2005) *Heterosexual Male Sexuality: Representations and Sexual Subjectivity*. Unpublished PhD Thesis, School of Psychology, University of Western Sydney, Sydney.

Murphy, P.F. (2001) *Studs, Tools, and the Family Jewels: Metaphors Men Live by*. Madison, WI: University of Wisconsin Press.

O'Neill, R. (2015) Whither critical masculinity studies? Notes on inclusive masculinity theory, postfeminism, and sexual politics. *Men and Masculinities*, 18(1), 100–120.

Reback, C.J. and Larkins, S. (2010) Maintaining a heterosexual identity: Sexual meanings among a sample of heterosexually identified men who have sex with men. *Archives of Sexual Behavior*, 39(3), 766–773.

Reis, E. (2013) Intersex surgeries, circumcision, and the making of "normal". In: Denniston, G.C., Hodges, F.M., Milos, M.F. eds. *Genital Cutting: Protecting Children From Medical, Cultural, and Religious Infringements*. The Netherlands: Springer, pp. 137–147.

Sherman, J. (2009) Bend to avoid breaking: Job loss, gender norms, and family stability in rural America. *Social Problems*, 56(4), 599–620.

Schwandt, T. A. (1996) Farewell to criteriology. *Qualitative Inquiry,* 2(1), 58–72.

Tonso, K.L. (2009) Violent masculinities as tropes for school shooters: The Montréal massacre, Columbine attack, and rethinking schools. *American Behavioral Scientist*, 52(9), 1266–1285.

Ward, J. (2015) *Not Gay: Sex Between Straight White Men*. New York: New York University Press.

Wassersug, R.J. (2009a) Passing through the wall: On outings, Exodus, angels, and the ark. *Journal of Religion & Health*, 483, 381–390.

Wassersug, R.J. (2009b) Mastering emasculation. *Journal of Clinical Oncology*, 27(4), 634–636.

Wassersug, R.J., McKenna, E. and Lieberman, T. (2012) Eunuch as a gender identity after castration. *Journal of Gender Studies*, 21(3), 252–270.

Watson, J. (2015) Multiple mutating masculinities: Of maps and men. *Angelaki*, 20(1), 107–121.

Webb, R.E. and Daniluk, J.C. (1999) The end of the line infertile men's experiences of being unable to produce a child. *Men and Masculinities*, 2(1), 6–25.

Wibowo, E., Wassersug, R., Warkentin, K., Walker, L., Robinson, J., Brotto, L. and Johnson, T. (2012) Impact of androgen deprivation therapy on sexual function: A response. *Asian Journal of Andrology*, 14, 793–794.

8   Conclusion
Conundrums and Concepts

Introduction

The authors' ambition for this book is to make a contribution to Gender Studies and to the development of theories of gender and sexuality. More specifically, we have focussed on the field of research often labelled as *Critical Studies on Men and Masculinities* (CSMM). During the last decade, this has been a growing research field, focusing on questions about men and masculinity in contemporary societies. The historical roots of this field of research can be found in men's increasing involvement in feminism and gender equality from the 1970s and onwards. Gradually, the field has developed from involving activists and feminist men towards an established academic subfield. Historically, discussions about men and masculinity, or more precisely about understanding masculinity as a social construction, are a relatively new phenomenon.

In Chapter 1, we drew upon the idea that cultural epistemologies provide the frames that are drawn upon to make sense of masculinity. The conundrums we have been investigating in this book lie at the intersection between attempts to develop concepts about changes, transformations and cultural shifts in the understanding of masculinity, on the one hand, and, on the other, a theoretical field leaning heavily on tools and concepts used to pinpoint what factors are actually counteracting our attempts to talk about changes. Thus, throughout this book we have been engaging with notions of transformation. We have seen that transformations taking place at individual, cultural and social levels impact on and shape men and masculinity. In some literature, especially in the context of self-help, such transformations are seen as making 'better men'. In other literature, especially that which is discussed in this book, there are also numerous examples of 'new' masculinities, and we find everything from metrosexual men to gender-equal fathers. In the context of society, we have seen that transforming men has a number of political implications, such as the development of more gender-equal societies. If transformations are key issues, then partly the purpose of this book has been to reflect on how this inflects the theoretical and conceptual tools that we have available.

A substantial part of this book is made up of the four chapters that address, respectively, the concepts of hegemonic masculinity, homosociality, homophobia and heteronormativity. When reading studies on men and masculinities, it seems almost impossible to avoid these concepts. Even if many researchers are critical of these concepts, and feel uncomfortable in this conceptual landscape, they still appear preoccupied with trying to adapt and reconfigure them. One of the reasons for this is that the concepts provide ways of understanding power relations. As indicated in Chapter 1, studies on men and masculinity have close connections with social movements that tend to theoretically prioritise fixed notions of social power. This power is deemed to operate in logical, predictable and *structured* patterns. Central to the formation of inequalities, hegemony, homosociality, homophobia and heteronormativity have been historically located within hierarchies of dominant/empowered (men) and subordinate/oppressed (women). Consequently, we argue that in order to develop and update theories of gender and masculinity, we need to confront and challenge the most usual definitions and configurations of these concepts.

We have struggled to de- and re-construct these concepts within a tension between structural and Post-structural approaches to power relations. In order to deepen our reflections of the common ways of framing and interpreting men and masculinities, we have allowed these chapters to lead up to Chapter 7, which challenges the template of 'masculinity' and the whole idea that we need to situate our studies in relation to the concept of masculinity. Engaging in a discussion on postmasculinity, we want to start a process of reflecting upon the premises for CSMM. The ambition is not to transgress this field of research or to settle this field of study, but instead to create movement and to open up a space for thinking through the main premises of the field. Therefore, the ambition throughout this book has been to open up the concepts investigated, showing the potential fruitfulness of trying to push the conceptual landscape in the direction of a Post-structural reading of men and masculinity. Structures are both limiting and enabling, and they constitute both stability and the conditions of the possibility for change. Thinking this way around the key concepts in this book, we can start to create spaces for imagining actual changes taking place in how men are positioning themselves in different societal spheres and relations. Thinking through hegemony also means that we need to study gradual changes in hegemonic structuration processes. However, in order to achieve this, we need to contextualise and get close to contemporary embodiments of masculinity and the transformations taking place.

The question of transformation through positions of stability and change is a thread throughout this book. How is it possible to reveal ongoing changes in terms of masculinity and power without concealing retentions, reconfigurations and restructuring of power? How is it possible to be able to examine and understand the constants of patriarchy, homophobia, and heteronormativity, and at the same time to be able to point towards possible and necessary change? It is our view that it is important to be able to capture at least potentialities for progressive change, because if we are not able to do this, we also implicitly accept that there is no possible way away from a patriarchal, homophobic, heteronormative society. Thus, we need concepts that are able to capture stability as well as change. In this book, we have tried to pinpoint and explore some of the theoretical and conceptual obstacles that stand in the way of such a project.

Conceptual Confusions and Theoretical Challenges

We have outlined in each of the chapters how theories and approaches to studies on men and masculinities have changed over time, as has the interest in studying and uncovering the possible part played by masculinity in understanding different social issues. Roughly, we draw out these changes in Chapter 2: from the idea of a biological or genetic 'real man', via theories on socialisation into static sex roles, to differentiations of masculinities and finally the queering of gender. Although the interest in research on men and masculinities has increased over the years, sometimes suggested to be an effect of societal change in, and sometimes a clash between, cultural epistemologies, it is still not obvious how, when and why masculinity is or should be considered important.

On the one hand, different approaches to masculinity are used in parallel, both in society and in research. Ideas of socialisation, and sometimes biological and genetic explanations and arguments, can be found in schools, social work, the medical field and of course the rise of some aspects of neuroscience. Concrete examples could be teaching practices aimed at boys, or the use of male role models for boys identified as being at risk. At the same time, transgender communities and Queer research are continuing to challenge such linear approaches to masculinity and femininity, both in everyday life and in research. On the other hand, there is also a tension between research still not paying attention to masculinity at all and research maybe paying too much attention to masculinity. In Chapter 2 we talked about school shootings, and how this tends to be explained without even considering the fact that almost every offender has been male. However, at the other end of the spectrum is research taking the connection between men and masculinity for granted, almost claiming that all male practices must be explained through a concept of masculinity.

Finally, studies on men and masculinities often rely upon the above-mentioned theoretical conceptions, that in themselves are somewhat of a conundrum, and very much linked together in studies on men and masculinities. The four Hs— hegemony, homophobia, homosociality and heteronormativity—tend to be used differently, sometimes in a more static and other times a more fluid way, creating confusion about how we can adequately capture power relations and inequalities, as well as their possible changes and fluidity. The chapter on hegemonic masculinity approaches these challenges by using fatherhood as an example, particularly with regard to how approaches to parental leave, gender and 'feminised' engagements with family, childcare and home differ between men. This is possible to interpret as ongoing change in relations between men and women, and men and men, as well as a possible change in terms of power relations. At the same time, it is possible to claim that these changes only create new venues to maintain power. Similarly, the chapters on heteronormativity, homosociality and homophobia all reveal tensions between using the different concepts to claim both stability as well as change.

Another thread and challenge that we address throughout the book is a theoretical tension between the local, often in terms of American or Western European localities, and global aspects of masculinities. The critique against Connell's initial theory on men and masculinities for universalising on the basis of research and experiences localised in a particular (Western) context is one example of this. Another is how not only hegemony but also heteronormativity, homophobia and homosociality theoretically seem to be framed inside a Western context. This becomes clear not only in terms of theory but also in terms of how theory tends to be used. Even when used in a non-Western context, the different theoretical concepts are still very much Western. This Western focus also becomes clear when reading about the emergence of different theoretical approaches to studies on men and masculinities in Chapter 2. Not only does it pose a challenge for future research; it has also posed a challenge when trying to uncover or visualise the conundrum of masculinity in other contexts than the Western.

A final theoretical challenge is found in how the different theoretical concepts seem to be closely intertwined and thus difficult to separate. Maybe this is most visible in the connection between homophobia and heteronormativity, but it is also traceable among the other concepts. Even in the discussion on post-masculinity and the example of 'dogging', one could argue that heteronormativity is very much an important part of the analysis. For instance, it could be argued that the men participating in sexual activities that deviate from a heteronormative norm still frame it within heteronormativity and a heterosexual format. At the same time, it prompts us to think about a notion of change taking place using existing language with different meanings. Throughout the book, we have discussed these theoretical challenges using various examples in a variety of settings, in order to draw us closer to unravelling the conundrum of masculinity. In the next couple of sections, we will pull the threads together and further clarify how to be able to use this theoretical landscape.

The Limits of the Conceptual Rethinking

Critical Studies on Men and Masculinities often relies heavily on the four 'H' concepts examined in the different chapters of this book. In our engagement with the concepts, we have stressed their confusions, epistemological differences and theoretical slippages. A principle conundrum throughout the book is how to conceptualise actual and empirically grounded transformations in masculinities and masculine subjectivities, and whether the concepts often used to capture men and masculinities are sufficient enough to grasp these transformations. Thus, one central task of exploration in the book is related to the relationship between the four 'H' concepts and the construction of masculinities.

Even though the concepts of hegemony, homosociality, homophobia and heteronormativity are often relevant to comprehending configurations of masculinities, we nevertheless stress the importance of approaching often-used definitions of the concepts with some caution and scepticism. Firstly, we argue that the concepts are sometimes used in a somewhat simplistic and structuralist way, hardly identifying complexity, ambivalence and contingency. Stuck or reduced to only gender and/or sexuality, the four 'Hs' do not always enable us to capture nuances and transformations in the configuration of masculinities. One way to challenge this approach is to relate the four 'Hs' to multiple power relations and categories. Hence, in some chapters we have stressed the importance of comprehending the presented concepts in relation to an intersectional approach. For example, in order to understand homophobia and its various expressions, we suggest that notions of class, ethnicity and nationality may also be of importance.

Furthermore, in the chapter on homosociality we discuss the possibility of gay/straight, gay/gay and mixed-race homosocial relations, thus extending the concept. We also include the often-forgotten concept of femininity when discussing homosociality. Moreover, the concept of hegemonic masculinity, at least in its initial usage, seems underdeveloped when it comes to, for example, ethnicity and notions of global masculinities. Contributing to a more complex understanding and visibility of contextual and contingent relations of power and subject positions, intersectionality stands out as an important tool when exploring men and masculinities. We cannot stress enough the significance of reflexivity with regard to how subjectivities around e.g. class, sexuality and ethnicity work through masculinity practices. Masculinities do not exist as exclusive categories but are constituted in complex interrelationships with other categories and power relations. The multiple discursive positions that research subjects occupy hence demand a close evaluation of the context in which we are conducting research.

Secondly, and related to the discussion on intersectionality, we also suggest that one as a researcher tries to avoid the assumption that the construction of masculinities is inevitably intertwined with the four 'Hs'. Even though, for example, homophobia often seems to play an important role in the configuration of masculinities, not least among young heterosexual men, we discuss and show how the constructions of masculinities do not inescapably rely on expressions of homophobia but instead rely also on seemingly inclusive and progressive relations. That said, the nature of masculinity is sometimes understood through the presence and absence of such concepts, thus re-positioning masculinity as a measureable trait. In Chapter 1 we identified how psychological approaches positioned themselves as being able to capture masculinity through measurable characteristics. There is a tendency, when using the four 'Hs', to do something similar. Furthermore, we also present examples of male horizontal homosociality, not necessarily imbued with heteronormative or sexist assumptions. Accordingly, we suggest that it is possible to construct masculinities without relying on the usual definitions of *hegemonic masculinity*, yet not beyond hegemony per se. Thus, we argue that hegemony may be reconfigured in a more desirable way. However, we also raise the question of whether these somewhat 'new', and supposedly more democratic, configurations of masculine subjectivities actually may maintain power and consequently underpin traditional hegemonic masculinity.

Thirdly, we suggest that it is problematic to assume that masculinities by necessity are related to male bodies and, consequently, that the four 'Hs' only relate to males. Leaning on a Post-structural approach, it is possible to think of the link between male bodies and masculinity as contingent and to recognise how female bodies may also enact masculinity. Although the male body seems to be the only legitimate body that masculinity can 'stick to' (Berggren, 2014), we, in accordance with Halberstam (1998), highlight female masculinities and stress the importance of recognising how masculinity can sometimes be a subject position also available for females to identify with. Symmetrically, this allows us to recognise femininity as a subjectivity that males can construct and embody. This approach destabilises gender categories through undermining their homogeneity and rejecting the distinctiveness of them. Seeking out subtle differences between and within identities helps us to highlight the highly contradictory constitution of differentiated masculinities.

Disconnecting masculinity from male bodies, i.e. moving beyond engendered bodies, is, however, a complex and uncertain project, but it carries perhaps a utopian idea. If the signs of masculinity become more and more disentangled from any taken-for-granted connection to male bodies, one could possibly consider this a democratisation as far as a broader field of subject positions becomes available to identify with. To some degree then, unpredictability and a greater fluidity might arise when it comes to power relations between women and men.

The final caveat that we wish to point out is to focus on the ways in which masculinity itself is sometimes used unproblematically. We have seen how the concept of masculinity is applied across the whole of the generational spectrum, from primary school boys through to older men. It is also possible to see a process in historical studies in which detailed and nuanced readings of men's practices are often reduced to masculinity alone. In some cases, the temporal specificity of manliness becomes transposed onto a trans-historical concept of masculinity. This can also be seen when masculinity is applied in a variety of different cultural contexts. Instead of localised versions of gender being used as the conceptual template through which to understand men, a Western concept of masculinity becomes applied, more often than not, to global South contexts. In this way, it is possible to understand masculinity operating as part of an academic imperialism, in which it works as a colonising concept. Therefore, whilst we have suggested a number of limitations to the four 'H' concepts, they thus resonate and inflect approaches to masculinity. At the same time, while it is important to apply critical reflexivity to masculinity and the four 'Hs', in the final part of this conclusion we return to the conundrum of masculinity.

The Landscape of Conundrum

Given this summary of the themes covered in this book, that is, the theoretical and methodological challenges we have pinpointed and how we have tried to tackle and to some degree transcend these, what can we say that this book has tried to accomplish as a whole on a more abstract level? If we draw a line through the book, we could say that starting with questioning the fruitfulness of assuming the presence of a form of injurious hegemonic masculinity in any, and all, contexts researched, we end up questioning the viability of the concept of masculinity in itself. Of course, such questioning should be read as precisely just that, i.e. a questioning and curious search for new ways of theorising what it means to be a man, and how masculine subjectivities are produced. It is not to preemptively establish that concepts such as hegemony, homophobia, homosociality, heteronormativity or even masculinity itself have no analytical purchase. Rather, it can be seen as an effort to interrogate the boundaries of these concepts and an urge not to assume their applicability in any, and all, settings.

One way of explicating where this puts us is by recourse to a Post-structural understanding of the notion of articulation. As Hall (1986, p. 53) has pointed out, the concept of articulation has a productive double meaning associated with it, in that it means both to express and to connect together. In addition, as Laclau and Mouffe (1985/2001, p. 105) point out, every such connection involves 'establishing a relation among elements such that their identity is modified as a result of the articulatory practice.' In other words, connecting two elements necessarily involves modifying the meaning of the two elements being connected. Now, following Glynos and Howarth (2007) in adopting articulation also as a methodological concept, we suggest that it is precisely such modifications we should pay attention to and be open to. To exemplify, when searching for hegemonic masculinity in a men's rugby team (Anderson and McGuire, 2010), we should be prepared to also adapt and reconfigure the notion of hegemonic masculinity when we articulate it with the empirical data we produce. Alternatively, when researching homophobia in an African context, we should not assume that we know what homophobia means beforehand but rather be open to having the meaning of homophobia modified when articulated with our empirical findings.

Of course, we should then also be able to acknowledge the limitations of the theoretical concepts that we import into empirical settings. Maybe we also have to be prepared to acknowledge that the concepts we bring with us are sometimes not particularly productive in helping us understand more of what it is going on in a specific setting. In one way, this is also how the book's last chapter can be read— as an explicit questioning of whether the concept of masculinity is still helping us understand the production of masculine subjectivities, or indeed gender relations more broadly. When we end up in circular arguments suggesting that what men do is masculinity because it is men that do it, and then position this masculinity as the cause of men's action, this might just suggest that the notion of masculinity is not helping us understand more than what we already knew beforehand (Holter, 2009).

As we have argued throughout the book, rather than clinging on to reified, monolithic and universalised notions of the four 'Hs', what is needed is greater precision, fewer assumptions and a greater sensitivity to local contexts. Picking up on the notion of masculinity as assemblage from the last chapter, we could then think of the four 'Hs' as often involved in assembling masculinity, but none of them as necessarily present, and no specific configuration of them (in relation to each other) given in advance. In this way we can, hopefully, avoid having complex and contradictory empirical findings 'crushed' under the pressure of heavy prefigured theoretical concepts. This is not to suggest, however, that we should all engage in purely data-driven, inductive research. Of course, theoretical concepts still need to guide our attention, but, in having done so, we should also let the complexities and particularities of the settings we investigate speak back to the concepts we bring to the analysis, and be generous enough to also allow our theoretical concepts be modified and reconfigured. At the heart of the interest in gendered notions of masculinity lies the idea that it is actually possible to change the way that men become men.

Throughout the book, when trying to define and understand men's behaviours and practices, we have adopted a range of strategies. One of those strategies has been to revise the concepts that are used to explain men and masculinity. We have done this through the four 'H' concepts, and, at the same time, we have sought to undermine the conundrum by deconstructing men's behaviour and the concept of men and masculinity. We have also recognised that there may be, across the world, a number of conundrums. It has become clear whilst writing this book that understanding how we make sense of men and masculinity through the notion of the conundrum might itself be limiting, and, by framing our arguments in the process of identifying a conundrum, we are immediately constrained and limited by how this is resolved. In conclusion, we understand the confusion and puzzlement that is associated with men and their practices as part of ongoing approaches to try to explore and understand what being a man means. Thus, by thinking through and holding onto a conundrum of masculinity, we continue to pursue greater knowledge and understanding about what it means to be a man.

References

Anderson, E. and McGuire, R. (2010) Inclusive masculinity theory and the gendered politics of men's rugby. *Journal of Gender Studies*, 19(3), 249–261.

Berggren, K. (2012) 'No homo': Straight inoculations and the queering of masculinity in Swedish hip hop. *NORMA—Nordic Journal for Masculinity Studies*, 7(1), 50–66.

Berggren, K. (2014) Sticky masculinity: Post-structuralism, phenomenology and subjectivity in critical studies on men. *Men and Masculinities*, 17(3), 231–252.

Glynos, J. and Howarth, D. (2007) *Logics of Critical Explanation in Social and Political Theory*. London: Routledge.

Halberstam, J. (1998) *Female Masculinity*. London: Duke University Press.

Hall, S. (1986) On postmodernism and articulation: An interview with Stuart Hall. *Journal of Communication Inquiry*, 10(2), 45–60.

Holter, Ø.G. (2009) Power and structure in studies of men and masculinities. *Norma, Nordisk tidskrift for maskulinitetsstudier*, 4(2), 132–150.

Laclau, E. and Mouffe, C. (1985/2001) *Hegemony and Socialist Strategy*. London: Verso.

Index

Printed in Great Britain
by Amazon

70417580R00095

The income approach to property valuation

THOMSON

The Income Approach to Property Valuation

Copyright © 1979, 1981 and 1989 Andrew Baum and David Mackmin

The Thomson logo is a registered trademark used herein under licence.

For more information, contact Thomson Learning, High Holborn House, 50-51 Bedford Row, London WC1R 4LR or visit us on the World Wide Web at: http://www.thomsonlearning.co.uk

British Library Cataloguing-in-Publication Data
A catalogue record for this book is available from the British Library

ISBN 1-86152-501-X

First edition 1979
Second edition 1981
Reprinted with corrections 1986
Reprinted 1987
Third edition 1989
This edition 1997
Reprinted 1998
Reprinted 2000 and 2002 by Thomson Learning

Printed in Croatia by ZRINSKI d.d.

The income approach to property valuation

Andrew Baum
David Mackmin
Nick Nunnington

THOMSON

Australia • Canada • Mexico • Singapore • Spain • United Kingdom • United States

Dear Mary,

I'm afraid that the publisher has said that this book has gone out of print.

Get your friend to try to find it second-hand.

Yours

Liam Donnell

www.abebooks.co.uk

HODGES FIGGIS
THE BOOKSTORE

56-58 Dawson Street
Dublin 2

Telephone (01) 677 4754
Facsimile (01) 679 2810
EMAIL   books@hodgesfiggis.ie

A Division of Waterstone's Booksellers Ireland Limited.
Company Registered No. 362624
Registered at 6 Fitzwilliam Square, Dublin 2.
VAT No: IE 6382624D

Contents

Preface to Fourth Edition

The first edition of this book was published in 1979. At that time we suggested that a lack of basic mathematical ability often prevented valuers from understanding modern or alternative approaches to valuation and, whilst not deriding the traditional market methods used by previous generations, we hoped that after reading this book trainees, the newly qualified and seasoned valuers would be in a better position to understand the alternative approaches to property valuation.

Over the intervening 15 years Baum and Mackmin has become a recommended text on a number of courses in the UK. The revisions to this edition, whilst reflecting changes in legislation and in the marketplace, are designed to assist the student rather than the practitioner.

Much has changed since the first edition and yet in many respects the basic methodology of the subject remains unaltered. The valuation methodology set out in the first edition is now taught as standard on most University courses, mathematical weaknesses have been overcome through the development of low-cost financial calculators, spreadsheets such as Lotus and Excel, and simple software packages for PC operation. The concepts remain, for some, problematic and in this edition revisions have been made to style and content to help those new to the subject to understand more readily the concepts underlying the valuation of real property.

In the first edition we argued the case for the use of discounted cash flow. Since then we have noted a growing international acceptance of DCF for property valuation. The UK, with its longer brokerage activity in the property investment market, still relies on conventional income capitalisation models. However, we sense a change of emphasis with the growth of Information Technology (IT) facilities and the strengthening of the economic analysis that now must underpin property valuations. The next edition may well treat the whole subject from a DCF perspective.

Education practice has also changed with the growth of IT which is reflected in this edition through the development of simple spreadsheets for use by student readers.

A more detailed critique of the income approach is contained in the Routledge sister publication Property Investment Appraisal by Baum and Crosby to which readers are referred.

During the course of these revisions the RICS published the Appraisal and Valuation Manual, the new red book. This has introduced new mandatory requirements for valuers and this edition has been revised in the context of these changes.

As in the third edition we have left many examples unadjusted for inflation as they are designed to illustrate points of principle rather than to reflect current market values.

Anyone who gives professional advice or makes an investment decision based on any part of this book does so entirely at his or her risk. It should not be presumed that the book represents the views of the Department of Land Management at the University of Reading or those of the School of Urban & Regional Studies at Sheffield Hallam University, and (needless to say) the responsibility for any error or ommission rests entirely with the authors.

Finally, we have taken this oportunity to integrate the study companion so that students now have the opportunity to measure their own learning and understanding.

David Mackmin, Nick Nunnington, Sheffield 1997.

Acknowledgements

We continue to thank Peter Byrne and David Jenkins who helped and encouraged us with the first edition. In this edition our thanks are due to RICS Business Services Ltd for permission to reproduce various extracts from the RICS Appraisal and Valuation Manual. To Circle Systems for permission to make use of their software in the preparation of Chapter 11 and Appendix C. In previous editions this chapter was prepared using software from Kel Computing which we equally commend to valuers. In Appendix B we include material originally provided by Gooch and Wagstaff but acknowledge that the style and contents of investment purchase reports have changed and are continuing to change.

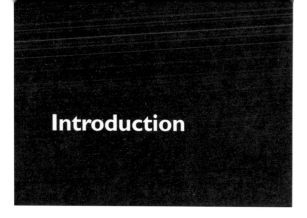

Introduction

Cairncross in his *Introduction to Economics* expresses his view that 'economics is really not so much about money as about some things which are implied in the use of money. Three of these-exchange, scarcity and choice-are of special importance.' Legal interests in land and buildings, which for our purposes will be known as property, are exchanged for money and are scarce resources. Those fortunates with surplus money have to make a choice between its alternative uses; if they choose to buy property they will have rejected the purchase of many other goods and services and will then have to make a choice between different properties.

Valuation is the vocational discipline within economics that attempts to aid that choice in terms of the value of property: that is, value within the framework of the specialised market that has evolved for the exchange of property rights, as well as value to a particular person or institution with known objectives, currently referred to as an appraisal or assessment of worth.

Property is purchased for use and occupation or as an investment; but in both cases the purchaser measures the expected returns or benefits to be received from the property against the cost outlay. The valuer's task is to express these benefits in money terms and to interpret the relationship between costs and benefits as a rate of return, thus allowing the investor to make a choice between alternatives.

Since 1945 the property and construction industries have grown in importance and property has been indiscriminately considered to be a 'safe' investment. The growth in pension schemes, life funds, property unit trusts and the like has completed the transition of the property market into a multi-million pound industry. As a result there has been a growth in demand for property to be valued and revalued for investors and for portfolio and asset valuation purposes.

Property as an investment is different to other forms of investment. The most obvious difference is its fixed location geographically and hence the importance of the quality of that location for the land's current or alternative uses as determined by its general and special accessibility and its interrelationship with other competing and complementary buildings, locations and land uses. Once developed, the quality of the investment is influenced by the quality of the permitted planning use and the quality of the physical improvements (buildings) on the site. In addition and essential to the assessment of exchange value is the quality of the legal title-is it freehold or leasehold? The owner of a freehold title effectively owns all the land described in the title deeds in perpetuity, including everything below it to the centre of the earth and everything above. Freehold rights may be restricted by covenants in the title and/or by the rights of others such as rights of way. A leaseholder's rights are limited in time, the length of the lease, and by the terms and conditions (covenants) agreed between landlord and tenant and written into the lease or implied or imposed by law or statute.

To be competent the valuer must be aware of all the factors and forces that make a market and are interpreted by buyers, sellers and market makers in their assessment of market price. In an active market where many similar properties with similar characteristics and qualities are being exchanged, a valuer will, with experience, be able to measure exchange value by comparing that which is to be valued with that which has just been sold. This direct or comparative method of valuation is used almost exclusively for the valuation of vacant possession freehold residential property. Differences in age, condition, accommodation and location can all, within reason, be reflected by the valuer in the assessment of value. Differences in size can sometimes be overcome by adopting a unit of comparison such as price per hectare or rent per square metre.

The more problematic properties are those for which there is no ready market; those which display special or unique characteristics; those which do not fully utilise the potential of their location and are therefore ripe for development, redevelopment or refurbishment; those that are tenanted and are sold as investments at prices reflecting their income generating potential; and leasehold properties.

For each of these broad categories valuers have developed methods of valuation that they feel most accurately reflect the market's behavioural attitude and which may therefore be considered to be rational methods.

In the case of special properties such as oil refineries, glassworks, hospitals and schools the usual valuation method is the cost or contractor's method. It is the valuer's method of last resort and is based on the supposition that no purchaser would pay more for an existing property than the sum of the cost of buying a similar site and constructing a similar building with similar utility written down to reflect the physical, functional and locational obsolescence of the actual building.

Properties with latent development value are valued using the residual or development (developer's) method. The logic here is that the value of the property (site) in its current state must equal the value of the property in its developed or redeveloped state less all the costs of development including profit but excluding the land. In those cases where the residual sum exceeds the existing use value then in theory the property will be released for that higher and better use.

All property that is income producing or is capable of producing an income in the form of rent, and for which there is both an active tenant market and an active investment market, will be valued by the market's indirect method of comparison. This is known as the investment method of valuation or the income approach to property valuation and is the principal method considered in this book.

The income approach and the income-based residual warrant special attention if only because they are the valuer's main weapon in the valuation of the most complex and highly priced investment properties.

The unique characteristics of property make property investment valuation more complex an art and science than that exercised by brokers and market makers in the market for stocks and shares. As stocks, shares and property are the main investments available there is bound to be some similarity between the pricing (valuation) methods used in the various markets and some relationship between the investment opportunities offered by each. A basic market measure is the investment yield or rate of return. The assessment of the rate of return allows or permits comparison to be made of investments within each market and between different investments in different markets. There is a complex interrelationship of yields and patterns of yields within the whole investment market, and in turn these yields are the key to pricing or valuation methods. Understanding market relationships and methods can only follow from an understanding of investment arithmetic.

Part One of this book therefore considers the basic investment arithmetic used by valuers. Part Two applies that knowledge to the valuation of income-producing property. Part Three considers some of the techniques used in the field of risk analysis. Throughout it is assumed that the reader has some knowledge of who buys property, why they buy it and what alternative investment opportunities there are, and also that he or she will have some knowledge of the nature of property as an investment. The reader should have some awareness of the social, economic and political factors that influence the market for and the value of the property.

Our purpose in writing this book has been aptly summarised, coincidentally, by Robert Chartham in *Sex Manners for Advanced Lovers*, which we misquote with apologies:

'What we are trying to aim at is to put forward suggestions of techniques which may not have occurred to some who have already transformed themselves into highly proficient (seasoned) valuers, in the hope that they will be encouraged to try them out to discover for themselves whether or not they are of any help to them, their partners or their clients.'

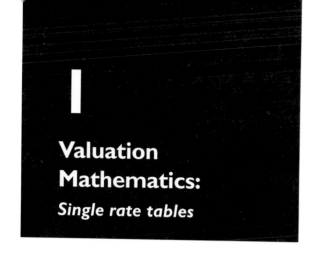

Valuation Mathematics:
Single rate tables

This book explores the function of property valuation with particular reference to property which is bought or sold as an investment. In order to be able to value an investment property a valuer must understand how the benefits to be enjoyed from the ownership of a freehold or leasehold interest in land can be expressed in terms of present worth.

To do this a valuer must have a working knowledge of the mathematics of finance and the theory of compounding and discounting future streams of income.

The basic concepts of financial mathematics examined in this chapter are defined below:

The six functions of £1

The amount of £1 (A) *another name for compound interest; that is, the future worth of £1 invested today allowing for compound interest at a given rate.*

The amount of £1 per annum (A £1 p.a.) *that is, the future worth of £1 invested at the end of each year accruing compound interest at a given rate.*

The annual sinking fund (ASF) *that is, the fraction of £1 which must be invested at regular intervals to produce £1 at a given point in the future with compound interest accruing at a given rate.*

The present value of £1 (PV) *that is, the present worth of £1 to be received in the future, discounted over a given period at a given rate of interest.*

The present value of £1 per annum (YP) *that is, the present worth of a series of payments of £1 due annually for a given period of time, discounted at a given rate of interest. This function is also known by valuer's as the years' purchase single rate.*

The annuity £1 will purchase *that is, the amount of money that will be paid back at the end of each year for a given number of years and at a given interest rate in return for £1 invested.*

The first chapter explores the mathematics behind these six functions and illustrates their application in the practice of property valuation.

Underlying assumptions and terminology

In this first section which deals with valuation mathematics the following standard notation is adopted:

i	=	interest, expressed as a decimal.
		i.e. $5\% = 5/100 = 0.05$
n	=	number of time periods, usually years.

There are several published valuation tables available which show the value of these and other functions for a range of interest rates and years. Some of these tables compute income as being received or invested quarterly as with many actual investments. However, in order to simplify this introductory chapter it is assumed that income is received or invested at the beginning or end of each year in one instalment.

It is also assumed that the tables work from the basis that the unit of money is always £1.

The amount of £1

The amount of £1 is simply another term for the familiar concept of compound interest. Consider the building society passbook set out below where the interest rate for deposits is at 10% per annum.

Date	Description	Receipts	Withdrawals	Balance
00 01JAN94	CASH 100.00		100.00	
01 31DEC94	INTEREST	10.00		110.00
02 31DEC95	INTEREST	11.00		121.00
03 31DEC96	INTEREST	12.10		133.10
04 31DEC97	INTEREST	13.31		146.41

As can be seen from the above the interest accumulates on both the original £100 invested and also on the interest added to it.

The formula to express this is therefore that if **£1** is invested for 1 year at i interest, at the end of that year it will have accumulated to $(1 + i)$.

At the end of the second year $(1 + i)$ will have earned interest at i; so at the end of the second year it will have accumulated to :

$(1 + i) + i(1 + i)$ which can be expressed as

$(1 + i)^2$

At the end of n years the accumulated sum will be

$(1 + i)^n$

where n is the number of years or other time period of accumulation.

Remember that interest is expressed as a decimal (i) or (r), e.g. 10% = 10 divided by 100 = 0.10

Example 1.1

Calculate the amount of £1 after 4 years at 10%.

$A = (1+i)^n$ $i = 0.10 ; n = 4$

$A = (1.1)^4$

   $= (1.1) \times (1.1) \times (1.1) \times (1.1)$

   $= 1.4641$

The calculation shows that £1 will accumulate to £1.47 after 4 years at 10% compound interest rate. Notice that if you multiply the figure produced by the formula in example 1 by 100, to show how £100 will accumulate, the figures accord with the building society passbook.

The amount of £1 per annum

This function is used to calculate the final value, with compound interest, of a series of payments made at regular intervals. Many investments follow this pattern. Consider for example another building society passbook set out below where this time the investor deposits £100 at the end of each year and interest is added at 10% per annum.

Date	Description	Receipts	Withdrawals	Balance
00 31DEC93	CASH 100.00		100.00	
01 31DEC94	INTEREST	10.00		110.00
02 31DEC94	CASH 100.00		210.00	
03 31DEC95	INTEREST	21.00		231.00
04 31DEC95	CASH 100.00		331.00	
05 31DEC96	INTEREST	33.10		364.10
06 31DEC96	CASH 100.00		464.10	
07 31DEC97	INTEREST	46.41		510.51
08 31DEC97	CASH 100.00		610.51	

The amount of £1 per annum table deals with this type of investment pattern. It shows the amount to which **£1**, invested at the end of each year, will accumulate at i interest after n years.

The table is simply a summation of a series of amounts of £1. If each £1 is invested at the end of the year, the nth £1 will be invested at the end of the nth year and will thus earn no interest whatsoever.
(Refer back to the building society passbook.)
Each preceding £1 will earn interest for an increasing number of years :

the $(n-1)$£1 will have accumulated for 1 year, and will be worth $(1+i)$;

the $(n-2)$£1 will have accumulated for two years, and will be worth $(1+i)^2$;

the first £1 invested at the end of the first year will be worth $(1+i)^{n-1}$.

This series of calculations when added together is expressed as :

$$1 + (1 + i) + (1 + i)^2 \ldots (1 + i)^{n-1}$$

This is a geometric progression and when summed it can be expressed as :

$$\frac{(1 + i)^n - 1}{i} = \text{formula for the amount of £1 per annum. (A £1 p.a.)}$$

Example 1.2

Calculate the amount of £1 per annum for 5 years at 10%.

$$A\ £1\ p.a. = \frac{(1+i)^n - 1}{i} \qquad i = 0.10\ ;\ n = 5$$

$$A\ £1\ p.a. = \frac{(1.10)^5 - 1}{i} = \frac{1.61051 - 1}{0.10}$$

$$= \frac{0.61051}{0.10} = 6.1051$$

Again note that by multiplying this figure by 100 to calculate the sum that £100 invested at the end of each year will accumulate produces the same figure as in the Building Society Passbook.

Example 1.3

If Mr A invests £60 in a building society at the end of each year, and at the end of 20 years has £4,323, at what rate of interest has this accumulated ?

Annual sum invested	£60
A £1 p.a. for 20 years @ i %	x
Capital Value (CV) of Investment at end of 20 years	£4,323

$$x = \frac{£4,323}{£60} = 72.05$$

If the reader refers to any of the published amount of £1 p.a. tables, it will be seen that 72.05 is the value for 20 years at 12%. This is the rate of compound interest at which this regular investment has accumulated.

Annual sinking fund

Property investors will often be required at some time in the future to meet a known expense. This may be some form of maintenance; for example, a building may require a new roof or service roads may require resurfacing.

Such obligations may be passed on to the tenant in the form of service charges, payable in addition to rent, which include the provision of a fund to be used for major works in the future. However, in some cases the landlord may be responsible for major repairs which cannot be recovered from the tenant. Such obligations should be reflected in the purchase price of the investment. In both scenarios a mechanism is required to estimate the magnitude and timing of the expense.

The investor could invest a lump sum immediately which with the accumulation of interest is designed to meet the estimated outlay when it arises. It may however be more effective to regularly set aside part of the income received from the investment (i.e. rent) in an account known as a sinking fund, which is planned to accumulate to the required sum when the expenditure is required.

Note that this situation is similar to the amount of £1 p.a. described above. As Example 1.4 demonstrates' the amount of £1 p.a. tables can be used to calculate the sum required to be set aside in a sinking fund to meet a known future expense.

Example 1.4

An investor is considering the purchase of a small shop in which the window frames have begun to rot. It is estimated that in 4 years' time they will require complete replacement at a cost of £1,850. The shop produces a net income of £7,500 p.a.

How much of this income should be set aside each year to meet the expense assuming the money is invested with a guaranteed fixed return of 7% per annum ?

Amount to be set aside	x
A £1 p.a. for 4 years @ 7 %	4.44
Cost	£1,850

$$£1,850 = 4.44x$$
$$x = £416.67\ p.a.$$

This annual sum is the sinking fund, or ASF

The use of annual sinking fund tables enables this sum to be calculated more easily.

Sum required	**£1,850**
ASF to replace £1 in 4 years @ 7%	**0.22523**
ASF	**£416.67 p.a.**

It can be seen that this calculation performs the function of the amount of £1 p.a. in reverse. In Example 1.4 the amount to be set aside was found by dividing the capital sum required by the amount of £1 p.a.

In the above, the annual sum was found by the product of the sum required and the ASF.

Therefore the ASF table is the reciprocal of the amount of £1 p.a.:

$$A \text{ £1 p.a.} = \frac{(1 + i)^n - 1}{i}$$

the amount of £1 (A) $= (1 + i)^n$

Therefore : $A \text{ £1 p.a.} = \frac{A - 1}{i}$

$$\text{ASF} = \frac{i}{(1 + i)^n - 1} = \frac{i}{A - 1}$$

Example 1.5

Calculate the ASF to accumulate to £1 after 5 years @ 10%

$$\text{ASF} = \frac{i}{(1 + i)^n - 1} = \frac{0.10}{(1.10)^5 - 1}$$

$$= \frac{0.10}{1.61051 - 1} = 0.1638$$

The present value of £1

The first three functions of £1 have shown how any sum invested today will be worth more than the same sum receivable at some future date due to the accumulation of compound interest. Therefore £1 receivable in the future cannot be worth the same as £1 at the present time. What it is worth will be the sum that could be invested now to accumulate to £1 at a given future date. This sum will obviously depend upon the time it is invested and the rate of interest it attracts.

If £1 were invested now at a rate of interest i for n years, then at the end of the period it would be worth $(1 + i)^n$.

If £x were to be invested now at i for n years and assuming it will accumulate to £1 :

Then $x(1 + i)^n = £1$

and $x = \frac{1}{(1 + i)^n}$

This is the formula for the present value of £1 (PV), and it is the reciprocal of the amount of £1

$$\text{PV} = \frac{1}{(1 + i)^n} = \frac{1}{A}$$

Proof :

PV £1 in 7 years @ 10%	=	**0.51316**
A £1 in 7 years @ 10%	=	**1.9487**
0.51316 x 1.9487	=	**1.00**

Example 1.6

If Mr. X requires a rate of return of 10%, how much would you advise him to pay for the right to receive £200 in 5 years' time ?

$$\text{PV} = \frac{1}{(1 + i)^n} = \frac{1}{(1.10)^5} = \frac{1}{1.6105}$$

$$= 0.6209 \text{ x £200} = \underline{£124.18}$$

i.e. £124.18 invested now at 10% per annum would accumulate with compound interest to £200 in 5 years' time.

The present value of £1 per annum

The amount of £1 p.a. was seen to be the summation of a series of amounts of £1. Similarly, the present value of £1 per annum is the summation of a series of present values of £1. It is the present value of the right to receive £1 at the end of each year for n years at i.

The present value of £1 receivable in one year is :

$$\frac{1}{(1+i)}$$

in two years it is :

$$\frac{1}{(1+i)^2}$$ and so the series reads :

$$\frac{1}{(1+i)} + \frac{1}{(1+i)^2} + \frac{1}{(1+i)^3} \cdots \frac{1}{(1+i)^n}$$

This is a further geometric progression which when summated can be expressed as :

$$\frac{1 - \frac{1}{(1+i)^n}}{i}$$ = the formula for PV £1 p.a.

As $$\frac{1}{(1+i)^n}$$ = PV

the PV £1 p.a. can be simplified to : $\frac{1 - PV}{i}$

Example 1.7

Calculate the present value of £1 per annum @ 5% for 20 years given that the present value of £1 in 20 years @ 5% is 0.3769

$$PV £1 p.a. = \frac{1 - PV}{i}$$

$$= \frac{1 - 0.3769}{0.05} = \frac{0.6231}{0.05}$$

$$= 12.462$$

Example 1.8

How much should A pay for the right to receive an income of £675 for 64 years if he/she requires a 12% return ?

Income	**£675**
PV £1 p.a. for 64 years @ 12 %	8.3274
Capital Value (CV)	**£5,621**

The present value of £1 p.a. is usually referred to by U.K. property valuers as the 'years' purchase'. The *Oxford English Dictionary* gives a date of 1584 for the first use of this phrase '*at so many years' purchase*' used in stating the price of land in relation to the annual rent in perpetuity. This term is sometimes confusing as it does not relate to the other terms. However, the terms are interchangeable and both will be used.

Obviously the PV £1 p.a. will increase each year to reflect the additional receipt of £1. However as this receipt is discounted into the future it will be worth less following the present value rule established above. The PV £1 p.a. in fact approaches a maximum value at infinity. However, as the example below shows, in fact the increase in PV £1 p.a. becomes very small after 60 years and is assumed to reach its maximum value after 100 years. In valuation terminology this is referred to as 'perpetuity'.

Example 1.9

In the formula $\frac{1 - PV}{i}$ what happens to PV as the time period increases?

What effect does this have on the YP figure ?

Table 1.1

Years	PV @ 10%	PV £1 p.a.@ 10%
10	0.3855	6.1446
20	0.1486	8.5136
30	0.0573	9.4269
40	0.0221	9.7791
50	0.0085	9.9148
75	0.00078	9.9921
100	0.00007	9.9993

From Table 1.1 two facts are clear ; the PV decreases over time and the YP (PV £1 p.a.) increases over time.

As **n** approaches perpetuity, notice that the PV tends towards 0 ; the present value of £1 such a long time in the future is reduced to virtually nothing.

Therefore if PV tends to 0 at perpetuity and

$$YP = \frac{1 - PV}{i}$$

YP at perpetuity will tend to : $\dfrac{1 - 0}{i}$

The formula for YP in perpetuity (YP perp) is therefore :

$$\frac{1}{i}$$

at a rate of 10% the YP perp $= \dfrac{1}{0.10} = \dfrac{10}{}$

Example 1.10

A freehold property produces a net income of £1,500 p.a. If an investor requires a return of 8%, what price should be paid? The income is perpetual: a YP in perpetuity should be used.

Income	£1,500	
YP perp @ 8%	12.5	$\left(\dfrac{1}{1.08} = 12.5\right)$
Capital Value	£18,750	

A further common valuation application of the present value of £1 p.a. is known as 'the years' purchase of a reversion to a perpetuity'. It shows the present value of the right to receive a perpetual income starting immediately (YP in perpetuity) and then defers that value (using the present value of £1) at the same rate of interest. It is useful to property valuers as often property will be assumed to revert to a perpetual higher income after an initial period, following a rent review.

 The years' purchase of a reversion to perpetuity table combines two functions :

it calculates the present value of a right to receive a perpetual income starting immediately (YP in perpetuity) and then defers that value (present value of £1)

at the same rate of interest.

YP rev. perp. = YP in perp. x PV £1

$$= \frac{1}{i} \ \text{x} \ \frac{1}{(1+i)^n}$$

$$= \frac{1}{iA}$$

Example 1.11

Calculate in two ways the present value of a perpetual income of £600 p.a. beginning in 7 years' time using a discount rate of 12%

Income	£600
YP perp. @ 12 %	8.33
Capital Value(CV)	£5,000
PV £1 in 7 years @ 12%	0.45235
CV	£2,262

or :

$$YP \ rev. \ perp. = \frac{1}{iA} = \frac{1}{i(1+i)^7} = \frac{1}{0.12(1.12)^7}$$

$$= \frac{1}{0.12(2.2107)} = \frac{1}{0.265284}$$

$$= 3.7695$$

Income	£600
YP rev. perp in 7 years @ 12%	3.7695
CV	£2,262

Note : the answer can also be found by deducting the YP for 7 years @ 12% from the YP in perpetuity @12%.

The use of this present value or discounting technique to assess the price to be paid for an investment or the value of an income-producing property ensures the correct relationship between future benefits and present worth; namely that the investor will obtain both a return on capital and a return of capital at the target rate or market-derived rate of interest used in the calculation.

This last point is important and can be missed when PV factors are summated to produce the PV of £1 p.a. and when this is renamed by valuers as the 'years' purchase'!

Example 1.12

An investor is offered five separate investment opportunities on five separate occasions of £10,000 in a year's time, £10,000 in 2 years' time, £10,000 in 4 years' time and £10,000 in 5 years' time, and seeks a return on each occasion of 10%.

What are the prices that should be offered for each investment :

| | Returns due in | | | | |
	1 year	2 years	3 years	4 years	5 years
	£10,000	£10,000	£10,000	£10,000	£10,000
PV £1 @ 10%	0.9090	0.8264	0.7513	0.6830	0.6209
	£9,090	£8,264	£7,513	£6,830	£6,209
A £1 @ 10%	1.1000	1.2100	1.3310	1.4641	1.6105
	£10,000	£10,000	£10,000	£10,000	£10,000

The answers of £9,090, £8,264, £7,513, £6,830, £6,209 show the prices that reflect the present worth of the investment today. The prices equate to the sum of money which if saved would have accumulated to £10,000 at the specified rate of interest at the appropriate period.

In other words in each case the investor is exchanging a sum of money today for a known future sum which will be equal to the sum of money today plus the interest forgone if the capital had been invested elsewhere at the same rate of interest.

Therefore, in each case the return on capital at 10% has been achieved and the initial capital has been returned.

Example 1.13

If the investor is offered all of the five investments in example 1.12 (i.e. an income for 5 years of £10,000), what should the investor pay now ?

The answer can be found by adding the individual discounted or present worth figures :

£9,090 + £8,264 + £7,513 + £6,830 + £6,209 = £37,908.

This can be calculated more directly by multiplying £10,000 by the PV £1 p.a. for 5 years @ 10%
(£10,000 x 3.7908 = £37,908)

Again the investor must achieve a return of capital, (the initial £37,908) and a return of 10% on the capital (that is the interest forgone). The proof is shown in the table below :

Year	Capital outstanding	Return @ 10%	Income	Return of Capital (Balance)
1	37,908.00	3,790.80	10,000	6,209.20
2	31,698.80	3,169.88	10,000	6,830.12
3	24,868.68	2,486.87	10,000	7,513.13
4	17,355.55	1,735.55	10,000	8,264.45
5	9,091.10	909.11	10,000	9,090.89

Note: rounding errors due to calculation to 2 decimal places only

Annuity £1 will purchase

This function shows the amount that will be paid back at the end of each year for n years at i, in return for £1 invested. It calculates what is known as the annuity that £1 will purchase.

An annuity entitles the investor to a series of equal annual sums. These sums may be perpetual or for a limited number of years.

When money is invested in a building society, interest accumulates on the principal which remains in the account. When an annuity is purchased, however, the initial purchase price is lost forever to the investor. The return from building society accounts is all annual interest on capital. The return from an annuity represents partly interest on capital but also partly the purchase price being returned bit by bit to the investor.

These constituent parts will be referred to as :

return on capital (interest) and ;

return of capital.

In an annuity the original capital outlay must be returned by the end of the investment. If not, how could the rate of interest earned by an annuity investment be compared with the rate of interest earned in a building society account?

The amount of an annuity will depend upon three factors : the purchase price, i and n.

Example 1.14

What annuity will £50 purchase for 5 years if a 10% yield is required?

Purchase sum	£50
Annuity £1 w.p. for 5 years @10%	0.2638
	———
Annuity	**£13.19**

The £13.19 has two constituent parts. The return **on** capital is 10% of the outlay, i.e. £5 p.a. This leaves £8.19 extra. This is the return **of** capital. But 5 x £8.19 does not return £50 because each payment is in the nature of a sinking fund which needs to be invested to attract compound interest (in this case 10%).

Proof :

ASF	£8.19
A £1 p.a. for 5 years @ 10%	6.1051
	———
CV	£50

Example 1.14 shows that the return **on** capital and return **of** capital are both achieved, as a sinking fund is inherent in the annuity.

Note :

Return **on** capital = i
Return **of** capital = **SF**

The formula for the annuity £1 w.p. is thus $i + SF$, where i is the rate of interest required and **SF** is the annual sinking fund required to replace the capital outlay in n years at i.

Example 1.15

Calculate the annuity £1 will purchase for 10 years @ 10%, if £6.1446 will purchase £1 at the end of each year for 10 years.

$$\text{£1 will purchase} \quad \frac{1}{6.1466} \quad = \quad \text{£0.1627}$$

Therefore the annuity £1 will purchase for 10 years @ 10% is £0.1627.

The annuity factor can also be calculated from the formula $i + SF$. As the sinking fund factor is the annual factor of £1 needed to build the return **of** capital, this is known technically as to amortise £1, so the total partial payment required for recovery of capital and for interest on capital must be the amortisation factor plus the interest rate.

Therefore the annuity £1 will purchase for 10 years at 10% is:

	$i = 0.1000$
plus the ASF to replace £1 in	
10 years @ 10%	$= 0.0627$
	———
	£0.1627

Many people interpret annuity to mean a life annuity, a policy issued by a life assurance company where the investor will receive for the rest of his/her life a given annual income in exchange for a given capital sum. The calculations undertaken by the life offices' actuaries have to take into account many factors - including life expectancy, which is determined by lifestyle. This is beyond the scope of this book, which is concerned with annuities related to property where the period of time the annuity will be paid is certain. However, before proceeding with more in-depth analysis of annuities there are a number of common terms which should be explained.

Annuity terminology

In arrears: This means that the first annual sum will be paid (received) 12 months after the purchase or taking out of the policy. The payments could be weekly, monthly, quarterly or for any period provided they are in arrears.

In advance: This means that the payments are made at the beginning of the week, month, year, etc.

An immediate annuity: The word 'immediate' is used to distinguish a normal annuity from a *deferred* annuity. An immediate annuity is one where the income commences immediately either 'in advance' or 'in arrears', whereas in the case of a deferred annuity capital is exchanged today for an annuity 'in advance' or 'in arrears', the first such payment being deferred for a given period of time longer than a year. In assurance terms one might purchase at the age of 50 a life annuity to begin at the age of 65. This would be a deferred annuity.

The majority of annuity tables are based on an 'in arrears' assumption.

The distinction between *'return on'* and *'return of'* capital is important in the case of life annuities because the capital element is held by the Inland Revenue to be the return of the annuitant's capital and therefore is exempt from income tax. In practice the Inland Revenue have had to indicate how the distinction is to be made. Quite clearly a precise distinction is not otherwise possible because of the uncertain nature of the annuitant's life.

The distinction in the case of certain property valuations undertaken on an annuity basis is important, because the Inland Revenue are not allowed to distinguish between 'return on' and 'return of' capital other than for life annuities. Thus tax may be payable on the whole income from the property and the desired return may not be achieved unless this factor is accounted for in the valuation.

Example 1.16a

What annuity will £4,918 purchase over 6 years at 6%?

	£4,918
Annuity £1 w.p. for 6 years @ 6%	0.2033
	£10,000 p.a.

Example 1.16b

What annuity will £1,000 purchase over 3 years at 10%?

	£1,000
Annuity £1 w.p. for 3 years @ 10%	0.4020
	£402 p.a.

Prove that the investor recovers his capital in full and earns interest from year to year at 10%.

Year	Capital outstanding	Interest @ 10%	Income	Return of capital
1	1,000		100	402	302
2	698	(1,000– 302)	69.80	402	332.20
3	365.80	(698 – 332.20)	36.58	402	365.42
		206.38	1206	999.62 *

* Error of 0.38 due to rounding

Example 1.17

What sum would have to be paid today to acquire an annuity of £1,000 for 6 years in arrears at 8% to begin in 2 years' time?

The 'in arrears' assumption means that the first £1,000 will be paid in 36 months' time.

0	0	0	1,000	1,000	1,000	1,000	1,000	1,000	£
Now	1	2	3	4	5	6	7	8	years

Annuity income	**£1,000**
PV £1 p.a. for 6 years @ 8%	4.622
Cost of immediate annuity	**£4,622**
Defer 2 years x PV £1 in 2* years @ 8%	0.857
	£3,961

* the PV table assumes payment in arrears

An annuity may be payable in advance.

This should cause no difficulty as the **PV of £1 p.a.** payable in advance at rate *i* for *n* periods is simply £1 plus the **PV of £1** per period, payable in arrears at rate *i* for (*n* - 1) periods.

Alternatively one can multiply the **PV £1 p.a.** in arrears for *n* periods by the factor (**1 + i**), *(see pp. 24 - 25)*.

Example 1.18

Calculate the capital cost of an annuity of £500 for 6 years due in advance @ 10%.

" in advance"

£500	£500	£500	£500	£500	£500
£500	£500	£500	£500	£500	£500

" in arrears"

Annuity income		**£500**
PV £1 p.a. for 5 years (*n*-1) @ 10%	3.79	
plus	1.00	4.79
		£2,395

or

		£500
PV £1 p.a. for 6 years @ 10%	4.3553	
x	1.1	4.79
		£2,395

9

Example 1.18 (cont.)

or £500 in advance for 6 years is £500 in arrears for 5 years plus an immediate £500 :

PV £1 p.a. for 5 years @ 10%	£500
	3.79
	£1,895
	+£500
	£2,395

Annuities may be variable. The present worth of variable income flows could be expressed as

$$V = \frac{I_1}{PV_1} + \frac{I_2}{PV_2} + \frac{I_3}{PV_3} \cdots + \frac{I_n}{PV_n}$$

Whilst it is possible to have a variable annuity changing from year to year it is more common to find the annuity changing at fixed intervals of time.

Example 1.19

How much would it cost today to purchase an annuity of £1,000 for 5 years followed by an annuity of £1,200 for 5 years on a 10% basis ?

Immediate annuity		£1,000	
PV £1 p.a. for 5 years @ 10%		3.79	£3,790
Plus deferred annuity		£1,200	
PV £1 p.a. for 5 years @ 10%	3.79		
PV £1 for 5 years @ 10%	0.62	2.3498	£2,820
			£6,610

It will be shown later that this approach is the same as that used by valuers when valuing a variable income flow from a property investment.

In the formula i + **SF**, i will remain the same whatever the length of the annuity. But the value of each year of the annuity will reduce as time increases due to the effect of **SF**. For a perpetual annuity, **SF** will be infinitely small, and tends towards 0. A perpetual annuity therefore = i.

Example 1.20

What perpetual annuity can be bought for £1,500 if a 12% return is required ?

Invested sum	£1,500
($i = 0.12$)	
Annuity £1 w.p. @ 12% perp.	0.12
	£180 p.a.

The formula for a perpetual annuity is i;

the formula for a year's purchase in perpetuity is $\frac{1}{i}$

and is therefore the reciprocal.

	Question :
	Is this true of all YPs ?
Annuity £1 w.p. for 5 years @ 10%	= 0.2638
YP for 5 years @ 10%	= 3.7908
	$3.7908 = \frac{1}{0.2658}$

The annuity £1 will purchase is therefore the reciprocal of the present value of £1 p.a.

It would follow that a second YP formula would hold,

i.e. $\dfrac{1}{i + SF}$

as the limited term annuity formula is i + **SF.**

This is easily proved.

Annuity £1 w.p. = i + **SF:**

hence capital x (i + **SF**)	=	**Income**
now income x **YP**	=	**Capital**

Therefore $\qquad$ **YP** $= \dfrac{1}{i + SF}$

This formula will be further discussed under Dual Rate Tables (see pp. 17 - 20).

Example 1.21

How much should A pay for the right to receive £1 p.a. for 25 years at 10%?

$$YP = \frac{1}{i + SF} = \frac{1}{i + \dfrac{i}{(1+i)^n - 1}}$$

$$= \frac{1}{0.10 + \dfrac{1.10}{(1.10)^{25} - 1}}$$

$$= \frac{1}{0.10 + 0.0101651} = \underline{£9.077}$$

Check

$$YP = \frac{1-PV}{i} = \frac{1 - 0.092296}{0.10} = \underline{£9.077}$$

The function of **SF** in this **YP** formula is exactly the same as that of **PV** in the original - that is, to reduce the value of the **YP** figure as **n** decreases. The years' purchase figure must include a sinking fund element, as the valuation of an investment involves equating the outlay with the income and the required yield, so that both a return on capital and a return of capital are received.

Example 1.22

Value an income of £804.21 p.a. receivable for 3 years at a required yield of 10%. Illustrate how a return on and a return of capital are achieved.

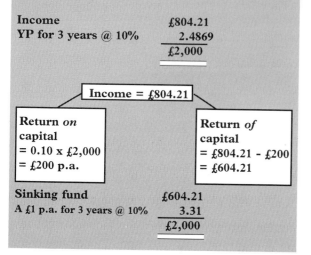

Income	£804.21
YP for 3 years @ 10%	2.4869
	£2,000

Income = £804.21

Return on capital
= 0.10 x £2,000
= £200 p.a.

Return of capital
= £804.21 - £200
= £604.21

Sinking fund	£604.21
A £1 p.a. for 3 years @ 10%	3.31
	£2,000

The return **on** and a return **of** capital can also be demonstrated by a table:

Year outstanding	Capital	Income	Interest on capital	Return of capital
1	£2,000	£804.21	£200	£604.21
2	£1,395.79	£804.21	£139.58	£664.63
3	£731.16	£804.21	£73.12	£731.09*

*Error of £0.07 due to rounding to two decimal places

A rate of return is received on outstanding capital (i.e. that capital which is at risk) only. The table assumes that some capital is returned at the end of every year so that the amount of capital outstanding reduced year by year. Interest on capital therefore decreases and more of the fixed income is available to return the capital outstanding. The last column shows how the sinking fund accumulates. **£604.21** is the first instalment: **£664.63** represents the second instalment of **£604.21** plus one year's interest at 10%. **£731.09** represents the third and final sinking fund instalment of **£604.21** plus one year's interest at 10% on **£1,268.84** (**£664.63** + **£604.21**).

The three summate to the original outlay of **£2,000.**

The above type of table is also used to show how a mortgage is repaid.

The use of single rate tables and mortgages

When a property purchaser borrows money by way of a legal mortgage it is usually agreed between the parties that the loan will be repaid in full by a given date in the future. Like anyone else lending money, the building society or mortgagee will require the capital sum to be repaid and will require interest on any outstanding amounts of the loan until such time as the loan and all interest are received. This is comparable to the purchase of an annuity certain from an assurance office. Indeed, conceptually, from the point of view of the mortgagee it is the purchase of an annuity. It follows that the mortgagee will require a return on capital and the return of capital.

The repayment mortgage allows the mortgagor (borrower) to pay back a regular sum each year, often by equal monthly instalments. Usually this sum is partly interest on capital, and partly return of capital. In the early years of the mortgage most of the payment represents interest on the loan outstanding and only a small amount of capital is repaid. But over the period of the loan, as more and more capital is repaid, the interest element becomes smaller and the capital repaid larger.

For the purpose of explanation, interest is assumed fixed throughout the term; this is becoming increasingly common in the more competitive mortgage market which has developed over recent years.

The distinction between *'return on'* and *'return of'* capital is of practical importance. Residential mortgagors may, up to certain limits, be allowed tax relief on interest paid but not on capital repaid. The distinction is even clearer in the case of the endowment mortgage, where interest is paid to the lender but capital is repaid by means of an assurance policy maturing at the end of the mortgage term. Tax relief may be allowed against the interest payments but not against the assurance premiums. The endowment mortgage tends to be cheaper (net of tax reliefs) at lower rates of interest and repayment mortgages cheaper at rates over 12% gross.

The valuer who can understand the concept of the normal repayment mortgage and can solve standard problems that face mortgagors and mortgagees should readily understand most investment valuation problems. The following examples are indicative of such mortgage problems.

Example 1.23

The sum of £10,000 has been borrowed on a repayment mortgage at 12% for 25 years.

(i) Calculate the annual repayment of interest and capital.

(ii) Calculate the amount of interest due in the first and tenth years.

(iii) Calculate the amount of capital repaid in the first and tenth years.

The formula for the annuity £1 will purchase is $i + \textbf{SF}$.

Its reciprocal, the PV £1 p.a. is $\dfrac{1}{i + \textbf{SF}}$ or $\dfrac{1 - \textbf{PV}}{i}$.

The mortgagee is effectively buying an annuity. There is in effect an exchange of £10,000 for an annual sum over 25 years at 12%. What is the annual sum?

Mortgage sum	£10,000
Annuity £1 w.p. for 25 years @ 12%	0.1275
Annual Repayment	£1,275

or £10,000 divided by PV £1 p.a. for 25 years @ 12%

$$\frac{£10,000}{7.8431} \quad = \quad £1,275$$

As interest in the first year is added immediately to capital borrowed, then:

£10,000 x 0.12 = £1,200 interest due in first year.

As the total to be paid is £1,275 so the amount of capital repaid will be £1,275 - £1,200 = £75 in the first year.

The amount of interest in the tenth year will depend upon the amount of capital outstanding at the beginning of the tenth year, i.e. after the ninth annual payment.

Although a mortgage calculation is on a single rate basis, as the formula is $i + \textbf{SF}$ one can assume that £75 p.a. is a sinking fund accumulating over 9 years at 12%.

	£75
Amount of £1 p.a. for 9 years @ 12%	14.7757
Capital repaid is	£1,108.1775

Capital outstanding is

£10,000 less £1,108 = £8,892

or **calculate the worth @ 12% of the right to receive 16 more payments of £1,275.**

	£1,275
PV £1 p.a. for 16 years @ 12 %	6.974
	£8,892

Capital outstanding is £8,892

Therefore, interest will be £8,892 x 0.12   =   £1,607

and capital repaid in year 10 is £1,275 - £1,607 = £208

In passing it may be observed that the capital repaid in year 1 plus compound interest @ 12% will amount to £208 after 9 years :

Year 1 capital	£75
Amount of £1 for 9 years @ 12 %	2.7731
Capital repaid in tenth year	£208

As interest on a mortgage is based on capital outstanding from year to year, the change in capital repaid from year to year must be at 12%.

	£75
Amount of £1 for 24 years @ 12 %	15.1786
Capital repaid in last year	£1,138

In many cases the rate of interest will change during the mortgage term. If it does, the mortgagor will usually have the choice of extending the term or repaying at a higher rate. More recently because of a high rate of interest, borrowers have borrowed on the longest possible term. Increases in the interest rate will then leave the borrower with no choice other than to increase the annual payment, as otherwise the mortgage would never be repaid.

Example 1.24

Given the figures in example 1.23 advise the borrower on the alternatives available if the interest rate goes down to 10% at the beginning of year 10.

Either: (a)   continue to pay £1,275 per annum and therefore repay the mortgage earlier

or: (b)   reduce the annual payment.

(a) No change in annual payment

Amount of capital outstanding at beginning of year 10 is (as before) £8,892.

This will be repaid at an annual rate of £1,275.

$$\frac{£8,892}{£1,275} = \text{PV } £1 \text{ p.a. for } n \text{ years @ } 10\% = 6.9739$$

Interpolation in the PV £1 p.a. tables at 10% gives *n* as between 12 and 13 years, i.e. the loan is repaid before the due date.

(b) Change in annual payment

Capital outstanding is	**£8,892**
Annuity £1 w.p. for 16 years @ 10%	**0.1278**
	£1,136

A change in interest at the beginning of year 10 means that, including the payment in year 10, there are 16 more payments due. The capital outstanding multiplied by the annuity £1 will purchase for 16 years, or divided by PV £1 p.a. for 16 years, at 10% (the new rate of interest) will give the new annual payment. This might be known as the annual equivalent of £8,892 over 16 years at 10%.

Currently tax relief on mortgage interest is available up to a mortgage ceiling of £30,000 per mortgaged property. This relief for basic tax payers is usually handled by the mortgagee under the mortgage interest relief at source scheme (MIRAS).

This chapter has explored the six single rate investment functions which form the most common basis of property valuations by the income approach and has indicated how the functions are used to assess both returns on various types of investments and borrowing by way of mortgages. The six basic functions and there associated formulae are set out below :

The amount of £1 :
used to calculate compound interest

$$A = (1 + i)^n$$

The amount of £1 per annum :
used to calculate the future worth of regular periodic investment

$$A \text{ £1 p.a.} = \frac{(1 + i)^n - 1}{i}$$

Annual sinking fund :
used to calculate the sum that must be invested annually to cover a known expense in the future at a known date

$$ASF = \frac{i}{A - 1} \qquad \frac{i}{(1 + i)^n - 1}$$

Present value of £1 :
used to calculate the present worth of sums to be received in the future

$$PV \text{ £1} = \frac{1}{A} \qquad \frac{1}{(1 + i)^n}$$

Present value of £1 per annum :
also known as the YP and used to calculate the present worth of a series of payments

$$PV \text{ £1 p.a.} = \frac{1 - PV}{i} \qquad \frac{1 - \dfrac{1}{(1 + i)^n}}{i}$$

$$OR \qquad \frac{1}{i + SF}$$

Annuity £1 will purchase :
used to calculate the annual sum given in exchange for an initial amount of capital

$$\text{Annuity £1 w.p.} = i + SF$$

Spreadsheet User

Spreadsheets are particularly useful for exploring the valuation tables and investment concepts outlined in this and the other chapters in Part One. These pages are designed for current but introductory users of Lotus 1-2-3 and Excel to help them use the spreadsheet as both a valuation tool and a means of exploring and understanding the concepts of valuation more fully.

Project I

Lotus or Excel can be used very effectively to generate your own set of valuation tables, which you can personalise to your own requirements, layout and style.

The example below shows how to construct a table for the Amount of £1 function. Only a small section of the spreadsheet is shown in the example : you should create the table for values of *i* between say 2% and 25% at 0.5% intervals and for 100 years. This project demonstrates the power of spreadsheets to repeat a calculation from a simple copy command. If you generate the whole table as indicated above the Amount of £1 calculation will be performed 4,700 times!

Tips :
* Plan the table carefully first, decide on its layout and presentation.
* Consider the logical sequence of the calculation and the parentheses required in the formula.
* You must fully understand the nature of relative and absolute cell references in order to understand how the single copy command generates the table by looking up the appropriate values of *i* and *n* in column **A** and row **2**.
* The symbol ^ is used to indicate to the power of.
* The table will require substantial compression to print on a single page. This is simple in Excel by clicking on the option to fit a single page in the Print dialogue box. In Lotus 1-2-3 (non-windows versions) you must use the **W.Y.S.I.W.Y.G.** add in to compress the page for printing.
* In the example below, the value of *i* is divided by 100 to express the value as a percentage as required in all valuation formulae . You could alternatively format the cells in Row 2 as a percentage and enter the values as **0.02, 0.025,** etc. The cell will be displayed as **2%, 2.5%,** etc. and you can remove the **/100** from the formula.

The following table shows the start of the Amount of £1 table . The whole table can be generated by copying the formula in cell C2 as a block for the whole table starting at cell C2 and extending for your chosen range of values of *i* and *n*. *NOTE : YOU ONLY HAVE TO ENTER THE FORMULA IN CELL C4 AND COPY TO GENERATE YOUR TABLE ! ; THE FORMULAE CONTAINED IN THE OTHER CELLS ARE SHOWN BELOW ONLY TO ILLUSTRATE HOW THE FORMULA CHANGES WHEN IT IS COPIED.*

	A	B	C	D	E	F
1			Interest (%)			
2			2	2.5	3	3.5
3	Years					
4	1		(1+(C$2/100))^$A4	(1+(D$2/100))^$A4	(1+(E$2/100))^$A4	(1+(F$2/100))^$A4
5	2		(1+(C$2/100))^$A5	(1+(D$2/100))^$A5	(1+(E$2/100))^$A5	(1+(F$2/100))^$A5
6	3		(1+(C$2/100))^$A6	(1+(D$2/100))^$A6	(1+(E$2/100))^$A6	(1+(F$2/100))^$A6
7	4		(1+(C$2/100))^$A7	(1+(D$2/100))^$A7	(1+(E$2/100))^$A7	(1+(F$2/100))^$A7
8	5		(1+(C$2/100))^$A8	(1+(D$2/100))^$A8	(1+(E$2/100))^$A8	(1+(F$2/100))^$A8

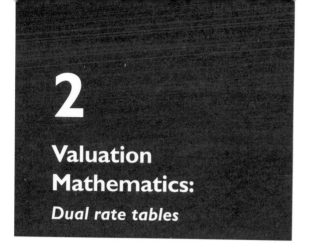

2

Valuation Mathematics:

Dual rate tables

In single rate annuity and years' purchase tables the sinking fund inherent in the formulae is providing for replacement *of* capital at the same rate per cent as the remunerative or investor's rate of return *on* capital. As such the sinking fund is notional and ensures that the correct value is assigned to the investment.

If the original capital outlay has to be replaced by the end of the life of the investment by reinvestment, for example if the investor wishes to maintain a given income flow by purchasing a comparable investment, this can be achieved by creating a sinking fund. Such a situation is rarely engineered in practice. Despite this fact, the conventional technique employed in the valuation of limited term property investments is founded upon this assumption.

The technique is only used by valuers to value wasting assets such as leasehold interests *(see Chapter 7)*. A freehold interest may be likened to saving in a building society (the principal is retained in the ownership of the investor) and all income represents a return on capital employed. A leasehold interest is a terminating or wasting asset and comes to an end after a given number of years. The sum originally invested is spent in return for an income for a given number of years. At the end of that time nothing remains.

In order, therefore, to compare the return from an investment in a leasehold interest with an investment in a freehold interest it is argued that the original outlay must be returned at the end of the lease so that a similar, equal income flow may be acquired. This process may continue into perpetuity so that a perpetual income may be enjoyed and the return becomes comparable with that receivable from a freehold investment.

There would seem to be no problem at first glance because a single rate YP includes a sinking fund to replace initial outlay. But two problems are encountered if an actual sinking fund is to be arranged. While a single rate YP

assumes that the sinking fund accumulates at the same rate as the yield from the investment, the rate of interest at which a sinking fund will accumulate does not necessarily relate to the yield given by the investment itself. Two rates may thus be needed. Second, the sinking fund must replace initial capital outlay and so the possible effect of tax on that part of the income that represents capital replacement cannot be ignored; nor can the effect of tax on sinking fund accumulations.

Because the sinking fund must be available at the required point in time with no doubt as to its security, a safe rate of interest is assumed to be earned by the sinking fund. In 1977/78 this fluctuated between 6-10% (building society rates) but valuers were using 2.5% - 4%, the practice of the 1930s. This low figure is often justified by the argument that the accumulation must be net of tax; but as building society accounts earn a higher return net of tax, are safe and are much more liquid than a sinking fund need be, so rates higher than 4% could be justified, but 4% is hardly ever exceeded in conventional valuations. During 1988 and in the early 1990s bank deposit accounts were again yielding as little as 2% net of tax on small deposits so the vagaries of the savings market will sometimes justify the adherence to a low net of tax accumulative rate. The overriding question lies not with the rate per cent but with the concept.

As already stated, there is no reason to suppose that the *'accumulative rate'* will equate with the yield from the investment or the *'remunerative rate'*. Where it does not, the YP figure will be *'dual rate'*.

The only formula for a dual rate YP catering for the difference in accumulative and remunerative rates is

$$\frac{1}{i + \text{SF}}$$

The formula $\quad \frac{1 - \text{PV}}{i}$

can only be used in the case of a single rate YP;

$$\frac{1}{i + \text{SF}}$$

can be used for single or dual rates.

In very rare cases annuities are calculated on a dual rate basis. This means that the investor requires a return on capital at one rate of interest but intends to recover his capital at a lower rate of interest.

Using the formula $i + SF$ the calculations are no more complex, initially, than those for a normal annuity.

Example 2.1

What annuity will £1,000 purchase if interest is at 10% but the return of capital is to be at 2.5% for 10 years?

i	= 0.1000
ASF to replace £1 in 10 years @ 2.5%	= 0.0892
	0.1892

therefore £1,000 x 0.1892 = £189.20

It will be noted that the dual rate introduces a different meaning of rate of return. Previously it was shown that the investor's return was normally assumed to be on capital outstanding from year to year. The dual rate assumes a return on initial capital throughout. Thus:

Capital	Interest @ 10%	ASF @ 2.5%
£1,000	£100	£89.20
£1,000	£100	£89.20
for each year from 1 to 10.		

The ten amounts of £89.20 have to be assumed to be reinvested in a fund accumulating at 2.5%. Thus:

	£89.20 p.a.
Amount of £1 p.a. for 10 years @ 2.5 %	11.2034
	£1,000

The investment is arithmetically perpetuated and it can be seen that on these terms a 10 year annuity of £189.20 p.a. is equal to a £100 perpetual annuity. The spendable income (total income less sinking fund) providing in each case a 10% return on the £1,000.

Example 2.2 How much would it cost to purchase today an annuity of £1,000 for 5 years followed by an annuity of £1,200 for 5 years on a 10% and 2.5% basis?

Annuity	£1,000	
PV £1 p.a. for 5 years @ 10% and 2.5%	3.445	£3,445
plus deferred annuity	£1,200	
PV £1 p.a. for 5 years @ 10% and 2.5%	3.445	
PV £1 for 5 years @ 10%	0.62	£2,563
		£6,008

Example 2.3

Value a limited income of £1,500 p.a. for 6 years where your client requires a yield of 11% and the best safe accumulative rate is 3%. Show how a return *on* and a return *of* capital are received.

Income	£1,500.00
YP for 6 years @ 11% and 3%	3.7793
Capital Value	£5,668.95

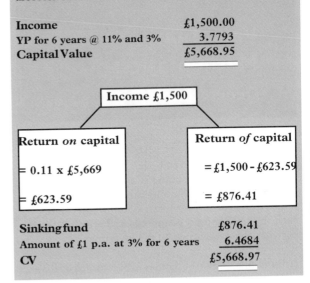

Return *on* capital	Return *of* capital
= 0.11 x £5,669	= £1,500 – £623.59
= £623.59	= £876.41

Sinking fund	£876.41
Amount of £1 p.a. at 3% for 6 years	6.4684
CV	£5,668.97

Sinking funds in dual rate YPs

The use of dual rate YPs assumes that sinking funds are taken out in practice. Such sinking funds are designed to replace the initial outlay on an investment. Because the sinking fund has to perform this function without question it is assumed to accumulate at a net-of-tax rate.

If an investor pays basic rate tax at 25%, and the rate of interest earned by the sinking fund is subject to this rate of tax, then a gross accumulative rate will be reduced to a net accumulative rate.

For example, where an ASF is £150 p.a. and the gross accumulative rate is 5% with tax at 25%, then:

After one year the interest earned is :

£150 x 5% = £7.50   but;

tax at 25% reduces this to (0.75 x £7.50) = £5.625.

£5.625 is only 3.75% of £150
so the gross rate of 5% has been reduced to a net accumulative rate of 3.75%.

Such a calculation is easily accomplished by applying a tax adjustment factor of **(1 - t)** to the original gross rate.

(where _t_ = the rate of tax expressed as a decimal)

If the required sinking fund instalment is calculated on gross instead of net rates of interest it will simply be inadequate whenever interest on the sinking fund is taxed.

Example 2.4

£1,000 must be replaced within 10 years. The accumulative rate is 6%: calculate the ASF.

Sum required	£1,000
ASF to replace £1 in 10 years @ 6%	0.075868
	£75.87

However the sinking fund is taxed at 25%. It will therefore actually accumulate at 6% (1 - t)

=	6 % (1 - t)	
=	6 % (0.75)	
=	4.5 %	

ASF	£75.87
A £1 p.a. for 10 years @ 4.5 %	12.29
Capital Value	£932.44

The sinking fund is insufficient to replace the initial outlay of £1,000, due to the effect of tax on the sinking fund accumulation. The SF must from the start be calculated in the light of the tax rate, i.e.

Sum required	£1,000
ASF to replace £1 in 10 years @ 4.5 %	0.08137
ASF	£81.37
A £1 p.a. for 10 years @ 4.5 %	12.29
Capital Value	£1,000

The sinking fund has this time been correctly calculated to accumulate after the effect of 25% tax on the interest accumulating in the sinking fund. Accumulative rates must be net of tax to compensate for this first effect that tax has on the accumulation of the sinking fund.

Dual Rate YPs and Tax

Tax also affects income from property. Rates of return from most investments are quoted gross of tax, because individual tax rates vary and net-of-tax comparisons may, as a result, be meaningless. The remunerative rate _i_% in a dual rate YP is therefore a gross rate of interest.

But a sinking fund is tied to the promise that it must actually replace the initial capital outlay, so that a comparable investment may be purchased. The effect of tax on the income cannot therefore be ignored.

Example 2.5a

Value a profit rent of £2,000 p.a. *(see Chapter 7)* receivable for 10 years using a remunerative rate of 10% gross and an accumulative rate of 3% net. The investor pays tax at 25p in the £ on all property income. Show how the calculation is affected.

Ignoring tax on income :	£2,000
YP for 10 years @ 10% and 3 %	5.341
Capital value	£10,682

But income is taxed @ 25p in the £1 :

Net income =	£2,000 x (1 - t)	
=	£2,000 (1 - 0.25)	
=	£2,000 (0.75)	
=	£1,500	

From this net income a net remunerative rate of 7.5% [10% (1 - _t_)] and a sinking fund to replace initial outlay must be found.

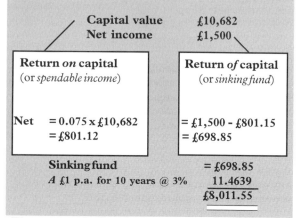

Sinking fund	= £698.85
A £1 p.a. for 10 years @ 3%	11.4639
	£8,011.55

The sum calculated above fails to replace the initial outlay of £10,682. *Why?*

Answer:

As the income is reduced by 25%, both spendable income and the sinking fund must be reduced by 25%. The spendable income then becomes a net spendable income representing a net return on capital and still conforms to the investor's requirements. But the net sinking fund must replace £10,682 - the fact that the gross sinking fund would notionally replace the initial outlay is no comfort for the investor left several thousand pounds short.

It must therefore be ensured that the net sinking fund still replaces the initial outlay.

Thus:

Gross sinking fund x (1 - t) = net sinking fund

Gross sinking fund = net sinking fund x $\frac{1}{(1-t)}$

If, having calculated the desired amount that should remain as a net sinking fund, this amount is multiplied by the 'grossing-up' factor of $\frac{1}{(1-t)}$

the required amount of net sinking fund will remain available after tax.

Thus:

Net SF x $\frac{1}{1-t}$ x (1 - t) = net SF

Clearly therefore more income must be set aside as gross sinking fund,

i.e. the net SF x $\frac{1}{(1-t)}$

This means that the amount of income remaining as spendable income will be reduced, and the investor's requirements of a 10% return will not be fulfilled. A new valuation is therefore required, reducing the price paid so that a grossed-up sinking fund may be provided and a 10% return (gross) can still be attained.

A new **YP** figure must be calculated using a 10% remunerative rate, a 3% net accumulative rate, and a grossing-up factor applied to the **SF** of $\frac{1}{(1-t)}$.

The dual rate **YP** formula adjusted for tax is therefore

$$\frac{1}{i + \left(SF \times \frac{1}{1-t} \right)}$$

In this case this becomes

$$\frac{1}{0.10 + \left(0.08723 \times \frac{1}{1-0.25} \right)}$$

$$= \frac{1}{0.10 + \left(0.08723 \times \frac{1}{0.75} \right)}$$

$$= \frac{1}{0.10 + 0.11630} = \frac{1}{0.2163}$$

$$= \underline{4.6232}$$

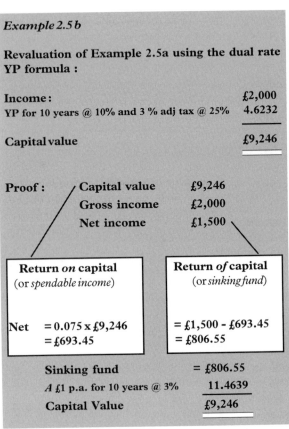

Example 2.5 b

Revaluation of Example 2.5a using the dual rate YP formula :

Income :	**£2,000**
YP for 10 years @ 10% and 3 % adj tax @ 25%	4.6232
Capital value	**£9,246**

Proof :	**Capital value**	**£9,246**
	Gross income	**£2,000**
	Net income	**£1,500**

Return *on* capital (or *spendable income*)	**Return *of* capital** (or *sinking fund*)
Net = 0.075 x £9,246 = £693.45	= £1,500 - £693.45 = £806.55

Sinking fund	**= £806.55**
A £1 p.a. for 10 years @ 3%	11.4639
Capital Value	**£9,246**

The result of using a tax-adjusted **YP** has been to reduce the capital value from £10,682 to £9,246. This has enabled the investor to gross-up the sinking fund to compensate for the effect of income tax and leave enough spendable income to provide a **10% gross** and **7.5% net** return on capital)

Summary

This chapter has explored the need to consider the replacement of capital where the investment has a limited life, such as a leasehold property investment which reduces in value as it approaches termination. The chapter illustrates the valuation theory of sinking funds which provide the mechanism for replacement of capital, to purchase a further investment when the existing investment terminates. In addition the effect of taxation on property incomes has been explored, showing the need to consider the effect of tax on both the spendable income and the sinking fund.

The formula for dual rate YP adjusted for tax is :

$$\frac{1}{i + \left(SF \times \dfrac{1}{1-t} \right)}$$

The effect of tax on a sinking fund is twofold :

1. **Tax is levied on the interest accumulating on the sinking fund.**

   To allow for this a *net accumulative rate* must be used.

2. **Tax is levied on the income from which a sinking fund is drawn.**

   So that the correct net sinking fund remains after tax a grossing-up factor is used.

   A tax-adjusted dual rate YP caters for this, and ensures that the correct valuation is made.

In the last chapter spreadsheet users were invited to generate their own set of valuation tables using the powerful copy function to generate a whole table from a single formula. However, spreadsheets can be used in the way set out in the project below to make tables redundant by incorporating the valuation mathematics to generate the capital value for any given income, interest rate, sinking fund rate, period and rate of tax.

Project 1

Using Lotus or Excel create an area for entry of the variables and display of the answers. An example is indicated below :

	A	B	C	D	E	F
1	Valuation Spreadsheet to calculate the capital value of a terminable					
2	income which is taxable :					
3						
4	**ENTER THE VALUATION DATA :**					
5						
6				Income	£	
7				Period (*n*)	(years)	
8				SF Rate (*i_s*)	%	
9				Interest rate (*i*) %		
10				Tax rate	(*t*) %	
11						
12				CAPITAL VALUE :		

In cell F12 you will need the formula for dual rate YP adjusted for tax which can be expressed with reference to the above cell layout as :

$$F6*(1/(F9 + (((F8 / (((1 + F8)\wedge F7) -1)) * ((1 / (1 - F10)))))))$$

Note: The above assumes that the cells F8,F9 & F10 are in a percentage format (see spreadsheet user 1); if not the values in the above formula require division by 100

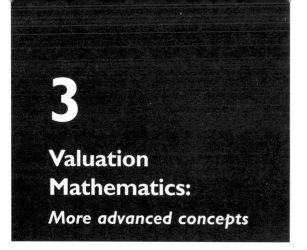

3

Valuation Mathematics:
More advanced concepts

The interrelationship of tables

The student's knowledge of this may be tested by problems requiring the use of information provided by one particular table to calculate a related figure from another table. A knowledge of the formulae is essential. It can be seen that the **amount of £1 (A)** is represented in each formula:

1 $PV = \dfrac{1}{A}$

2 $A\ £1\ P.A. = \dfrac{A - 1}{i}$

3 $ASF = \dfrac{i}{A - 1}$

4 $YP = \dfrac{1 - \dfrac{1}{A}}{i}$ or $\dfrac{1}{i + \dfrac{i}{A - 1}}$

5 $A\ £1\ w.p. = i + \dfrac{i}{A - 1}$

6 $A = (1 + i)^n$

It can also be seen from the above that the six tables fall into three sets of reciprocals : 1 & 6
2 & 3
4 & 5

It is the thorough understanding of this and the nature of the formula that provides the key to the solution of the following type of problem.

Example 3.1.

Showing your workings, calculate to four places of decimals:

(i) **PV £1 p.a. @ 5% for 20 years** using the figure given in the valuation tables for PV £1, 20 years @ 5%.

$PV = \dfrac{1}{A}$: $PV\ £1\ p.a. = \dfrac{1 - PV}{i}$

PV £1 in 20 years @ 5% $= 0.37689$

PV £1 p.a. for 20 years @ 5% $= \dfrac{1 - 0.37689}{0.05}$

$= \dfrac{0.62311}{0.05}$

$= 12.4622$

(ii) **ASF** necessary to produce £1 after 15 years @ 3% using the amount of £1 table.

$ASF = \dfrac{i}{A - 1}$ A £1 15 years @ 3% = 1.558

ASF to replace £1 in 15 years @ 3% $= \dfrac{0.03}{1.558 - 1}$

$= 0.0538$

(iii) **YP 70 years @ 5% and 2.5%** given that the ASF to produce £1 in 70 years @ 2.5% = 0.0053971.

$YP = \dfrac{1}{i + SF}$ where i is the remunerative rate and SF is the annual sinking fund to produce £1 for n years @ i

$= \dfrac{1}{0.05 + 0.0053971}$

$= \dfrac{1}{0.0553971}$

$= 18.0515$

Some problems may not allow simple substitution.

Example 3.2

Given that A £1 p.a. for 7 years @ 4% = 7.8983, find YP for 7 years @ 4%.

$$\text{A £1 p.a.} = \frac{A - 1}{i} \qquad \text{ASF*} = \frac{i}{A - 1}$$

Therefore $\quad \text{A £1 p.a.} = \dfrac{1}{\text{SF}}$

$$\text{YP} = \frac{1}{i + \text{SF}}$$

the value of SF in this formula is the reciprocal of the amount of £1 p.a. for 7 years @ 4%, i.e. 7.8983

Therefore $\quad \text{YP} = \dfrac{1}{0.04 + \dfrac{1}{7.8983}}$

$$= \frac{1}{0.04 + 0.1266} = \frac{1}{0.1666} = \underline{6.00}$$

* ASF is the same as SF

Example 3.3

Given that **ASF 16 years @ 4%** = 0.04582, find the annuity £1 will purchase for 14 years @ 4%.

$$\frac{\text{A £1 for 16 years @ 4\%}}{\text{A £1 for 2 years @ 4\%}} = \text{A £1 for 14 years @ 4\%}$$

$$\text{ASF} = \frac{i}{A - 1} = 0.04582$$

$$A - 1 = \frac{0.04}{0.04582} = 0.873 \qquad A = 1.873$$

$$\frac{1.873}{(1 + i)^2} = \text{A £1 for 14 years @ 4\%}$$

$$\frac{1.873}{(1.04)^2} = \frac{1.873}{1.0816} = 1.7317$$

Thus A £1 w.p. for 14 years @ 4 % $= i + \dfrac{i}{A - 1}$

$$= 0.04 + \frac{0.04}{0.7317 - 1}$$

$$= 0.04 + \frac{0.04}{0.7317} = 0.04 + 0.05467$$

$$= \underline{0.09467}$$

The problem may be complicated further by changing the relevant number of years. This obviously presents a considerable difficulty. It is no longer sufficient just to isolate A, as it will represent the wrong number of years in the annuity figure.

In the compound interest formula $(1 + i)^n$, n is the exponent and the expression means that $(1 + i)$ is multiplied by itself n times. Exponents have certain properties and a knowledge of these can be useful when manipulating the various valuation formulae.

The properties of exponents

1   **Any number raised to the zero power equals 1**

2   **A fractional exponent is the root of a number**

$$(1 + i)^{\frac{1}{2}} \text{ or } (1 + i)^{0.5} = \sqrt{(1 + i)}$$
$$(1 + i)^{0.2} = \sqrt[5]{(1 + i)}$$

3   **When a number being raised to a power is multiplied by itself the exponents are added**

$$(1 + i)^4 \times (1 + i)^6 = (1 + i)^{10}$$
and $\quad (1 + i)^{10} \div (1 + i)^5 = (1 + i)^5$

Nominal and effective rates of interest

The rates of return provided by different investments are usually compared by means of the annual rate of interest quoted. For example, building societies usually quote net rates of interest earned in savings accounts, such as 10% per annum, representing the return provided by the investment. Sometimes, however, such information should be qualified by the frequency of payment of interest. Where interest is not paid annually, the quoted rate of interest will often be misleading.

For example, building society A pays 10% per annum, interest paid annually. 10% per annum in this case is the quoted or stated rate, which is called the *nominal* rate of interest. Because interest is paid annually, 10% is also the actual rate of interest earned in one year or the ***effective*** rate of interest.

Consider, on the other hand, building society B which pays 10% per annum with interest paid half-yearly. 10% per annum paid half-yearly indicates that two instalments of 5% per 6 months are actually paid. Hence the nominal rate of 10% per annum will differ from the effective rate of interest, as the interest paid after 6 months will itself earn interest over the second half of the year.

The total accumulation of £1 invested in an account for one year will therefore by $£(1.05)^2 = £1.1025$. Interest is 10.25 pence, accumulated on £1 invested. The effective rate of interest is therefore **10.25%**, and building society B is more generous than building society A.

Investments are therefore best compared by means of the annual effective rate of interest. Building societies, banks and all other finance companies are required to disclose this annual percentage rate (**APR**). The APR may be based on sums which include arrangement costs.

Incomes in advance and non-annual incomes

The issue here is how should a valuer deal with the valuation of incomes received in advance? Most years' purchase valuation tables assume that the unit of income is received at the end of the year. The same may apply to **PV** and **A £1 p.a.** tables.

However, this is not always a realistic assumption. Rent from property is usually paid in advance. Tables giving *'in arrears'* figures may be used alongside common sense to provide related *'in advance'* figures.

1 **PV £1**: normally assumes that the sum is to be received at the end of the year n. If the sum is received at the start of year n instead, this will coincide with the end of year $(n - 1)$.

   Thus the **PV of £1 receivable in advance**

$$= \frac{1}{(1 + i)^{n-1}}$$

2. **Amount of £1 p.a.** normally assumes that each £1 is invested at the end of each year. If this becomes the start of each year instead an extra £1 will accumulate for n years - but the £1 paid at the end of the nth year will now be paid at the start of year n. The series becomes :

$$(1 + i)^n + (1 + i)^{n-1} \ldots (1 + i)^2 + (1 + i)$$

this can be summated to :

$$\left(\frac{(1 + i)^{n+1} - 1}{i} \right) - 1$$

3. **Year's purchase or PV £1 p.a.** usually assumes income to be received at the end of each year. But if it comes in advance, the series will read

$$1 + \frac{1}{(1 + i)} + \frac{1}{(1 + i)^2} \cdots \frac{1}{(1 + i)^{n-1}}$$

and this can be summated to

$$\frac{1 - \frac{1}{(1 + i)^{n-1}}}{i} + 1$$

Example 3.4

Calculate YP for 6 years @ 10% in advance.

$$\frac{1 - \frac{1}{(1 + 0.10)^{6-1}}}{i} + 1$$

$$= \frac{1 - \frac{1}{1.6105}}{0.10} + 1 = 3.79 + 1 = \underline{4.79}$$

Alternatively, this could be given by
YP for 5 years @ 10% + 1: (3.79) + 1 = 4.79, or by
YP for 6 years @ 10% x (1 + i).

In this book so far i has always represented an annual interest rate. But, the formulae can be used for alternative interest rate periods which are commonly used in property investment transactions. It must be ensured however that i and n relate to the same time period.

The time period can be anything; so for example if the interest rate i is quarterly, the time period n must represent quarterly periods:

i.e. for 1 year n would equal 4.

The same logic may be applied to all six functions as specified at the beginning of this chapter.

Incomes receivable quarterly in advance

It was stated at the beginning of this chapter that some valuation tables are based on the assumption that income may be received or invested quarterly.

At the current time it is much more common to find income from property (rent) paid in advance. In fact such income is usually paid quarterly in advance, and this is the basis of valuation tables by **Bowcock and Rose**. By far the most common application of such a basis is to years' purchase tables.

The formula for the years' purchase to be applied to an income receivable quarterly in advance, single rate, is:

$$YP = \frac{1 - \dfrac{1}{(1+i)^n}}{4\left[1 - \dfrac{1}{\sqrt[4]{(1+i)}}\right]}$$

where i is the annual effective rate of interest.

For example, the single rate years' purchase, quarterly in advance, at an annual effective rate of 10% for 20 years, is **9.038**, compared with the equivalent annual in arrears years' purchase of **8.5136**, reflecting the advantages of receiving income both earlier and more regularly.

The formula for the years' purchase to be applied to an income receivable quarterly in advance, dual rate with a tax adjustment, is:

$$YP = \frac{1}{4\left[1 - \dfrac{1}{\sqrt[4]{(1+i)}}\right] + \dfrac{4\left[1 - \dfrac{1}{\sqrt[4]{(1+s)}}\right]}{[(1+s)^n - 1][1-t]}}$$

where i is the annual effective remunerative rate, s is the annual effective accumulative rate, and t is the tax rate.

For example, the dual rate years' purchase, quarterly in advance, at an annual effective remunerative rate of **10%**, an annual effective accumulative rate of **3%**, adjusted for tax at **40%**, for **20** years is **6.3555**, compared with the annual in arrears equivalent figure of **6.1718**.

It is strictly correct that such factors should be applied to incomes which are received quarterly in advance, in order that it is demonstrable that the yield indicated by the valuation is actually provided by the investment. The use of other tables might provide valuations which are acceptable in the market, but it should be noted that such valuations are based upon slightly misleading rates of return.

Continuous compounding

When interest is added more frequently than annually, the compound interest $(1 + i)^n$ is adjusted to :

$$\left(1 + \frac{i}{m}\right)^{mn}$$

where m is the number of times per year that interest is added, i is the nominal rate of interest per year and n is the number of years.

If, for example, the nominal rate of interest is 100% per annum, then within the formula i becomes 1, and £1 invested for one year will accumulate to

$$£ \left(1 + \frac{1}{m} \right)^{m}$$

The greater the number of times in the year that interest is added, the greater will be the total sum at the end of the year: but there must be a limit, because while the number of periods becomes infinitely large the rate of interest per period becomes infinitely small.

Potentially, m might tend towards infinity. This would imply the immediate reinvestment of earned interest, or *continuous compounding*.

Mathematically the maximum sum to which £1 could compound in 1 year at 100% per annum is given by the following series:

$$1 + \frac{1}{1} + \frac{1}{1 \times 2} + \frac{1}{1 \times 2 \times 3} + \frac{1}{1 \times 2 \times 3 \times 4} \cdots \frac{1}{m!}$$

which is a convergent series summating to 6 places, to **2.718282**.

Now to return to the general case :

$$A = \left(1 + \frac{1}{m} \right)^{mn}$$

Let $\dfrac{i}{m} = \dfrac{1}{t}$

then t is the reciprocal of the rate of interest (m) period.

As the number of payments per year becomes larger and tends towards infinity, t does likewise and interest can be said to be *compounding continuously*.

Then $A = \left(1 + \dfrac{1}{t} \right)^{mn}$

$m = ti,$

so $A = \left(1 + \dfrac{1}{t} \right)^{nti}$

or $A = \left[\left(1 + \dfrac{1}{t} \right)^{t} \right]^{in}$

as t tends towards infinity :

$\left(1 + \dfrac{1}{t} \right)^{t}$ becomes e (see above).

Thus **£1** invested at i with interest compounding continuously over n years will accumulate to e^{in}.

Example 3.6

To what sum will £1 compound over 2 years @ 10% per year nominal rate of interest assuming continuous compounding ?

$$e^{in} = 2.718282^{(0.1)(2)}$$

$$= 2.718282^{(0.2)}$$

$$= \sqrt[2]{2.718282}$$

$$= \underline{£1.221}$$

£1 accumulating at 10% per year with interest added annually would only compound to $(1.10)^2$ or £1.21.

The present value of £1 $= \dfrac{1}{(1+i)^n}$

or $(1+i)^{-n}.$

It follows then that where interest is compounding continuously :

The present value of £1 $= e^{-in}$

The foregoing demonstrates that the rate of interest used in calculations of compounding and discounting must be *the effective rate for the period*.

This chapter has demonstrated the interrelationships between the six functions of £1. It has expained the important concept of effective rate of interest per interest earning period and illustrated how the formulae for the six functions of £1 can be amended to cover payments made in advance and where interest is due quarterly or at other frequencies.

The PV of £1 receivable in advance:

used to calculate present value where the sum is received at the start of the year

$$= \frac{1}{(1+i)^{n-1}}$$

The amount of £1 per annum receivable in advance:

used to calculate the future worth of regular periodic

investment made a the start of each year

$$= \left(\left(\frac{(1+i)^{n-1} - 1}{i} \right) \right) - 1$$

Present value of £1 per annum or YP receivable in advance:

used to calculate the present worth of a series of payments received in advance

$$= \frac{1 - \frac{1}{(1+i)^{n-1}}}{i} + 1$$

YP single rate, income receivable quarterly in advance :

$$= \frac{1 - \frac{1}{(1+i)^{n}}}{4 \left[1 - \frac{1}{\sqrt[4]{(1+i)}} \right]}$$

In the previous chapter spreadsheet users were invited to construct a spreadsheet to value an income using the dual rate YP adjusted for tax for any values of n, i, i_s and t. The same principles of construction can be applied to the concepts and formulae explored in this chapter. The example below is used to construct a spreadsheet to value income receivable quarterly in advance. Spreadsheet users should try to apply the solution to all the formulae explored in this chapter.

Project 1

Using Lotus or Excel create an area for entry of the variables and display of the answers.

An example is indicated below :

	A	B	C	D	E	F
1	Valuation Spreadsheet to calculate the capital value of an income					
2	receivable quarterly in advance :					
3						
4	ENTER THE VALUATION DATA :					
5						
6				Income	£	
7				Period (*n*)	(years)	
8			Annual effective	Interest rate (*i*) %		
9						
10						
11						
12				CAPITAL VALUE :		

In cell F12 you will need the formula for **YP** applied to an income receivable quarterly in advance, single rate which can be expressed with reference to the above cell layout as :

$$F6*((1-(1/((1+F8)^{\wedge}F7)))/(4*(1-(1/((1+F8)^{\wedge}0.25)))))$$

Note : The above assumes that cell F8 is in a percentage format; if not, the values in the above formula require division by 100

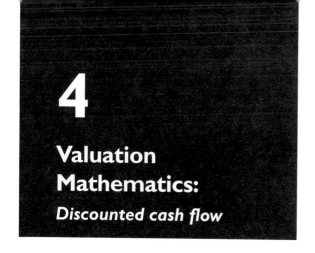

4

Valuation Mathematics:

Discounted cash flow

Discounted Cash Flow (**DCF**) is an aid to the valuation or analysis of any investment producing a cash flow. In its general form, it has two standard products - **NPV** and **IRR**.

Net present value (NPV)

Future net benefits receivable from the investment are discounted at a given *'target rate'*. The sum of the discounted benefits is found and the initial cost of the investment deducted from this sum, to leave what is termed the net present value of the investment, which may be positive or negative. A positive **NPV** implies that a rate of return greater than the target rate is being yielded by the investment; a negative **NPV** implies that the yield is at a rate of return lower than the target rate. The target rate is the minimum rate which the investor requires in order to make the investment worth while, taking into account the risk involved and all other relevant factors. It will be governed in particular by one factor: the investor's cost of capital.

Investments may require the initial outlay of a large capital sum, and investors will often be forced to borrow money in order to accumulate that sum. The interest to be paid on that loan will be the investor's cost of capital at that time. It is clear that the rate of return from an investment where the initial capital has been borrowed should be at least equal to the cost of capital, or a loss will result.

An alternative way of looking at this is that the investor will always have alternative opportunities for the investment of his capital. Money may be lent quite easily to earn a rate of interest based on the cost of capital. The return from any investment should therefore compare favourably with the opportunity cost of the funds employed, and this will usually be related to the cost of capital.

For these reasons, the target rate should compare well with the cost of capital. From this basis, a positive or negative **NPV** will be the result of the analysis and upon this result the investment decision may be made.

Example 4.1

Find the **NPV** of the following project, using a target rate based on a cost of capital of **13%**.

Outlay £10,000

	Income	PV £1 @ 13%	Discounted sum £
Returns in year 1	5,000	0.8849	4,425
Returns in year 2	4,000	0.7831	3,133
Returns in year 3	6,000	0.6930	4,158
			£11,716
		Less outlay	£10,000
		NPV	£1,716

The investment yields a return of **13%** and, in addition, a positive **NPV** of **£1,716**. In the absence of other choices, this investment may be accepted.

However, it is more usual for the investment decision to be one of choice.

Example 4.2

An investor has **£1,400** to invest and has a choice between investment **A** and **B**. The following returns are anticipated:

Income flow	A	B
	£	£
Year 1	600	200
2	400	400
3	200	400
4	400	600
5	400	600

The investor's target rate for both investments is 10%, the investments are mutually exclusive (only one of the two can be undertaken); which investment should be chosen?

Income flow **A**

	Income	PV£1@10%	Discounted sum
Year 1	600	0.9091	545
2	400	0.8264	330
3	200	0.7513	150
4	400	0.6830	273
5	400	0.6209	248
			£1,546
		Less outlay	£1,400
		NPV	£146

Example 4.2 (cont.)

Income flow B

	Income	PV£1@10%	Discounted sum
Year 1	200	0.9091	182
2	400	0.8264	330
3	400	0.7513	300
4	600	0.6830	409
5	600	0.6209	373
			£1,594
		Less outlay	£1,400
		NPV	£194

From this information investment **B** should be chosen.

Each investment gives a return of **10%** plus a positive **NPV**:

B produces the greater **NPV**   £194
compared to **A**   £146.

If either investment had been considered to be subject to more risk, this fact should have been reflected in the choice of target rate.

In example 4.2 both investments involved the same amount of capital or initial outlay. However, this will not always be the case, and, when outlays on mutually exclusive investments differ, the investment decision will not be so simple. An **NPV** of £200 from an investment costing £250 is considerably more attractive than a similar **NPV** produced by a £25,000 outlay.

How can this be reflected in an analysis?

A possible approach is to express the **NPV** as a percentage of the outlay.

Example 4.3

Which of these mutually exclusive investments should be undertaken when the investor's target rate is **10%** ?

Investment A	Investment B
Outlay £5,000	Outlay £7,000

Income flow

Year 1	£3,000	£4,000
Year 2	£2,000	£3,000
Year 3	£1,500	£2,000

Example 4.3 (cont.)

Income flow A

	£	PV£1@10%	Discounted sum
Year 1	3,000	0.9091	2,727
2	2,000	0.8264	1,653
3	1,500	0.7513	1,127
			£5,507
		Less outlay	£5,000
		NPV	£507

Income flow B

	£	PV£1@10%	Discounted sum
Year 1	4,000	0.9091	3,636
2	3,000	0.8264	2,479
3	2,000	0.7513	1,503
			£7,618
		Less outlay	£7,000
		NPV	£618

At first sight, B might appear to be more profitable, but if the **NPV** is expressed as a percentage of outlay the picture changes.

$$A = \frac{£507}{£5,000} \times 100 = 10.14 \%$$

$$B = \frac{£618}{£7,000} \times 100 = 8.83 \%$$

On this basis **A**, and not **B**, should be chosen.

The NPV method is a satisfactory aid in the great majority of investment problems but suffers from one particular disadvantage. The return provided by an investment is expressed in two parts - a rate of return, and a cash sum in addition which represents an extra return. These two parts are expressed in different units which may make certain investments difficult to compare.

This fault is not present in the following method of expressing the results of a DCF analysis

The internal rate of return (IRR)

This is the discount rate which equates the discounted flow of future benefits with the initial outlay.

It produces an NPV of 0 and may be found by the use of various trial discount rates.

Example 4.4

Find the IRR of the following investment.

Outlay £6,000 : Returns Year 1 £1,024
Year 2 £4,000
Year 3 £3,000

Trying 10% :

Year	£	PV£1@10%	Discounted sum
1	1,024	0.9091	931
2	4,000	0.8264	3,306
3	3,000	0.7513	2,253
			£6,490
		Less outlay	£6,000
		NPV	£490

At a trial rate of **10%**, a positive NPV results. £490 is too high - an **NPV** of 0 is the desired result. The trial rate must be too low, as the future receipts should be discounted to a greater extent.

Trying 16% :

Year	£	PV£1@16%	Discounted sum
1	1,024	0.8621	931
2	4,000	0.7432	2,972
3	3,000	0.6407	1,923
			£5,778
		Less outlay	£6,000
		NPV	- £222

This time the receipts have been discounted too much. A negative **NPV** is the result, so the trial rate is too high. The **IRR** must be between 10% and 16%

Trying 14% :

Year	£	PV£1@14%	Discounted sum
1	1,024	0.8772	899
2	4,000	0.7695	3,076
3	3,000	0.6750	2,025
			£6,000
		Less outlay	£6,000
		NPV	£0,000

As the **NPV** is **0** in *example 4.4*, the **IRR** must be **14%**.

Calculation of the **IRR** by the use of trial rates will be difficult when the **IRR** does not happen to coincide with a round figure, as in the following illustration.

Outlay £4,925

Trying 11% :

Year	Cash Flow £	PV£1@11%	Discounted sum
1	2,000	0.9009	1,802
2	2,000	0.8116	1,623
3	2,000	0.7312	1,462
			£4,887
	Less outlay		£4,925
	NPV		-£38

The trial rate is too high :

Trying 10% :

Year	£	PV£1@10%	Discounted sum
1	2,000	0.9091	1,818
2	2,000	0.8264	1,652
3	2,000	0.7513	1,503
			£4,973
	Less outlay		£4,925
	NPV		£48

The IRR is therefore between 10% and 11%.

Published tables may not give PV figures between 10% and 11%; the continued use of trial rates to make a more accurate estimation of the IRR will therefore be impracticable. The analysis has shown that the IRR lies between 10% and 11%, but the accuracy of such an analysis is limited.

A graph of NPVs plotted against trial rates will usually take the form shown in *Figure 4.1* below.

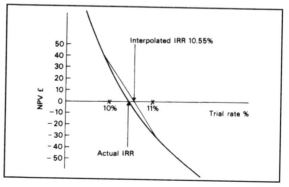

33

The graph shows how the **IRR** (producing an **NPV** of 0) lies between **10%** and **11%**.

If the graph is drawn accurately, it will be possible to estimate the **IRR** in this way. This process is both difficult and time-consuming and will not guarantee complete accuracy. The graph takes the shape of a gentle curve and although a straight line may be assumed between two sufficiently close trial rates and the **IRR** estimated to a fair degree of accuracy, it is not precise. This process is known as linear interpolation.

Linear interpolation can also be carried out by the use of the following formula, which simply assumes a straight-line relationship between the trial rates and the resulting **NPVs**.

IRR = Lower trial rate

$$+ \quad \frac{\text{NPV at lower trial rate}}{\text{NPV at lower trial rate} + \text{NPV at higher trial rate}}$$
(**ignoring signs**)

x Difference in trial rates.

In this case the lower trial rate is **10%**; the higher trial rate is **11%**; the **NPV** at the lower trial rate is £48 and the **NPV** at the higher trial rate is -£38.

The difference in trial rates is **1%**

$$\text{IRR} \quad = \quad 10\% + \frac{48}{48 + 38} \quad \text{x } 1\%$$

$$= \quad 10\% + \frac{48\%}{86}$$

$$= \quad 10\% + 0.558\% \quad = \underline{10.558\%}$$

This result is a more accurate representation of the geographical interpolation, which yielded a result of **10.55%**.

This method will provide a satisfactory answer in the majority of cases. However, it must be borne in mind that a graph of **NPVs** plotted against trial rates will result in a curve, and not a straight line between two points. Because of this, linear interpolation is inaccurate to a certain extent, and the result should not be expressed to too many decimal places.

An IRR of **10.56%** will be sufficiently reliable and precise for most purposes. Such calculations, however, are more readily undertaken using an investment calculator, the correct figure being **10.56087452%**.

Comparative use of NPV and IRR

When analysing a range of investments **NPV** and **IRR** results may be compared, in some cases conflicting results may arise and additional analysis may be needed to determine the best choice of investment.

Example 4.5

On the basis of **NPV** and **IRR** methods rank the following investments, using a rate of **10%** in each case.

Investment A Outlay £5,000		Investment B Outlay £10,000	
Income:	£	**Income:**	£
Year 1	600	Year 1	3,342
Year 2	2,000	Year 2	3,342
Year 3	4,000	Year 3	3,342
Year 4	585	Year 4	3,342

(a) NPV analysis : (Trial rate 10 %)

Investment A:

		£	PV£1@10%	Discounted sum
Year	1	600	0.9091	545
	2	2,000	0.8264	1,653
	3	4,000	0.7513	3,005
	4	585	0.6830	399
				£5,602
			Less outlay	£5,000
			NPV	£602

Investment B:

		£	PV£1@10%	Discounted sum
Year	1	3,342	0.9091	3,120
	2	3,342	0.8264	2,836
	3	3,342	0.7513	2,578
	4	3,342	0.6830	2,344
				£10,878
			Less outlay	£10,000
			NPV	£878

On the basis of the NPV analysis, the investor should choose investment B which has the highest NPV.

Example 4.5 (cont.)

(b) IRR analysis : It is clear from the **NPV** analysis that each investment has an **IRR** exceeding **10%** because the **NPV** is positive.

Investment A :

Trying 15%

Year	£	PV£1@15%	Discounted sum
1	600	0.8696	522
2	2,000	0.7561	1,512
3	4,000	0.6575	2,632
4	585	0.5718	334
			£5,000
		Less outlay	£5,000
		NPV	£0,000

Investment B :

Trying 14%

Year	£	PV£1@14%	Discounted sum
1	3,432	0.8772	3,011
2	3,432	0.7695	2,639
3	3,432	0.6750	2,317
4	3,432	0.5921	2,033
			£10,000
		Less outlay	£10,000
		NPV	£0,000

On the basis of the IRR analysis, the investor should choose investment A, because it has the highest IRR.

In this example the **IRR** and **NPV** methods give different rankings.

Which investment should be chosen?

In investment **B**, an extra £5,000 has been employed. This can produce certain extra benefits. To analyse the situation futher it is necessary to tabulate the difference in cash flows between investment **A** and **B** .

	A	B	B - A
Outlay	£5,000	£10,000	£5,000
Receipts :			
Year 1	£600	£3,432	£2,832
Year 2	£2,000	£3,432	£1,432
Year 3	£4,000	£3,432	-£568
Year 4	£584	£3,432	£2,848

Incremental analysis

The final column could be called the increment of **B** over **A**. This in itself becomes a cash flow on which an **NPV** or **IRR** analysis could be carried out. The cost of capital is **10%**, and, as it has been assumed to represent the investor's target rate, it is also assumed that this is a rate of return that could be earned elsewhere.

If the increment earns a return of less than **10%**, the investor would be wise to invest £5,000 in project **A** and obtain **10%** interest elsewhere with the remaining £5,000.

Another way of looking at this is to remember that the cost of capital also represents the cost of borrowing money. If the investor's £10,000 has been borrowed, a return of less than **10%** on the increment of £5,000 of project **B** over project **A** means that the loan charges on this £5,000 are not being covered and the loan of the second £5,000 was not worth while.

However, if the increment can be shown to produce a return in excess of **10%**, the loan charges will be covered. Investment B thus uses the whole £10,000 to good effect. If project **A** were chosen, the extra £5,000 could only earn **10%**, as it is assumed that no return in excess of the cost of capital could be earned without incurring an extra element of risk.

Such analysis is called *incremental analysis:*

Incremental flow:

	£	PV£1@10%	Discounted sum
Year 1	2,832	0.9091	2,575
2	1,432	0.8264	1,183
3	- 568	0.7513	- 427
4	2,848	0.6830	1,945
			£5,276
			- £5,000
		NPV[1] =	£ 276

The **IRR** of the increment exceeds **10%**, so investment **B** should be chosen. The first £5,000 employed is as profitable as it would be if used in investment **A**; the second £5,000 is used more profitably than is possible elsewhere. **B** is therefore preferable to the investment of £5,000 at the cost of capital rate of interest of **10%**.

Discounted cash flow tables in certain sets of valuation tables are simply extensions of the **present value of £1** and **present value of £1 per annum tables**: this illustrates the point that DCF is nothing more than a present value exercise.

[1] Any project incorporating frequent sign changes can produce more than one IRR due to the polynomial nature of the underlying equation.

Summary

4

This chapter has demonstrated the use of the PV function to assess the acceptability of investment opportunities measured against an investors target rate of return. In those cases where the results of an NPV and an IRR analysis conflict an incremental analysis may be undertaken to assess the return on any additional capital used.

The discounted cash flow process has two key components :

- *A Net Present Value calculation (NPV) discounts the net benefits of an investment using the present value function at the investor's target rate or opportunity cost of capital rate.*

  The initial outlay is deducted from the NPV and if the resultant sum is positive then the investment is acceptable at the target rate used.

- *An Internal Rate of Return (IRR) represents the investments return and is calculated by trial and error or through the use of an iterative process using investment calculators or spreadsheets. Generally the higher the IRR the better the investment opportunity given the same risk assessment.*

- *Care needs to be taken in accurately assessing the benefits and timing of such benefits, including any terminal or resale value at the end of the cashflow.*

- *Cash flows with negative sums arising during the life of the investment may produce multiple values of IRR.*

Spreadsheet User

Spreadshets are ideally suited to financial modelling, the application of discounted cash flow solutions and the calculation of internal rates of return. Indeed most spreadsheets have financial functions such as NPV and IRR built in to save time and trouble. However, as explained below the use of the built-in functions must be undertaken carefully as they may not operate in the way in which the user expects.

Project I

You are evaluating a scheme which will cost £80,000 immediately and generates the following cash flow at the end of each year :

Year I	£10,000
Year 2	£25,000
Year 3	£35,000
Year 4	£30,000
Year 5	£20,000

Calculate the Net Present Value of the Scheme and the Internal Rate of Return.

I: Construct a spreadsheet which calculates the Net Present Value.
Use the Present Value of £I formula in cell E5 and copy this formula to cells E6:E9.
In cell F5 enter the formula D5*E5 and copy to cells F6:F9.
To calculate the Net Present Value in cell F10 use the formula = sum(F4:F9)

(the use of the in-built Net Present Value and Internal Rate of Return functions are explored on page 36.)

	A	B	C	D	E	F
I						
2			Year		P.V £I@10%	Discounted sum
3						
4		Expenditure		-80000		-80000
5		Income	I	10000	0.9091	9091
6			2	25000	0.8264	20661
7			3	35000	0.7513	26296
8			4	30000	0.6830	20490
9			5	20000	0.6209	12418
10			NET PRESENT VALUE =			8957
11						
12			INTERNAL RATE OF RETURN =			13.90%

Project I (cont.)

The present value can be calculated directly from the cash flow and target rate using the **NPV** function.

The NPV function in Lotus :   @NPV(rate,range)   *the net present value of a series of cashflows (range), at the discount rate*

The NPV function in Excel :   NPV(rate,range)   *the net present value of a series of cashflows (range), at the discount rate*

Note : in both **NPV** functions it is assumed that the first cashflow occurs at the end of the first period, and subsequent cashflows at the the end of each subsequent period. In many property and other examples the user will wish the outlay to occur at the beginning of the first period as in this example.

Try calculating the **NPV** in Project I using the **NPV** function in a spare cell expressed as :

In Lotus I-2-3 :   @NPV(0.1,D4:D9)   *In Excel 4 :*   NPV(0.1,D4:D9)

the figure produced is £8,143 : which differs from our calculation using the present value formula.

This undervaluation is caused because the **NPV** function is treating the outlay of £80,000 as occurring at the end of Period 0 not at the beginning.

To use the **NPV** function in Lotus or Excel it needs to be modified if, as in most cases, the initial outlay occurs at the beginning of period 0.

The initial cashflow must be isolated so the **NPV** function in Project I must be modified to :

In Lotus I-2-3 :   -80000+@NPV(0.1,D5:D9)   *In Excel 4 :*   =-80000+NPV(0.1,D5:D9)

and the same result as the original calculation using the present value formula should result.

2:   Calculating the IRR.

The **IRR** function in both Lotus and Excel uses the iteration technique to calculate the discount rate at which the **NPV** for a given cash flow is equal to 0:

The IRR function in Lotus :   @IRR(guess,range)   *the internal rate of return of a series of cashflows (range), the guess rate being used only to start the iteration process.*

The IRR function in Excel :   IRR(range,guess)   *the internal rate of return of a series of cashflows (range), the guess rate being used only to start the iteration process.*

To calculate the **IRR** in Project I enter the following in a spare cell :

In Lotus I-2-3 :   @IRR(0.1,D4:D9)   *In Excel 4 :*   =IRR(D4:D9,0.1)

Note : for the **IRR** function to work there must be at least one positive and one negative value in the cashflow. Problems may occur where the cashflow is non-standard and changes sign several times.

Questions: part one

1: A sum of £250 is invested at 9.5% for 15 years. What sum will there be at the end of 15 years?

2: A capital sum of £1,500 is needed in 10 years. How much must be invested today assuming a compound rate of 8.5?

3: A mortgage of £40,000 is arranged at 8%. What is the annual repayment if the term is for 30 years?

4: A sum of £1,000 is invested at the end of each year and earns interest at 16%. How much will this accumulate to in 10 years' time?

5: How much must be invested each year at 6% compound interest to produce £2,500 in 16 years' time?

6: You have expectations of becoming a partner in private practice in 10 years' time. This will cost you £25,000.

   a) How could you provide for this?

   b) How much would it cost at 12%?

   c) How much would it cost today saving at 12%, if inflation is increasing the cost at 12%?

7: a) If you save £200 a year for 10 years in a building society at 7%, how much will you have at the end of ten years?

   b) If you added a further sum of £2,000 at the beginning of year 5, how much would you have at the end of 10 years?

   c) If you do (a) and (b) and leave it to accumulate for a further 5 years, how much will you have?

8: A shop is let at £10,000 a year for 5 years after which the rent will rise to £50,000 in perpetuity. What is its value on an 8% basis?

9: 8% Treasury Stock are selling at £80 per £100 face value certificate. What is the true rate of return if the stock has exactly 5 years to run to redemption?

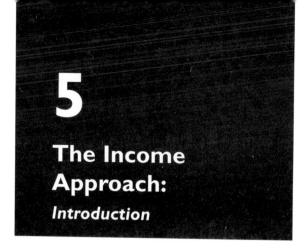

5

The Income Approach:

Introduction

Introduction

Valuation by direct capital comparison with sales in the market is the preferred method of valuation for most saleable goods and services. Valuation by this method is reliable provided that the sample of comparable sales is of sufficient size to draw realistic conclusions as to market conditions. This requires full knowledge of each transaction. Such a situation rarely exists in the market for investment property, and in the absence of directly comparable sales figures the valuer turns to the investment method. The investment method is used for valuing income-producing property whether freehold or leasehold, because as a method it most closely reflects the behaviour of the various parties operating in the property market.

Initially, the valuer considers the level of income or net benefits to be derived from the ownership of an interest in property, because investors are primarily concerned with the income and the risks attaching to that income when making investment decisions.

Valuation was earlier summarised as the estimation of the future benefits to be enjoyed from the ownership of a freehold or a leasehold interest in land or property, expressing those future benefits in terms of present worth. The valuer must therefore be able to assess these future net benefits *(income)* and be able to select the appropriate rate of interest in order to discount these benefits to derive their present value. The income approach to property valuation requires the valuer to concentrate on the assessment of the income pattern and the rate(s) of interest to be used to discount that income-flow.

Definitions

In a discipline that is derived from urban economics and investment analysis one would expect to find some common agreement as to the meaning of terms used by practitioners. This does not exist, so that additional problems may arise when advice is given to investors who are more acquainted with terms used by other financial advisers. The advice of the most expert valuer is of minimal value if it is misinterpreted, so a definition of terms used from hereon may be useful.

The explanations and definitions that follow may not achieve universal acceptance but are adhered to within this text and where indicated are mandatory on members of the RICS, ISVA and IRRV.

The question of value definition has bemused valuers and philosophers for centuries. It is recorded that Plato described 'the notion of value as the most difficult question of all sciences.' [1] An early definition is set out in the 1938 edition of Mustoe, Eve and Ansteys Complete Valuation Practice:

'In ordinary speech the "value" of a thing means the amount of money which that thing is worth in the open market. The valuer, whether he is valuing real property or chattels or livestock, endeavours to assess each article in terms of pounds, shillings and pence; to him "value" means the amount of money for which property will exchange' (Mustoe, Eve, Anstey 1938).

Considerable difficulties emerged in the 1970s and again in the 1990s, over the meaning and definition of value. The RICS addressed the issues through the Asset Valuation Standards Committee in the 1970s and reviewed the issue through a working party set up in 1993 under Michael Mallinson. Some of the recommendations of the Mallinson report have been accepted by the R.I.C.S. who now require valuers to use the following definitions *(see Appendix A for further details)*.

Market Value

This definition is the one adopted by the International Valuation Standards Committee (IVSC) and is considered by the RICS to be equivalent in its application to Open Market Value (see below).

'The estimated amount for which an asset should exchange on the date of valuation between a willing buyer and a willing seller in an arm's length transaction after proper marketing wherein the parties had each acted knowledgeably, prudently and without compulsion' (PS 4.1.1). [2]

---

1 *Real Estate Appraising in Canada, The Appraisal Institute of Canada.*

2 *Here and elsewhere in the text PS refers to the practice statements set out in the Appraisal and Valuation Manual, RICS, 1995.*

The definition is detailed in PS 4.1 and valuers must report to clients the fact that the valuation is based on the definition and its interprative commentary.

Open Market Value (OMV)

'An opinion of the best price at which the sale of an interest in property would have been completed unconditionally for cash consideration on the date of valuation, assuming:

> *(a) a willing seller;*
>
> *(b) that, prior to the date of valuation, there had been a reasonable period (having regard to the nature of the property and the state of the market) for the proper marketing of the interest, for the agreement of price and terms and for the completion of the sale;*
>
> *(c) that the state of the market, level of values and other circumstances were, on any earlier assumed date of exchange of contracts, the same as on the date of valuation;*
>
> *(d) that no account is taken of any additional bid by a purchaser with a special interest; and*
>
> *(e) that both parties to the transaction acted knowledgeably, prudently and without compulsion' (PS 4.2.1).*

Existing Use Value

'This definition is used as the basis for valuing property for financial statements where the property to be valued is occupied for the purpose of a business. It follows the OMV definition with the addition of two further assumptions :

> *(f) the property can be used for the forseeable future only for the existing use; and*
>
> *(g) that vacant possession is provided on completion of the sale of all parts of the property occupied by the business (save that, solely where the property is owned by a public or other non-profit making body for the delivery of a service, it is to be assumed that the property will continue to be occupied or let for its existing use)'*
> *(PS 4.3.1).*

Estimated Realisation Price: (ERP)

'An opinion as to the amount of cash consideration before deduction of costs of sale which the valuer considers, on the date of valuation, can reasonably be expected to be obtained on future completion of an unconditional sale of the interst in the subject property assuming :

> *(a) a willing seller;*
>
> *(b) that completion will take place on a future date specified by the valuer to allow a reasonable period for proper marketing, (having regard to the nature of the property and the state of the market);*
>
> *(c) that no account is taken of any additional bid by a purchaser with a special interest;*
>
> *(d) that both parties to the transaction acted knowledgeably, prudently and without compulsion.' (PS 4.5.1).*

Further definitions are set out in PS 4.

Whenever a valuation is prepared on an **ERP or ERRP** basis (other than on a standard form provided by the client) the valuer must also provide an opinion of **MV or OMV.**

Value in exchange

This is market value. If a good or service is incapable of being exchanged for other goods or services it has no market value.

Calculation of Worth

'The provision of a written estimate of the net monetary worth at a stated date of the benefits and costs of ownership of a specified interest in property to the instructing party, and reflecting the purpose(s) specified by that party.'

The extent to which the calculation of worth, at the stated date, differs from OMV should be set out clearly and under no circumstances should a calculation of worth be described as a valuation.

Price

Price is a historic fact except when qualified in such a phrase as **'offered at an asking price of ...'** Under perfect market conditions value in use would equate with value in exchange and price would be synonymous with value. The property market is not perfect and price and value cannot always be said to be equal.

Valuation

This is the art or science of estimating the value of interests in property. According to the dictionary, the word 'valuation' is interchangeable with the word 'appraisal'. The latter word is used by Baum and Crosby (1995) as a source term covering both the assessment of market value and ERP and for the estimations of worth. The latter is better considered as analysis. In the market the term 'appraisal' is sometimes used in reference to the 'Appraisal of a Development Scheme' or as implying a process that is more comprehensive than a mere opinion of value. For clarity this text uses the terms valuation and analysis.

Valuation is further defined by the RICS in the Appraisal and Valuation Manual as **'the provision of a written opinion as to capital price or value, or rental price or value, on any given basis in respect of an interest in property, with or without associated information, assumptions or qualifications'**.

Valuation report

This is the formal presentation of the valuer's opinion in written form. As a minimum it must contain a sufficient description to identify the property without doubt; a value definition; a statement as to the interest being valued and any legal encumbrances; the effective date of the valuation; any special feature of the property or the market that the valuer has taken special note of; and the value estimate itself. **(See Appendix B.)**

These definitions may be confusing to the reader and not obviously that important, but in practice they may be very important. Even more important is the valuer's instruction and the importance of communication between valuer and client. **'How much is it worth?'**, **'What price should I offer?'**, **'Is it worth £x million?'**, **'What figure should we include in our accounts for the value of our property assets?'** and **'Is that the same as their market worth?'**, are questions which may give rise to different responses from the valuer and might result in the valuer expressing different opinions for the same property interest for different purposes. The base or definition must be clarified at the time of agreeing instructions and must be confirmed in the valuation report **(see 'Valuation**

Process'). p46

Further commentary on these definitions and other bases of valuation are set out in **Appendix A**.

It is important for the valuer to have a clear understanding with the client regarding the most appropriate bases of valuation, be it:

- **Market Value (MV)**
- **Open Market Value (OMV),**
- **Open Market Value for the Existing Use (OMVEU),**
- **Open Market Value of the existing use by a Registered Housing Association (OMVEU-RHA),**
- **Open Market Value for Alternative Use (OMVAU),**
- **Estimated Realisation Price (ERP),**
- **Estimated Restricted Realisation Price (ERRP),**
- **Estimated Realisation Price for the existing use of a fully equipped operational entity valued having regard to trading potential, or**
- **Depreciated Replacement Cost (DRC).**

In terms of this book and the methods set out herein the terms 'value' or 'valuation' refers to the assessment of **Market Value, Open Market Value** or **Estimated Realisation Price** unless otherwise stated.

The Investment Method

The investment method is a method of estimating the present worth of the rights to future benefits to be derived from the ownership of a specific interest in a specific property under given market conditions. In property valuation these future rights can usually be expressed as future income (rent) and/or future reversionary capital value. The latter is in itself an expression of resale rights to future benefits. The process of converting future income flows to present value capital sums is known as capitalisation, which in essence is the summation of the future benefits each discounted to the present at an appropriate market-derived discount rate of interest. The terms *discount rate* and *capitalisation rate* are increasingly preferred to 'rate of interest', 'interest rate' or 'rate of return'. The use of the term 'rate of interest' should be restricted to borrowing, being the rate of interest charged on borrowed funds.

In *Chapter 1* a distinction was made between return on capital and return of capital. The interest rate or rate of return refers to return on capital only and is sometimes referred to as the remunerative rate to distinguish it from the return of capital or sinking fund rate. Technically a discount rate ignores capital recovery but in general valuation usage discount rate and capitalisation rate are synonymous and are assumed to mean any annual percentage rate used to convert a future benefit (income flow or lump sum) into a present worth estimate.

It is necessary to discount future sums at a rate to overcome :

- liquidity preference

- time preference

- the risks associated with uncertainty about the future.

Some of these risks have been identified by Baum and Crosby:

- Tenant risk   - Voids
               - Non payment of rent
               - Breach of Covenants

- Sector risk   Type specific: *Retail, Offices* Location specific

- Structural risk   Building failure Accelerated depreciation or obsolescence

- Legislation risk   New laws specific to property that might affect usability, rents, etc.

- Taxation risk   Possibility of future taxes on property

- Planning risk   planning policy may impinge upon performance *e.g. new roads, pedestrianisation*

- Legal risk   undiscovered issues affecting title

To which must be added the uncertainty associated with the macro economy and inflation. A capitalisation rate reflects all these factors and more and is referred to as an all risks yield (**ARY or Cap rate**).

In its simplest form income capitalisation is merely the division of income (I) by the annual rate of capitalisation (R).

A rate of capitalisation is expressed as a percentage - say **10%** - but as was stated in Chapter 1 all financial analyses and calculations require this ratio to be expressed as a decimal.

Therefore :

10% becomes 0.10,

and 8% = 0.08, and thus

Value (V) = I / i

The capitalisation factor in valuation is termed **years' purchase (YP)** *(see Chapter 1).*

The capitalisation of an infinite income, dividing by a market rate of capitalisation, is a simple exercise known as capitalisation in perpetuity. Where, however, the income is finite, then allowance must be made for recovery of capital. Two concepts exist in UK valuation practice: the internal rate of return and the sinking fund return. Each allows for the systematic return of capital over the life of the investment, but each approach is based on different assumptions.

The internal rate of return assumes that capital recovery is at the same rate as the return on capital i. It reflects the normal investment criterion of a return on capital outstanding from year to year and at risk, with the capital being returned from year to year out of income. Where capital recovery is at the same rate as the risk rate the table used is the **present value of £1 per annum (YP single rate)** which in turn is the reciprocal of the **annuity £1 will purchase**. Thus any finite income stream can be treated as an annuity calculation. This concept is the more acceptable because the present worth of any future sum is that sum which if invested today would accumulate at compound interest to that future sum, and hence the present worth of a number of such sums is the sum of their present values.

If the sums are equal and receivable in arrears then

$$V = I \times \frac{1 - PV}{i}$$

If the sums vary from year to year then :

$$V = \sum \frac{I1}{(1 + i)} + \frac{I2}{(1 + i)^2} + \frac{I3}{(1 + i)^3} \cdots \frac{In}{(1 + i)^n}$$

Mathematically there need be no distinction between the two concepts as capital recovery can always be provided within a capitalisation factor by incorporating a sinking fund to recover capital:

$$PV £1 \text{ p.a.} = \frac{1}{i + SF}$$

But if it can be shown that investors insist on a return on initial outlay throughout the life of the investment, then the sinking fund concept is the more acceptable. Further, if it can be shown that investors expect a return of capital at a different rate to the return on capital then this can be allowed for in the formula (see page 17).

The arithmetic manipulation of figures in capitalisation exercises is not, of course, valuation.

Valuation is a process which requires careful consideration of a number of variables before figures can be substituted in mathematically proven formulae. Any assessment of present worth or market value can only be as good as the data input allows and that factor is dependent upon the education, skill and market experience of the valuer. Ability to analyse and understand the market is of paramount importance.

Valuation has been likened to a science, not because of any precision that may or may not exist, or because in part it involves certain basic mathematics, but because the question *'How much?'* poses a problem that requires a solution.

The scientific approach to problem solving is to follow a systematic process. There may well be short cuts within the process. Indeed the discounting exercise itself, because it is repetitive, can frequently be carried out by pre-programmed calculators and computers. Short cuts exist if data are already available, but adoption of a systematic approach provides the confidence that full account has been taken of all the factors likely to affect the value of a property. This systematic approach is outlined in the Valuation Process.

Valuation process

First the valuer should define the problem.

'What are the client's real requirements?'

'Why does he/she want a valuation?'

'What is the purpose of the valuation?'

These questions should establish whether the client requires a market valuation, or a valuation for company asset purposes, insurance, or rating.

The date of the valuation must be ascertained. If a value is required for book purposes at a certain date, an 'in advance rental' may require an 'in arrears' valuation and vice versa.

Following the Mallinson report the RICS has reconfirmed the need for the valuer to clarify and agree conditions of engagement; that is, to confirm the clients instructions and to do so in writing. This stage in the process is a mandatory requirement for RICS, ISVA and IRRV members, the details are set out in the practice statements (*see Appendix A*).

Having established the fact that the instructions are within the valuer's competence and having confirmed the instructions, the valuer needs to arrange to inspect the property and to collect all the data needed for the valuation.

Within specific economic and market conditions the valuer will be considering five principal qualities:

● **the quality of the legal title.**

● **the quality of the location.**

● **the quality of the building.**

● **the quality of the lease(s).**

● **the quality of the tenant(s) in occupation or those that can be assumed in the case of a new or owner-occupied property.**

The following schedule and *Figure 5.1* provide some idea of the mass of data that needs to be collected and assessed in order to arrive at an objective opinion of the property's marketable qualities' which in turn colour the valuer's judgement as to the income generating capabilities of the property and its suitability as an investment.

The property:	Site measurements
	Building measurements:
	External, internal, number of floors
	(In accordance with RICS code of Measurement Practice)
	Elevation, orientation
	Services:
	heating, lighting,
	air conditioning, lifts, etc.
	Age and design
	Suitability of premises for present use
	Adaptability
	Accessibility to markets, amenities, labour
Legal:	Interest to be valued
	Freehold or leasehold
	Details of title restrictions such as:
	restrictive covenants
	Details of any leases or sub-leases, tenants, rent levels, lease terms
Planning:	Permitted uses
Economic:	General
	State of economy

Economic (cont.)	Regional and local
	Population structure
	Average wages
	Principal employment
	State of local industry
	Economic base of area
	Level of unemployment
	Town and regional growth prospects
	Transportation, existing and planned
	Current planning proposals
	Building societies, savings banks and general level of investment in the town and region
	Position of town in regional hierarchy
Market:	**Total stock of similar property**
	Comparison of subject property to the stock
	New stock in course of construction and planned
	Vacancy rates
	General level of rents and rates
	Tenant demand for similar property
Alternative investments:	**Other properties**
	Stocks and Shares
Legislation:	**Planning control**
	Landlord and tenant control over rents and security of tenure.
	Privity of contract
	Safety, health and working conditions and controls.
	European Union Directives

This significant amount of data is collected for analysis if considered significant in terms of value. The valuer needs to know what other properties are in the market, whether they are better in terms of location, etc., who are in the market as potential purchasers and as potential tenants, and whether the market for the subject property is active.

To collect the level of information required entails either very sound local knowledge, or the need to make enquiries of the local planning authorities, rating authorities, highway authorities, transport companies and local census statistics.

Thus one finds that the major firms of surveyors and valuers will now hold on file considerable detailed information on the City and West End of London, including in some instances very detailed street-by-street information, and similar information on the main provincial cities. This information source is kept up to date by research members extracting relevant information from national and local papers, local council minutes, etc.

Figure 5.1 **Factors determining investors' yield requirements and market capitalisation rates.**

General level of interest rates
Economy / Government Policy / Alternative Investment Opportunities

Legislation
Planning / Landlord & Tenant / Building Health / Fire / Working Conditions Environmental / EU

Age and condition of building
Repairs / Fashion / Adaptability

Inflation
Rental Growth Capital growth

Location
Accessibility Markets Labour

Security
Tenant / Rent Lease Terms

Taxation
Rates / Income / Corporation / CGT / CTT

Liquidity
Ease / Cost of transfer

Volatility
Sensitivity to market change

Management
Tenant Mix / Service Charges Lease Responsibilities

Having collected the information shown above, it is then necessary to consider the market.

'A major danger in assessing the direct property market lies in failing to identify the main segments into which the market is divided according to the value, reversionary terms, etc. ... of a property'.[3]

The valuer must be able to identify :

- **the most probable type of purchaser**

- **the alternative comparable properties on the market**

- **the current level of demand within that sub market, and**

- **any new construction work in hand.**

3 *Greenwell & Co. Property Report, October 1976.*

These and other questions will indicate what market data are required as preparatory material for the valuation. A particular concern to valuers is the need to identify the possibility of the property containing deleterious materials and/or of the site being contaminated. The valuer needs to alert the client to the possibility that the valuation report will contain a number of exclusions or caveats, the recommended caveats are contained in the RICS Practice Statements.

The most difficult aspect in an income capitalisation exercise is the determination of the correct capitalisation rate. Every property investment is different, and if the available data on sales are insufficiently comparable then it may become difficult to justify the use of a selected rate. Thus if a property with a 7 year rent review pattern sells on a 7% basis then this can be assumed to be the market capitalisation rate for that type of property let on 7 year review with the first review at a comparable date in the future and with a comparable level of rental increase.

If the subject property differs in any respect then the valuer will need to seek better comparables or will have to adjust that rate to reflect the differences between the old property and the subject property.

The valuation process can be redefined[4] as shown in *Figure 5.2*

Figure 5.2	The Valuation Process

Assess gross income from lease or estimate gross income potential from the market

Deduct

Allowances for voids

equals

Effective gross income

Deduct

Allowances for outgoings on repairs, insurance, management and any other operating expenses or non-recoverable service costs including rates

equals

Implied net income	Contracted net income

Capitalised (with reversion if appropriate) to produce estimate of total present value

[4] see The Appraisal Process by D.H. Mackmin.

Within this process the three main variables likely to have the greatest effect on the final estimate of value can be identified: income *(rent)*, operating expenses, and capitalisation rate. It is our presumption that a valuer practising in a well-run valuation department will be able to provide reliable figures for these items readily, and should be able to substantiate these figures from available analysed data.

Income or rent

Capitalisation is the expression of future benefits in terms of their present value. Valuation therefore requires the valuer to consider the future: but current UK valuation practice reflects a distrust of making predictions. The convention has developed of using initial yields on rack rented property as the capitalisation rates to be applied to current estimates of future rental income, thereby building into the capitalisation rate the market's forecast of future expectations. The forecast is still made but the valuer has avoided any explicit statement. American appraisers consider this approach to be outmoded and argue that it should only be used if a level constant income flow is the most probable income pattern. In other circumstances they recommend the use of a Discounted Cash Flow Approach.

The RICS research report *(Trott, 1980)* on valuation methods recommended the use of growth explicit models for investment analysis and suggested that a greater use should be made of growth explicit DCF models in the market valuation of property investments.

This view is supported by *Baum and Crosby (1995)*, and the **RICS Appraisal and Valuation Standards Board** has set up a working party to *'drive forward work on the production of modified all-risk yield methodologies'*.

Whenever the investment method is to be used, whether in relation to tenant-occupied property or owner-occupied property, an initial essential step is the estimation of the current rental value of that property. If the property is already let this allows the valuer to consider objectively the nature of the present rent roll. Initially the most important task must be the estimation of rental income.

If the property is owner-occupied then it is necessary to assess the imputed rental income. The assessment requires analysis of current rents being paid, rents being quoted and the vacancy rate of comparable properties.

This assessment should for preference be carried out in accordance with the RICS definition of Open Market

Rental Value (OMRV) as follows:

'An opinion of the best rent at which a new letting of an interest in property would have been completed at the date of valuation, assuming;

(a) a willing landlord;

(b) that, prior to the date of valuation, there had been a reasonable period (having regard to the nature of the property and the state of the market) for the proper marketing of the interest, for the agreement of the rent and other letting terms and for the completion of the letting;

(c) that the state of the market, level of values and other circumstances were, on any earlier assumed date of entering into an agreement for lease, the same as on the date of valuation;

(d) that no account is taken of any additional bid by a prospective tenant with a special interest;

(e) a stated length of term and stated principal conditions applying or assumed to apply to the letting and that the other terms are not exceptionally onerous for a letting of the type and class of the subject property;

(f) that no premium passed and that any rent free period is in respect only of the time which would have been needed by the incoming tenant to make the subject property fit for occupation; and

(g) that both parties to the transaction acted knowledgeably, prudently and without compulsion.' (PS 4.9.1).

It will be seen later that this differs to the statutory definition in the **Landlord & Tenant Act 1954** and will differ to many sets of assumptions set out in existing leases. In assessing the rental value of a property the valuer needs to check the basis for such calculations before turning to the market for supporting evidence *see Figure 5.3.*

Figure 5.3   Rental Basis

Situation:	Basis:
Lease renewals of business premises under Landlord & Tenant Act 1954	s.34 Landlord & Tenant Act 1954
Rent Reviews	Rent Review clause within current lease
Vacant Property, owner occupied property or where a reversion to a new letting can be assumed.	PS 4.9.1
Estimates of OMRV	PS 4.9.1

Detailed analysis of the letting market must precede analysis of a specific letting. Thus if it can be demonstrated within the market for office space that such space users will pay a higher rent for ground floor space than for space on a higher floor then this may be reflected in the way in which a letting of a whole office building is analysed in terms of rent per square metre. If the rent of luxury flats and apartments can be shown to have a closer correlation with the number of bedrooms than with floor area then analysis might be possible on a per bedroom basis.

If floor area is to be used then continuing analysis will indicate whether or not bids are influenced by, for example:

the size and quality of:

- entrances,

- shared areas,

the provision of:

- air conditioning

- car parking

- security

- lifts

communal facilities:

- recreation, leisure, food

- banks, cash points

- first aid

Reliable estimates of current rents can only flow from analysis of rents actually being paid, and under no circumstances should a valuation be based on an estimate of rent derived from analysis of an investment sale where there is no current rack rent passing. This is because rent analysed in this manner depends upon the assumption of a capitalisation rate.

For example, if the only information available on a transaction is that a building of **500 m²** has just been sold for **£50,000** with vacant possession, the only possible analysis is of sale price per square metre.

In most cases analyses of rent being paid should be on the basis of net lettable space, but agricultural land is often quoted on a total area basis inclusive of farm dwellings and buildings.

Net lettable space becomes more meaningful if it is taken to mean the net area of the building suitable for use for the purpose let as defined in the **RICS Code of Measurement**. This definition excludes circulation space within the building such as stairwells, landings, lifts and ancillary facilities such as wash rooms. The rent analysed on this basis reflects the quantity and quality of the facilities provided, which should of course be noted on any data record sheet for future use. The precise set of rules for measuring buildings of different use types will vary from valuer to valuer and from area to area, but the old adage *'as you analyse so should you value'* should be adhered to in terms of building measurement.

There is a growing tendency for shop premises to be let at a fixed rental plus a percentage of profit or turnover. Where a valuation is required of property let on such terms full details of total rents actually collected, checked against audited accounts for a minimum of 3 years, should be used as the basis for determining income cash flows for valuation purposes.

Where evidence is provided from outside the valuer's own sources it should be presented in the format specified in the RICS Appraisal and Valuation Manual.

Due to the heterogeneous nature of property it is customary to express rent in terms of a suitable unit of comparison thus:

Agricultural land	*rent per hectare*
Office and factory premises	*rent per square metre*
Shops	*rent per square metre overall or per square metre front zone*

The measurement of retail premises: zoning

Three alternative approaches have been developed for analysing shop rent:

**overall analysis,
arithmetic zoning and
natural zoning.**

a) Overall analysis

The rent for the retail space is divided by the lettable rental space to obtain an overall rent per m². This is a simple approach but is complicated by the practice of letting retail space together with space on upper floors used for storage, sales, rest rooms, offices or residential accommodation at a single rental figure. In these circumstances it is desirable to isolate the rent for the retail space.

Some valuers suggest there is a relationship between ground floor space and space on the upper floors - this will only be the case where the user is the same or ancillary (e.g. storage). Here custom or thorough analysis will indicate the relationship, if any, between ground floor and upper floor rental values. Where the use is different the rent of the upper floor should be assessed by comparison with similar space elsewhere and deducted from the total rent before analysis. Thus if the upper floors comprise flats then the rent for these should be assessed by comparison within the residential market and then deducted from the total rent.

Overall analysis tends to be used for shops in small parades and for large space users. In the latter case it is reasonable to argue that tenants of such premises will pay a pro rata rent for every additional square metre up to a given maximum. The problem here is that what one retailer might consider to be a desirable maximum could be excessive for all other reailers. Such a point should be reflected as a risk accounted for by the valuer in his selection of capitalisation rate.

b) Arithmetic zoning

This approach is preferred in many cases to an overall rent analysis because, in retailing, it is the space used to attract the customer into the premises that is the most valuable (namely the frontage to the street or mall). Again the rent for the retail space should be isolated before analysis.

Example 5.3

Analyse the rent of £50,000 being paid for shop premises with a frontage of **6 m** and a depth of **21 m**.

Overall = £50,000 $\div$ 126 (6 x 21) = **£396.82 per m²**

Zoning: *Assume zones of 7 m depth and £x per m²*
rent for Zone A

Then	Zone A = 6 x 7	= 42 m² at £x	= 42.0x
	Zone B = 6 x 7	= 42 m² at £$\frac{1}{2}$x	= 21.0x
	Zone C = 6 x 7	= 42 m² at £$\frac{1}{4}$x	= 10.5x
			73.5x

$$£50,000 \div 73.5 = x$$
$$£680.27 = x$$

The rental value for Zone A is therefore £680 per m²

The observant reader will realise that the space could be divided into any number of zones. Different regions and different retail centres display different trading patterns, and whilst a common convention is to use two zones and a remainder with Zone A and B of 7 m depth other practices will be found. Custom and practice do not necessarily reflect market behaviour and adapting different zones and zone depths for analysis can produce considerable variations in opinion as to rental value for a given location. A current concern is the proposed switch from imperial measures where 20-foot zones or their equivalent metric figure may be replaced by depths expressed initially in metres e.g. 6m/7m Zone A depths. The arithmetical implications on rental analysis and hence opinions of rental value are very real; but rents do not vary because of variations in the zones used by valuers, they vary because of variations in trading potential.

Certainly in practice retailers do not see the premises divided into rigid zones. Every rental estimate must be looked at in the light of the current market and common sense - who would be the most probable tenant for premises 7 m wide by 100 m deep? Is there any user who operates in such space, or is the last 50 m waste or valueless space for most retailers in that locality?

c) Natural zoning[5]

This method can only effectively be used to analyse rents within a shopping street or centre where information is available on a number of units, as it requires comparison between units. As previously explained the rents for retail space must be isolated from the rent for the premises as a whole.

The rent of two adjoining premises, one of **6 m x 21 m**, let at **£50,000** per annum, the other **8 m x 25 m**, let at **£65,000** per annum can then be considered.

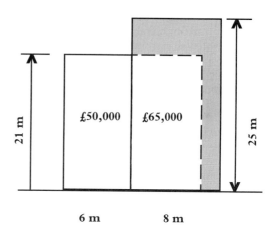

The method here argues that if retailers are paying £50,000 for **6 m x 21 m** and £65,000 for **8 m x 25 m** then £15,000 represents the rent for the area hatched in the sketch. Even here the logic may collapse if somewhere within the parade there is a shop **6 m x 20 m** let at £67,500 per annum.

In terms of the rental analysis of retail space, warehouse accommodation and factory space, the valuer needs to have a sound knowledge of the specific requirements of different retailers and of different manufacturers.

Where one is dealing with standard shop units, for example within a shopping mall, the unit of comparison can often be left as the 'shop unit'. Rent will be a factor of location/position and not size.

[5] See R. Emeny and H.M. Wilks, 'Principles and Practice of Rating Valuation', Estates Gazette, 1982.

The developing technique, although not yet found to be any more satisfactory than those listed, is multi-variate analysis when the dependent variable rent is considered against a number of independent variables which could include size, location, distance from car parks, bus station, etc.

It would be ideal if all rental estimates could be based on true comparables, i.e. those of the same size, design, facilities, location, etc. This is rarely the case in practice. With experience, adjustments can be made for some of these variations, but wherever possible estimates of rent should be based on close comparables.

As far as office records are concerned, strict procedures should be adhered to so that the format of data is consistent. In this respect it is recommended that all rents are analysed net of landlord's outgoings (see below) and that apart from obvious factors such as the address of the property the record should contain details of facilities included (e.g. central heating, air conditioning) and the lease terms.

The valuer must be in possession of all the facts of a given letting before any rental figure can be analysed. In the case of residential and commercial property statute intervenes to protect the tenant in several ways *(see Chapter 10)*. Thus a tenant of business premises who carries out improvements would not expect to pay an increase in rent for these improvements on the renewal of the lease. The valuer must therefore know the basis upon which a given rent was agreed before he can make proper use of the information. An earlier lease might have been surrendered or the tenant might have undertaken to modernise the premises. Either of these could have resulted in a rental lower than a market rental being agreed between the parties. And of increasing concern is the lease definition of rent where there is provision for a rent review - there is almost certainly a difference between 'full market rental' and a 'reasonable rent', the latter inferring something less than the maximum rent achievable if offered in the open market.

The RICS has produced proformas where rental evidence is obtained from other valuers. These have been prepared to ensure that valuers seeking information from another professional will be provided with all the data necessary to arrive at a reasoned analysis.

It is arguable that the rent agreed for a 20-year lease without review will differ from that agreed for the same lease with 10-year, 7-year or 5-year reviews. Whether these rents would be higher or lower will depend upon whether the rental market is rising or falling *(see Chapter 9)*. For preference, comparability should entail estimating rents from analyses of lettings with similar review patterns. If this is not possible it must be remembered that capitalisation is the discounting of income flows at a market derived rate and that it is the combination of income and discount rate which produces the estimate of present value.

The need in a weak letting market for landlords to offer inducements such as fitting out costs and rent-free periods indicates the need for valuers to be in full possession of all the facts before reaching any conclusion on market rents being paid.

Crudely a rent of **£50,000 p.a.** agreed for a property for a period of **5** years with no rent payable for one year would be viewed by the market as a rent of **£40,000 p.a.**

(£50,000 x 4 years ÷ 5 years) = £40,000

The landlord's argument is that the rental value is **£50,000** a year but it has been waived for 12 months.

Other inducements can be considered in a similar way. Thus **£100,000** given for fitting out the building might be treated as equivalent over 5 years to a reduction of **£20,000** a year, i.e., the rental value without the **£100,000** would have had to fall to **£30,000** a year to induce a letting.

The main issue with all such inducements is assessing the period of time to which the inducement applies. The authors' opinion is that it should apply only to the period up to the first full rent review. Strictly speaking a discounting approach should be adopted to reflect the time value of money.

Rental value will also be affected by a number of other lease clauses. Particular attention should be paid to those dealing with alienation - assignment and subletting; user; repair and service charges. Although the **Landlord and Tenant Act 1988** now ensures that landlords do not unduly delay the granting of consents in conditional cases, the position in relation to an absolute prohibition on alienation remains unchanged. In the latter case there will be an adverse effect on rents. User restrictions in shopping centres and multiple tenanted commercial property can have a beneficial effect on rents, but where they are too restrictive they will have a detrimental effect on rents.

The Landlord & Tenant (Covenants) Act 1995 has amended the Law on Privity of Contract. It allows landlords to define in a lease the qualifications of acceptable assignees and whilst 'reasonableness' remains a factor, some leases will be seen to be more onerous than others due to such legally permitted restrictions.

Responsibility for repairs and the nature of any service charge provisions must be considered twice: firstly to see if they are affecting market rents, and secondly to see if they leave the landlord with a liability which must be estimated and deducted as a landlord's expense before capitalisation. (For valuation purposes rent must be net of VAT.)

Landlords' expenses

Where investment property is already subject to a contracted lease rent, and/or where it is customary to quote rents for a specific type of property on gross terms, it is essential to deduct landlords' outgoings (operating expenses) before capitalising the income. Investment valuations must be based on net income. This means an income net of all the expenses that the owner of an interest in property is required to meet out of the rents received from ownership of that interest in that property other than tax.

Expenses may be imposed upon the landlord by legislation, or they may be contractual, as in an existing lease. But an inspection of the property may suggest that, though neither party is statutorily or contractually liable, there are other expenses that will have to be met by the owner of that interest in the property. The valuer must identify all such liabilities and make full allowance for them in the valuation. In order to do this, reference must be made to all existing leases in respect of the property.

The principal items of expenditure can be broadly classified under the headings of insurance, management, taxes, running expenses and repairs. Of these only the cost of complying with repairing obligations should cause any real difficulty in accurate assessment.

Insurance

The valuer armed with plans and his own detailed measurements of the building will be able to estimate or obtain an accurate quotation for all insurances, particularly fire insurance. Fire insurance is an extremely involved subject, complicated by the variation in insurance policies offered. A valuer should therefore be acquainted with the terms and conditions of policies offered by two or three leading insurance companies and should always assess the insurance premium in accordance with those policies.

If reinstatement value is required this can be referred to a building surveyor or preferably a quantity surveyor, or may be based on adjusted average figures extracted from Spon's *Architects' and Builders' Price Book*. Due to the 'averaging provisions' of most policies it is better to be over-insured than under-insured, and hence to overestimate rather than underestimate this item.

Quotations for other insurances necessary on boilers, lifts, etc., can always be obtained from a broker or insurance company.

A deduction for insurance will rarely be necessary as the lease will usually contain provisions for the recovery of all insurance charges from the tenant in addition to the rent. In most cases the wording of a 'full repairing and insuring lease' leaves the responsibility for insurance with the owner, but the cost of the insurance with the tenant.

Management

This refers to the property owner's supervising costs equivalent to the fee that would be due to a management agent for rent collection; attendance to day-to-day matters such as the granting of licences to assign/sub-let or to alter the premises; inspections of the premises, and instructions to builders to carry out repairs. It is frequently considered to be too small to allow for in the case of premises let to first class tenants on full repairing and insuring terms. The valuer must use discretion but it is suggested that if the valuer's firm would charge a fee for acting as managing agents, then a similar cost will be incurred by any owner of the property and a deduction for management should therefore be made.

The fee may be based on a percentage of rents and service charges collected or on a negotiated annual fee. The practising valuer will be aware of the appropriate market adjustments to make, based on current fees charged by managing agents. Where VAT is payable on rents it will impose an additional management cost which will be reflected in the fees negotiated by the managing agents. Where the management fee is recoverable as part of a full service charge no deduction need be made in a valuation of the landlord's interest.

Taxes

The Uniform Business Rate (UBR) is paid by the occupier of business premises. Inspection of the lease will indicate the party to that lease who has contracted to meet the 'rates' demand. If premises are let at an inclusive rental (i.e. inclusive of UBR) then rates should be deducted. If let exclusive then no deduction is necessary. If the letting is inclusive and there is no 'excess rates clause' then the deduction must represent the average annual figure expected up until the end of the lease or next review, not a figure representing current rates.

If an excess rates clause is included then the sum to be deducted is the amount of rates due in the first year of the lease or the lowest sum demanded during the current lease. This is because such a clause allows for the recovery from the tenant of any increase in rates over and above the amount due in the first year of the lease.

Other *'rates'* may include water rates, drainage rates, and rates for environmental and other purposes.

It has always been the custom in the UK to value before deduction of tax on the grounds that income and corporation tax are related to the individual or company, and not to the property. However, if market value implies the most probable selling price, there is automatically an implication of the most probable purchaser. The valuer without this knowledge cannot be held to be assessing market value; thus it is held by some that the tax liability of the most probable purchaser should be reflected in the valuation *(see Chapter 8)*.

For simplicity, no deduction will be made for tax in most of this text.

Running expenses

Where the owner of an interest is responsible for the day-to-day running of a property such as a block of flats, and office building let in suites, or a modern shopping centre, a deduction from rent may be necessary to cover the cost of items such as heating, lighting, cleaning and porterage. Current practice is to include provision for a separate service charge to be levied to cover the full cost of most running expenses.

The valuer must therefore inspect the leases to check the extent to which such expenses are recoverable. Older leases tend to include partial service charges, in which case the total income from the property should be assessed and the total cost of services deducted.

All the items falling under the general head of 'running expenses' are capable of accurate assessment by reference to current accounts for the subject property; by comparison with other properties; by enquiry of electricity, gas and oil suppliers; by enquiry of staff agencies; and so on. The valuer operating within a firm with a large management department is at a distinct advantage, as that department should be able to provide fairly accurate estimates based on detailed analyses of comparable managed property.

Where a full service charge is payable this is usually adjustable in arrears. In other words, the annual service charge is based on last year's expenses. During periods of rapidly rising costs the owner will have to meet the difference between service cost and service charge, and if this is a significant recurrent amount it represents a reduction in the owner's cash flow and should be taken into account in a valuation.

Increasingly these points are being met by more complex service charge clauses and schedules which provide for interim increases; for example to cover the uncertain energy element in running expenses.[6]

Repairs

A detailed consideration of existing leases will indicate those items of repair that have to be met by the landlord out of rental income. The sum to be deducted from an annual income before capitalisation must be an annual averaged figure. Thus liability to redecorate a building every 5 years should be estimated and averaged over the 5 years. A check should be made against double accounting - if the cost of repairs to boilers, lifts, etc., is covered by a service charge then no allowance should appear under repairs for such items. If indeed the cost of redecoration is recoverable by a direct proportionate charge to tenants then no deduction need be made.

Where an allowance has to be made every effort is required to estimate the amount as accurately as possible. An excess allowance will lead to an undervaluation, inadequate allowance to an overvaluation.

Advice, if needed, should be obtained from builders and building surveyors as well as by comparison with other known repair costs for comparable managed property.

Essential works

Any obvious immediate renewals or repairs as at the date of the valuation should be allowed for by a deduction from the estimate of capital value to reflect the cost (*see Chapter 9*).

Averages and percentages

Valuers should use averages with care. An example of this is the use of average heating costs per square metre. The valuer is required to value a specific property, not an average property. The requirement is to estimate the average annual cost of heating that specific property. Some valuers, texts, and correspondence courses suggest that it is a reasonable approach to base insurance

---

[6] *The statutory requirements relating to service charges and management charges in residential property are complex. Readers involved or interested in the residential sector must refer to all current Housing and Landlord and Tenant legislation.*

premiums and repair costs on a percentage of full rental value. This approach is not recommended unless the valuer can prove that the figure adopted is correct. A percentage allowance may be widely inaccurate; a High Street shop could be worth £100,000 a year and a block of 20 flats could be worth £100,000 a year, but the latter will almost certainly cost more to keep in repair. Two properties may let at identical rents, but one may be constructed of maintenance-free materials, the other more cheaply constructed with short-life material. A thousand square metres of space in Oxford Street, London, and in Exeter, Devon, may cost the same to maintain but could have very different full rental values. A large old building may let at the same rent as a small modern building, and clearly the repairs will differ.

Similar points may be made in respect of the use of percentages to estimate insurance premiums.

Voids

Where there is an over-supply of space within a given area the probability of voids occurring when leases terminate is increased. If a single investment building is let in suites to '*n*' tenants, voids may occur sufficiently regularly for a valuer to conclude that the average occupancy is only, say, **95%**. In such cases, having estimated the full rental value, the figure should be reduced to the level of the most probable annual amount. Voids are less likely to affect operating expenses so a pro rata allowance on operating costs should not be made. Indeed in some exceptional cases it may have to be increased to allow for empty rates, non-recoverable service costs and additional security.

In the case of a building let to a single tenant, a void is only likely to occur at the end of the current lease. If this is a reasonable expectation then the income pattern must be assumed to be broken at the renewal date for the length of time considered necessary to allow for finding a new tenant. Additional allowances may have to be made for negative cash flows if empty rates and other running expenses have to be met by the owner during this period.

The time taken to renew leases to current tenants and to negotiate rent reviews can represent a significant loss to a landlord. New leases will contain 'interest' clauses to cover interest lost on rent arrears, and delayed settlement of reviews and renewals.

In other cases the valuer may wish to adjust rental income down to reflect the fact that agreement is unlikely to coincide with the rent review or lease renewal date.

Purchase expenses

Rent charges

In the few cases where rent charges occur these should be allowed for in a valuation by making a capital deduction. The sum to be deducted is the redemption cost, calculated in accordance with the **Rent Charges Act, 1977.**

Stamp duty, solicitors' fees, etc.

It has long been valuation practice when giving investment advice to include in the total purchase price an allowance to cover stamp duty, solicitors' fees, and any other expenses to the purchaser occasioned by the transaction including VAT. This in total currently amounts to **2.75 - 3%** of the purchase price.

It should be remembered that analysis of a transaction might also take these expenses into account to reveal the purchaser's yield on total outlay rather than the yield realised on the purchase price alone.

It is current practice in investment valuation work to express value net of these sums. However, MV, OMV and ERP are normally expressed without deduction for selling expenses.

Income Capitalisation or DCF

The first step in the income approach is to identify the actual net rent being paid (Net Operating Income: **NOI** in North American appraisal practice), and the current open market rent in net terms.

The second step is to determine the most appropriate basis of discounting the income; that is, whether to use:

- **Non-growth Discounted Cash Flow.**

- **Growth explicit Discounted Cash Flow.**

- **Conventional Income Capitalisation.**

- **Rational or real value methods.**

In an active property market the valuer will be able to determine an appropriate capitalisation rate *(all risks yield)* from the analysis of sales of comparable properties.

For a property to be comparable it will need to be:

- similar in use

- similar in location

- similar in age, condition, design, etc. (i.e. to have similar utility value)

- similar in quality of tenant

- let on similar lease terms.

Where a property sale meets most but not all of these criteria the experienced valuer with good market knowledge will be able to adjust the capitalisation evidence obtained from the market for any variations.

Experience or knowledge here means knowing:

- **the current players in the market**

- **who is selling which type of property and why**

- **who is buying which type of property and why**

- **the current state of the market and the underlying reasons for it rising or falling**

- **the national, regional and local economic situation.**

Analysis of current sales prices must be undertaken on a consistent basis, the valuer needs full details of the transaction in order to assess the capitalisation rate net of purchase costs.

Example 5.4

An office building is currently let at its open market rent of £100,000 a year net of all outgoings with rent reviews every 5 years. It has just been sold for £1,250,000. **Assess the capitalisation rate.**

$$\frac{100,000}{1,250,000} \times 100 = 8\%$$

In practice the transaction may have been completed at a price to produce a return of 8% on total acquisition cost to the purchaser and thus £1,250,000 would represent price plus fees hence:

let purchase price = £x
let purchase costs = 3%

then $1.03x$ = £1,250,000
       x = £1,213,592
and capitalisation rate = 8.24%

A variation in capitalisation rate of 0.25% can be very significant at the lower rates.

Thus:

Income	£100,000
YP perp @ 4.25%	23.52941
	£2,352,941

Income	£100,000
YP perp @ 4.00%	25.0
	£2,500,000

Here the **0.25%** variation represents **£147,059** or a variation in value of **5.88%.**

The market evidence and market knowledge will allow the valuer to express an opinion on capitalisation rates with some confidence and to be able to make 'intuitive' or professional adjustments for variation between the subject property and the market evidence:

market evidence

8%

less than 8 %	8% plus
superior property	*inferior property*

In some cases the property will display qualities which add to and detract from the quality of the investment. Thus a property may be in a marginally better location but may be marginally less efficient having only **75%** net to gross floor area compared to the normal **80%** for the market.

The subtleties of market intuition cannot be taught, they have to be acquired from experience.

Where the property sold is producing a rent (income) below full rental value, and there is an expectation of an early reversion, the capitalisation rate can be found by trial and error or iteratively using a financial calculator.

This is an IRR calculation (see p.32) and the rate percent found is called an equivalent yield (see p.65).

> **Q** *A freehold shop let at its open market rental value of £75,000 a year with rent reviews every 5 years has just been sold for £1,250,000. Assess the market capitalisation rate.*

P. 193

> **Q** A freehold office let at £30,000 a year with 2 years to the next rent review has just been sold for £553,000. The current estimate of open market rent is £40,000. Assess the equivalent yield.

p.184

those properties displaying an income pattern which is out of line with the normal expectations in the market-place.

The use of DCF and conventional capitalisation approaches are considered in Chapters 6 and 7 for free-hold and leasehold properties.

Discounted Cash Flow (DCF)

All income capitalisations are a simplified form of DCF. Thus the capitalisation of **£100,000** a year in perpetuity at **8%** can be shown to be the same as discounting a perpetual (for ever) cash flow of **£100,000** receivable at the end of each year in perpetuity (see p. 6).

Nevertheless there are growing arguments for using a cash flow approach for all income valuations - in particular a DCF approach. This

- provides clearer meaning to investors, bankers and professional advisers

- can incorporate regular and irregular costs such as fees for rent reviews, lease renewals, voids, etc.

- can allow for expected refurbishment costs

- can incorporate adjustments for obsolescence.

DCF is the normal basis in North America where property is frequently let on gross rents with provision for landlords to recoup increases in certain service costs but not all.

Additionally, DCF methods may be a preferred approach when dealing with new developments which are not expected to achieve full potential for several years following practical completion.

The current use of the term 'DCF' by UK valuers generally refers to the use of a modified DCF. (Rational Method) or Real Value approach to valuation. Some valuers believe these methods should be used for all valuations whilst others see their use being reserved for

The key steps in the income approach to property valuation are:

- *Agree purpose of valuation, basis of value and other terms and conditions with the client.*

- *Assess current net operating income.*

- *Assess income potential based on comparable evidence of current lettings.*

- *Assess appropriate capitalisation rate.*

- *Consider use of cash flow layout in order to incorporate specific allowance for fees, depreciation, etc.*

- *Complete the valuation and prepare a full report or where agreed with the client a short report in accordance with the RICS Appraisal and Valuation Manual.*

6

The Income
Approach:

Freeholds

The main legal interests bought and sold in property are freehold and leasehold interests. As investments, the former have an assumed perpetual life span although on many occasions the valuation should include a reversion to site value at the end of the building's economic or physical life; the latter have a limited life span fixed by the lease term. Having identified the interest to be valued the valuer must then determine not only the current income but also future income and the income flow pattern.

Two distinct approaches have developed for assessing the open market value of an income-producing property.

The first, as already indicated *(Chapter 4)*, is to assume a level continuous income flow and to use an overall or all-risks capitalisation rate derived from the analysis of sales of comparable properties let on similar terms and conditions (i.e. 5-year or 7-year rent review patterns) to calculate present worth.

The second has been named the **discounted cash flow (DCF)** approach.

The first or normal approach is favoured by many on the grounds that it is more correctly a market valuation. As such it relies on an active property market and an ability to analyse and obtain details of comparable capitalisation rates. Those in favour of the DCF approach argue that, when there is insufficient activity within the defined sub-market, valuation can still be undertaken on the DCF approach and, further, that most valuers using the normal approach fail to recognise the sub-markets involved.

For example, it is assumed that if initial yields on rack rented properties are, say, 7% then the capitalisation rates to be used for valuing property with an early reversion to a rack rent can be closely related to 7%. The argument against this is that if there is no evidence of capitalisation rates from sales of investments with early reversions it may be because there is no market for such investments.

The strongest criticisms of the normal approach are that it fails to specify explicitly the income flows and patterns assumed by the valuer, and growth implicit all risk yields are used to capitalise fixed tranches of income. The DCF approach requires the valuer to specify precisely what rental income and expenses are expected when, and for how long. The valuer is therefore forced to concentrate on the national and local economic issues likely to affect the value of the specific property as an investment. There may after all be properties in a depressed economy for which rental increases in the foreseeable future are very unlikely.

The DCF approach accepts the idea of the opportunity cost of investment funds. Opportunity cost implies that a rate of return must be paid to an investor sufficient to meet the competition of alternative investment outlets for the investor's funds. This is the basis of the riskless rate of discount, a riskless rate being assumed to compensate for time preference only. Any investment with a poorer liquidity factor or higher risk to income or capital value will have to earn a rate over time in excess of the riskless rate. Analysts tend to adopt as their measure the current rate on 'gilt edged' stock. These are generally held to be fairly liquid investments and are safe in money terms if held to redemption. Additionally, if they are sold at a loss, or at a gain, it can be reasonably assumed that there will have been a similar movement in the values of most other forms of investment. Property, being considerably less liquid, is expected to achieve a return over time of **1-2%** above the going rate on gilt edged stock, or higher in the case of poor-quality properties or locations.

The DCF method requires the valuer to '*forecast*' rents and to discount those rents at a rate sufficiently higher than the riskless rate to account for the additional risks involved in the specific property investment. 'Forecast' here does not mean prediction nor does it necessarily imply a projection based on extrapolating or extending the past into the future. It is an estimate of the most probable rent due in '*n*' years' time based on sound analysis of the past and present market conditions. The current preference seems to be to assess an implied growth rate for rent from the relationship between all risk capitalisation rates and gilts plus a risk premium of **1-2%**.

Capitalisation and DCF approaches will be used in problems relating to the valuation of freehold interests in property. The examples will indicate the approach adopted.

Capitalisation and DCF methods

The technique of converting income into a capital sum is extremely simple. In the case of freehold interests in property the income will have the characteristics of an annuity which may be fixed, stepped, falling or variable.

A fixed or level annuity

If the income is fixed for a period much in excess of 60 years or in perpetuity, or if a property is let at its rack rental and there is market evidence of capitalisation rates, then it can be treated as a level annuity in perpetuity.

Net income $\div i$ = Capital value

Net income x $\dfrac{1}{i}$ = CV

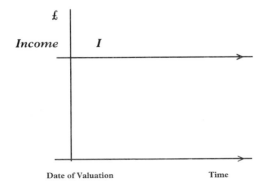

Income I

Date of Valuation   Time

Example 6.1

A shopping centre was developed on a war-damaged central site in 1955. The site was let by the local authority to the developer on a lease for **150** years at a ground rent of £10,000 a year.
The lease has no break clauses or rent review clauses.

- **Fixed Income of £10,000**

- **Unexpired Term 110 years as at 1995 valuation date**

- **Reversion 2105**

- **Capitalisation rate 12%**

  £10,000 ÷ 0.12 = £83,333

Example 6.1 (cont.)

A conventional valuation would appear as :

Net Income	**£10,000 per annum (p.a.)**
YP in perpetuity at 12% (Present value of £1 pa in perpetuity at 12%)	8.33
Estimated Market Value	**£83,333**

A perpetuity approach is used because the discount factor for 110 years is equivalent to that in perpetuity (see p.6).

There may be market comparables to support the capitalisation rate of **12%**. But in the absence of evidence this rate can be compared to that achievable as a return on irredeemable government stocks with an adjustment for any extra risks or security attaching to the property investment. Investments of this nature are very secure in money terms but not in real terms. The money security is provided by the fact that the ground rent is secured by the rents paid by the occupying tenants to the developer and by the fact that the lease would be forfeited in English Law on non-payment.

A similar approach can be adopted for properties currently let at their open market rental.

Example 6.2

Value a freehold shop in a prime trading position let at its full rental value of **£20,000** per annum on full repairing and insuring terms. The lease is for **20** years with reviews every 5 years. Similar properties are selling on the basis of an all risks yield (**ARY**) or capitalisation rate of **5%**

Rent	**£20,000**
YP perpetuity @ 5%	**20**
CV	**£400,000**

Notes:

1. Where the lease is only for 20 years' but it can be assumed that it would continue to let readily and that full rents will be receivable then it can be treated as a perpetual income. Such an assumption could not be made if the trading position was under threat from planned development such as an out-of-town centre.

2. Although the rent is reviewable every 5 years there is no need to provide for this explicitly in a capitalisation approach if at each reversion the rent would also be equivalent to today's market rental value of £20,000.

3. All property incurs a management cost but customarily when property is let on FRI terms no deduction is made for management.

4. For some purposes the costs of acquisition (survey fees, legal fees and Stamp duty) will be deducted to arrive at a net value. Where the net value plus fees adds up to £400,000, £20,000 will represent a return on total outlay of 5% *(see Chapter 12)*. The return on net value would be greater than 5%.

Example 6.3

If the rent in *example 6.2* is payable in advance and the market is still looking for a **5%** investment the valuation becomes:

Rent	£20,000
YP perpetuity @ **5% in advance**	21
	£420,000

Notes:

1   £420,000 is being paid for the right to receive an immediate £20,000 and thereafter £20,000 at the end of each year. This could only be the case if the valuation was undertaken on the rent due date. In such a case it is not the terms of the lease but the date of the valuation and the rent payment date that guides the valuer. In property sales the contract will usually provide for rental apportionment as between vendor and buyer *(see Bornand, 1988).*

2   Similar points and changes can be made to reflect quarterly rental arrangements.

Valuers are being encouraged to represent their investment valuations as cash flows as this is a more familiar format for accountants and investment analysts.

Period	Net Income	PV £1 @ 5%	NPV
1	20,000	0.95237	19,047.6
2	20,000	0.90703	18,140.6
3	20,000	0.86384	17,276.8
4	20,000	0.82270	16,454.0
5	420,000*	0.78353	329,082.6
			400,001.6

(* £420,000 represents the resale value at the end of year 5 being the right to continue to receive £20,000 p.a. thereafter in perpetuity plus the rent due at the end of year 5 of £20,000.)

This structure set out on a spreadsheet allows the valuer to revalue using a range of capitalisation rates where there may be some degree of uncertainty as to the market capitalisation rates *(see Spreadsheet User 6 at the end of this chapter)*. The structure can also be lengthened and developed to reflect growth.

The use of non-conventional methods is inappropriate where there is ample evidence of recent transactions and where the capitalisation is of a property let at the current open market rental value on current lease terms, however the following examples are included to indicate the development of the Short-Cut DCF/Equated Yield and Real Value Methods.

Short-cut DCF method

In *example 6.2* no account was taken of the fact that in year 5 there would be a review of the rent to the open market rental value.

Fixed interest securities are considered to be risk-free; even more so where the value (stock face value) is index linked.

If at the time of valuation property of a particular type and quality is selling on a **5%** basis and risk-free stock can be purchased to achieve a return of **10%** then the market for property must be implying an expectation of growth.

Thus £100 invested in stock at **10%** will be producing £10 per year when the same invested in property is producing **5%** or £5 per year. This represents a loss of £5 a year whilst the investor is accepting the greater risks attached to the purchase of property. If these greater risks warrant a **2%** adjustment the property investor should be looking for an overall return of **12%** (**10%** + **2%**). The difference between **5%** and **12%** is known as the *'reverse yield gap'*, being the opposite of the normal expectation that investors' returns rise as risks rise. The gap must be made good through growth.

The necessary level of growth can be calculated using DCF techniques, and a number of formulae and tables have been produced to simplify the process. In the above paragraph an annual growth rate of **7%** might be inferred (**12%** - **5%** = **7%**) but in the case of property incomes (growth) in rent can only be recovered at rent reviews which are rarely annual, more frequently 5 yearly but sometimes every 3 years or every 7 years.

Given the rates of **12%** and **5%** the following growth rates would be implied given the following different Rent Review patterns:

Rent Reviews every:	Implied growth (12% and 5% p.a.)
3 years	7.32
5 years	7.64
7 years	7.93

Source: Donaldsons Investment tables.

The same figures can be calculated from any one of a number of formulae:

$$K = e - (ASF \times P)$$

where

K   = the capitalisation rate expressed as a decimal,

e   = the overall return or equated yield expressed as a decimal,

ASF   = the annual sinking fund to replace £1 at the overall or equated yield over the review period (t), and

P   = the rental growth over the review period from which the implied rate of rental growth can be calculated.

Some commentators prefer the formulation:

$$(1 + g)^t = \frac{\text{YP perp. at K - YP } t \text{ years at } e}{\text{YP perp. at K x PV } t \text{ years at } e}$$

or

$$g = [\sqrt[t]{(1 + (1-\frac{K}{e}) ((1 + e)^t - 1))}] - 1$$

So given that **K = 0.05 (5%), e = 0.12 (12%)** and **t = 5 years**

then $0.05 = 0.12 - (0.1574097 \times P)$

$0.1574097 \; P = 0.12 - 0.05$

$0.1574097 \; P = 0.07$

$P = 0.07 / 0.1574097$

$P = 0.444699$ **(44.47% over 5 years)**

The nature of compound interest was outlined in **Chapter 1.** Here there is an implied growth in rent, **'P'**, over 5 years of **44.47%** and therefore:

$$P = (1 + g)^t - 1$$

where g = growth per annum expressed as a decimal and

t = the rent review period (5),

1 + P must equal $(1 + g)^t$ to give

1.444699	$= (1 + g)^5$
$1.444699^{0.2}$	$= (1 + g)$
[(or $\sqrt[5]{1.444699}$	$= (1 + g)$]
1.076355	$= (1 + g)$
Therefore g	$= 1.076355 - 1$

$$g\% = 7.6355\%$$

The figure 7.6355% represents the implied annual average rental growth in perpetuity.

The steps in the Short-cut DCF method can now be stated:

- Discount the current rent to the next review or lease renewal at the overall rate or equated yield. This is logical as there can be no growth in a rent fixed by legal contract (the lease) for a term of years.

- Multiply the Estimated Rental Value **(OMRV)** by the amount of £1 for the period to review at the implied rate of rental growth.

- Discount (capitalise) the future market rent in perpetuity at the capitalisation rate **(All Risks Yield)** and discount the capitalised value on reversion for the intervening period at the overall or equated yield

The issues to be resolved are

- Assessment of **ARY** (Capitalisation Rate)
- Assessment of Overall Yield (Equated Yield)

Example 6.4

Revalue the property in *Example 6.2* using a Short-cut DCF approach.

		£20,000	
PV £1 p.a. for 5 years @ 12% (YP)		3.6047	
			£72,094

		£20,000	
Amount of £1 in 5 years @ 7.6355%		1.4447	
Implied Rent in 5 years		£28,894	

PV £1 p.a. in perp. @ 5%	20		
PV £1 in 5 years @12%	0.56743		
		11.3486	
			£327,906
			£400,000

The value is identical to the normal income capitalisation because of the underlying assumptions incorporated in the implied growth formula. This could be set out as a cash flow over a number of years if preferred by the client.

The figure of **£28,894** does not represent a forecast of the rent to be expected in **5** years' time. It is simply an expression of future rental derived from the market's implications of purchasing risk investments below risk free rates. It represents the rental needed in 5 years' time to recoup the loss of return (income) during the next 5 years in order to achieve an overall return **2%** higher than the given risk-free rate.

> **Q** *Freehold shops in prime locations let on FRI terms, with rent reviews every 5 years' are selling on an initial yield (ARY) of 6%. If investors' target rates are 1% above gilts which stand at 8% what is the implied growth rate?*

Real Value method

Neil Crosby developed a real value approach based on earlier work of Dr Ernest Wood and has become the principal exponent of this technique. The technique is similar to the Short-cut DCF Method in that it values the current rent at the equated yield. Where it differs is that it retains the reversionary rent at today's open market rental value but discounts the reversionary capital value at the *Inflation Risk Free Yield* (**IRFY**).

When using any of the capitalisation techniques the valuer needs to assess the nature of the rental agreement as set out in the lease to ascertain, in the light of current market conditions, the extent to which the rental income is inflation proof.

- **Where rental income is completely inflation prone - that is where it is fixed with no expectation of change - the equated yield should be used in the discounting process.**

- **Where rental income is completely inflation proof the IRFY should be used.**

This process reflects the fact that between rent reviews the real value of the income may be falling.

The steps in the method follow the DCF Method in assessing the implied growth rate; from this the valuer calculates the **IRFY** from the formula:

$$\frac{e - g}{1 + g}$$

in this example

$$\text{IRFY} = \frac{0.12 - 0.076355}{1.076355}$$

$$= \frac{0.043645}{1.076355}$$

$$= 0.0405488 \ (\times 100\%)$$
$$\text{say } 4.055\%$$

The valuation becomes :

		£20,000	
PV £1 p.a. for 5 years @ 12% (YP)		3.6047	
			£72,094

		£20,000	
PV £1 p.a. in perp. @ 5%	20		
x PV £1 in 5 years @ 4.055%	0.81975		£327,900
			£399,994

Both the DCF and Real Value models overcome some of the key criticisms of conventional valuation when valuing property currently producing less than their open market rental value.

Conventional methods as set out in the next section:

1. **Overvalue the fixed term income through the use of a capitalisation rate rather than the equated yield.**

2. **Undervalue the reversion by using open market rents expressed in today's market terms rather than reverting to future rents.**

Point 1 is covered in both non-traditional methods by using the equated yield. Point 2 is covered in the DCF method by capitalising the assumed implied future rent using the capitalisation rate and by deferring using the equated yield; in the real value method by deferring the capitalised current rent at the **IRFY**.

Income patterns

A 'stepped' annuity

If the income is fixed by a lease contract for '*x*' years and is then due to rise, either by reversion to a rack rental to be valued, for simplicity, in perpetuity, or to rise to a higher level for '*y*' years, then reverting to a rack rental in perpetuity, the valuation may be treated as an immediate annuity plus a deferred annuity in one of two ways. The first is referred to as a *term and reversion*, the second as the *layer method*.

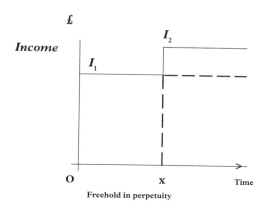

Having estimated I_1 and I_2 as accurately as possible, the critical factor is the capitalisation rate *i%* which need not remain the same throughout. If it does remain the same, then each approach will produce the same value estimate.

Example 6.5

If the property in *example 6.2* is let at £10,000 per annum on **FRI** terms with 2 years to run to a review the valuation could appear as:

Term and reversion

Term	£10,000	
YP 2 years @ 5%	1.86	
		£ 18,600
Reversion	£20,000	
YP perp. @ 5%		
x PV £1 in 2 years @ 5%	18.14	£362,800
		£381,400

Layer

Layer	£10,000	
YP perp. @ 5%	20	£200,000
Top slice	£10,000	
YP perp. @ 5% x PV £1 in 2 years @ 5%	18.14	£181,400
		£381,400

Notes:

1. Because all the capitalisation and deferment or discounting rates have been left at 5% both conventional methods produce the same value figure.

2. In this case YP x PV of 18.14 comes from the YP of 20 multiplied by the PV factor of 0.9070. It could have been found by using the YP of a reversion to a perpetuity table or deducting the YP for 5 years from the YP in perpetuity *(see Chapter 1)*.

Here again a cash flow would represent this as :

End of Year	Net Income	PV £1 at 5%	NPV
1	10,000	0.95238	9,523.80
2	10,000	0.90703	9,070.30
3	420,000	0.86384	362,812.80
			£381,406.90

Some valuers still insist on using different rates to reflect some personal view on security of income. This can be dangerous and can produce very peculiar results. This can apply to either of the traditional approaches as illustrated below.

Term and Reversion

Term	£10,000	
YP 2 years @ 4%	1.89	£18,900
Reversion	£20,000	
YP perp. def'd 2 years @ 5%	18.14	£362,800
		£381,700

Layer

Layer	£10,000	
YP perp. @ 4%	25	£250,000
Top slice	£10,000	
YP perp. def'd 2 years @ 5%	18.14	£181,400
		£431,400

The variation in the term and reversion is negligible and in a valuation would not be material when expressed as an opinion of, say, **£380,000**. In the layer method, failure to appreciate the effect of the change results in an underlet property being valued higher than the equivalent fully let property *(see example 6.2)*. This cannot be correct. Practising valuers generally avoid such an error by capitalising the layer income at the **ARY** and increasing the rate on the top slice.

The reason for valuers wishing to change rates within a valuation rests with the historic evolution of the methods and the changing economy as reflected in the investment market *(see Baum and Crosby, 1995)*.

Valuers in the nineteenth century were primarily dealing with rack rented properties, largely agricultural, at a time when inflation was relatively unknown. A realistic and direct comparison could be made between alternative investments such as the undated securities *(gilts)* issued by government, the interest on deposits and farmland. The latter, being more risky, was valued at a percentage point or so above the secure government stock. Other property, such as residential and the emerging retail properties, were more risky but were let on long leases so they could be capitalised in perpetuity, again at an appropriate higher rate.

In the 1930s the depression made any contracted rent a better or more secure investment than an unlet property and there was real fear that at the end of a lease the tenant would seek to redress the position by requesting a lower rent or by vacating. Logic suggested the use of a lower capitalisation rate for secure contracted rents than unsecured reversions.

This approach continued unchallenged until the 1960s. In the meantime the market had changed in many ways and with the rise of inflation the investment market had identified a crucial difference between fixed-income investments such as gilts and those where the owner could participate in rental and capital growth such as equities and rack rented properties.

This change was noted in the market and the reverse yield gap emerged. Nevertheless, valuers continued to use a capitalisation approach, varying yields to reflect the so-called security of income of contracted rents, the argument being that a tenant would be more likely to continue to pay a rent which was less than the estimated rental value because it represented a leasehold capital value *(see Chapter 7)*. The market did not appear to recognise that the technique of the 1930s was one of using rates to reflect money risk, whereas those post the appearance of the reverse yield were capitalisation rates which reflected money risks and expectations of growth.

There are currently many arguments for not varying capitalisation rates in simple conventional valuations, but two will suffice. By the 1960s the property market for income-producing properties was being dominated by the major institutions.

Valuers offering property investment opportunities were increasingly required to specify:

(a) the initial or year one rate of return, and

(b) the investment's internal rate of return.

The former acted as a cut-off rate as actuarial advice at that time required all investments, depending upon the fund, to produce a minimum return - frequently *3-4%*. The second caused confusion for valuers used to using perhaps four or five rates in a multiple reversionary property. The confusion arose because few valuers understood the concept of **IRR,** few knew how to calculate it, and in the 1960s there was nothing more sophisticated than a slide rule to aid with calculations.

The profession took a little longer to recognise that if the capitalisation rate is held constant it becomes the expected **IRR**. It can also be shown that for many term and reversion exercises using variable rates the **IRR** - now popularly called the equivalent yield - is almost the same as the **ARY**. As a result many valuers, whether using the term and reversion or layer method, now use an equivalent or same yield approach. It is, however,

important to distinguish between the terms 'equivalent' yield and 'equated yield'.

In Donaldson's Investment Tables it is stated that:

'The equated yield of an investment may be defined as the discount rate which needs to be applied to the projected income so that the summation of all the income flows discounted at this rate, equals the capital outlay ... whereas an equated yield takes into account an assumed growth rate in the future annual income, an equivalent yield merely expresses the weighted average yield to be expected from the investment in terms of current income and rental value, without allowing for any growth in value over the period to reversions.'

Secondly it can be shown that variable rates pose their own problems.

Bowcock (1983) uses a simple example of two properties each let at £100 per annum but one with a review in 5 years and the other with a review in 10 years, both with a reversion to £105 per annum.

Traditionally the solution might appear as:

Term	£100	
YP 5 years @ 9%	3.8897	
		£388.97
Reversion	£105	
YP perp. def'd		
5 years @ 10%	6.2092	£651.96
		£1040.93

Term	£100	
YP 10 years @ 9%	6.4177	£641.77
Reversion	£105	
YP perp. def'd		
10 years @ 10%	8.8554	£404.82
		£1046.59

Clearly, there is something wrong with a method which places a higher value on the latter investment, which includes a 10-year deferred income, than the former with a 5-year deferred income. In practice, this potential error is not noted by valuers, who subjectively adjust their rates to reflect (a) their view of the extent of the security of income, namely the ,difference between contracted rent and full rental value, and (b) the risk associated with the period of waiting up to the rent review.

Some critics have also drawn attention to the problems of selecting the correct deferment rate in a variable yield valuation. Customarily the reversion has been deferred at the reversionary capitalisation rate. If this is done then it can be shown that the sinking fund provision within the YP single rate formula (at **9%** in the above example) is not matched by the discounting factor(**10%** in the example) ; as a result the input rates of return of **9%** and **10%** will not be achieved. This can be corrected by deferring the reversion at the term rate.

The discerning valuer must conclude that it is safer and more logical to adhere to the same yield or equivalent yield approach. It is also the easiest yield to extract from sales evidence as the calculation is identical to that of the **IRR**. On a same yield basis there is no distinction to be made between the two capitalisation methods. However, the term and reversion seems the most acceptable theoretical method and preferable for valuations involving lease renewals when a void allowance or refurbishment cost may need to be built in. It is also easier to handle if outgoings have to be deducted. The layer method is possibly simpler and useful when handling certain investments where clients wish to know what price has been or is to be paid for the top slice.

Valuers are still faced with the problem of finding comparables. The more unusual the patterns of income the more difficult it is for the valuer to judge the correct capitalisation rate.

For example, *what would be the right equivalent yield to use for a property let at £10,000 p.a. with a reversion to £20,000 p.a. in 15 years?*

In these cases an equivalent yield approach is likely to be criticised when the yield used is lower than the opportunity cost of capital or gilt yield for investments with a fixed income running for **15** or more years.

The position today is that investments with growth potential sell on a low yield basis compared to the fixed income returns on government stock. But the risk position has not changed, as all property is still riskier than holding cash or gilt stock. Thus if gilts are at, say, **12%** a property investor should arguably be looking for **13-14%**. Purchasing at **5%** is forgoing at least £8 per £100 invested per annum. Few people offered employment at £13,000 per annum would reject it in favour of one at £5,000 per annum unless they were certain that over a specified contract term the loss of £8,000 per annum would be compensated by regular and substantial increases in salary. The same is true of property. So capitalising at **5%** must imply rental growth in perpetuity and the first criticism of the equivalent, or same yield approach for reversionary investments is that it fails to indicate rental growth explicitly by reverting to current rental values.

Also, both the term income and the reversion are capitalised at the same **ARY** implying the same rental growth when clearly a lease rent is fixed by contract for the term. The only substantive arguments in defence of the equivalent yield approach are simplicity and that purely by chance it may overvalue the term just sufficiently to compensate for the undervaluation of the reversion *(see Baum and Crosby, 1995)*. The modified DCF and Rational approach have been developed to overcome these criticisms.

Example 6.6

Using the facts from *example 6.5,* revalue on a modified DCF basis assuming the **FRV** of £20,000 is based on a normal 5-year review pattern and that an equated return of **12%**. is required

The implied growth rate is 7.6355% (see p.62)

This implies that the rent in 2 years' time would need to be:

£20,000 x amount of £1 at 7.6355% for 2 years

£20,000 x 1.5854 = 23,170.80, say £23,170

The property can now be revalued on a contemporary basis, in this case using a modified short-cut DCF or Rational Method *(Baum and Crosby, 1995, provide a full critical comparison).*

Short-cut DCF

next 2 years	£10,000	
YP 2 years @ 12%	1.6901	
		£16,901
Reversion to	£23,170	
(£20,000 x *A* £1		
@ 7.6355% for 2 years)		
YP perp. @ 5 %	20	
	£463,400	
PV £1 @ 12% for 2 years	0.7972	
		£369,422
		£386,323

The difference in opinion in practice on such a short reversionary property would be less significant as the valuations would probably be rounded to **£382,000** and

£385,000 respectively. However, it can be seen how the term and reversion produces a nearly acceptable solution by overvaluing the term by £1,699 (£18,600 - £16,901) which to some extent compensates for the undervaluation of the reversion of £6,622 (£369,422 - £362,800).

The short-cut DCF now reads like an investment valuation as all contracted income is discounted at a money market rate and the reversion is to an expected, albeit implied, rent, not today's rental value.

The importance of this issue is greater when considering a longer reversionary property.

Example 6.7

Assuming the same facts as *examples 6.5 and 6.6* but assuming a reversion in 15 years.

Conventional
Term and reversion

	£10,000	
YP 15 years @ 7%	9.1079	
		£91,079
	£20,000	
YP perp. @ 7%	14.2857	
	£285,714	
PV £1 in		
15 years @ 7%	0.3624	
		£103,542
		£194,621

A capitalisation rate of 7% has been used rather than 5% in order to reflect the difference between an investment with a long reversion and one with a short reversion.

However :
£20,000 x Amount of £1 @ 7.6355% for 15 years
£20,000 x 3.02 = £60,306.34

Modified DCF

	£10,000	
YP 15 years @ 12%	6.8109	
		£68,109
	£60,306	
YP perp. @ 5%	20	
	£1,206,120	
PV £1 in 15		
years @ 12%	0.1827	
		£220,358
		£288,467

Here a subjective assessment had to be made as to the appropriate equivalent yield to use for a 15-year deferment. The modified **DCF** assesses the fixed lease income at the equated yield or opportunity cost, the reversion is to the implied rent in **15** years' time and the value is deferred at the equated yield. If the DCF is arithmetically more correct (and it is) then an equivalent yield of less than 5.25% would have to be used to arrive at a figure of £288,467. It is extremely difficult in the absence of true comparables to arrive at a correct equivalent yield subjectively, but that appears to be the favoured approach and may involve the use of money rates for discounting the fixed term.

Currently, though, it is not possible to say that a modified DCF approach must be the preferred approach. It may be the more rational approach in that it is possible to argue that investors should be indifferent between the short and long reversionary properties if they are expected to produce the same equated yield. But this is difficult to support if the market is substantially discounting long reversions through the subjective approach of their investment surveyors; implying inconsistency over the choice of equated yields. The modified **DCF** can be proved by using a full projected cash flow over, say, **100** years, discounted at **12%** as in *Table 6.1*.

Table 6.1

DCF to 100 years allowing for a rental growth at 7.6355% discounted at an equated yield of 12% and providing for a reversion to future capital value in year 100. This would bring the value figure more into line with the modified DCF.

Period (years)	Income x A £1 @ 7.6355%	PV £1 p.a. @ 12 %	PV £1 @ 12 %	Present value
0–15	10,000	6.8109	-	68,109
16–20	60,306	3.60477	0.18269	39,714
21–25	87,124	3.60477	0.10367	32,558
26–30	125,868	3.60477	0.05882	26,688
31–35	181,842	3.60477	0.03337	21,874
36–40	262,706	3.60477	0.01894	17,936
41–45	379,532	3.60477	0.01074	14,693
46–50	548,310	3.60477	0.00609	12,037
51–55	792,144	3.60477	0.00346	9,880
56–60	1,144,410	3.60477	0.00196	8,085
61–65	1,653,329	3.60477	0.00111	6,615
66–70	2,388,566	3.60477	0.00063	5,424
71–75	3,450,761	3.60477	0.00036	4,478
76–80	4,985,314	3.60477	0.00020	3,594
81–85	7,202,282	3.60477	0.00011	2,855
86–90	10,405,137	3.60477	0.00006	2,250
91–95	15,032,301	3.60477	0.000037	2,005
96–100	21,717,164	3.60477	0.000021	1,644
100	434,343,280	3.60477	0.00001	4,343
			Value	£284,782

In practice such contemporary methods seem to be rejected in favour of the market methods. That implies that although valuers do not make the market they do in some instances have a strong influence. Current market practice favours the simple equivalent or same yield approach.

This creates the probability that investors will conclude that some valuers are overvaluing, or undervaluing, properties and will sell or purchase in the market at market prices to take advantage of such market imperfections.

Throughout this section it must be remembered that the growth rates used are implied and that the figures derived in no way predict the future. They merely provide the valuer with an additional tool with which to examine and, as will be seen later, to analyse the market. Such implied rents must be critically examined against the reality of the marketplace and realistic economic projections.

Example 6.8

Value freehold shop premises let on lease with 4 years to run at £7,000 per annum. The tenant pays the rates and the insurance and undertakes internal repairs. It is worth £12,500 per annum net today and rental values for this type of property are continuing to rise in this area.

Assumptions:

1   **Current capitalisation rates on rack rented comparable premises are 8%.**
2   **Rents are due annually in arrears.**

Market Valuation:

Gross income per annum for 4 years		£7,000	
Less landlord's outgoings			
External repairs and decorations[1]	£650		
Management at 5% of £7,000[2]	£350	£1,000	
Net income		£6,000	
Years' purchase for 4 years @ 7%[3]		3.39	£20,340
Plus reversion in 4 years to[4]			
Net income		£12,500	
YP in perp. def'd 4 years @ 8%[5]		9.19	
		£144,875	
Estimate of capital value			£135,215
Value (say) £135,000[6]			

Notes:

1   Based on office records, etc.
2   Based on fees charged by management department for comparable properties and net of reasonable VAT.
3   The relationship between the rates here and later (7% and 8%) depends upon a number of assumptions as to the true behaviour of the market. The argument here is that the £6,000 is more secure in money terms, hence a lower rate is used.
4.   In a normal market valuation the reversion is to full rental value (FRV) as estimated in today's terms. There is no deduction here as it is a net rent, although some valuers could allow for management at say 1-2% of rent collected.
5   YP in perp. deferred = YP perp. at 8% x PV £1 in 4 years at 8% or YP perp. at 8% less YP for 4 years at 8%.
6   This final estimate is rounded as no valuer can truly value to the nearest £; figures of this magnitude would bear rounding to the nearest £1,000.

The idea of reducing the term capitalisation rate by 1% to reflect money security is almost certainly inappropriate during inflationary periods. Money security should give way to a reflection of purchasing power risk. Some purchasers will not differentiate between a property let below rack rental and one let at rack rental, because there is no real difference provided the sum paid for the investment reflects the difference in current income and any difference in expectation of future rental change. But, on the latter point, is it reasonable to use the same discount rate for both the capitalisation of, and the 4-year deferment of, the reversionary income?

A number of valuers would comment that this rate and the deferment rate should be higher by **1-2%** to reflect the greater uncertainty of receiving the future increased income. Of the two, the concept of increasing the deferment rate may seem the most logical as **8%** could be applied to £2,500 if it was receivable today. But those who defend the former method argue that it results in an overvaluation of the term which helps to compensate for the undervaluation of the reversion.

The point here in practice, and as indicated in the question, is that if the rent of £12,500 is continuing to rise the true rent in 4 years' time will exceed £12,500 and the reversion has therefore been undervalued. Those who favour a **DCF** approach would argue that neither approach is defensible because, assuming the opportunity cost of money is **12%**, capitalisation rates of **7%** and **8%** and deferment rates of **8%** imply a particular expectation of growth in the incomes over the periods involved.

The particular rates used in the examples may fortuitously have produced a result which is close enough to the correct value of the property.

A modified DCF approach may be preferred or used as a check.

A comparable conventional layer method valuation employing different rates may be laid out as in *example 6.9.*

Example 6.9

Layer income	£6,000	
YP perp. @ 7%	14.29	
		£85,740
Marginal income [1]	£6,500	
YP perp. def'd 4 years @ 8% [2]	9.19	
		£59,735
Estimate of capital value		£145,205

Value (say) £145,000

Notes:

1. Reversionary income of £12,500 minus initial (layer) income of £6,000.

2. Parry's Valuation Tables (*Estates Gazette*) 8th edition, page xxiii, lays down a rule for adjusting the capitalisation rates in a layer method valuation to produce the same figure of value as in example 6.3. The method requires the capitalisation rate for the marginal income $(I_2 - I_1)$ to be found from the ratio of $(I_2 - I_1)$ to the difference between the existing rent capitalised as if in perpetuity and the full rental value, also capitalised as if in perpetuity. But, as the method requires the valuer to make an initial assumption concerning the appropriate term and reversion rates it is much simpler to carry out a term and reversion valuation.

An equivalent yield valuation may be derived from either approach to find the single equivalent rate of interest which, if applied to both term and reversion (or layer and marginal) income, will produce the same valuation.

Example 6.10

Valuation (term and reversion)		£135,215
Term:		
Net income	£6,000	
YP 4 years @ x %	a	£A
Reversion:		
Net income	£12,500	
YP perp. def'd 4 years @ x %	b	£B
	£(A+B) =	£135,215

By trial and error, x % may be found. In this case it is approximately 7.97%. This is the equivalent yield.

Valuation (equivalent yield)		
Term:		
Net income	£6,000	
YP 4 years @ 7.97%	3.31	£19,860
Reversion:		
Net income	£12,500	
YP perp. def'd 4 years @ 7.97%	9.23	£115,375
		£135,235

Valuing throughout at 8% produces:

£6,000 x 3.3121 + £12,500 x 9.18787 + £19,872 + £114,848

= **£134,720 or say £135,000.**

This suggests that making a 1% allowance from the **ARY** for security of income is of minimal consequence.

An equated yield valuation is a valuation which employs DCF techniques. This may be combined with a conventional valuation approach as a short cut or carried out fully as previously illustrated.

The conventional capitalisation approach is perfectly acceptable under normal conditions where property is let on normal terms with regular rent reviews, and where there is evidence of capitalisation rates. In such cases it is most logical to use an equivalent yield approach, whether it be in the format of the term and reversion, or the layer, method.

Where the income pattern is not normal, there is a strong case for using the DCF approach. DCF directs the valuer to concentrate upon an explicit consideration of the net current and future incomes, and upon the correct rate of interest to use to discount that specified cash flow.

A falling annuity

This can be treated in a similar manner to a rising annuity using either of the previous methods.

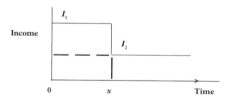

Many valuers would adopt the layer method so that a higher capitalisation rate could be used for the income that will cease ($I_1 - I_2$) as it is considered to be at greater risk.

The issue of falling incomes is not new but the recession has produced a number of over-rented properties which create a hybrid form of the falling annuity.

Example 6.11

Value a freehold office building let at £10,000 p.a. with 5 years to the review. The current rental value is £7,500 p.a. *(The rental pattern is illustrated below.)*

The valuer's immediate response is 'will rents rise to the contracted level by the review date?' If he/she feels confident in saying yes, then the valuation problem is removed and £10,000 p.a. could be treated as a perpetual income provided a current capitalisation rate can be derived from market comparables.

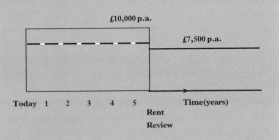

The second question is whether the tenant can insist on a lower rent at the review date. If there is an upwards-only rent review clause then this might preclude a fall in rent.

The valuer's conventional solution to a terminating income is to use the layer method assessing the income to be lost on a dual rate basis thus *(see p.17 and Chapter 7):*

Continuing income	£7,500		
YP perp. @ 8%		12.5	
			£ 93,750
Plus income to be lost	£2,500		
YP for 5 years @ 8% and 3% adj. tax @ 40%		2.54	£6,350
			£100,100

The philosophy here is that only £2,500 for 5 years will cease and that the capital value assigned to this income must be recovered at the low, safe sinking fund rate of 3% after allowing for the incidence of taxation on that part of the income which represents capital recovery.

But the use of 8% implies a growth in the £7,500 from today, which is clearly false because it has already been implied that there will be no increase for at least 5 years.

Alternatively the £2,500 could be capitalised at a higher single rate, but in both instances there is a danger of double counting as the use of 8% during the term implies that the figure of £7,500 is growing and so a part of the term income has been valued twice.

The valuer needs to distinguish the genuine terminating income from that which may represent a temporary shortfall. Thus a building with a time limited planning consent may display an income pattern which is going to fall and this reduction will not be recovered until the lower valued use has, through real and inflationary growth over several years, risen to the higher value use. In these cases a hybrid capitalisation may be necessary to reflect not only the fall in income but also the variations in *'risk'* attaching to the tranches of income arising from different uses.

The 1979 edition of this book suggested that a DCF approach would be the preferred solution to the falling income problem. Crosby, Goodchild and others have developed this approach to the valuation of the over-rented property.

The steps in the solution are:

1. **Assess the implied rental growth rate from comparable investment properties let at their open market rental value.**

2. **Calculate the point in time when current open market rental value will exceed the current contracted income.**

3. **Capitalise the contracted rent up to the cross-over point or first review thereafter at the equated yield.**

4. **Capitalise the implied market rent at the equivalent yield (ARY) from the date taken in step 3 in perpetuity discounted for the period of waiting at the equated yield.**

Solution to example 6.11 using the Crosby approach :

1. **ARY from comparable properties are 8%.**

2. **Equated yield is 12%.**

3. **Implied rate of rental growth given $e = 0.12$ and $k = 0.08$ is 4.63%.**

4. **7,500 x Amount of £1 in 'n' years at 4.63% = £10,000**

$$7,500 \times 1.334 = £10,000$$

$$\therefore \quad (1 + 0.0463)^n = 1.334$$

$$n = \sqrt[n]{1.334}$$

$$n = >6<7$$

$$\underline{\underline{\text{say } 6.5 \text{ years}}}$$

5.   In this example, given an upward only rent review in 5 years, the rent will remain at £10,000 at the first review. The valuer must exercise judgement to decide the most probable date for a review to occur. In this case the valuation might be:

Rent	£10,000	
YP 7 years @ 12%	4.5638	
		£45,638

Rent		£10,000	
YP perp. @ 8%	12.5		
PV £1 in 7 years			
@ 12%	0.45235		
		5.6543	£56,543
			£102,181

If the lease was due to terminate after 5 years then the implied rent at that time could be calculated at the implied growth rate of **4.63%**. *Then:*

£7,500 x amount of £1 in 5 years at 4.63% = Implied rent in year 5.

The contracted rent would be valued at the equated yield for 5 years with a reversion to the lower rent in year 5. Here there are practical difficulties for the valuer as most landlords would wish to retain the higher rent by payment of a reverse premium in order to underpin future rent reviews, but valuers must always be conservative in their assumptions in an open market valuation or estimation of realisation price.

Whilst theoretical solutions to this problem can be found using implied growth rates and DCF techniques these may not truly reflect behaviour in the marketplace and the valuer must not let the mathematics override market judgements. In particular future rents calculated using implied growth rates over the short term must not be used as a substitute for market analysis. The latter may well suggest minimal change in rental value over the short term.

The problem of falling incomes becomes more acute in the secondary and tertiary markets; that is, when considering over-rented properties in non-prime locations, or with non-prime tenants. Here market capitalisation rates will generally be gilt rates or higher and the valuer will have to use his or her best judgement in circumstances where the calculation of implied growth is unrealistic and impracticable.

Q **Value a freehold warehouse.**
A comparable property on the same business park let at its open market rental value of £42,500 has just been sold for £472,000. The subject property is similar in size but was let on a reduced (inducement) rent of £30,000 three years ago. There is a rent review in 2 years' time. Assess the ARY and value the warehouse. Demonstrate the use of modified DCF and Real Value approaches on the basis of an equated yield requirement of 12% P.184

Baum and Crosby (1995) suggest that *'for a property over-let to a very secure covenant under a lease with more than 15 years unexpired (on upwards only rent reviews), the term yield could be determined in comparison with a fixed income gilt plus a small risk margin for property illiquidity but without the traditional risks of property such as uncertainty for future income flow'*. An interesting 1990s observation which flows logically from earlier observations that 'valuers in the nineteenth century were primarily dealing with rack rented properties, largely agricultural at a time when inflation was relatively unknown. A realistic and direct comparison could be made between alternative investments such as undated securities (gilts) issued by government. Property being more risky was valued at a percentage point or so above the secure government stock.'

In some respects history is repeating itself. It is again reasonable to argue that the original *'term and reversion'* valuation may be appropriate in some circumstances. Thus an over-rented property may show little prospect of income change to the owner until a future lease renewal at which point best estimates or implied growth may suggest a market rental above the current contracted rent. The future rent may appear to be less secure as it will depend on a new letting or lease renewal and at such a date in the future that further rental growth may be unlikely due to depreciation. A market conventional approach might be to capitalise the term at say 1% above comparable gilts reflecting current income security of the tenant in occupation, and the reversion at 2% above gilts to reflect the greater risk attached to the reversion including the risk of a letting void.

The reader is reminded that, whilst detailing income valuation methods and the links between conventional and DCF techniques, the real task is the identification of the risks associated with the property to be valued, which requires research into future expectations (forecasting) as well as observation of the current market and market transactions.

A variable annuity

It is fairly rare to find a completely variable income from property, i.e., one where the income changes from year to year. But the suggested technique is to treat the calculation as an **NPV** calculation, treating each payment as a separate reversion and discounting each to its present value at an appropriate rate of discount *i.*

Advance or arrears

It has always been the custom to assume annual 'in arrears' income flows and annual rates for capitalisation purposes. There is, however, a growing tendency, as property is let on 'in advance' terms, to value on such a basis. In this respect it is essential to determine the valuation date at the commencement, as in many cases this will fall between rental payments. Technically this is still an 'in advance' valuation as the assumption of open market value will generally imply an apportionment of rents received 'in advance' as at the date of completion of a sale, and for valuation purposes the valuation date may be treated as a sale completion date.

Second, it is necessary to be certain that in this respect the lease terms are being enforced. It is common to find rent due on 1 January *'in advance'* being paid at a date later than 1 January.

Third, one should not lose sight of the fact that *'in advance'* means one payment due immediately, i.e. its present value is the sum due, and thereafter the same sum is due for *n* periods in arrears.

The crucial point is the relationship between the income and the discount rate. The latter must be the correct 'effective' rate for the particular income pattern. For preference this should be derived from market analysis of comparable *'quarterly'*, *'yearly'*, *'in advance'* or *'in arrears'* transactions as investors may not in fact be prepared to accept the same effective rate. If the appropriate comparable evidence is not available, then an *'in arrears'* rate can be transposed to (say) an effective *'quarterly in advance'* rate or a *'quarterly in advance'* income changed to an 'annual in arrears' income.

It should be noted that the use of *'quarterly in advance'* valuation tables for the valuation of incomes received on this basis may be questioned, as it is very rare that the valuation date will coincide exactly with the date when an instalment of rent is due. The income pattern may in fact resemble a 'quarterly in arrears' income.

If a property valuation is analysed on a precise basis, allowing both for the correct apportionment of rent as at the date of valuation and for the correct timing of future rents, then the rate of return will be higher than the rate per cent adopted in the valuation on an 'annual in arrears' basis. This realisation has encouraged some valuers to switch to *'quarterly in advance'* valuations using published tables or programmed calculators and computers. Where this is done, valuers must be sure that they adopt the proper market relationship between income patterns and yields of comparables in their valuation work.

When the whole market relates to *'quarterly in advance'* lettings and all valuers are analysing yields on a precise basis, then the market yields adopted by valuers for capitalisation work will be correct for *'in advance'* valuations. Until then the valuer needs to be fully aware of the basis of the quoted market yield before transposing it to an *'in advance'* valuation.

The reader should note that as the assessment of rental value, outgoings and capitalisation rates are all opinions, switching to *'in advance'* valuation tables will not in itself achieve a better opinion of value. Attempts at such arithmetic accuracy may be spurious.

Save where stated, the *'annual in arrears'* assumption has been used in all examples. This assumption is still commonplace in valuation practice, but accurate investment advice requires that estimation of the exact timing of income receipts is necessary in order to assess yields accurately. The use of spreadsheets enables the valuer to incorporate an accurate calendar within any valuation or analysis programme.

On examination it will be noted that certain property investments resemble certain other forms of investment and they can be distinguished by the future pattern of returns. Thus, property let on long lease without review could be compared to an irredeemable stock.

Owner-occupied freehold commercial properties are comparable to equity shares, whereas freehold properties let on a short lease or with regular rent reviews (whilst in a sense resembling equity investments) must also reflect the stepped income pattern. Short fixed-income leasehold interests are comparable to any fixed-term investment such as an annuity.

Recognition of these relationships is essential if the valuer is to make correct adjustments to the capitalisation rates to be used in a valuation where the income pattern produced by the property is out of line with current market evidence.

Sub-markets

Open market value and estimated realisation price are market concepts, hence a detailed knowledge and understanding of the sub-markets will be a prerequisite for every market valuation. The valuer will need to know the key players in each market and sub-market.

As an indication the following sub-markets can be noted:

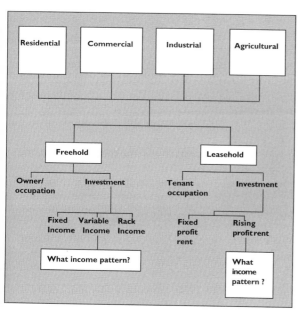

The valuation of leasehold interests is considered in the following chapter.

Summary

- *All freehold income valuations are based on the principal of discounting future net benefits to their present worth.*

- *Two broad methods are used:*

  Conventional capitalisation at the All Risks Yield or Equivalent Yield

  Contemporary DCF / Equated yield or Real Value approaches.

  Both can be expressed in Cash Flow Format.

- *Conventional methods are used where there is good evidence of capitalisation rates from the market.*

- *Contemporary methods are used where there is good evidence of capitalisation rates but where it is desirable to express rental changes explicitly AND*
  * for the assessment of worth to a client given the client's target rate
  * where there is poor market evidence - for example, in the case of long reversions and over-rented properties.

- *Assessment of implied growth rates for use in contemporary methods relies in part on market evidence of capitalisation rate and on the valuer's ability to interpret the market's requirements in terms of equated yields. Baum has demonstrated that variations in the latter are less significant than expected for most valuations.*

- *Assessment of implied growth rates must not be confused with forecasts of future rents based on econometric projections.*

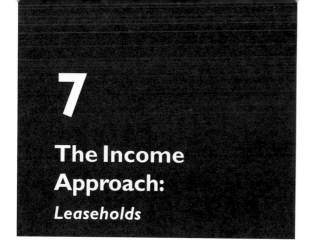

7

The Income Approach:

Leaseholds

The problem of valuing leasehold interests in property has been vexing valuers for many years. In most other countries the debate is now closed, but in the UK there is still considerable disagreement between those who regard the *'dual rate'* (sinking fund) or reinvestment approach to be correct and those who would seek to treat a leasehold as they would treat any investment requiring analysis or valuation.

In this section the different views are set out with comments, and whilst the view of the authors may be apparent it would be wrong without empirical evidence to state categorically that one or other approach is the right one. Our advice is to identify the sub-market, identify the most probable type of purchaser, and as far as possible adopt methods that parallel the investment aims of that most probable purchaser group.

A number of facts are not in dispute, namely:

1. A leasehold interest is of finite duration.

2. In investors' terms a lease can only have a market value if it produces an income and if it is assignable. The leasehold income is the profit rent, the rent actually received or potentially receivable less the rent payable to the superior landlord.

3. The profit rent must be adjusted for any expenses payable by the interest holder, but irrecoverable from the sub-lessee.

4. Where tax on income is payable, the capital cost of acquiring a finite investment has to be recovered out of the taxed income.

5. The mathematical formulation of the years'

purchase single rate may be equated with the years' purchase dual rate $\left(\dfrac{1}{i + SF}\right)$ so that capitalisation of an income using either single or dual rate provides the investor with a return on initial outlay plus replacement of capital in a sinking fund, on the assumption of compound interest within the rates used.

The crux of the problem is how the purchaser of a leasehold interest should or does allow for capital recovery.

Dual rate adjusted for tax

The reasons generally given for valuing leaseholds on the dual rate basis for recoupment (recovery) of capital by reinvestment in a sinking fund at a low safe rate are:

1. **That an investor requires a return on initial outlay throughout the lease term at the remunerative rate.**

2. **That all capital must be recovered by the end of the lease term and that to be certain of doing this reinvestment in a sinking fund accumulating at a low, safe, net-of-tax rate must be undertaken.**

3. **That by so doing the investor has equated the finite investment with an infinite (freehold) investment in the same property base, i.e., the spendable income is perpetuated *(see Chapter 2).***

Example 7.1

Estimate the value of a 4-year unexpired lease. The profit rent is **£100** per annum net.

Net of outgoings profit rent	£100	
YP for 4 years @ 10% and 3%		
adj. tax @ 40%	2.00	
		£200

Proof:

Annual sinking fund to replace £1 @ 3% in 4 years	= 0.239	
∴ ASF to replace £200	= 200 x 0.239	
	= £47.80	

Within conventional dual rate valuations two schools of thought are apparent. Initially both accept that the risk, or remunerative, rate for a leasehold should be a minimum of **1-2%** above the appropriate freehold rate. This is to allow for the additional problems of reinvesting in a sinking fund, reinvesting the accumulated sinking fund at the end of the lease term, and for the additional risks inherent in a leasehold investment relating to restrictions imposed by the lease terms and possible dilapidations. This philosophy would have been sound in the late nineteenth and early twentieth centuries when leases were for long terms of **99** years or more. To assume some constant magical relationship today is inconsistent with the philosophy of market valuations, unless market transactions justify that rate.

Both schools assume that reinvestment must be at a low, net-of-tax rate and that the sinking fund premium or instalment must be met out of taxed income. But the schools seem to differ on the nature of the sinking fund.

The original theory is that capital replacement in order to be guaranteed must be in effect **'assured'** Hence reinvestment is assumed to be made in a sinking fund policy with an assurance company. Such a policy is a legal contract. The total sum assured will be paid out on the due date if all premiums have been met. The rate of accumulation is assumed to be between **2.5%** and **4%**. Such a policy is unaffected by any changes in tax rates, as such changes will only affect the investor's investment income.[1]

The second school argues in favour of reinvestment at safe rates. These will not necessarily be guaranteed but could conceivably include regular savings in a post office account, bank deposit account, or building society savings or investment accounts.

A potential 'danger' is that the valuer can be implying an effective gross return on the sinking fund greater than the remunerative rate used in a valuation. Conventionally a **6%** freehold yield might become a **7%** leasehold yield, but **7%** and **4%** with a tax rate of **50p** in the **£1** would imply that the investor could invest in a sinking fund and initially be better off than by purchasing the leasehold interest. It can be seen that the profit rent must grow at a rate sufficient to compensate for the opportunity cost of investing at **7%** gross and not at **4%** net.

This would be perfectly tenable under certain market conditions.

Both approaches rely on the argument that the purchaser of a leasehold investment is unlikely to have the opportunity to reinvest at the remunerative rate. Apart from the fact that there is no need to reinvest if the investor accepts a return on capital at risk, there is the obvious point that relatively safe rates, albeit variable, are readily available for regular saving.

Further, purchasers of leasehold investments invest in more than one unit, and may receive sufficient income each year to purchase further leasehold investments. The leasehold investor is then better advised to reinvest in further leaseholds (or freeholds) rather than in a sinking fund.

Historically there may have been some justifications for the dual rate approach. In the eighteenth, nineteenth and early twentieth century leaseholds had long terms (frequently ground leases or improved ground leases with no rent reviews), and were therefore comparable to freehold investments. Initially they were valued single rate at **0.5 - 2%** above the freehold rate to reflect the additional risk arising from lease covenants etc.

[1] If a policy is taken out and a re-sale occurs part way through the term, the insured must either continue to pay the annual premium or accept a paid-up policy. In the latter case there would be a shortfall in capital recovery.

The problem emerged in the 1920s and 1930s when lease length began to fall and when the gap between safe and risky investments became greater. This was in part a reflection of depression in the economy.

It was also a time when purchasers of leases were individuals buying for occupation rather than to hold as investments; there were few large investors in the market. By the mid-1930s valuers were split between single rate and dual rate, although writers still made the point that sale prices could be analysed on either basis. The need to demonstrate parity with freeholds began to dominate, as did the concern for capital recovery when safe investments were yielding so little.

For those who were seeking protection and perpetuation through reinvestment there was the added difficulty of finding reinvestment opportunities for small annual sums other than in a bank or post office. The result was a growing rationale for the conventional dual rate approach.

The position post-1960 was very different as inflation became part of life. Nevertheless, the dual rate method survived virtually unchallenged other than for the universal acceptance of the need for the tax adjustment. It survived with the low sinking fund even though most savers could achieve much higher returns than the 4% maximum used by valuers. It survived even though few sinking fund policies were taken out, even though occupiers were depreciating leaseholds as wasting assets in their accounts and even though investors accepted that they effectively provided for capital replacement by reinvestment in a general sense rather than on a per property basis.

A final point is that where the investment is made with borrowed funds or partially borrowed funds (e.g. 60% mortgage) reinvestment at the rates adopted in valuations by certain valuers will certainly be at levels lower than the interest charged on the borrowed capital. Clearly the investor would be better advised to pay off part of the loan rather than reinvest in a sinking fund.

One of the most disturbing elements of dual rate valuation practice is its concentration on today's profit rent and its failure to consider the future, in particular its failure to reflect the unique gearing characteristics of longer leaseholds. Taking, for example,

Property A held for 20 years at **£10,000 p.a.** without review and sub-let with 5-year reviews for **£20,000 p.a.**,

and

Property B similarly held at **£80,000 p.a.** and sub-let at **£90,000 p.a.**,

the conventional dual rate approach would place the same value on both as they both produce a profit rent of **£10,000 p.a.**

This completely hides the fact that with rental growth at any rate per cent the profit rents after each rent review grow at different rates. This problem of gearing can only be solved by valuing the head rent and occupation rent separately and by adopting a DCF or real value approach. Conventional dual rate methodology would, if applied constantly to every situation, provide the investor with some phenomenal investment opportunities and result in some vendors grossly underselling their investments.

The dual rate method was considered in depth in the RICS research report *(Trott, 1980)* and by **Baum and Crosby 1995**. A general conclusion being that it will continue to be used because 'that is how the market does it'; however, for investment advice a DCF approach should be adopted and, indeed, should always be used to check the dual rate approach to avoid the possibility of incorrect sales advice.

> **Q** Value a leasehold profit rent of £20,000 for 4 years using 8% and 3% adj. tax at 40% and prove that a return on capital at 8% and a return of capital at a net rate of 3% is achieved.

Variable profit rents

Variable profit rents present special problems in valuations where the sinking fund rate of return adopted is lower than the investment risk rate (remunerative rate).

The valuation of a leasehold investment may involve a variable profit rent in the following cases:

1. **Where a leaseholder lets property to a sub-lessee for part only of the unexpired term. In this case there will be a fixed profit rent for 'n' years and a reversion to a different level of profit rent in 'n' years.**

2. **Where a leaseholder lets property to a sub-lessee for the full unexpired term with a proviso for rent reviews in 'n' years to a**

known sum or to full rental value.

3. **Where a leaseholder has a right to a new lease under the Landlord and Tenant Act 1954 Part II, and where the rent for the new lease must be at full rental value adjusted for goodwill and/or approved improvements carried out by the lessee.**★

> ★ See Landlord and Tenant Act 1954 Part II and Law of Property Act 1969
> Wherever a leasehold valuation is required the valuer should exercise care in determining the true net profit rent, special attention being given to the allowance for expenditure of repairs and insurance when a sub-letting has taken place on terms differing from the head lease.

In some cases the profit rent will be rising, while in others it will be falling. In both cases anomalies occur if, in the assessment of present worth, the flow of income is treated as an immediate annuity plus one or more deferred annuities, assessed on a dual rate basis. The valuation should be treated as an immediate variable annuity.

Whilst the valuer's subjective adjustments to the remunerative rates used in the three cases may well differ, the particular problem of variable profit rents will remain and is fully illustrated in the following problem.

Example 7.2

Using as an example a profit rent of £1,800 for 2 years rising to £2,000 for 5 years, demonstrate the problems encountered when valuing rising profit rents on a conventional dual rate basis.

Demonstrate the alternatives to this approach.

Leasehold rate at FRV: 10% and 3% adj. tax @ 40%

Conventional valuation:★
Term:

Profit rent	£1,800	
YP for 2 years @ 9% and		
3% adj. tax @ 40%	1.0977	
		£1,976

Reversion:

Profit rent	£2,000	
YP for 5 years @ 10% and		
3% adj. tax @ 40%	2.416	
	£4,832	
PV £1 in 2 years @ 10%	0.8265	
		£3,994
		£5,970

> ★ The use of variable remunerative rates causes further problems as does the deferment of the reversions at the reversionary remunerative rate. These issues can be overcome by adopting a same yield approach.

What are the problems?

None is apparent from this valuation, but compare the valuation of the following profit rent of **£1,800** receivable for 7 years (5 years plus 2 years):

Profit rent	£1,800
YP for 5 years @ 10% and	
3% adj.tax @ 40%	3.1495
	£5,669.10

Notice that the second investment is valued at £300 lower than the first.

But what is the real difference?

The first investment produces an extra £200 for 5 years deferred for 2 years.

Profit rent	£200
YP for 5 years @ 10% and	
3% adj. tax @ 40%	2.416
	£483.2
PV £1 in 2 years @ 10%	0.8265
	£400.0

The difference in the two valuations is £300, yet the difference in rent is worth **£400.**

There is obviously some kind of error.

The error can be demonstrated in the same manner much more dramatically.

Take two profit rents with a 20-year life.
One is of **£1,000** for the whole period; the other rises to **£1,100** after 10 years (and is therefore more valuable).

(1)			(2)		
Profit rent	£1,000		Profit rent	£1,000	
YP for 20 years @ 10% and 3% adj. tax @ 40%	6.1718		YP for 10 years @ 9% and 3% adj. tax @ 40%	4.2484	£4,248
	£6,172		Reversion to	£1,100	
			YP for 10 years @ 10% and 3% adj. tax @ 40% x PV £1 in 10 years @ 10% (4.0752 x 0.386)	1.573	£1,730
					£5,977

The inferior investment is valued more highly by the conventional dual rate method, and the error becomes embarrassing.

It can be demonstrated without any need for comparison that an error does exist by checking that the sinking fund actually replaces the initial outlay. This will be done with reference to the original valuation.

Term

CV	£5,970
Income	£1,800

Spendable income
0.09 x £5,970
= £537.3

Sinking fund
£1,800 - £537.3
= £1,262.7 gross
= 0.6 (£1,262.7) net
= £757.6

A £1 p.a. for 2 years @ 3%	2.03
	£1,538

This **£1,538** will then be allowed to accumulate interest for 5 more years, the period of the reversion.

	£1,538	
A £1 in 5 years @ 3%	1.1593	= **£1,783 replaced**

Reversion:

CV	£5,970
Income	£2,000

Spendable income
0.10 x £5,970
= £597

Sinking fund
£2,000 - £597
= £1,403 gross
= 0.6 (£1,403) net
= £842

A £1 p.a. for 5 years @ 3%	5.3091
	£4,470 replaced

Total replacement of capital

£1,783 + £4,470 = **£6,253**

Compare **£6,253** with an initial outlay of **£5,970** and it can be seen that there is an over-replacement of capital.

Why?

It can be shown that the replacement of capital for both term and reversion, when examined separately, is perfectly correct.

Term:

CV	£1,976
Income	£1,800

Spendable income
0.09 x £1,976
= £178

Sinking fund
£1,800 - £178 = £1,622 gross
x 0.6
£973.2 net

A £1 p.a. for 2 years @ 3%	2.03
Term capital replaced	£1,976

Reversion:

CV	£4,832
Income	£2,000

Spendable income
0.10 x £4,832

= £483.2

Sinking fund
£2,000 - £483.2 =
£1,516.8 gross
x 0.6
£910.08 net

A £1 p.a. for 5 years @ 3%	5.3091
Reversion capital replaced	£4,832

It follows that the error must arise from the addition of term and reversion. This produces an extra accumulation of sinking fund resulting in an over-replacement of capital. The deferment of the reversion by a single rate PV is another expression of the same error. It is often said that the error results from the provision for two sinking funds or the interruption of the desired single sinking fund. As a result the methods that have been devised to deal with this error attack the problem by attempting to ensure that the initial capital is accurately replaced by the sinking fund.

Method 1: The sinking fund method

The problem which has been identified above is that the conventional dual rate method of valuing leasehold interests does not provide for accurate replacement of capital. The sinking fund method ensures that this must happen, its premise being that capital value is equal to the amount replaced by the sinking fund. The method calculates the amount of the net sinking fund and its accumulation which must necessarily be equal to the capital value of the investment.

Let CV = x

Term: Rent = £1,800
Gross sinking fund = Income - spendable income

$= £1,800 - 0.09x$

(Return on capital = remunerative rate of 9%: return on capital = $0.09x$)

Net sinking fund $= (£1,800 - 0.09x)(0.6)$
$= £1,080 - 0.054x$

Reversion:

Rent $= £2,000$
Gross sinking fund $= £2,000 - 0.10x$
Therefore :
Net sinking fund $= £1,200 - 0.06x$

Calculate accumulation of net sinking funds:

Term: $£1,080 - 0.054x$

A £1 p.a. for
2 years@ 3%   2.03
A £1 in 5 years @ 3%   x 1.1593
            2.3534

$£2,541.65 - 0.127x$

Reversion: $£1,200 - 0.06x$
A £1 p.a. for 5 years
@ 3%   5.3091

$£6,370.29 - 0.31285x$

Adding the term and reversion equations together

$£8,912.57 - 0.4455x$

The capital value should equal the amount replaced and therefore x should equal the sum of the sinking fund accumulations.

So:

$x = £8,912.57 - 0.4455x$

$1.4455x = £8,912.57$

Therefore

$x = £6,165.74$

This method can be checked by checking the accumulation of sinking funds on term and reversion.

Term:

CV	£6,166
Income	£1,800

Spendable income	Sinking fund
0.09 x £6,166	£1,800 - £554,94 = £1,245.06 gross
= £554.94	x 0.6
	£747.04 net

A £1 p.a. for 2 years @ 3%   2.03
A £1 in 5 years @ 3%   1.1593
                2.354

£1,758.07

Reversion

CV	£6,166
Income	£2,000

Spendable income	Sinking fund
0.10 x £6,166	£2,000 - £616.6 = £1,383.40 gross
= £616.60	x 0.6
	£830.06 net

A £1 p.a. for 5 years @ 3%   5.3091

£4,406.87

Capital replaced   £6,164.94*

---

*   The marginal error here is due to the initial rounding to £6,166 and subsequent rounding in the calculations.

Method 2: The annual equivalent method[2]

The purpose of this second method is to find that fixed income which would be equivalent to the rising profit rent which is to be valued.

Equivalent incomes for both term and reversion are found and valued separately to allow for the use of different remunerative rates on term and reversion.

It was originally suggested that the rate of interest used to capitalise and de-capitalise both incomes when finding the annual equivalent should be the accumulative rate, and this will be the approach that will be adopted, although it is open to question at the present time due to the problem of choosing a reasonable accumulative rate.

---

[2] The current teaching of this and the sinking fund method is attributed to Dr M.J. Greaves previously of Reading University and the National University of Singapore.

A *Capitalise at low safe rate:*

Term:

Income	£1,800
YP for 2 years @ 3%	1.9135
	£3,444

Reversion:

Income		£2,000
YP for 5 years @ 3%	4.5797	
PV £1 in 2 years		
@ 3%	x 0.9426	4.3168
		£8,633

B *Find annual equivalent income:*

Term:

£3,444 ÷ YP for 7 years @ 3%

= £3,444 ÷ 6.2303

= £552.78

Reversion:

£8,633 ÷ YP for 7 years @ 3%

= £8,633 ÷ 6.2303

= £1,385.65

C *Capitalise annual equivalents at market capitalisation rate*

Term:

Income	£552.78	
YP for 7 years @ 9% and		
3% adj. tax @ 40%	3.2519	£1,797.59

Reversion:

Income	£1,385.65	
YP for 7 years @ 10% and		
3% adj. tax @ 40%	3.1495	£4,364.10
		£6,161.69

D *Proof:*
Term:

CV	£1,797.59
Income	£1,800

Spendable Income	Sinking fund
0.09 x £1,797.59	£1,800 - £598.19* = £1,201.81 gross
= £161.78	x 0.6
	£721.09 net

Reversion:

CV	£4,364.10
Income	£2,000

Spendable income	Sinking fund
0.10 x £4,364.10	£2,000 - £598.19* = £1,401.81 gross
= £436.41	x 0.6
	£841.09 net

* Total spendable income at 9% and 10% on term and reversion is
£598.19 (£161.78 + £436.41).

Check sinking fund accumulations:

Term:

		£721.09
A £1 p.a. for 2 years @ 3%	2.03	
A £1 in 5 years @ 3%	x 1.1593	2.354
		£1,697

Reversion:

		£841.09
A £1 p.a. for 5 years @ 3%		
	5.3091	£4,465
		£6,162*

* Error due to rounding.

The proof employed in the sinking fund approach is not applicable in this case, where term and reversion must be kept separate when checking the sinking fund accumulation. In the first approach spendable income differs over term and reversion; but in the annual equivalent method, spendable income remains the same. If the remunerative rates were the same over term and reversion then either proof may be used, but when they differ; the annual equivalent valuation can only be checked by the particular approach outlined above.

Method 3: The double sinking fund method[3]

This, the original of the three methods discussed here, involves more detailed arithmetic. The required sinking fund to replace a capital value of x is deducted from income to leave the amount of spendable income that will be enjoyed.

The spendable income is then capitalised.

[3] This method is attributed to A.W. Davidson one time Head of Valuation at Reading University.

This ignores the sinking fund accumulation, which is then added back to produce a similar equation to that which is solved in the sinking fund approach.

A constant sinking fund is ensured by this approach, overcoming the conventional method's fault.

1 Let CV = x Then:

sinking fund to replace x = ASF to replace £1 in 7 years at 3% x x

$$= 0.1305064x$$

Gross up for tax @ 40% $= 0.1305064x \left(\frac{1}{1-t} \right)$

$$= 0.1305064x \times \frac{1}{0.6}$$

$$= 0.2175106x$$

Therefore

Spendable income is £1,800 – 0.2175106x for term.
Spendable income is £2,000 – 0.2175106x for reversion.

2 Capitalise the spendable income

Term:

Income	£1,800 – 0.2175106x
YP for 2 years @ 9%	1.7591
	£3,166.38 – 0.3826228x

Reversion:

Income	£2,000 – 0.2175106x

YP for 5 years @ 10% 3.7908
PV £1 in 2 years
@ 10%   0.8264463
                                    3.133
                        £6,265.79 – 0.6814372x

Adding the term and
reversion   £9,432.17 – 1.06406x

This (£9,432.17 minus 1.06406x) is the present value of the spendable income provided by the investment. It has been capitalised by a single rate YP which contains an inherent sinking fund at the remunerative rate. The capital value of the spendable income could thus be reinvested at the end of 7 years, while another sinking fund has been provided to replace the capital value of the whole income flow - x. There are therefore two

sinking funds, hence the name of the method.

An alternative view is to remember that income is split into two parts when it is received for a limited period - spendable income and sinking fund. It follows that capital value can be split into capitalised spendable income and capitalised sinking fund. Having found the first of these constituents the second should be added to give the total value of the investment.

What, then, is the present capital value of the sinking fund?

It replaces x in 7 years.

Its present value is x deferred for 7 years at the investor's remunerative rate(s): **9%** for 2 years and **10%** for the remaining 5.

3 Replaced CV = x

PV £1 in 5 years @ 10%	0.6209213	
PV £1 in 2 years @ 9%	0.84168	
		0.522617
		0.522617x

Thus if x is the capital value **CV**, then x must be equal to the total of **1**, **2** and **3**.

x	= £9,432.17 - 1.06406x + 0.522617x
x	= £9,432.17 - 0.541443x
1.541443x	= £9,432.17
x	= £6,119.05

Proof:

Term:

CV	£6,119.05
Income	£1,800

Spendable income	Sinking fund
0.09 x £6,119.05	£1,800 – £550.71 = £1,249.29 gross
= £550.71	x 0.6
	£749.57 net

Reversion:

CV	£6,119.05
Income	£2,000

Spendable income	Sinking fund
0.10 x £6,119.05	£2,000 – £611.91 = £1,388.09 gross
= £611.91	x 0.6
	£832.85 net

Check sinking fund accumulations:

Term:	£749.57
A £1 p.a. for 2 years @ 3% 2.03	
A £1 in 5 years @ 3% x 1.1593	2.354
	£1,764.02
Reversion:	£832.85
A £1 p.a. for 5 years @ 3%	5.3091
	£4,421.68
	£6,185.70

(compare with CV of £6,119.05)

The proof suggests that capital value is not accurately replaced. But the rationale of the method must ensure accurate replacement of capital, and this leads to the conclusion that this method suffers from another fault. This is that although rates of return of **9%** on the term and **10%** on the reversion are required they are not accurately provided by this valuation.

There is an over-replacement of capital and consequently the interest is undervalued, as in the conventional method, but to a reduced degree.

	CV	Replaced CV
Conventional dual rate:	£5,970	£6,253
Sinking fund:	£6,166	£6,165
Annual equivalent:	£6,162	£6,162
Double sinking fund:	£6,119	£6,186

It is therefore possible to conclude that the sinking fund and annual equivalent methods best overcome the problem posed by the conventional method of valuing variable profit rents as they appear to provide for accurate replacement of capital and correctly allow for the required rate of return to be provided.

However, even the apparent accuracy of these solutions cannot be relied upon in all circumstances.

For example, the sinking fund method becomes unworkable if the term income is particularly low; the spendable income over the period becomes negative, and considerable problems arise.

Harker, Nanthakumaran and Rogers (1988) of Aberdeen University in their discussion paper on *'Double sinking fund correction methods'* support the sinking fund method and suggest a resolution to the negative spendable income problem.

A popular alternative to these methods is the Pannell method. In this method the capital value of the variable profit rents are found by capitalising each on a single rate basis using the appropriate leasehold remunerative rates. The annual equivalent of the product is then found by dividing through by the YP for the full unexpired term at the remunerative rate or the average of the rates used. This annual equivalent can then be capitalised on a dual rate basis for the full term.

Because the use of dual rate valuations can be seen to lead to difficulties, single rate leasehold valuations may be put forward as an alternative. But even single rate valuations may be prone to error where more than one rate of interest is used *(see p.65)*.

Nonetheless, the potential for arithmetic error in a single rate valuation is considerably less, and this type of valuation of leaseholds will now be considered.

> **Q** A shopping centre currently produces rents of £2.5million with rents due for review in 3 years to £3.25million and thereafter every 5 years.
>
> The centre is held leasehold with 60 years of the lease to run with one rent review of the ground rent in 10 years' time. The ground rent is currently £50,000 p.a. and the rent review is fixed at 5% of the shop rentals.
>
> Set out skeleton valuations of the headlease using a conventional dual rate approach at 8% and 3% with tax at 40p and a (DCF) approach on the basis of a freehold target rate of 10%.

Single rate valuation of leaseholds

If a single rate approach is to be used in a marketplace where purchasers are liable for tax on incomes then capital recoupment must be provided for out of taxed income. To do this the inherent sinking fund element must either be adjusted for tax, or tax deducted from the profit rent.[4] The latter approach is adopted here.

Example 7.3

Estimate the present worth of a profit rent of £100 for 4 years. Tax is at **40%** and the investor requires a net of tax return of 7.75%.

Profit rent	£100
Less tax at 40p	40
Net of tax profit rent	£60
YP for 4 years @ 7.75%	3.33
	£200

The investor will obtain a return on his/her capital of **7.75%** net and will recover his/her capital in full at **7.75%**. Whether or not part of the income is reinvested is immaterial, as the investor has the opportunity of accepting a partial return of capital at the end of each year.

Year	Capital outstanding	Net income	Return on capital @ 7.75%	Return of capital
1	£200	£60	£15.50	£44.5
2	£155.5	£60	£12.05	£47.95
3	£107.55	£60	£8.335	£51.66
4	£55.89	£60	£4.33	£55.67*
				£199.78

*Error due to rounding of figures

Two valuers valuing an income of £100 would therefore both agree on a figure of £200. But valuer **A** would argue that the investment represented a **10%** gross return allowing for replacement of capital at **4%** net (see above **example 7.1**) whilst valuer **B** given the information on income, tax and purchase price of £200 would argue that the only acceptable method of

[4] See Chapter 8 for consideration of net valuation

investment analysis where purchase price is known is to find the internal rate of return which over 4 years is, in this case, approximately **35%** on gross income (**see p 86**). No doubt investors do like to make investment decisions on like criteria and one might therefore suggest that the reason why some investors will buy leasehold interests is simply that they do show a high **IRR**.

'As you analyse, so should you value.'

This tenet is often used by valuers as an argument in support of the retention of the dual rate approach to leasehold valuations. It is equally useful in advocating the use of single rate leasehold valuations.

Example 7.4

A 5-year leasehold investment producing a profit rent of **£1,000 p.a.** has been sold for **£2,584**. Analyse this market evidence and value a 50-year profit rent of **£1,000 p.a.**

A Dual rate: analysis

Income	£1,000
YP for 5 years @ x% and 3%	
adj. tax @ 40%	2.584
	£2,584

Solve by tables or formula to find x:
x = 8%

Income	£1,000
YP for 50 years @ 8% and 3%	
adj. tax @ 40%	10.551
	£10,551

B Single rate: analysis

Income	£1,000
YP for 5 years @ x%	2.584
	£2,584

Solve by tables or formula to find x:
x = 26%

Valuation

Income	£1,000
YP for 50 years @ 26%	3.845
	£3,845

The result of switching from a dual rate to a single rate basis is a valuation which is impossible to reconcile with market evidence. On current experience, it is much more likely that a price nearer to £10,551 would be paid for the 50-year investment.

Because of this inconsistency, because conventional dual rate valuations are adjusted for tax, and because the tax position of the purchaser is a vital factor in the market for leaseholds, the analysis and valuation should be carried out net of tax *(see Chapter 8).*

Example 7.4 (cont.)

C Single rate (net of tax): analysis

Income	£1,000
Less tax @ 40%	£400
Net income	£600
YP 50 years @ 5.1%	18.0
	£10,800

It can therefore be concluded that an alternative to dual rate valuations, which provides valuations consistent with current market experience, does exist: the single rate, net-of-tax approach. It must be emphasised that the switch from dual rate to single rate will necessitate a change in the remunerative rates used, and that the difference between the freehold rates used with the (equivalent gross) leasehold rates for similar properties will be greater than the conventional 1-2% adjustment *(see p.73).* A differential of 2-4% will be more appropriate to reflect the additional loss of security incurred by removing the assumption of a sinking fund accumulating at a low, safe rate.

The use of net single rate valuations of leasehold interests avoids the great majority of technical problems identified in the earlier discussion of dual rate valuations. The problem of choosing the appropriate rate of tax remains, as does the problem of deriving an appropriate leasehold capitalisation rate from a very diverse market.

Tax adjustment rate

What rate of tax should be used to adjust a gross profit rent to a net rent, or to gross-up a sinking fund to allow for tax?

The answer normally given is to use standard rates of income or corporation tax but the problem is more complex due to the presence of non tax payers such as pension funds and charities. The valuer's task is generally to determine market value, this implies a sale to the most probable purchaser, which implies some knowledge of the market and therefore sufficient knowledge to adjust, both for analysis and valuation, at a rate appropriate to the most probable purchaser.

However, as tax is levied at different rates for different investors, an average tax rate **(e.g. 40%)** is used to reflect market interaction. But analysis of leasehold investments from a client's point of view must be carried out at that client's net-of-tax rate.

Example 7.5

'Short leasehold investments are sound investments for charities because of their tax advantage.' Discuss.

Apart from the point that charities are more interested in income over the long term than short term, a number of points can be made. If the statement is true then charities must comprise a sub-market for this kind of investment. In that case the valuer needs to reflect the fact that the income is probably tax free; that they would be ill-advised to reinvest in a sinking fund policy with an assurance company because they will probably have difficulty in recovering the tax element on the 4% net accumulations of the policy; and that they would be best advised to reinvest in the safest gross funds[5] to avoid delay in recovery of taxed interest or dividends.

Example 7.6

Analyse the sale of a £100 profit rent for 4 years at a price of £200 from the point of view of a gross (i.e. non-tax-paying) fund.

$$\frac{£200}{£100} = \text{multiplier of 2}$$

(a)   Assume reinvestment in an equivalent safe gross fund at, say, **8%**. Therefore the sinking fund to recover £200 will be:

£200 x ASF to replace £1 in 4 years at 8%

= £200 x 0.22
= £44

The gross spendable income	= £100 - £44
	= £56
Therefore	
The gross return	= $\frac{56 \times 100}{200}$
	= 28%

[5] The term 'safe gross funds' is used here to indicate any investment where interest or dividends are paid without deduction of tax.

(b)　Without a reinvestment assumption analyse to find the internal rate of return.

Solve :
$$\frac{1 - \left[\dfrac{1}{(1+i)^4} \right]}{i} = 2$$

The present value of £1 p.a. in 4 years at 35% = 2, and therefore the IRR is 35%.

Charities, because of their tax position, may be interested in short leasehold investments, because, if they can buy at prices determined by absolutely conventional approaches the effective return will be sufficiently high to compensate for the disadvantages of the investment.

Categories of leasehold investment

There are a number of identifiable categories of leasehold interests, each of which requires a different approach due to the specific sub-market and profit rent pattern.

1 Long leaseholds, over (say) 30 years, at a fixed head rent.

Where the head lessee is in occupation or has sub-let on a short lease the investment may be treated as one with potential income growth, i.e. a rising profit rent. Whether a dual rate or single rate approach is followed, the risk rate (remunerative rate) will probably be comparable to that for freehold rack rented properties with similar rent review patterns, but **1-2%** higher.

If the head lease is for a term certain in excess of 40 years, then it could be treated as directly comparable to the freehold, because the length of time involved reduces the sinking fund (recoupment of capital) to a very small percentage of the profit rent, which becomes nearly all spendable income, as in the case of a freehold investment. But the problem of gearing must be noted and a split valuation used as a check, if not as the method.

2 Fixed profit rent

Where the head lessee, or predecessor in title, has sub-let the property for the full unexpired term of the head lease without rent review, the profit rent is fixed. The

valuation must reflect this factor and the profit rent must be capitalised at an appropriate cost of capital rate. This effectively allows for the depreciating worth of each year's income in terms of purchasing power. A single rate approach is frequently the most effective method.

3 Occupation leases

If the most probable purchaser is a potential occupier then, although an investment valuation may be adopted, care must be taken to see that it reflects the objectives of that type of purchaser. For example, if the lease of retail premises in a prime trading position is to be sold with the benefit of vacant possession then the purchaser will very likely be another retailer. Retailers will not be looking for a property investment return of $x\%$ on the imputed profit rental; they will be seeking a first class outlet for their goods. Their bids are likely to be well above that of most property investors, indeed, analyses of such sales may produce very unusual rates of return whichever way the analysis is undertaken.

Summary

7

The historical evolution of the dual rate method is now shrouded in the mists of time. Textbooks and journals of the time move from single rate to dual rate with very little explanation and with virtually no consideration of the fact that it hinges on the acceptance of a return on initial outlay throughout the life of the investment. A concept apparently unique to the UK leasehold property investment market.

The emergence of the tax adjustment factor is better documented and is relevant to all short-term investments, however valued, where tax is charged on that element of income which is essentially capital recoupment.

Part of the market is still as reluctant today to return to single rate as it was initially to shift from it to dual rate. A strength of dual rate lay in the ability to compare returns from freeholds with leaseholds. The reluctance today may be the fear of the unknown arising from the unique nature of every leasehold investment and the pressure on the valuer to find a unique solution. The solution lies in the proper use of discounting techniques where the unique growth expectations can be explicitly accounted for.

In summary dual rate methodology can be criticised because

- sinking funds *per se* are not available in the market;

- leaseholds as investments are not directly comparable to freeholds and remunerative rates cannot be taken as 1-2% above freehold rates;

- accumulative rates do not appear to be market sensitive. 4% has been used when safe rates have been as high as 12% and when they have been below 4%;

- it is not possible to devise a dual rate adjusted for tax from market sales unless at least 2 of the 3 variables are assumed by the valuer (tax rate, SF rate and/or remunerative rate);

- dual rate analysis of variable geared profit rents is similarly impossible;

- there is an arithmetic error in dual rate when used for valuing variable profit rents.

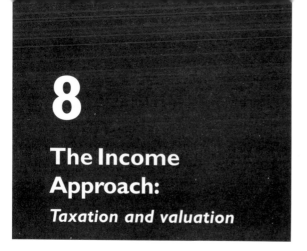

8

The Income Approach:

Taxation and valuation

It is customary in valuation to ignore the effects of income tax, on the grounds that investors compare investments on the basis of their gross rates of return. This may well be an acceptable criterion where tax affects all investments and all investors in a like manner. Although this is not the case in the property market only a few valuers would argue that tax should always be deducted from income before being capitalised at a net-of-tax capitalisation rate (a *'true net approach'*).

One of the most important points to note is that where the income from property is all *return on capital* (that is, true spendable income), gross and net valuations will produce the same value estimate. Where part of the income is a part return of capital this, other than in the case of certain life annuities, is not exempt from taxation and in such cases the gross and net approaches may produce a different value estimate.

In addition, certain investments will produce fairly substantial growth in capital value over a relatively short term, due to a growth in income. In these cases, if the investment is resold, Capital Gains Tax **(CGT)** may be payable on the gain realised.

Example 8.1

Explain what is meant by '*net rates of interest*' and discuss their uses in valuation, using numerical examples.

A net rate of interest is interest earned on deposited monies after the deduction of an allowance for the payment of tax on the gross interest earned. Here the phrase refers to any net-of-tax rates.

Thus **£1,000** deposited with a bank, for example, earning interest at the rate of **10%** per annum would, with tax at **40p in the £(40%)**, produce a net rate of **6%** $(10 \times (1 - t))$ where t is 0.4. As far as the valuer's use

of the valuation tables is concerned, the switch from gross to net valuations should cause no problems. Thus, the present value of £1 in 5 years at **10%** gross allowing for **tax at 40p** in the **£** can be found in tax-adjusted tables to be **0.74726**, or in unadjusted tables at **6%** $(10 \times (1 - t))$ where t is 0.4 to be 0.747258. It should be obvious that where **£100** is invested at **10%**, and tax is payable, compounding can only take place at the net-of-tax rate.

It is also obvious that, where an investor is a taxpayer paying tax on all investment income at **40%**, the actual return after tax will be reduced. The significance of this is not lost on investors, who always have full regard to their net-of-tax returns. When considering property investments, it is therefore necessary to consider whether valuations should also be based on net-of-tax incomes and yields.

For simplicity of illustration a tax rate of 50% is used in some of the examples.

Incomes in perpetuity

The formula for capitalising an income in perpetuity is income divided by *i*.

If the gross income is **£1,000** and the gross capitalisation rate is **10%** then:
£1,000 $\div$ **0.10 = £10,000**.

If tax is payable at 50p in the £ then

$$1,000 \times \left(\frac{1 - t}{1} \right) \div 0.10 \times \left(\frac{1 - t}{1} \right)$$

$$= 500 \div 0.05 = £10,000$$

Clearly as the numerator and denominator are multiplied by a constant $\frac{1 - t}{1}$

then they can be divided through by that constant.

Hence, $I \div i = \dfrac{I \times \dfrac{1 - t}{1}}{i \times \dfrac{1 - t}{1}}$

No difference in value estimate will occur, because the income is perpetual and is all return on capital.

Finite or terminable incomes

An income receivable for a fixed term of years may have a present value which can be assessed on a single or dual rate basis, gross or net of tax.

Consider an income of £1,000 receivable for five years on a **10% gross** basis with tax at **50%**.

A Single rate

	Gross	Net of tax at 50p
	£1,000	£500
	PV £1 p.a. for 5 years@ 10%	PV £1 p.a. for 5 years@ 5%
	3.7908	4.32955
	£3,790	£2,164

Here there is a clear difference between the two figures which can be seen to result from the tax adjustments that have been made.

$$I \times \frac{1 - \dfrac{1}{(I+i)^n}}{i}$$

cannot be equated with

$$I(1-t) \times \frac{1 - \dfrac{1}{(1+i(1-t))^n}}{i(1-t)}$$

Here, part of the £1,000 income is a return of capital. If tax is payable at 50p in the £, then only £500 is available to provide a return on capital and a return of capital. A purchase at £3,790 would be too high to allow for the returns implied if tax is at 50p. Where tax is payable, replacement of capital (purchase price) must be made out of taxed income.

In order to preserve the gross rate of **10%** for investment comparison the valuation can be reworked, recognising that the return on capital is at **10%** and the return of capital is at a net rate out of taxed income. i is therefore **0.10** and the ASF in the formula is at **5%** adjusted for tax.

$$1,000 \times \frac{1}{0.10 + \left(0.1809 \times \dfrac{1}{1-t}\right)} = £2,165$$

or set out as a valuation:

	£1,000
YP for five years @ 10% and 5% adj. tax @ 50%*	2.165
	£2,165

* Formula =	$\dfrac{1}{i + ASF}$	therefore becomes	$\dfrac{1}{0.10 + \left(0.1809\left(\frac{1}{1-t}\right)\right)}$
=	$\dfrac{1}{0.10 + 0.3618}$	= 2.165	

The gross valuation has been adjusted to equate with the net valuation. Where there is a tax liability, the net valuation is deemed to be more correct because capital cost must be recovered out of taxed income.

Capital outstanding		10% gross	Capital recovered (£1,000 - 10% - 50p in £) tax
1	2,165.00	216.500	391.75
2	1,773.25	177.325	411.3375
3	1,361.91	136.190	431.90
4	930.01	93.000	453.50
5	476.50	47.650	476.175*
			£2,165

* Error due to rounding.

B Dual Rate

The realisation that capital cost may have to be recovered out of taxed income has, for many years, been recognised in the valuation of leasehold property and has resulted in the production of dual rate tax-adjusted tables. Assuming that £1,000 is the profit rent produced by a leasehold interest, and adopting the same gross yield of **10%**, a sinking fund at **3%** and tax at **50%**, the following gross and net valuations may be made.

	Gross
	£1,000
YP for 5 years @ 10% and 3% adj. tax @ 50%	2.098
	£2,098

	Net
	£500
YP for 5 years @ 5% and 3%	4.196
	£2,098

The net valuation is of an income of £1,000 less tax at 50%, namely £500. With a gross rate of return of 10%, the net rate must be 5% and, as the sinking fund rate is also assumed to be net, allowance has already been made for tax on the sinking fund accumulations. As the whole income has been netted no further tax adjustment is needed (*see Chapter 2*).

The gross valuation becomes in effect a net valuation, because it assumes both a net accumulative rate and a grossing-up factor to allow for the incidence of tax on that part of the income representing capital recovery.

Thus in two cases - incomes receivable in perpetuity, and leasehold interests - the normal valuation approach has been shown to be equivalent to the true net approach, apparently obviating any dilemma. However, problems arise when considering deferred incomes, or cases where property is let below full rental value.

Deferred incomes

A deferred income is one due to commence at a given date in the future.

Example 8.2

Calculate the present worth of an income of £2,000 per annum in perpetuity due to commence in 5 years' time. A 10% gross return is required, and tax is payable at 50%.

	Gross		Net
	£2,000		£1,000
YP perp. @ 10%	10	YP perp. @ 5%	20
	£20,000		£20,000
PV £1 in 5 years		PV £1 in 5 years	
@ 10%	0.6209	@ 5%	0.7835
	£12,418		£15,670

Again, it can be seen that capitalisation in perpetuity gross and net each produce the same value of £20,000 in 5 years' time, but, by further discounting to allow for the 5 years deferment, the gross and net valuations produce different results clearly arising from the deferment factors of **0.6209** and **0.7835**.

Obviously a purchaser would wish to pay only £12,418, *but what of the vendor?*

Assuming initially that capital gains are not taxable, one can see that an investment purchased for £12,418 held

for 5 years and sold for £20,000 is a 10% investment.

£12,418 x amount £1 for 5 years at 10% = £20,000

But if an investor were to deposit £12,418 in an income-producing investment, the 10% return of £1,241.80 in year one would be taxed. From a taxpayer's point of view, a **10%** return, all in capital growth with no tax would be better than 10% all in income subject to taxation.

If there was no **Capital Gains Tax (CGT)** capital growth investments would be very attractive to high rate taxpayers, to such an extent that prices could be pushed up to the point of indifference, i.e. until the capital growth investment is equated with an income investment. In this example, if tax is at **50p** in the £, a taxpayer would get the same return after tax from depositing £15,670 at **10%** gross as from purchasing £2,000 p.a. in perpetuity deferred 5 years for £15,670.

The introduction of **CGT** in 1965 reduced the tax-free element of capital growth but did not lessen the belief held by some valuers that the net approach was still correct. It is recognised that the incidence of all taxes should be reflected in an investor's true return. Therefore, if tax is material to investors' decisions in the marketplace it should be allowed for in a valuation.

To explain a need for net valuation, a single question needs to be posed.

'If investors are assured of a 10% gross return and pay tax at 50%, are they expecting a 5% net-of-tax return?'

To this one could add a supplementary question.

'Are investors interested in their return net of tax?'

It cannot but be assumed that as the Inland Revenue have a prior claim then investors must have some regard to the net-of-tax income.

Rising freehold incomes

Combining the £1,000 income for 5 years with the £2,000 income commencing in 5 years and continuing in perpetuity, the result will be a normal term and reversion valuation.

Using the figures from the preceding examples, the

gross and net valuations produce these results:

	Gross	Net
Value of £1,000 for 5 years	£3,790	£2,164
Value today of reversion to £20,000	£12,418	£15,670
	£16,208	£17,834

(In such cases, the net valuation will always be higher than its gross equivalent)

The gross valuation of £16,208 may be analysed in two parts: an expenditure of £3,790 to acquire £1,000 for 5 years coupled with an expenditure of £12,418 for £20,000 in 5 years' time. In the absence of income tax, the investor readily achieves his 10% return: but what of his 5% net return?

After tax on income, the investment will have the following cash flow:

Year	Cash flow
1	£500
2	£500
3	£500
4	£500
5	£20,500

This is the cash flow assumed for the **5%** net valuation, and the investor would achieve a **5%** return at an acquisition cost of £17,834. Therefore at £16,208 the investment must be showing a better return than **5%**. If investors only expect a net return of **5%**, valuing gross may result in vendors' interests being undersold.

Gross funds

The term '*gross funds*' is used today to describe any investor exempt from income, corporation and/or capital gains tax. These are principally charities, local authorities, approved superannuation funds, friendly societies and registered trade unions. Other institutions, such as insurance companies, enjoy partial relief by being assessed at a lower rate. Many first-class property investments are now held by gross funds, which are an increasingly large part of the property market - so much so that co-ownership schemes in agricultural investment and in commercial investment have been carefully created to allow small and large funds to buy, as co-owners, substantial single investments in property while still preserving their tax-exempt status.

If the most probable purchaser in the market is a gross

fund then the sub-market is one of gross funds. Because they pay neither income nor capital gains tax, the return to them will be both their gross and net return. Valuations within this sub-market must be based on analysis of comparable transactions, which suggests that no adjustments should be made for tax.

Net or gross?

Because a difference in the valuation may result when valuing net or gross of tax, the problem therefore remains.

Should the valuation be net or gross?

There is no categorical answer: a number of points may, however, be made.

1. In certain cases a net valuation will not produce an accurate estimate of market value, as every potential purchaser may have a different tax liability.

2. A net valuation should be carried out when advising a purchaser of his maximum bid for an investment when his required net-of-tax return is known.

3. In certain sub-markets the market is dominated by non-taxpayers. In these cases a gross valuation will produce the same valuation as a net valuation allowing for tax at 0%.

Capital gains tax (CGT)

The introduction of **CGT** in 1965 had an immediate impact on the property market. Initially it reduced the obvious benefit of investing in properties with high capital growth expectations such as freeholds with early substantial reversions. The market soon adapted to the changes but although there were pleas from a few to move to a net-of-tax approach to valuation the market responded with a simple adjustment to the ARY to account for this new risk element.

Reversionary properties still remained more attractive to individuals because of the differences between the **CGT** tax rate and the very high personal tax rates.

The introduction of indexation provisions in the **Finance Act 1984** and the revision of those provisions in the **Finance Act 1988**, whereby only gains in excess of the indexed *(retail price index)* gains were to be taxed, increased the attractions of capital growth investments. The reduction in tax rates to two bands and the provision to tax gains at the same rate as that for taxing a taxpayer's income have eroded the advantages of growth investments over income investments.

The remaining tax advantages are:

1. CGT is charged on net gains, i.e. after deduction of purchase and sale costs and allowable expenses.

2. CGT is charged on the gain after adjustment for indexation.

3. CGT is charged on the gain after deducting the taxpayer's tax free allowance.

4. The tax demand may be up to 2 years after the gain is realised.

5. CGT may, in some cases, be deferred through roll over relief.

For all these reasons individuals with a **40%** tax liability may still favour the highly reversionary properties in preference to rack rented properties. But it is probably the ability of the right property to outpace inflation that attracts the private investor.

For the major investors the changes in indexation provisions have made it easier to take decisions to sell than previously. But because property is normally purchased as a long-term investment any gain is likely to be deferred many years and will not therefore have a significant bearing on purchase price. In addition, *'rollover-relief'* may be possible, effectively postponing any **CGT** and, in any event, for certain classes of investor their exemption from **CGT** makes them a market in their own right.

There may, however, be obvious cases where property is to be purchased with the intention of realising a capital gain at a specific date in the future. Where the purchasers in the market are likely to have the same intent or where investment advice is to be given to a specific client it might be necessary to reflect CGT in the valuation.

Summary
8

- Income capitalisation of property is usually undertaken on a before tax basis.

- Tax on income has no effect where all income is return on capital.

- Tax may need to be reflected where investments are terminable in the short term and tax is a factor in the market place.

- Tax is potentially significant when valuing leasehold investments.

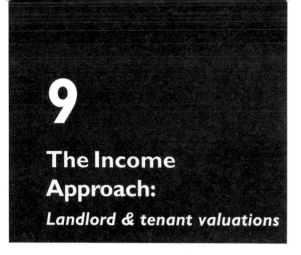

9

The Income Approach:

Landlord & tenant valuations

The income approach to property valuation centres particularly on the relationship between landlord and tenant. This chapter examines several of the valuation problems raised by this relationship.

Premiums

A premium is a lump sum paid by a tenant to a landlord in consideration for a lease granted at a low rent, or for some other benefit. *'At a low rent'* signifies a rent below full rental value, and the other benefits will be as a rule, financial, having the same effect as a reduction in rent.

Examples of this are the tenant paying for repairs that would normally be the landlord's responsibility, and the tenant financing the extension of the property without being charged an increase in rent.

A premium is often paid on the grant or renewal of a lease, but there may be more than one premium, payable at any time during the lease term. It entails a cash gain coupled with a loss of rent for the landlord because the usual result of charging a premium will be a letting at less than full rental value. The landlord is therefore selling part of his income.

The tenant will be paying a lump sum in return for a lease at a rent below full rental value, effectively buying a profit rent.

Why pay a premium?

The payment of a premium has many advantages to a landlord, and few to the tenant. It could be concluded that premiums will usually be paid where there is a seller's market, i.e. where there is competition among prospective tenants to secure an agreement with the prospective landlord.

The advantages to a landlord are several.

1. Although the amount of the premium will reflect the discounting of future income, an immediate lump sum receivable instead of a future flow of income is often more attractive due to the 'time value of money'. The landlord may prefer a lump sum in order to meet an immediate expense or to make any kind of cash investment.

2. Receipt of a lump sum immediately may reduce the diminishing effect that inflation has on the value of future income in real terms, especially if rent review periods are longer than is favourable to the landlord.

3. A premium may have tax advantages, but these are substantially reduced now that income and capital gains are taxed at the same rate.

4. A premium should increase the landlord's security of income. Once the tenant has paid a premium, he has invested money in his occupation of the premises in expectation of making an actual or notional profit rent. As a result he is more likely to remain in occupation of the premises and should be a more reliable tenant. Some of the risk attached to the investment from the landlord's point of view may be reduced.

The advantages to a tenant are less well-defined.

1. A premium may be useful as a loss or deduction to be made from profits when being assessed for income tax or capital gains tax.

2. Paying a premium may be advantageous to a tenant when his/her financial circumstances are such that he/she prefers to part with capital in order to reduce future recurring expenses.

However, the landlord will usually enjoy the greater benefits. When a property attracts many prospective tenants a landlord may demand and receive a premium in addition to rent. Valuers must be careful to note that this represents the capital value of the extra rent, above market rent, that such excess competition can sometimes generate. The following section deals with the assessment of premiums for rents forgone.

Valuation technique

A premium entails a loss to the landlord of part of the income and a gain to the tenant of a profit rent. The amount of the premium should be calculated so that each party is in virtually the same position as if full rental value were to be paid and received.

The gain/loss of rent, capitalised over the period for which it is applicable, should be calculated to be equal to the amount of the premium. It is conventional practice to use full freehold rates to capitalise the landlord's loss of rent and full leasehold rates to capitalise the tenant's gain of profit rent, presumably on the basis that each party by definition is to be in the same position as if full rental value were being paid and received.

The following three examples assume :

- **a freehold rate of 10%,**
- **leasehold rates of 11% and 3% with tax @ 40p,**
- **a full rental value of £2,500,**
- **premiums payable at the start of the lease and no rent reviews.**

Example 9.1

What premiums should **A** charge on the grant of a 21-year lease to **B** at a rent of **£1,500 ?**

Full rental value	£2,500		
Rent agreed	£1,500		

Therefore :

A's loss of rent	=	£1,000		
YP for 21 years @ 10%		8.6487	=	£8,649

Example 9.2

A grants the above lease. What premium should B offer?

Full rental value	£2,500
Rent agreed	£1,500

Therefore :

B's gain of profit rent =	£1,000		
YP for 21 years @ 11% and 3% adj. tax @ 40%	5.9481 =	£5,948

The problem of valuing freehold interests single rate and leasehold interests dual rate is here presented. In practice one would expect negotiation between parties to reach a compromise sum, which may be found by the following methods:

1　**Average final offers:**

$$\frac{£8,649 + £5,948 = £7,298.5}{2} \quad say \; £7,300$$

2　**Average YPs:**

$$\frac{8.6487 + 5.9481 = 7.298}{2}$$

x difference in full and agreed rents of £1,000

$$= £7,298$$

In most cases the tenant is due to take occupation and the notional nature of the profit rent is not taxable, and so some valuers will adopt a gross approach to the leasehold calculation bringing the figures much closer together
**(i.e. £1,000 x YP 21 years @ 11% and 3%
= £1,000 x 6.9027 = £6,903).**

Example 9.3

A grants **B** a lease for **28 years.**
A premium of **£18,000** is to be paid.
What rent should be fixed?

Again, a compromise must be reached.
Taking the average of two YP figures can save an unnecessary stage in the calculations, so this approach will be adopted.

	A	**B**
Full rental value	£2,500	£2,500
Agreed rent	x	x
YP 28 years	9.3066 (10%)	6.7194 (11% and 3% adj. tax @ 40%)

Average YP	9.3066	+	6.7194
		2	

$$= 8.013$$

Then	8.013 (£2,500 − x) =	£18,000
	£20,032.5 − 8.013x =	£18,000
	8.013x =	£2,032.5
	x =	£253.65 p.a.

The gain or loss of rent is ($£2,500 - x$). When capitalised by using an average **YP**, this is the average capitalised gain or loss of rent and is thus the value of the premium. The unknown, x, can then be calculated.

As has already been suggested, a tenant's repair, improvement or extension may be treated as a premium.

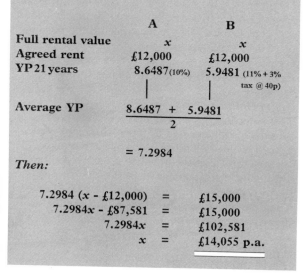

Example 9.4

A grants to **B** a 21-year lease at a rent of £12,000 p.a. which is below full rental value. **B** has to repair the property at the commencement of the lease as part of the contract at a cost of £15,000.

Estimate the full rental value.

	A	B
Full rental value	x	x
Agreed rent	£12,000	£12,000
YP 21 years	8.6487 (10%)	5.9481 (11% + 3% tax @ 40p)

$$\text{Average YP} \quad \frac{8.6487 \ + \ 5.9481}{2}$$

$$= 7.2984$$

Then:

$$7.2984 \ (x - £12,000) = £15,000$$
$$7.2984x - £87,581 = £15,000$$
$$7.2984x = £102,581$$
$$x = £14,055 \text{ p.a.}$$

(The cost of repairs is in the nature of a premium for which B expects a reduced rent. ($x - £12,000$) is the gain/loss of rent, and multiplying this by the average **YP** gives the average capitalised gain or loss of rent.)

This figure of £14,055 must be the full rental value of the premises on these assumptions. This was never a negotiated figure, as it was a known market fact borne in mind by both parties during the negotiations. But the use of the average YP is necessary as the rent of £12,000 would have been arrived at by negotiation.

Whilst this is a useful theoretical analysis the reader is reminded that it is a very poor way of establishing rental value and is generally unacceptable to the courts or an arbitrator.

The conventional investment method can give rise to answers that are hard to accept. In **examples 9.1** and **9.2 A** required £8,649 to compensate for the loss of rent. **B** could only afford to offer £5,948, as this was all the gain of profit rent was worth. An agreement at £7,300 would thus make both parties unhappy. But it must be remembered that dual rate valuations using a remunerative rate **1%** higher than for freehold valuations inevitably cause lower valuations of the interest, and that dual rate valuations are net in a gross form.

Another approach is the **'before and after valuation'**. From the freeholder's point of view, whenever a lease at a low rent is granted the market value of the property may be depreciated by a sum greater than the initial premium calculation suggests. In **example 9.1** £8,649 is the premium but the payment of £8,649 alters the nature of the investment from a growth income of £2,500 to a fixed income of £1,500 for 21 years with a reversion to **FRV** in **21** years' time.

Thus the respective capitalisation rates may differ. If this is the case, a **'before and after valuation'** is needed.

Before		
FRV		£2,500
YP perp. @ 10%		10
		£25,000
After		
Rent reserved	£1,500	
YP 21 years @ 12%* 7.562		
		£11,343
Reversion to	£2,500	
YP rev. perp. after		
21 years @ 10%	1.35	
		£3,375
Estimated capital value		£14,718

£25,000 - £14,718 = **Premium of £10,282**

* Cost of capital or money rate as income is fixed for 21 years.

A further problem to be overcome is that the freeholder has indeed lost precisely £1,000 per annum but the tenant has gained a rising profit rent starting at £1,000 per annum. Traditional valuation methods do not fully reflect this factor. It seems reasonable to question the use of dual rate valuations in such problems and in the valuation of leasehold interests in general **(see Chapter 7)**. A truer picture of real gain and real loss requires an explicit DCF approach.

Emerging in the 1990s has been the concept of reverse premiums. Typically an owner of property reluctant to appear to be letting the whole or part of a property below historic rental levels has offered a premium to a tenant on taking a lease. Similarly tenants occupying overrented property have had to offer premiums when sub-letting the whole or part. The valuation key is to recognise that a reverse premium is a payment from landlord to tenant whilst premiums are normally payments from tenants to landlords. The principles behind their calculation are similar and a before and after valuation is recommended to reflect the market attitude to properties when the rent is being held artificially above normal market rents.

> **Q** Calculate the premium to be paid when shop property (5% ARY) is to be let at £50,000 on 5-year normal lease term when the open market rental value on similar terms is £75,000.

Future costs and receipts

P. 189

A study of conventional techniques of deferring future costs raises a number of further questions which are examined shortly.

The deferment of future receipts is relatively straightforward. Often an investment will provide a capital sum at some given time in the future. An example of this is a premium payable during the currency of a lease. This is part of the investment and could therefore be discounted at the remunerative rate.

Example 9.5

A lets 10 High Street to **B** for 21 years at £13,925 p.a. In addition, a premium of £15,000 is payable at the end of the lease. **FRV is £15,000 p.a.** Value **A**'s interest.

Assuming a freehold rate 10%

Rent	£13,925	
YP for 21 years @ 9%	9.2922	
		£129,393
Rent	£15,000	
YP rev. perp. after 21 years @ 10%	1.35131	
		£20,269
Premium	£15,000	
PV £1 in 21 years @ 10%	0.13513	
		£2,027
Estimated capital value		£151,689

This approach implies that future fixed receipts should be discounted at the remunerative rate and added to the freehold value. In which case the premium of £15,000 varies in value according to the quality of the investment. This conventional approach cannot be accepted.

The present worth of any known future sum must be found by reference to money market rates.

Future capital costs will often arise out of investment in property. Conventional valuation practice distinguishes two types of future capital cost.

1 Liabilities.

These may have to be incurred for some reason and are a cost to the investor, often being legally enforceable. They must be allowed for in a valuation. Examples are premiums to be paid in the future; a sum to be spent on dilapidations at the end of the lease; or work that must be carried out under fire regulations, etc.

The investor must make certain that the cash required for the liability is available at the relevant time. Any accumulation must therefore be risk-free, and it follows that conventional practice recommends the discounting of liabilities at the accumulative rate. The use of the accumulative rate is not acceptable *per se* but the rationale of using a safe net of tax rate is sound.

2 Expenditure.

This is optional and will only be undertaken if it provides a sufficient return. This *'sufficient return'* is taken for convenience to be the rate of return that the investment as a whole provides. Thus expenditure is discounted at the remunerative rate.

The distinction may be of vital importance to investment decisions.

Example 9.6

B offers £1,000 to **A** for the leasehold interest. **A** receives a profit rent of £380 **p.a.** with 14 years remaining and no rent reviews on head- or sub-lease. **A** has agreed to carry out repairs at a cost of £1,000 in 4 years' time. Should **B**'s offer be accepted?

Assuming a leasehold rate of 11% and 3% adj. tax @ 40%:

Profit rent	£380 p.a.	
YP for 14 years @ 11% and 3% adj. tax @ tax @ 40%	4.8183	
		£1,830
Less: Cost of repairs		
(1) *Liability ?*	£1,000	
PV £1 in 4 years @ 3%	0.8884	
		£888.4
Estimated capital value (1)		£942
or :		
(2) *Expenditure ?*	£1,000	
PV £1 in 4 years @ 11%	0.65873	
		£658.7
Estimated capital value (2)		£1,172

The distinction is obviously vital. If the cost is treated as a liability then the offer is accepted but not if treated as an expenditure. In many cases the decision is an arbitrary one, the effect of which can be sizeably reduced by the use of realistic '**safe**' money rates.

A further problem now emerges and that is the estimation of future expenditures and liabilities when they are not known or fixed in monetary terms at the date of valuation. For example, an expected major renewal in 4 years' time can only initially be estimated on the basis of cost today. But the deduction to be made from open market value in good condition must be an amount the market considers fairly reflects the current condition. Where the future sum is fixed in monetary terms then a present value calculation at a realistic monetary safe rate is satisfactory. Where it is a current estimate then the valuer must consider whether the costs will increase at a faster rate than that which can be safely earned on savings.

If the expenditure is likely to rise at **10%** per annum and money can be saved to earn interest at **10%** per annum, then the wisest solution is to deduct the full cost from today's value. If money can earn interest at a higher rate than the estimated inflationary increase in costs then a discounted sum can be deducted. If costs are rising faster than money rates then it would be logical to deduct the full cost now and indeed to have the repairs or renewals undertaken now. However, unless the work is essential as at the date of valuation, it may be as realistic to simply write down the value in sound condition by an appropriate factor.

Extensions and renewals of leases

The occupier or tenant of business premises will often be anxious to remain in occupation because a business move might involve considerable expense, loss of trade and loss of goodwill, resulting in a large loss of profit. In these circumstances tenants will be keen to negotiate an extension of the lease, a renewal of the existing lease on similar terms, or the grant of a completely new lease on different terms. Similarly landlords anxious not to lose a tenant may commence negotiations for a new lease 2 to 3 years prior to the end of a lease and ahead of the statutory or contractual date for service of notice to terminate the lease.

The problem of a tenant who approaches the landlord as the lease draws to an end provides very little difficulty. The landlord will require a rent approaching, or at, full rental value, and the tenant will expect to pay it, because that is what it would cost to lease a comparable property. But finding alternative accommodation is not an easy operation, and business decisions are prudently taken well in advance. It is thus more usual for a tenant to approach the landlord well before the termination of the existing lease and when they do, a valuation problem will arise. If the tenant approaches the landlord during the currency of the lease with a proposal to renew that lease immediately for an extended period, it will follow that the tenant is offering to surrender the current lease. (Such problems are often called '***surrender and renewals***'.)

If, as is probably the case, a profit rent or a notional profit rent has arisen, then any surrender will be a surrender of valuable leasehold rights in the property. The tenant would be ill-advised to accept a new lease at full rental value.

The landlord, on the other hand, is not likely to agree to any indiscriminate extension of the tenant's profit rent because the anticipated reversion to full rental value will already be reflected in the open market value of the freehold. Negotiations must be conducted to see that following the surrender and lease renewal there is no diminution in the value of the landlord's or of the tenant's interests in the property.

Valuers acting for both parties will be checking the position from both sides on the basis that the present interest should equal the proposed interests. This will involve four or more valuations.

Example 9.7

A tenant occupies premises on a 21-year lease with **2** years to run at **£15,000** a year. The tenant wishes to surrender this lease for a new lease for **15** years with rent reviews every **5** years.
The **OMRV** on **FRI** terms for **15** years with 5-year reviews is **£30,000**.
Freehold ARY is **7%**.

Present interest **TENANT**		Present interest **FREEHOLDER**	
OMRV	£30,000		£15,000
Rent payable	£15,000	YP 2 years	
		@ 7%	1.8080
			£27,120
Profit rent	£15,000		£30,000
YP 2 years @ 8%		YP perp. @ 7%	
and 3% tax		x PV £1 in 2	
@ 40%	1.1099	years @ 7%	12.4777
	£16,648		£374,331
			£401,451

Example 9.7 (cont.)

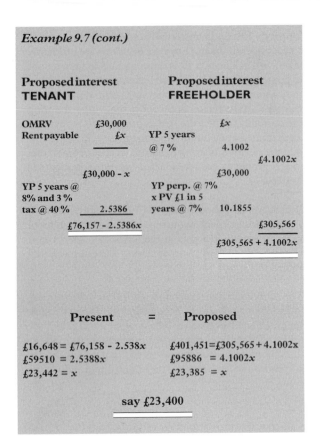

Proposed interest TENANT		Proposed interest FREEHOLDER	
OMRV	£30,000		£x
Rent payable	£x	YP 5 years @ 7%	4.1002
			£4.1002x
	£30,000 – x	£30,000	
YP 5 years @ 8% and 3% tax @ 40%	2.5386	YP perp. @ 7% x PV £1 in 5 years @ 7%	10.1855
	£76,157 – 2.5386x		£305,565
			£305,565 + 4.1002x

Present	=	Proposed
£16,648 = £76,158 – 2.538x		£401,451=£305,565 + 4.1002x
£59510 = 2.5388x		£95886 = 4.1002x
£23,442 = x		£23,385 = x

say £23,400

The landlord requires a minimum premium of £23,385, while the tenant can afford to offer £23,442. Negotiation between the parties will take place. A split at around £23,400 may be the result, or the parties may settle at a figure nearer the landlord's or tenant's figure depending upon their negotiating strength and the state of the market.

It must be pointed out that the above type of solution may result in a tenant's bid being lower than the landlord's minimum requirement. If the gap is sufficiently large, the proposals may be shelved. Considerable forces of inertia will, however, normally conspire to produce an agreement if the shortfall is of a minor nature: for examples, the landlord, if satisfied with the tenant, may wish to save the advertising and legal fees involved in finding a new tenant. And the old tenant will have many reasons, already discussed, for being prepared to make a small loss in order to carry on in occupation of the premises.

Example 9.8

T occupies 6 High Street, holding a lease from L at a rent of £2,000 p.a. FRI with 8 years remaining. T requires a new 40-year lease, starting immediately, and proposes to carry out improvements to the premises in 3 years' time at an estimated cost of £12,000 which will increase full rental value by £2,500 p.a.

As a condition of the present lease, L requires that T pays a premium of £1,000 in 5 years' time. It is proposed that under the new lease T should pay a premium of £3,000 immediately and £5,000 after 20 years.

7 High Street is an identical property and has recently been sold on a **10%** basis. It has just been let on a 21-year lease at a rent of £6,000 p.a. FRI with a premium of £15,000 payable at the start of the lease by the lessee.

It is agreed that the rent for *6 High Street* should increase by **50%** halfway through the proposed term.

Acting between the parties, assess what rent should be fixed under the proposals.

This problem is rather involved and includes examples of everything discussed in this chapter. It must be read and analysed extremely carefully before being attempted, and its implications must be fully realised. For example, if improvements costing £12,000 will increase FRV by £2,500 per annum, this is a fact that cannot be ignored when assessing the value of the landlord's present interest, because it might be possible for him to obtain possession in 8 years' time and carry out the said improvement.

It will be necessary to calculate the full rental value of *6 High Street* from the information given concerning *No 7*.

FRV of 7 High Street =	£6,000
	+ annual equivalent of £15,000 premium.

(£6,000 is a reduced rent to compensate for the premium. The full rental value will thus be £6,000 plus the value of the premium spread over the 21-year term.)

From the landlord's point of view =

$$£6,000 + \frac{£15,000}{\text{YP for 21 years @ 10\%}^\star}$$

From the tenant's point of view =

$$£6,000 + \frac{£15,000}{\text{YP for 21 years @ 11\%} \text{ and 3\% adj. tax @ 40\%}}$$

★Property (freehold) sold on a 10% basis.

Example 9.8 (cont.)

YP for 21 years @ 10%	= 8.6487
YP for 21 years @ 11% and 3% tax @ 40%	= 5.9481

$$\text{Average YP} = \frac{8.6487 + 5.9481}{2} = 7.2984$$

$$\frac{£15,000}{7.2984} = £2,055 \text{ p.a.}$$

Therefore

FRV = £8,055 FRI

A Landlord's present interest

Rent	£2,000 p.a.
YP for 8 years @ 9%	5.5348
	£11,070

Reversion (1):
If landlord does not carry out the possible improvements.

Rent	£8,055 p.a.
YP rev. perp. after 8 years @ 10%★	4.665
	£37,577

Reversion (2):
Assuming landlord does carry out the improvements, and assuming the delay is short enough to involve no appreciable loss of rent.

Rent	£10,555 p.a.
YP rev. perp. after 8 years @ 10%★	4.665
	£49,239

★Both rents are full rental values, although they differ in magnitude, the security of income is assumed unchanged.

The figure of **£49,239** can only be achieved by an expenditure of **£12,000** in 8 years' time and therefore value today must be reduced accordingly.

Cost of improvements	£12,000
PV £1 in 8 years @ 10%★	0.4665
	£5,600

★This is 'expenditure' and discounted (possibly erroneously) at the remunerative rate.

This leaves a net present value for the reversion of £43,639 (£49,239 - £5,600).

Reversion (2) is more valuable so the landlord would improve, and the value of the freehold interest is this increased sum.

Estimated capital value	
£11,070 + £43,639 =	£54,709

In addition, a premium is payable after 5 years:

Premium	£1,000	
PV £1 in 5 years @ 10%	0.621	
		£621
Estimated capital value		£55,330

B Landlord's proposed interest

Rent		x
YP for 20 years @ 9%		9.1285
		$9.1285x$

Reversion to rent		$1.5x$★

★Rent increased by 50%.

YP for 20 years @ 9.5 %	8.8124	
PV £1 in 20 years @ 9.5%	0.1628	
	1.4348	
		$2.1523x$

Reversion to FRV	£10,555★	
YP rev. perp. after 40 years @ 10%	0.221	
		£2,333

Plus premiums:	1 Immediately		£3,000
	2 In 20 years	£5,000	
	PV £1 in 20 years @ 10%	0.14864	
			£743
			$11.2808x + £6,076$

★Rent as increased by tenant's proposed improvements.

Present interest	= proposed interest
£55,330	= £6,076 + 11.2808x
£49,354	= 11.2808x
£49,354 ÷ 11.2808	= x
£4,375 p.a.	= x

C Tenant's present interest

Rent received	£8,055	FRI
Rent paid	£2,000	FRI
Profit rent	£6,055	

YP for 8 years @ 11% and		
3% adj. tax @ 40%	3.3622	

CV		£20,358
Less premium	£1,000	
PV £1 in 5 years @ 7%*	0.713	
		£713

* Liability: so use a realistic, low, safe, net accumulative rate. This rationale obviously raises a question mark about a dual rate YP using an accumulative rate of 3%; but to amend that would involve the reappraisal suggested in Chapter 7.

Net CV		£19,645

D Tenant's proposed interest

Rent received	£8,055
Rent paid	x
Profit rent	£8,055 - x

YP for 3* years @ 11% and	
3% adj. tax @ 40%	1.5403

CV	£12,407 - 1.5403x

* After 3 years T improves the premises and increases FRV.

Reversion to:

Rent received	£10,555
Rent paid	x
Profit rent	£10,555 - x

YP for 17 years @ 11% + 3%	
adj. tax @ 40%	5.3594
PV £1 in 3 years @ 11%	x 0.7312
	3.9188

CV	£41,363 - 3.9188x

Reversion to:

Rent received	£10,555
Rent paid	1.5x
Profit rent	£10,555 - 1.5x

YP for 20 years @ 11% + 3%	
adj. tax @ 40%	5.8131
PV £1 in 20 years @ 11%	x 0.124
	0.7208
CV	£7,608 - 1.0812x

Adding the constituent elements of the valuation together :

$$£12,407 - 1.5403x$$
$$£41,363 - 3.9188x$$
$$£7,608 - 1.0812x$$

Total	£61,378 - 6.5403x

Less

1 Improvements

	£12,000	
PV £1 in 3 years @ 11%*	0.7312	
		£8,774

*Expenditure.

2 Premium now

	£3,000

3 Premium in 20 years

	£5,000	
PV £1 in 20 years @ 7%*	0.2584	
		£1,292

*Liability .

	£13,066

New total CV:

	£48,312 - 6.5403x

Present interest = proposed interest
£19,645	= £48,312 - 6.5403x
6.5403x	= £28,667
x	= £4,383 p.a.

Minimum L will accept:	£4,375 p.a.
Minimum T can offer:	£4,383 p.a.
Agreement between	
parties of (say):	£4,380 p.a.

Example 9.8 is as originally set out in the first edition and is included here in the same form to illustrate how the traditional or conventional valuer would approach this complex problem. It is obvious that the advice to landlord and tenant based on such calculations could be wrong. Provided the basis is supported by market evidence the valuers could argue that the figures are reasonable reflections of the current market. The reader's eyebrows should have risen over the last few pages and the red pen used frequently for marginal comment. The tutor need search no further for new problems; they are all here if the issues are reconsidered

on an equated yield, modified cash flow approach, or on a full DCF basis.

The valuer must have regard to and take account of all the peculiarities of conventional valuation, the problems of future liabilities entered at current costs, the problems of long reversionary leases without rent reviews and the way in which a surrender and renewal can alter the market's perception of both the freehold and leasehold interests.

Q An office building was let 30 years ago for 40 years without a rent review clause in the lease, at £10,000 a year.

It is now estimated that the building would let in the market at £100,000 a year.

Similar office buildings in the vicinity that are let at market rentals have been sold recently on an 8% basis.

Calculate: *p 184*

(a) the rent to be paid on the surrender of this lease for a new 25-year lease with 5-year rent reviews.

(b) the price the landlord should pay the tenant to secure a new 25-year lease to the tenant at **OMRV**.

Marriage value

Where a property is split into multiple interests, either physically or legally, or both, each of the newly created interests will have a market value. The total of these values will not necessarily equate with the market value of the freehold in possession of the whole property. In such cases, an element of what is known as *'marriage value'* might be shown to exist.

The following example will serve to demonstrate this.

Example 9.9

A is the freeholder of an office block, the full rental value of which is **£28,000 p.a.** on FRI terms.

Fourteen years ago **A** let the whole to **B** on a 40-year lease at a rent of **£10,000 p.a.** on FRI terms without a rent review.

B sub-let to **C** 6 years ago, at a rent of **£18,000 p.a.** FRI for a term of 25 years without rent review.

Value all interests.

B wishes to become the freeholder in possession of the office block.

Advise him on the sum to be offered for the interests of A and C.

How much should they accept?

Valuation of current interests:
(Freehold rate 10%)

*1 A's interest:**

Rent	£10,000	
YP for 26 years @ 9%	9.929	
		£99,290
Reversion to FRV:	£28,000	
YP rev. perp. after		
26 years @ 10%	0.839	
		£23,492
	Total	£122,782

*Traditional term and reversion.

2 B's interest:

Rent received:	£18,000
Rent paid:	£10,000
Profit rent:	£8,000

YP for 19 years @ 10% and 3%
adj. tax @ 40%   6.0112
                          £48,090

Reversion to rent received

	£28,000
- Rent paid	£10,000
Profit rent	£18,000

YP for 7 years @ 11% and 3%
adj. tax @ 40%   3.0533
PV £1 in 19 years @ 11%   0.1377
                          £7,567

Total	£55,657

3 C's interest

Rent received	£28,000
- Rent paid	£18,000
Profit rent	£10,000

YP for 19 years @ 11% and 3%
adj. tax @ 40%   5.6703

Estimated value	£56,703

The total value of all interests at present is:
£122,782 + £55,657 + £56,703, i.e. £235,142.

B wishes to become freeholder in possession. How much will this be worth now that the full rental value can be received immediately and in perpetuity.

FRV	£28,000
YP perp. @ 10%	10
	£280,000

Notice that the total value of all interests at present is only £235,142: there will be what is called a marriage value created by the merger of interests of £44,858.

How is this marriage created, and where does it arise?

Capital value is the product of two things: income and a capitalisation factor. It follows that the marriage value must arise from one or both of these.

1. Income: Does this change upon merger of the interests? In the case of the freehold in possession, the total income passing is £28,000. When A, B and C have interests in the property A receives £10,000, B makes a profit rent of £8,000 and C makes a profit rent of £10,000. The total of rents and profit rents passing is therefore £28,000.

This holds for any year. The total of rents and profit rents will always be full rental value, because what the freeholder loses by way of rent, someone else gains as profit rent.

2 Capitalisation factor: Does this change? The freehold in possession is valued by applying a single rate YP to the whole £28,000. But when the interests are split, the profit rents earned by B and C are valued by dual rate YPs, adjusted for tax.

This leads to a lower capital value:

YP for 10 years @ 10%	= 6.1446
YP for 10 years @ 10% and 3% adj. tax @ 40%	= 4.0752

The effect of splitting the freehold in possession into three interests has been to reduce the total value of the block owing to the effect of valuing the leasehold interests dual rate. When leasehold and freehold interests are merged to create a freehold in possession, the total value is increased because the whole income is valued single rate.

This increase in value created by the merger is known as marriage value.

Marriage value	£44,856
C	£56,703
B	£55,658
A	£122,783
Unencumbered freehold:	£280,000

The merger of interests will create additional value and so B can offer £224,342 for the interests of A and C. B's present interest is worth £55,658: the freehold in possession will be worth £280,000 and the gain £224,342 (£280,000 - £55,658).

But how much should B offer to A and to C?

What price should A and C ask for their interests?

B's first move will be to buy either **A**'s or **C**'s interest. The maximum **B** will be able to offer to **A** is the gain to be made from the transaction. If **A**'s interest is purchased the freeholder will only be subject to **C**'s underlease.

Value of B + A

Rent	£18,000	
YP for 19 years @ 9%	8.9501	
	£161,101	
Reversion to	£28,000	
YP rev. perp. after		
19 years @ 10%	1.635	
	£45,780	
Total		£206,881

B's present interest is worth £55,658: the gain will be £206,881 - £55,658 = £151,223 and this is the maximum that can be offered to **A**. The minimum that **A** will accept will be the market value of £122,783. Assuming that **A** and **B** will employ valuers who will be aware of both figures agreement will be reached between these two boundaries.

The difference between these figures is:

£151,223 - £122,783 = £28,440
and is the marriage value between A and B.

It can also be found in the following way.

A, before the transaction, had an interest worth £122,783; **B** had an interest worth £55,658. This totals £178,441. The value of the combined interest is £206,881; and the difference between these two figures is £28,440, the marriage value.

B's next step will be to acquire the interest of C. It must be noted that **B** now has an interest, as freeholder, worth £206,881. By acquiring **C**'s interest, **B** becomes the freeholder in possession with an interest valued at £280,000. The gain that **B** stands to make is therefore:

£280,000 - £206,881 = £73,119

This is therefore the maximum that **B** could offer to **C**.

The minimum that **C** will accept will be the market value of £56,703. There will again be negotiation between these two figures. The difference between these two figures is £16,416, i.e. the marriage value between **B** and **C**.

This may also be obtained by summating the present interest of **B** and **C** (£206,881 and £56,702 = £263,584) and deducting this from **B**'s new interest worth £280,000.

£280,000 - £263,584 = £16,416.

Note that the total marriage value was found to be **£44,856.**

This is split between **A** and **B** and **B** and **C**:

Marriage value A + B:	£28,440
Marriage value B + C:	£16,416
Total marriage value:	£44,856

This term *'marriage value'* usually refers to the above, the result of the merging of interests in the same property. It can also be used to describe the extra value created by a merger of two properties.

Example 9.10

B is the owner of a derelict house on a small site. On its own, the site is too small to be profitably developed, but could be used as a parking space. A is in a similar position next door. The area is zoned for shopping use and an indication has been given that planning permission would be given to construct a small shop covering both sites.

Assess the price that B could offer to A for the freehold interest in his property, and a reasonable sale price.

Value of B's present interest:

Rent for parking, say	£50.00 p.a.
YP perp. @ 15%	6.67
CV	£333.50

Value of proposed merged site:

this might be valued by using a *'residual valuation'* (see Chapter 11) but market evidence indicates that similar sites have been selling for £3,000.

Maximum B can offer	= £3,000 - £333.50
	= £2,666.50
say	£2,650
Minimum A will accept	£333.50

A price will be reached by negotiation between these

two figures. A marriage value of **£2,333** (**£3,000** - **£667**) has been created in this case, by a merger of sites.

Throughout this chapter, traditional approaches to valuation have been followed. Elsewhere, a number of these approaches have been questioned. It is therefore necessary to emphasise that it is the valuer's role to assess open market value. If the valuer feels confident that he can substantiate the particular approach adopted by reference to the market, then marriage value in multiple interest investments may well exist; but the valuer must be certain of this market fact. He must beware that it is not based on false assumptions and fortuitous mathematics.

For example, an approach adopted in the USA for valuing leasehold investments in property could be loosely described as the *'difference in value'* method. The logic used is that if a property has a rental value of **£28,000** a year, and on that basis has a market value of **£280,000** but due to the grant of certain leases is currently worth only **£122,782**, then the value of the leasehold investments is **£280,000** less **£122,782**. On this basis marriage value does not exist.

This, then, is one extreme. At the other, consider the value of a very short leasehold interest. The value is likely to be low owing to the short term and the problem of dilapidations. The freehold interest would, however, reflect fully the loss of rental until review and in such a case genuine marriage value would exist.

It should be emphasised that the single rate valuation of leasehold interests (*see Chapter 7)* will, in the absence of any significant adjustment of capitalisation rates, greatly reduce any apparent marriage value, and may produce valuations which have greater affinity with market realities. So too can the use of a real value or DCF equated yield approach.

A discussion of marriage value could not be complete without some mention of *'break-up'* values. This in essence is the opposite of marriage value and recognises that different investors have different needs, objectives, risk preferences and tax positions. As one might purchase a company as a whole and then sell off separately the component parts to realise a higher total value so one might buy a freehold interest in a property and through careful sub-division of title realise a higher total value. The idea is really no more complex than that of lotting a large estate. This again emphasises the need to couple a thorough knowledge of the discounting technique with a thorough knowledge of the property market. A particular issue here is the whole question of unitisation of single property investments. The market will dictate whether 1,000 units in a **£10 million** property will be worth **£10,000** per unit or more than

£10,000 per unit or less than **£10,000** per unit. The relationship need not remain constant so that under some market conditions greater value may be realised by buying out all the unit holders and reselling as a whole in the open market.

The test is not :   **do the calculations suggest that marriage value exists?**

but :   **does the market evidence prove that marriage value exists?**

Full rental value: non-standard reviews constant rent theory

How much rent should be paid under a lease with non-standard rent review periods so as to leave the two parties in the same financial position as if they had agreed on a standard term?

In times of rental increases, or, indeed, decreases, the rent review pattern will affect the full rental value of a property, a concept so far regarded as being inflexible. It will be to the landlord's advantage in times of rental growth to insist upon regular rent reviews. Conversely, if he is burdened or presented with an arrangement whereby few, or no, rent reviews are provided for in the lease, then he may require a higher initial rent as compensation.

Two situations may arise where such compensation may be applicable. Firstly, a new lease may be arranged without the prevalent rent review pattern. For example, in a market where 3-yearly reviews are normally accepted, a new lease may be granted with 7-yearly reviews. In such a case the landlord might ask for a higher initial rent.

Secondly, the problem might arise at a rent review where the period between reviews is the result of previous negotiations. For example, a 42-year lease granted 21-years ago with a single midterm review will present problems if 3-yearly reviews are currently accepted, and again the landlord might have to ask for a higher reviewed rent as compensation.

Several methods have been devised to deal with this problem in a logical manner. One method was illustrated in a letter by *Jack Rose* to the *Estates Gazette*, **3 March 1979, at page 824**.

This method is designed to produce a single factor, k, which is applied to the full rental value on the usual pattern, to arrive at the compensatory rental value. This is formulated as:

$$k = \frac{(1+r)^n - (1+g)^n}{(1+r)^n - 1} \times \frac{(1+r)^t - 1}{(1+r)^t - (1+g)^t}$$

where k = multiplier,
r = equated yield,
n = number of years to review in subject lease,
g = annual rental growth expected, and
t = number of years to review normally agreed.

Example 9.11

What rent should be fixed at a rent review for the remaining 7 years of a 21 year lease of shop property, when rents are expected to rise at **12%** per annum and 3-yearly reviews are prevalent in the market?

An equated yield of **15%** based on the return provided by undated government stock with an adjustment for risk should be used, and the full rental value with 3-yearly reviews would be **£15,000 p.a.**

$$k = \frac{(1+0.15)^7 - (1+0.12)^7}{(1+0.15)^7 - 1} \times \frac{(1+0.15)^3 - 1}{(1+0.15)^3 - (1+0.12)^3}$$

$$= \frac{2.660 - 2.211}{1.66} \times \frac{0.521}{1.521 - 1.405}$$

$$= 0.2705 \times 4.4914$$

$$= 1.2149$$

Rent to be charged:

£15,000 x 1.2149 = £18,224 p.a.

There is growing evidence in the property market that the rent review pattern in a lease has a considerable effect upon the rents required by landlords, and the above is an attempt to make such adjustments logically. This method, and the others suggested, are adaptations of discounted cash flow techniques to valuation problems. It must be concluded that the use of DCF in all valuations will remove all of the inconsistencies referred to in this chapter as well as those problems identified in *Chapters 5, 6 and 7*, and is the ultimate and logical refinement of *'the income approach'*.

> **Q** Rents on 5-year rent review patterns are £25,000 a year. What rent should a landlord expect if the property is to be let with rent reviews every 3 years. Use a growth rate of 5% an equated yield of 10%.

The logic behind the DCF approach is difficult to defeat but the market is reluctant to move into the uncharted area of market forecasting. The valuer is trying to establish on the basis of the market rental value for a specific fixed term what the rent should be for a longer or shorter fixed term. The first is assumed to equate with the actual annual rentals each year for the term discounted to their present worth and re-assessed as a fixed annual equivalent sum. The second is the projection or shortening of the actual expected annual sums re-expressed as an annual equivalent. This process can only be undertaken on the basis of an assumed (but hopefully research-supported growth rate) or on the basis of an implied growth rate *(see Chapter 13)*.

The latter approach is more questionable in this exercise because the implied rental growth figures are long-term averages to be used for the purpose of valuing non-market rent review patterns. Either the landlord or the tenant would be concerned if the actual rental value rose at a higher or lower rate than the implied average growth rate. For an uplift rent the valuer is trying to determine the appropriate growth rate for that specific property. There is then, an argument in favour of using forecasted growth rates based on thorough research for assessing uplift rents rather than merely using implied rates.

In arbitration cases it is a question of presenting the strongest supportable case for or against the uplift, the arithmetical assessment is only a starting point.

In the case of non-normal rent reviews the courts have adopted a simple **10-15%** increase for a longer review or increased the market rental by a factor for each additional year over the normal rent review evidence in preference to a DCF approach.

The examples in this chapter do not reflect the statutory rights of landlords and tenants which may have to be taken into account and are considered in Chapter 10.

Summary

9

- Premiums are payable by tenants to landlords to ensure a letting at below market rental or for other reasons.

- Reverse premiums are payable by landlords to tenants or by tenants to sub-tenants to secure deals above market rentals.

- Premiums are generally assessed on the basis of value equations. Both parties should be neither better off nor worse off, and a before and after valuation is preferred.

- At the end of a lease either landlord or tenant may seek to secure a new lease in exchange for the surrender of the old lease. Neither party should be any better or worse off following the surrender and renewal, and a present v proposed interest calculation is normally used.

- Constant rent theory argues that a landlord should be no worse off over time by letting on an extended rent review pattern, but the market places an upper limit of 10-15% on the uplift negotiable for long rent review periods.

10

The Income Approach:

The effects of legislation

In the examples shown in the text it has been assumed that landlords and tenants are generally free to negotiate whatever lease terms they find acceptable for a particular tenancy of a property. In particular it has been assumed that they are free to agree the amount of rent to be charged for the premises and that in most cases the landlord can obtain vacant possession at the termination of the current lease. This is not always the case in the UK and the valuer must have regard to the provisions of the **Landlord and Tenant Acts** and the various **Rent and Housing Acts** as they affect properties occupied for business and residential purposes. **The Agricultural Holdings Acts** are of similar importance in the case of agricultural property, but agricultural property is not considered in this text.

The predominant feature of all landlord and tenant legislation is that it amends the normal law of contract as between landlord and tenant giving tenants substantial security of tenure (the right to remain in occupation following the termination of a contractual agreement) and setting out statutory procedures for determining and/or controlling the rents that a landlord can charge a tenant for the right to occupy a property. (The subject matter of this chapter is discussed in more detail in **Statutory Valuations**.)

Business premises

The most important statutes affecting business premises are the **Landlord and Tenant Act 1927 Part I** and the **Landlord and Tenant Act 1954 Part II** as amended by the **Law of Property Act 1969 Part I**.

These statutes primarily affect industrial and commercial property, but the expression 'business' includes a trade, profession or employment and includes any activity carried on by a body of persons whether corporate or unincorporate. This definition as set out in *Section 32*, **Landlord and Tenant Act 1954 Part II** is sufficiently broad to include some types of occupation which would not normally be regarded as business occupations, such as a tennis club (see *Addiscombe Garden Estates Ltd and another* v. *Crabbe and others, Queen's Bench Division (1958) 1 QB 513*).

Compensation for improvements

Under the **Landlord and Tenant Act 1927 Part II** the tenant of business premises is entitled 'at the termination of the tenancy, on quitting his holding, to be paid by his landlord compensation in respect of any improvement (including the erection of any building) on his holding made by him or his predecessors in title, not being a trade or other fixture which the tenant is by law entitled to remove, which at the termination of the tenancy adds to the letting value of the holding' (*Section 1*, **Landlord and Tenant Act 1927**).

This right does not extend to improvements carried out before **25th March 1928,** nor to improvements 'made in pursuance of a statutory obligation, nor to improvements which the tenant or his predecessors in title were under an obligation to make, such as would be the case where a tenant covenanted to carry out improvements as a condition of the lease when entered into' (*Section 2*, **Landlord and Tenant Act 1927**). Except that those made after the passing of the 1954 Act 'in pursuance of a statutory obligation' will qualify for compensation (*Section 48*, **Landlord and Tenant Act 1954**).

The tenant will normally require the consent of the landlord before carrying out alterations or improvements, or alternatively they may apply to the court for a certificate to the effect that the improvement is a 'proper improvement' (*Section 3*, **Landlord and Tenant Act 1927**).

It should be noted under *Section 19(2)*, **Landlord and Tenant Act 1927 Part II** that 'in all leases...containing a covenant, condition or agreement, against the making of improvements without licence or consent, such covenant...shall be deemed...to be subject to a proviso that such licence or consent is not to be unreasonably withheld...' *Section 49* of the **1954 Act** renders void any agreement to contract out of the **1927 Act**.

Compensation payable is limited under *Schedule 1* of the **Landlord and Tenant Act 1927** to the lesser of:

1. The net addition to the value of the holding as a whole as a result of the improvement; or

2. The reasonable cost of carrying out the improvement at the termination of the tenancy, subject to a deduction of an amount equal to the cost (if any) of putting the works constituting

the improvement into a reasonable state of repair, except as so far as such cost is covered by the tenant's repairing covenant.

Further, 'in determining the amount of such net addition regard shall be had to the purposes for which it is intended the premises shall be used after the termination of the tenancy' (*Section 1(2)*, **Landlord and Tenant Act 1927**). For example, if the premises are to be demolished immediately then the improvements are of no value to the landlord and no compensation would be payable. But if the premises are to be demolished in, say, 6 months' time and there is a temporary user planned then compensation would be based on the net addition to value of the improvements for that 6 month period. If the landlord and tenant fail to agree as to the amount of compensation, the matter can be referred to the county court. Where a new lease is granted on the termination of the current lease no compensation can be claimed at that point in time. Both the **1927 Act** and the **1954 Act** provide that the rent on a new lease shall exclude any amount attributable to the improvements in respect of which compensation would have been payable *(see '(c)', p.111).*

Thus the initial problem to be solved by a valuer when instructed to value business premises is the extent to which they have been improved by the tenant and the extent to which these may become compensatable improvements under the provisions of the **Landlord and Tenant Act 1927.**

Example 10.1

Value the freehold interest in office premises currently let at £5,000 on full repairing and insuring terms with **6 years** of the lease unexpired. The current full rental value on full repairing and insuring terms is £10,000. Improvements were carried out by the tenant and these have increased the market rental value by £1,000 and would cost today an estimated £8,000 to complete.

Value the premises on the assumption that the tenant will vacate on the termination of the present lease and will be able to make a valid claim for compensation under the **Landlord and Tenant Act 1927.**

Current net income	£5,000	
YP for 6 years @ 8%	4.62	
		£23,100
Reversion in 6 years to	£10,000	
YP perp. deferred 6 years @ 8%	7.87	
		£78,700
		£101,800

Less compensation under Landlord and Tenant Act 1927 for improvements being the lesser of:

(a) Net addition to the value

Increase in rental attributable to improvements:

	£ 1,000
YP perp @ 8%	12.5
	£12,500

(b) Cost of carrying out improvements

	£8,000
Therefore compensation is	£8,000
x PV £1 for 6 years @ 8%	0.63
	£5,040

(b) is the lesser amount,

Therefore

Value of freehold allowing for payment of compensation to tenant =	£101,800 – 5,040
	£96,760
say	£96,750

As shown elsewhere this traditional equivalent yield valuation raises some basic issues: first is the whole question of implicit versus explicit growth valuation models, the second is the validity of using current estimates of changes in rental value attributable to the improvements and of using current costs for assessing the compensations when the actual compensation will have to be based on figures applicable in 6 years' time. This is a further argument for at least checking the valuation by reference to a true DCF approach.

It could be argued that the £8,000 should not be discounted as in effect it is the equivalent cost of the future amount discounted.

Security of tenure

In accordance with the provisions of *Section 24(1)* of the **Landlord and Tenant Act 1954** tenants of business premises are granted security of tenure; however, the parties may contract out of these provisions. Tenancies to which this part of the Act applies will not come to an end unless terminated in accordance with the provisions of **Part II** of the **Act**, so that some positive act by the landlord or tenant needs to be taken to terminate a tenancy. Where notice to terminate is served by the landlord he must give at least 6 months' notice and not more than 12 months' notice. Such notice cannot come into force before the expiration of an existing contractual tenancy. Thus in the case of most leases of business premises the earliest date a landlord can serve notice on a tenant is 12 months prior to the contractual termination date. If notice is not served the tenancy continues as a statutory tenancy at the contracted rent until terminated by notice.

The Act further provides that a tenant has the right to the renewal of his lease. If the landlord wishes to obtain possession he may oppose the tenant's request for a new tenancy only on the grounds set out in the Act.

Section 30(1) states the following grounds on which a landlord may oppose an application:

(a) where under the current tenancy the tenant has any obligations as respects the repair and maintenance of the holding that the tenant ought not to be granted a new tenancy in view of the state of repair of the holding, being a state resulting from the tenant's failure to comply with the said obligations;

(b) that the tenant ought not to be granted a new tenancy in view of his persistent delay in paying rent which has become due;

(c) that the tenant ought not to be granted a new tenancy in view of other substantial breaches by him of his obligations under the current tenancy, or for any other reason connected with the tenant's use or management of the holding;

(d) that the landlord has offered and is willing to provide or secure the provision of alternative accommodation for the tenant, that the terms on which the alternative accommodation is available are reasonable having regard to the terms of the current tenancy and to all other relevant circumstances, and that the accommodation at the time at which it will be available is suitable for the tenant's requirements, including the requirement to preserve goodwill, having regard to the nature and class of his business and to the situation and extent of and facilities afforded by the holding;

(e) Where the current tenancy was created by the sub-letting of part only of the property comprised in a superior tenancy and the landlord is the owner of an interest in reversion expectant on the termination of that superior tenancy, that the estimate of the rents reasonably obtainable on separate lettings of the holding and the remainder of that property would be substan-

tially less than the rent reasonably obtainable on a letting of that property as a whole, that on the termination of the current tenancy the landlord requires possession of the holding for the purpose of letting or otherwise disposing of the said property as a whole, and that in view thereof the tenant ought not to be granted a new tenancy;

(f) That on the termination of the current tenancy the landlord intends to demolish or reconstruct the premises comprising the holding or a substantial part of those premises or to carry out substantial work of construction on the holding or part thereof, and that he could not reasonably do so without obtaining possession of the holding;

(g) Subject as hereinafter provided, that on the termination of the current tenancy the landlord intends to occupy the holding for the purposes, or partly for the purposes, of a business to be carried on by him therein, or as his residence.

To oppose an application under that last mentioned ground **(g)** the landlord must have been the owner of the said interest for at least 5 years prior to the termination of the current tenancy. **Section 6** of the **Law of Property Act 1969** extends **Section 31(g)** of the **1954 Act** to companies controlled by the landlord and **Section 7** of the **Law of Property Act 1969** has altered the effects of **31(f)** of the **1954 Act** so that a landlord wishing to oppose the grant of a new tenancy under that ground must now not only prove his intent to carry out substantial works of alteration but also that it is necessary to obtain possession in order to complete such works. Thus if a landlord can demolish and rebuild without obtaining possession and if the tenant is agreeable or willing to co-operate then the courts will allow the tenant to remain in possession.

Section 32 of the **Landlord and Tenant Act 1954**, whilst requiring the new lease to be in respect of the whole of the building, has now been amended by **Section 7** of the **Law of Property Act 1969**, which adds **Sections 31(A)** and **32(1)(A)** to allow a court to grant a new tenancy in respect of part of the original holding where the tenant is in agreement.

Compensation for loss of security

When a landlord is successful in obtaining possession the tenant may be entitled to compensation under **Section 37** of the **Landlord and Tenant Act 1954**. *'Where the Court is precluded...from making an order for the grant of a new tenancy by reason of any of the grounds specified in paragraphs (e), (f) and (g)... the tenant shall be entitled on quitting the* holding to recover from the landlord by way of compensation an amount determined in accordance with the following provisions of this section...'

The amount of compensation payable will be **2** times the rateable value of the holding if for the whole of the **14** years immediately preceding the termination of the tenancy the premises have been occupied for the purposes of a business carried on by the occupier or if during those **14** years there had been a change in the occupation and the current occupier was the successor to the business carried on by his predecessor. In all other cases the amount of compensation shall be the rateable value of the holding (these multipliers were revised in **1990**).

Under *Schedule* 7 of the **Local Government and Housing Act 1989** and the **Landlord and Tenant Act 1954 (Appropriate Multipliers) Order** 1990, the multiplier under *Schedule 37 (2)* is still **three** if the relevant date is before **1 April 1990**. It is **one** if the relevant date is after **1 April 1990**. These are doubled in appropriate cases. In some cases removal expenses will be paid if part of the property is domestic. Transitional arrangements provide for a multiplier of **eight** where the landlord's notice is given after **31 March 1990** but before **1 April 2000** and the tenancy was in existence or was contracted before **1 April 1990** and the tenant has exercised an option for compensation to be based on the Rateable Value as at **31 March 1990**.

Terms of the new lease

Where a new lease is granted then the new rent payable will normally be in accordance with the provisions of *Section 34* of the Act, particularly when the parties are in disagreement and the matter is referred to the county court for settlement.

The Law of Property Act 1969 has amended *Section 34* so that:

'*the rent payable under a tenancy granted by order of the Court under this part of this act shall be such as may be agreed between the landlord and tenant or as, in default of such agreement, may be determined by the court to be that at which, having regard to the terms of the tenancy (other than those relating to rent), the holding might reasonably be expected to be let in the open market by a willing lessor, there being disregarded:*

(a)   any effect on rent of the fact that the tenant has or his predecessors in title have been in occupation of the holding;

(b)   any goodwill attached to the holding by reason of the carrying on thereat of the business of the tenant (whether by him or by a predecessor of his in that business);

(c)   any effect on rent of any improvement carried out by the tenant or predecessor in title of his otherwise than in pursuance of an obligation to his immediate landlord (see LPA amendment below);

(d)   in the case of a holding comprising licensed premises any addition to its value attributable to the licence, if it appears to the court that having regard to the terms of the current tenancy and any other relevant circumstances the benefit of the   licence belongs to the tenant.'

Items **(a)**, **(b)** and **(c)** are those that valuers have most frequently to reflect in valuations of business premises.

Items **(a)** and **(b)** cause particular difficulty in assessment for, whilst it is simple to explain the meaning of these requirements, it is often extremely difficult to assess them in practice. Under item **(a)** the valuer must demonstrate that, for example, premises have a rental value as defined in the Act of £**5,000,** but in the absence of the protective legislation the occupying tenant would bid £**5,500,** in order that the overbid of £**500** must be disregarded.

Similarly under item **(b)** if it can be demonstrated that the premises are worth £**5,000** but to any other tenant carrying on the same business are worth £**5,500** then the £**500** of business goodwill must be disregarded.

Section 1 of the **Law of Property Act** has extended the meaning of *Section 34 (c)* to include tenants' improvements carried out at any time within 21 years of the renewal of the tenancy.

All the other terms and conditions of a new tenancy shall be as agreed between the parties, but if the parties cannot agree then *Sections 33* and *34* of the **Landlord and Tenant Act 1954** require the court to restrict the terms of the tenancy to 14 years with appropriate rent reviews (**Law of Property Act 1969** *Section 2* which adds *sub-section 3* to *Section 34* of the 1954 Act).

The Law Commission has proposed a number of amendments to the **1954 Act** but as yet none have been enacted. In particular it is proposed that the **14** year period be amended to **15** years. In practice a growing number of lease renewals are for terms of **10, 15, 20 or 25** years depending upon market conditions and tenants desires and negotiating strengths.

Example 10.2

Assuming the facts as stated in *example 10.1*, value the freehold interest and assume the tenant is granted a new 14-year lease with a rent review in the **7th** year and that the improvements were completed **3** years ago. The first step to resolve this problem requires the setting out of the income flow. Some valuers find it simpler to construct a cash flow diagram (**see below**). In **6** years' time the lease is due for renewal, at a rental ignoring the worth of the improvements (**Landlord and Tenant Act 1954**).

But there is some doubt as to the rent that could be charged at the rent review after 7 years. According to the **Law of Property Act** it would seem that no account should be taken of the value of the improvements for a period of **21** years.

If this argument applies then the rent on the review must once more be at a figure excluding any value attributable to the improvements provided a *S.34* disregard or equivalent is included in the rent review clause. This reasoning, coupled with the specific provisions in the **Landlord and Tenant Act 1954**, would effectively result in no account being taken of the improvements at any time during the whole of the new lease.

Thus the cash flow will be as shown below :

21 years' Law of Property Act improvement

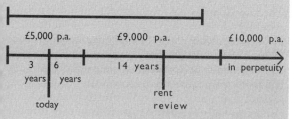

Solution, assuming cash flow as shown above
(and see notes following the valuation)

Current net income	£5,000	
YP for 6 years @ 7%	4.76	
		£23,800
First reversion to S.34 rent	£9,000	
YP for 14 years @ 7%	8.75	
PV £1 in 6 years @ 7%	0.67	
		£52,762
Second reversion to FRV	£10,000	
YP perp. def'd 20 years @ 7%	3.69	
		£36,900
		£133,462

If a **21**-year period elapses prior to a rent review date then the full rental value of the improved premises could be charged from the review date.

This would appear to be contrary to the **1954 Act** as originally drafted which clearly intended that the effects on rent of any improvements should be disregarded for the whole of the new tenancy of **14** years.

Whilst some confusion apparently exists, a number of points are becoming obvious from the decisions reached in a number of Landlord and Tenant cases.

First, the legislation relates quite clearly to the determination of *'rent payable under a tenancy granted by order of the Court'*, and this can only occur on renewal of a lease and not on a rent review.

Second, the Act uses the word *'reasonable'* which suggests that the rent as determined need not be the maximum possible rent.

Third, the rent on any review will be determined in accordance with the appropriate clauses in the lease and, unless there is specific reference to *Section 34* of the **Landlord and Tenant Act 1954** or a specific statement that improvements carried out during an immediately preceding lease, or within **21** years of the review date, are to be disregarded, the review rent may fully reflect the current rental of the property as improved.

Professional advisers are therefore forewarned when acting for tenants to see that rent review clauses in leases are sufficiently worded to protect their clients (see RICS/Law Society model rent review clause .) When licences for improvements are granted they should also confirm that the effect on rental value of the improvements will be disregarded on review or renewal of the current lease.

If this advice is followed then tenants may avoid any repetition of *Ponsford and Others* v. *HMS Aerosols Ltd, 1977, Estates Gazette 243: 743* where tenants of a factory rebuilt the premises which had been destroyed by fire, at the same time substantially improving the property with the landlord's consent. Shortly after rebuilding, the rent was due for review.

The wording of the lease and licence was such that the Court of Appeal held that the tenants would have to pay rent in respect of the improvements, the cost of which they had borne themselves. The wording of the lease, together with the wording of any licences, will determine the factors to be taken into account when assessing the rent to be paid on review. A similar situation would occur if a tenant were to carry out improvements without the proper licence of the landlord.

(Readers are also referred to *English Exporters (London) Ltd* v. *Eldonwall Ltd. (1973) Ch 415.*)

When valuing business premises, or advising tenants of business premises, the valuer must have regard to all the terms and conditions of the lease and to the relevant statutory provisions.

In practice, negotiations and/or court proceedings may result in the new rent commencing many months after the termination of a current contractual lease. *Section 64* of the **1954 Act** further provides that any new terms, including those relating to rent, may only commence **3** months after the court application has been 'finally disposed of'. This can lead to a considerable loss of income for the landlord.

The **Law of Property Act 1969** added a new section, *24A*, to the **1954 Act**.

(1) The landlord of a tenancy to which this part of this Act applies may:

    (a)   **if he has given notice under section 25 of this Act to terminate the tenancy; or**

    (b)   **if the tenant has made a request for a new tenancy in accordance with Section 26 of this Act; apply to the court to determine a rent which it would be reasonable for the tenant to pay while the tenancy continues by virtue of Section 24 of this Act, and the court may determine a rent accordingly.**

(2) A rent determined in proceedings under this section shall be deemed to be the rent payable under the tenancy from the date on which the proceedings were commenced or the date specified in the landlord's notice or the tenant's request, whichever is the later.

From a valuer's viewpoint the interesting aspects of these provisions relate to the assessment of the amount of this interim rent.

Section 24A(3) contains the following direction:

In determining a rent under this section the court shall have regard to the rent payable under the terms of the tenancy, but otherwise subsections (1) and (2) of Section 34 of this Act shall apply to the determination as they would apply to the determination of a rent under that section if a new tenancy from year to year of the whole of the property comprised in the tenancy were granted to the tenant by order of the court.

A number of principles were established in the **Eldonwall** case and endorsed in *Fawke* v. *Chelsea (Viscount) (Estates Gazette 250:855).* The valuer is effectively urged to determine a rent for a hypothetical yearly tenancy. *Ratners (Jewellers) Ltd* v. *Lemnoll Ltd (Estates Gazette 255:987)* illustrates this point, emphasising acceptance of the principle that, having determined a normal market rent under the terms of **Section 34,** the valuer should discount this rent to reflect the 'year-to-year' nature of the tenancy. We doubt whether the debate is closed.

Readers should be aware that, due to the hypothetical year-to-year assumption, the interim rent may be lower than the current rent passing, and are reminded that the formula employed in *Chapter 9, example 9.11,* may be used to determine the annual equivalent rent. Bowcock's *Property Valuation Tables* may also be employed to this end, both methods being more rigorous than the crude discount methods currently used. However, this general expectation may be contradicted by market evidence of annual rents exceeding fixed term rents.

The Law Commission recommendation is that tenants should also have the right to serve notice for the determination of an interim rent. The 1990s market has been one where many landlords have sought to continue with a contracted rent for as long as possible rather than serve notice which would lead to a reduction in rent. In these over-rented cases the tenant is prevented from serving an interim rent and should therefore take action to serve a S. 26 notice to terminate the tenancy at the earliest date.

Landlord and tenant negotiations

It is important to appreciate that whilst the Landlord and Tenant Acts are there to protect the tenant on termination of his lease, many tenants will seek to negotiate new leases before their current leases expire.

The Landlord and Tenant Acts give the tenant increased bargaining strength and full regard should be given to these statutes when advising a landlord or tenant on the terms for a new lease.

Example 10.3

A tenant occupies shop premises on a lease having 2 years to run at £6,000 p.a. net. Ten years ago she substantially improved the property. The full rental value of the property today as originally demised would be £10,000 but as improved it is worth £14,000. The tenant wishes to surrender her present lease for a new 15-year lease with 5 year reviews; the landlord has agreed in principle and you have been appointed as independent valuer to assess a reasonable rent for the new lease.

As outlined in **Chapter 9**, this requires consideration from the tenant's and landlord's points of view on a 'before and after' basis.

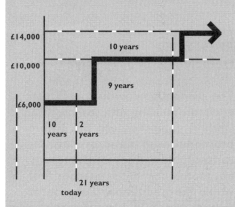

Note: The 21-year rule will run out after 9 years of the new lease and OMRV can be charged from the rent review in year 10; that is, in 12 years' time.

Value of freeholder's present interest if he does not accept surrender of the lease:

Current income	£6,000	
YP for 2 years @ 7%	1.8080	
		£10,848

Reversion to FRV subject to S.34(c) L&T Act 1954 Part II and assuming a new 15-year lease with review agreed	£10,000	
YP for 10 years @ 7%	7.02	
PV £1 in 2 years @ 7%	0.87	6.10
		£61,000

Reversion to FRV	£14,000	
YP perp. def'd 12 years @ 7%	6.34	
		£88,760
Value of present interest		**£160,608**

(If the assumption here is that a review after 5 years would be permitted by the courts then one must further assume that professional advisers would see that the rent review clause fully reflected the intention of the **L & T Act 1954 Part II** as amended by the **Law of Property Act 1969**.)

Value of freeholder's proposed interest:

Let rent to be reserved for new 15-year lease = £x per annum

Proposed rent	£x	
YP 5 years @ 7%	4.10	4.10x

Reversions to FRV	£14,000	
YP perp. def'd 5 years @ 7%	10.185	
		£142,590

Value of future interest:	£142,590 + 4.10x .

On the assumption that the freeholder should be no better off and no worse off the value of his present interest must be equated with the value of his future interest:

$$\text{Present interest} = \text{proposed interest}$$
$$£160,608 = £142,590 + 4.1x$$
$$£160,608 - £142,590 = 4.1x$$
$$£18,018 = 4.1x$$
$$£4,394 = x$$

Value of tenant's present interest assuming no surrender:

FRV to tenant	£14,000	
Less rent reserved	£6,000	
Profit rent	£8,000	

YP for 2 years @ 8% and 3% adj. tax @ 40%	1.10	
		£8,800

Reversion to	£14,000	
Less S.34 rent reserved	£10,000	
	£4,000	

YP for 10 years @ 8% and 3% adj. tax @ 40p	4.437	
PV £1 in 2 years @ 8%	0.857	
	3.80	£15,210

Value of present interest	**£24,010**

Value of tenant's proposed interest:

Note: After the rent review in 10 years the rent rises to £14,000

Let rent to be reserved for new 15-year
lease = £x per annum,
then new profit rent is:

FRV to tenant	£14,000
Less rent reserved	
	x
Profit rent	£14,000 − x
YP for 5 years @ 8% and 3% adj. tax @ 40p	2.5386
Value of proposed interest	£35,540 − 2.5386x

Present interest	=	proposed interest
£24,010	=	£35,540 − 2.5386x
2.5386x	=	£35,540 − £24,010
2.5386x	=	£11,530
x	=	£4,541

Here it would seem reasonable for the parties to accept a rent for a new 15-year lease, on surrender of the present 2-year term, of, say, £4,500 per annum with a full rent review after 5 years.
But these valuations should be cross-checked with a DCF approach.

Q

Your client owns the freehold interest in an office building.
The building has a ground floor and four upper floors and the whole is let on full repairing and insuring terms for a term of 21 years without reviews. The lease has 3 years to run at £150,000 p.a.

The building originally contained only a ground and two upper floors but the tenant agreed as a condition of the lease to add a third floor. This work was com-

Q (cont.)

pleted within 2 years of the grant at a cost of £150,000. Seven years ago a mansard roof was added at a further cost of £50,000. All these works were approved by the landlord.

There are 400m^2 on each of the ground, first, second and third floors but the top floor has an area of only 250m^2.

Office space is letting at £200 per m^2. Where there is no lift, the rent on upper floors is £150 per m^2.

The property is assessed for rating at RV £350,000.
Freehold equivalent yields are 7%.

The tenants now wish to refit and equip the building with new carpets, lighting, computer, etc. but before proceeding wish to improve their security of tenure. They would prefer to buy the freehold but as a second best would like to surrender their present lease for a new 20-year full repairing and insuring lease with reviews every 5 years.

Advise the freeholder,
(ignoring VAT) :

a) on the rent that could be expected in 3 years' time;

b) on the price that should be asked for the freehold interest;

c) on the rent that should be asked for the proposed 20-year lease

d) on the amount of compensation due to the tenant if possession was recovered.

Residential property

Over 65% of homes in England and Wales are now owner-occupied and the appropriate method for the valuation of such freehold residential property is that of direct capital comparison *(Mackmin: Valuation and Sale of Residential Property, Routledge 1994).*

However, there are still many individuals and families occupying tenanted property both on a furnished and an unfurnished basis. The capital value of such properties may be assessed by using the income approach.

The period since the **Housing Act 1980** has seen a number of changes in political attitude towards the public and private sectors of the rented housing market. A large number of public sector tenants exercised their right to buy under the Act and are now home owners. But the hoped-for stimulus for the private sector never materialised.

The **Housing Act 1988** made further significant changes to the law relating to public and private sector housing, including Housing Associations.

The important changes in the private sector relate to the extension and amendment of the law concerning assured and shorthold tenancies.

As from 15 January 1989 all existing and new assured tenancies come under the 1988 Act and the previous system of protected shorthold tenancies has been replaced by a new scheme of assured shorthold tenancies.

Recently the right to enfranchise has been significantly extended by the **Leasehold Reform Housing and Urban Development Act 1993**. This complex Act has brought new opportunities for leaseholders of both houses and flats to enfranchise.

Private sector tenancies

Residential investment properties in the private sector can be grouped under the following heads:

1. Assured tenancies under the **Housing Act 1988.**

2. Assured shorthold tenancies under the **Housing Act 1988.**

3. Tenancies subject to protection under *Part I* of the **Rent Act 1977 (the 1977 Act)**, generally referred to as regulated furnished or regulated unfurnished tenancies, including those tenancies previously known as controlled tenancies by *Section 64* of the **Housing Act 1980 (the 1980 Act)**. Tenancies in this category must have been 'entered into before, or pursuant to a contract made before, the commencement of the **Housing Act 1988**, i.e. 15 January 1989.

4. Tenancies of dwelling-houses with high rateable values (*Schedule 1.2*, **1988 Act**).

5. Tenancies where the landlord remains resident in another part of the same building *(Schedule 1(10)*, **1988 Act).**

6. Tenancies at a low rent (*Schedule 1(3)*, **1988 Act**). Such tenancies may be protected under the **Landlord and Tenant Act 1954, Part I.**

7. Tenancies with enfranchisement rights under the **Leasehold Reform Act, 1967** as amended by the **Housing Acts of 1969, 1974 and 1980**, and by the **Leasehold Reform, Housing and Urban Development Act 1993**.

(A further minor group of (formerly controlled) tenancies which are partially business lettings cannot become regulated tenancies (**1977 Act, Section 24(3)** and will fall to be considered under *Part II* of the **Landlord and Tenant Act 1954.)**

Each is considered below in terms of the valuation implications of the legislation relating to each category. Those involved with the letting and management of residential property are referred specifically to the above legislation and to the **Housing Act 1988** and the **Landlord and Tenants Acts of 1985 and 1987**.

Assured tenancies

The **1980 Act** introduced a new class of tenancy in the private sector known as the assured tenancy. This was intended to encourage the institutional investor to build new homes to let on the open market.

Few tenancies were, in fact, created under the **1980 Act**, largely due to the restriction of the provisions to new dwellings provided by 'approved' landlords. Under the **1988 Act** all new tenancies of residential property, other than those statutorily excepted by *Schedule 1*, will be assured tenancies.

The **1988 Act** created a completely new scheme but borrows heavily from the **1977 Act** and from the **1954 Landlord and Tenant Act**. The working of the scheme broadly parallels that of the **1954 Act** in terms of tenant protection, but grounds for possession as set out are very similar to those found in the **1977 Act**. These tenancies may be granted at market rents.

It is too soon to judge how successful the new scheme will be in stimulating the private rented sector of the residential market, but the reaction of investors to the many business expansion schemes floated after the **1988 Finance Act** provides hope for the government. If a new market is created then its success will depend upon the relationship between vacant possession values and the investment value of the same property subject to an assured tenancy.

The valuation of residential property subject to an assured tenancy is likely to be on an income approach, but it will be some time before there is sufficient confidence in the market for valuers to assess capitalisation rates and market rents. The income approach is likely to be the preferred approach because of the security of tenure provisions in the Act.

Section 5 specifies that such tenancies can only be brought to an end with a court order and to obtain such an order the landlord(s) must follow the procedures set out in the Act and specify the ground(s) for possession which must be one or more of those set out in *Schedule 2* to **the 1988 Act**. In the case of grounds 1-8 inclusive, the court, if satisfied, must order possession; in all other cases the court may order possession.

The effect of these provisions is to create tenancies for residential property and hence residential investments of a continuing nature with strong similarities to business tenancy investments for which an income approach is appropriate.

Assured shorthold tenancies

The **1980 Housing Act** introduced the concept of shorthold tenancies, but the 1980 provisions have been superseded by those set out in the **1988 Act**.

An assured shorthold tenancy must be for a minimum period of 6 months. A prescribed notice must be served on the tenant prior to the grant of the tenancy stating that the tenancy is to be a shorthold tenancy. In addition to the grounds for possession specified in the **1988 Act** for assured tenancies, the landlord is entitled to bring an immediate action for possession provided the tenancy has expired and provided all the correct notices have been served. The courts in such cases have to grant possession.

This added ability to recover possession suggests that such properties will be valued on the basis of capitalised term income plus a reversion to vacant possession capital value.

Tenancies created before 15 January 1989 and subject to the provisions of the Rent Act 1977

A regulated tenancy is one falling within the rateable value limits of £400 and £200 or £1,500 and £750, and since the Rent Act 1974 the same regulations now apply both to furnished and unfurnished tenancies, save where there is a resident landlord. No new regulated tenancies can now be created.

The main Act dealing with regulated tenancies is the **Rent Act 1977**. A regulated tenancy may be contractual or statutory. That is, a lease or an agreement for a lease may exist, or the tenant may be *'holding over'* and exercising his statutory rights.

The **1965 Rent Act** introduced the new concept of 'fair' rent and this is now consolidated in the **1977 Act**. *Section 70* of the **1977 Act** sets out the rules for determining a 'fair' rent, the most important feature being that the effect on rental value of the scarcity of residential accommodation within an area must be ignored.

A *'fair'* rent will in areas of undersupply be lower than the rent one would expect if the premises were offered in the open market in the absence of the **Rent Acts**.

The **Rent Act** also requires that, in determining what is or would be a fair rent, regard shall be had to all the circumstances, and in particular to the age, character, locality and state of repair, of the dwellinghouse and, if any furniture is provided for use under the tenancy, the quantity, quality and condition of the furniture. But the following must be disregarded:

(a)   any disrepair or defect attributable to a failure by the tenant to comply with the terms of the tenancy;

(b)   any improvement carried out by the tenant otherwise than in pursuance of the terms of the tenancy (renewal of fixtures will be classed as improvements);

(c)   any improvement to the furniture made by the tenant under the regulated tenancy or as the case may be any deterioration in the condition of the furniture due to any ill-treatment by the tenant.

The **1968 Rent Act** as amended by subsequent legislation provides for the appointment of Rent Officers in all local authority areas. Landlords and tenants both have the right to apply to the Rent Officer at any time, notwithstanding the existence of a contractual tenancy, for a rent to be registered. On receipt of an application for registration the Rent Officer inspects the premises, usually calls a meeting between landlord and tenant and subsequently notifies the parties of his intention to register a fair rent. Fair rents are registered exclusive of rates and on the assumption that the tenancy is subject to *Sections 11-14* of the **Landlord and Tenant Act 1985**[1]. Either party may appeal to the Rent Assessment Committee.

Once a rent has been registered it remains the maximum recoverable rent for 2 years save for permitted variations to cover extra rates borne by the landlord and increases where separate service charges exist.

Re-application during the 2 years is only allowed on the grounds that there has been a change in the condition of the dwellinghouse or the terms of the tenancy. In all other cases the rent remains fixed for 2 years or until such later time that a rent is re-registered.

As far as the valuation of properties subject to regulated tenancies is concerned, the important points to note are as follows.

1.   **The recoverable rent is restricted to the level of a 'fair rent'.**

2.   **The rent can only be increased after 2 years.**

3.   **On the death of the original tenant the tenancy may be transferred twice. The second succession will be to an assured tenancy. The rules on succession have been amended by Schedule 4 of the 1988 Act.**

There is still an active market for this type of investment, particularly where a portfolio of such properties is offered for sale. Those active in this market will be aware that a percentage of vacant possession value, between **25%** and **50%** in most cases, is used to assess market value when the income approach might only produce realistic market valuations by the use of very low capitalisation rates.

In a number of special cases, the tenancy will be held to be outside the Rent Acts, or, provided the correct notices are served at the commencement of the tenancy, the courts have a mandatory power to grant repossession. Examples of such tenancies are: holiday lettings, lettings by educational establishments to students, lettings by absentee owners and lettings of properties purchased for retirement.[2]

In those cases where the tenancy is excepted by the Rent Act 1977 or where the court must order possession under that Act or the 1988 Act, and it is reasonable to assume that vacant possession can be obtained, the property should be valued by direct capital comparison.

Tenancies with high rateable values

The total number of tenanted houses and flats falling within this category represents a very small percentage of the whole, but still comprises an important sector of the market, particularly in central London. To be unprotected the rateable value of the tenancy as at 23 March 1965 must have exceeded £400 if situated in Greater London or £200 if situated outside London. If the property was not tenanted prior to 1 April 1973, when the current valuation list came into force, or after 15 January 1989, then the figures are £1,500 and £750 respectively.

The valuation of such properties requires the capitalisation of the current contracted net income, plus, the reversion to capital value, or the capitalisation of the reversionary net income, the latter and the capitalisation rate being assessed by reference to current market evidence. The capitalisation rate will therefore reflect the market's view

---

[1] Under these sections landlords of residential premises let for terms of 7 years or less are responsible for structural repairs, exterior repairs and repairs to services, water, gas and electricity; this extends to certain fixtures such as WC, baths and basins. The liability of landlords has been further generally extended by the Defective Premises Act 1972 (see also S.116, Housing Act 1988).

[2] Schedule 15, 1977 Act as amended by 1980 Act, see also Schedule 1, 1988 Act.

regarding the possibility of such properties becoming assured tenancies.

As many of these properties will be in blocks of flats, special attention must be given to the calculation of landlord's outgoings and in terms of freehold valuations of blocks of flats to the **Landlord and Tenant Act 1987**, which gives tenants the collective right to buy under specific conditions.

Resident Landlords

The **Rent Act 1974** introduced a new special class of tenancy where the landlord resides in the same building. Such tenancies, whether of furnished or unfurnished premises, now fall under the **1977 Rent Act.**

The important feature of a resident landlord letting is that although the tenant enjoys limited protection from eviction (**1977 Act, Protection from Eviction Act 1977 and the 1980 Act**) the landlord, or, on the landlord's death, the landlord's personal representatives, can recover possession. Repossession may take 3 to 12 months through County Court procedures (**1980 Act**): the basis of valuation of such a property is therefore vacant possession value, deferred for 3 to 12 months, arguably the maximum period. The income approach is not, therefore, of particular relevance to this class of investment.

If created after 15 January 1989 it will be excluded from being an assured tenancy by *Schedule 1* (similar provisions apply to circumstances where board and lodging is provided) and will therefore be valued on a vacant possession basis.

Tenancies on long leases

The **Leasehold Reform Housing and Urban Development Act 1993** has considerably amended the right of tenants with long leases (over 21 years) of both houses and flats. The term 'house' has a specific definition (see **Leasehold Reform Act 1969**) but the normal interpretation of the word is used in this text

Houses

Almost all long lessees of houses satisfying a number of qualifying conditions now enjoy the right to acquire the freehold title to their home - the right to enfranchise. Some have a right to request a 50-year extension to their leases.

All tenants seeking to enfranchise must satisfy the following conditions:

- **Must be a long lease - i.e. originally granted for a term of years exceeding 21.**

- **The property must be a 'house' as defined.**

- **The tenant must have resided in the house for the last 3 years or for at least 3 years in the last 10 years.**

- **The rent must be a low rent as defined.**

Up until 1993 there was a further test based on Rateable Value or after the abolishment of Rateable Value for residential property a capital value equivalent under the **References to Rating (Housing) Regulations 1990**. The **1993 Act** removed the rateable value limit for enfranchisement but it may be relevant for determining the enfranchisement price.

The low rent tests before modification required:

- **The rent at the commencement of the tenancy not to exceed two-thirds of the rateable value if the tenancy commenced between August 1939 and April 1963 or**

- **To be less than two-thirds of the rateable value on the appropriate day if the tenancy was entered into before April 1990 or**

- **The rent must be below £1,000 (London), £750 (elsewhere) if the tenancy commenced on or after 1st April 1990**

The new test for those tenants which fail the old test is that

- *The rent* **must not exceed two-thirds of the letting value of the property on the date of commencement of the tenancy if it begins before 1st April 1963, or**

- **the rent must not exceed two-thirds of the rateable value on the relevant date (usually date of commencement of the tenancy) if the tenancy commenced after April 1963 but before April 1990, or**

- **in any other case the rent must not exceed £1,000 (Greater London) or £750 (elsewhere).**

The **1993 Act** also extended the right to enfranchise to tenancies commenced before 18 April 1980 and which were previously capable of being determined by notice following a death or marriage .

The **1993 Act** builds upon the **1967 Act** as amended and earlier precedents set by the Land Tribunal.

The legislation contains a number of exceptions and valuers are advised to always obtain the clients' solicitors' advice before preparing valuations based on expectation of enfranchisement.

Valuers may need to reflect the enfranchisement provisions in the following cases:

- **Valuations of Freehold interests when the tenant enjoys the right to enfranchise.**

- **Valuation of long leases where the tenant enjoys the right to enfranchise**

- **Assessment of enfranchisement price for freeholders and/or leaseholders.**

Because of the rights now vested in tenants of long leases of houses the market for such leases has been distorted as, too, has the market for freehold investment opportunities where lessees enjoy enfranchisement rights. The valuer in this specialist sub-market must have regard to market activity as well as to concepts built around enfranchisement prices.

Enfranchisement price is assessed under the 'original' method of the **1967 Act** if the RV is below **£1,000** in Greater London or **£500** elsewhere on the appropriate day.

1. 'Original Method'

The price to be paid on enfranchisement under *Section 9* of the **1967 Act** is the market value of the landlord's interest on the assumption that the tenant had acquired a 50-year extension of his lease under the Act. *Section 82* of the **1969 Housing Act** amended *Section 9* so that the tenant's own bid for the freehold is to be disregarded. This is markedly different to the assumptions under the **1993 Act**.

Example 10.4

A holds a ground lease of a London house at a ground rent of £20 per annum with 25 years unexpired. The fair rental value of the house is **£2,000 p.a.**
Freehold houses of a similar type have sold for **£25,000.** By comparison the bare site would appear to be worth **£10,000.** The rateable value was £450 on the appropriate day.

Advise A on the price he would have to pay to enfranchise.

Landlord's interest:

Ground rent	£20 p.a.	
YP for 25 years @ 8%★	10.675	
		£213.50

Reversion to modern ground rent:

Site value: £10,000
('cleared site' approach)

$$\text{Modern ground rent} \quad = \quad \frac{£10,000}{\text{YP perp. @ 8%}}$$

$$= \quad \frac{£10,000}{12.5}$$

$$= \quad £800 \text{ p.a.}$$

or Freehold value £25,000.

Value of site say 40% = £10,000 ('standing house' approach).

Modern ground rent as before =	£800 p.a.	
YP perp @ 8%★★	12.5	
PV £1 in 25 years @ 8%	0.146	
	1.825	
		£1,460
Estimated value		£1,673.50

★ The Lands Tribunal has always accepted yields of 6-9% on ground rents.

★★ Although the reversion is to a 50-year lease, followed by a reversion to a fair rent, the Tribunal has always accepted the assumption of a perpetual ground rent.

Example 10.5

Using the facts of *example 10.4* advise A if the site has a worth of £40,000 for redevelopment purposes.

Landlord's interest (as before):	£1,673.50

Plus: Marginal development value

£40,000 – £10,000	=	£30,000
PV £1 in 25 years @ 8%		0.146
		£4,380
		£6,053.50

Less: Compensation to tenant for loss of notional extended lease:

Rent received	£20,000 p.a.
minus modern ground rent	£800 p.a.
Profit rent	£1,200 p.a.
YP for 50 years @ 13% and 3% adj. tax @ 40%	6.9072
PV 1 in 25 years @ 13%	0.047102
	£390.42
Estimated value	**£5,663.08**

---

2. 'New Method' 1993 Act

The price under the **1993 Act,** and for those properties which qualified under earlier legislation but had a rateable value above £1,000 in Greater London or £500 elsewhere, will be calculated in accordance with *S. 9(1A)* of the 1967 Act. There is no assumption as to a 50-year extension and marriage value is to be taken into account. The latter is to be a minimum of 50% of the sum arising from the merger of the freehold and leasehold interests.

The landlord is also entitled to compensation for any loss or damage due to:

'*(a) any diminution in value of any interest of his in other property resulting from the acquisition of his interest in the house and premises, and*

(b) any other loss or damage which results from acquisition of his interest to the extent that it is referable to his ownership of any interest in other property'

This proviso means that a landlord can claim, among other things, for loss of development value.

A typical valuation would take the following form:

Pro forma for assessing Enfranchisement Price under the 1993 Act

Freeholder's Present Interest

Ground rent	£	
YP for __ years at __ %	_____	
		£A

Plus reversion to

(a) Open market Capital Value £

less
allowance for risk of tenant holding over under L & T 54 Part I[3] - £ _____

x PV £1 in __ years at __ % _____

or

(b) OMRV (not ground rent) £
YP perp at _ %
x PV £1 in _ years at 0% _____

Add reversionary value	£B
Value of Freehold £A + £B =	£C

Plus Marriage Value

Open Market Capital Value FH with vacant possession £D

Value of lessee's interest

Open Market Capital Value of Leasehold prior to Enfranchisement £E

or

Investment Value of Leasehold Interest being:

OMRV £

---

[3] Under the 1954 Act tenants of long leases had limited statutory rights to remain in occupation. The rent in the case of a tenancy terminating before 15 January 1999 would be a fair rent, after that date it would be to the open market rent. The valuer needs to adapt a most probable stance based on the facts.

Less ground rent	£
Profit rent	£

**YP 00 years at __% and
__% adj. for tax @ __**

$$£F$$

Then marriage value =

$$£D - (£C + £E \text{ or } £F) = \quad £$$

Enfranchisement Price =

**£C   + Minimum of 50%
of marriage value   =   £**

Plus

diminution in value of
Freeholder's other investments   £

Plus   Freeholder's Costs   £

£

Flats

Under the **Landlord and Tenant Act 1954 *Part I*** tenants of flats on long leases at low rents enjoyed minimal rights of security of tenure. The **1954 Act** is amended by the **Housing Act 1980,** and the **Local Government and Housing Act 1989** allowed such tenants to remain in possession as statutory tenants paying a *'fair'* rent if their tenancy expired before 15 January 1999 or open market rent if it expired after 1999.

However, under the **Landlord and Tenant Act 1987**, tenants of blocks of flats were granted the right to acquire the freehold in their property under limited conditions; namely

- **a prior right if the freeholder sought to sell the interest.**

- **in the event of the tenants proving mismanagement (as defined) by the freeholder.**

Qualifying conditions were restrictive but the basis of the price was the normal market value of the freeholder's interest subject to the tenancies.

The **1993 Act** has added to the 1987 provision to acquire by creating the right to 'collective enfranchisement' and by granting tenants the individual right to an extended lease of 90 years at a peppercorn rent subject to the payment of a premium to the freeholder.

The market response is that the complexity of the legislation may well dissuade tenants from exercising their rights of collective enfranchisement. The valuer is again advised to seek the client's solicitor's advice before preparing any valuations under the Act.

In the simplest collective enfranchisement scenario the enfranchisement price will be based upon:

- **The value of the freeholder's present interest subject to the long leases.**

  **This would be made up of :
  (i) Ground rents capitalised
  (ii) Reversion to Open Market Capital Value of the flats deferred for the unexpired terms of the leases, or capitalised market rents deferred for the unexpired terms of the lease.**

- **Marriage value of a minimum of 50% being the difference between:**

  (i) Freehold Vacant Possession value of the whole property and

  (ii) The value of the encumbered freehold interest as above plus the value of the leasehold interests in the flats.

- **Plus any Diminution in value of Freeholder's other interests, including Development Value.**

- **Plus costs.**

Where not all the tenants qualify or wish to participate, and/or where other property is included in the enfranchise or where some units are leased back to the freeholder, the calculation becomes far more complex.

The Housing Act 1996 further amends the 1987 Act and rights of enfranchisement. It alters the low rent test; extends rights to tenancies failing the low rent test if the lease exceeds 35 years; redefines the basis for valuing the freeholders' interest and for calculating premiums for the extension of leases.

Readers are referred to specialist texts in this area of valuation and to Guidance Note 15 (GN 15) in the Appraisal and Valuation Manual (RICS 1995).

Summary

10

When undertaking valuations of business property valuers must note:

- Tenants may be protected by the Landlord & Tenant Act 1954.

- Tenants may have the right to compensation under the Landlord and Tenant Act 1927.

- Tenants undertaking improvements are entitled to receive the rental benefit of these improvements for a minimum period of 21 years.

- Tenants may be entitled to claim compensation if repossession occurs.

When undertaking valuations of residential property valuers must note:

- The market for tenanted residential property is influenced by the legislation that provides varying degrees of security to tenants on short leases and enfranchisement rights to tenants on long leases.

- The valuer must, in conjunction with the client's solicitor, identify the nature of the tenancy, and the specific statutory rights of landlord and tenant, before offering any valuation advice.

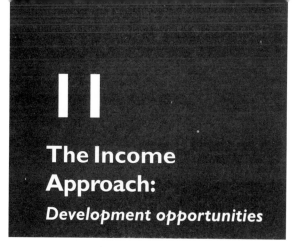

11

The Income Approach:

Development opportunities

In relation to the *'income approach'* residual valuations and development appraisals require the valuer to assess and capitalise the potential income stream from a proposed development which does not yet exist.

Development potential may be released following an input of capital:

- **In the case of a bare or underdeveloped site where planning permission for development has been, or is likely to be, obtained.**

- **In the case of an existing building for refurbishment or where planning permission has been, or is likely to be, obtained for a change of use.**

- **In the case of an existing building where planning permission has been, or is likely to be, granted for its demolition and replacement.**

The preferred valuation approach must remain one of direct capital comparison.

However, it is in the market for property with development potential that the most difficulty in finding good comparable evidence is experienced. In the investment market, the income approach is the most suitable and widely used alternative to direct capital comparison.

In the market for property with development potential an adaptation of the income approach, known as the 'residual method', is the most widely used technique.

The residual method

The conventional approach to a residual valuation is based upon a very simple concept. The value of the completed project less all of the costs incurred in the project is equal to the residual valu,. *or:*

$$\boxed{\begin{array}{c}\text{Gross}\\\text{Development}\\\text{Value}\end{array}} - \boxed{\begin{array}{c}\text{All Costs}\\\text{and}\\\text{Profit}\end{array}} = \begin{array}{c}\textbf{RESIDUAL}\\\textbf{VALUE}\end{array}$$

The value of the completed project is usually known as the *Gross Development Value*. This is the capital value of the finished development and is usually found by capitalisation of the projected income from the scheme.

The costs of development include all of the costs of construction, including professional fees (Architects, Quantity Surveyors, etc.), the cost of borrowing the capital to undertake the scheme, and the developer's profit. The surplus that remains after deducting all of these costs from the projected value is the residual value of the bare site or site and buildings to be redeveloped.

Example 11.1

A plot of land has planning permission for the erection of **7,000 m²** (gross) of office space on five floors.

The development will be completed in **2 years** from now and rents are expected to average **£120 per m²** (net).

Building costs are expected to average **£400 per m²**, excluding fees.

Prepare a valuation to advise a prospective developer of the maximum bid to be made for the site.

(Comparable evidence of prices obtained for similar sites is not available.)

Gross development value:

7,000 m² (gross) x 85%*   = (say) 6,000 m² (net)

6,000 m² @ £120 per m² p.a. = £720,000 p.a.
YP perp. @ 7%   14.29

                                      £10,285,714
                                      ————————

*Reduction for non-usable space of 15%.

Example 11.1 (cont.)

Gross development value c/o: £10,285,714

Less costs:

(a) Building costs:
7,000 m² @
£400 per m²   £2,800,000

(b) Architects and
quantity surveyors
fees @ 12.5 % of
building costs   £350,000

Total building costs:
                £3,150,000

(c) Finance costs:
15% p.a. for 2 years
on 50% of total
building costs
(£1,575,000 x (1.15)²)
- £1,575,000 =   £507,937

(d) Legal fees,
estate agents' fees
and advertising
upon disposal:

@ 2% GDV =   £205,714

(e) Promotion say: £50,000

(f) Developer's profit:
@ 15% GDV   £1,542,857

Total costs: £5,456,508

Residual: £4,829,206

Let site value = x

Legal and valuation fees on
site purchase @ 3% = 0.03x

Total accumulated debt after
2 years @ 15% p.a. = 1.03x(1.15)²

1.03 x(1.15)² = £4,829,207
1.362x = £4,829,207

Site value = £3,545,673

The use of the residual method varies according to the stage of the development process. The above calculation is very generalised in its assumptions and the technique is often criticised as a method of determining land value.

Where it is used to assess the value of bare sites for rating or statutory purposes it is often divorced from the realities of actual development and has been criticised by the Lands Tribunal, whose members denounced the method as *'far from a certain guide to values'* (*Cuckmere Brick Co. Ltd and Fawke* v. *Mutual Finance Ltd (1971) EG 218:1571*) and have suggested that *'once valuers are let loose upon residual valuations, however honest the valuers and however reasoned their arguments, they can prove almost anything'* (*First Garden City Ltd* v. *Letchworth Garden City Corporation (1986) EG 200:123*).

However, as will be explained later in this chapter, where the technique is used to appraise projects where land has been purchased for a known sum and a quantity surveyor has provided accurate cost information the technique is more robust.

Example 11.1 can be used to illustrate the dangers of the generalised assumptions built into the simple residual valuation.

For example the finance for development is calculated on only **50%** of the total construction costs to reflect the phased drawing down of borrowing over the development period. This assumption will hold true if the payments to contractors follow an equal distribution pattern similar to that shown in *Figure 11.1* for the traditional office building. However, if the building involved a portal steel frame which brings the development costs forward, the expenditure pattern may change to that shown in *Figure 11.1* for an industrial building. This destroys the 50% assumption and an expenditure of this pattern should assume funding on around 75% of the total building costs.

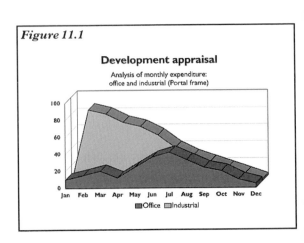

Figure 11.1

Development appraisal

Analysis of monthly expenditure:
office and industrial (Portal frame)

The need for accurate cash flow based projections of building costs are therefore essential for accurate residual valuations.

In addition to being subject to generalised assumptions the final value is very sensitive to small variations in key variables - particularly the yield, rental values and building costs.

To illustrate this problem note the effects on the residual value calculated in *example 11.1* with the changes to the key variables as shown in *Figure 11.2*.

Figure 11.2

Illustration of the sensitivity of the residual site value calculated in Example 11.1 to changes in key variables.

Original site value	£3,545,673
Site value when yield only increased by 0.5%	£3,120,825
Site value when rents only increased by 10%	£4,184,426
Site value when building costs only increased by 10 %	£3,280,977

A further problem facing valuers has been the difficulty of handling an increasing number of variables such as VAT, fees, etc. in the valuation exercise when carried out manually. Currently many development surveyors use spreadsheets or computer software packages which do not remove the basic criticism but their flexibility and speed of operation enables valuers to check each appraisal for sensitivity and avoid generalisations in the assumptions to achieve greater confidence in their opinions of value.

Example 11.1 has been reappraised using a package prepared and marketed by Circle Systems[1] which is one of several programs now available to valuers.

The report produced by the system is set out in **Appendix C**, together with notes on the assumptions and methodologies used.

[1] See *Estates Gazette* No.9524 pp.70-73, 17 June 1995 for a review of the Circle System by John Kirkwood.

The traditional residual approach can therefore be significantly improved with the application of computers through sensitivity analysis and more complex treatment of the underlying assumptions.

However, although packages such as Circle allow for complex phasing of developments by the linking of parts and areas of schemes together they still rely heavily on assumptions made about the distribution of payments and receipts.

The need for adoption of the cash flow approach

Cash flow modelling is now a standard feature of most development appraisal systems and its use is encouraged to counter the difficulties and criticisms described above.

These are especially useful when dealing with large phased developments such as business parks or major residential schemes. The cash flow approach also allows the valuer to take into account the financial status of the client and to provide a more accurate and realistic financial appraisal. For example, joint ventures or schemes involving equity finance may require differential interest rates and complex flows of income which cannot be accommodated in a traditional appraisal.

As the valuation profession is being encouraged to be more conscious of the needs of its clients the cash flow approach should be more widely adopted to ensure that the financial situation of the client is accurately modelled within the appraisal.

The cash flow approach explained

Testing the traditional residual results against cash flow models suggests that the greater variability occurs with phased developments such as low-rise residential schemes where cash in-flows coincide with cash outflows. The variation in result is less pronounced with the relatively simple one-off development, especially those with a project term of 12 months or less.

In the absence of alternative development schemes, it is almost certain that the cost of borrowing money will be at least as high as the rate of interest that the developer could earn on excess funds. It is therefore reasonable to conclude that the developer should pay off debts as soon as income is produced by the development.

The developer will pay considerable attention to his likely cash flow and his likely maximum borrowing requirement over the building period. A cash-flow table will provide full information concerning these two points, and will allow for the accurate estimation of finance charges. In very complex multiuse schemes the development surveyor and quantity surveyors may be able to use cash flow analysis to re-schedule the detailed timing of development to improve the overall return on capital.

Systems such as Circle allow the user to construct a monthly cash flow from the original residual valuation which can then be edited to reflect more accurate data provided by quantity surveyors or to explore the effects of adjusting the cash flow. The program provides the user with a full DCF analysis of the project and can also be converted into a Lotus 1-2-3 spreadsheet file.

The example below illustrates the cash flow approach using a simple manual calculation:

Example 11.2

A site has the benefit of planning permission for the erection of a block of **20** flats, totalling **1,100** square metres of space.

The value of each completed flat is estimated to be **£100,000**, using comparable transactions, but flat prices are expected to continue to rise at **5%** per annum.

Building costs are estimated at **£800** per m^2 and are expected to rise at **0.5%** per month. It is expected that **5** flats will be sold in each of months **9–12** and that building costs will be evenly distributed over a 12-month building period.

Architects' and quantity surveyors' fees will be payable in two instalments in months **6** and **12** at **10%** of the building costs.

Agents' and solicitors' fees will be charged on sale at **1%** of the sale price of each flat, and the developer will require a profit of **15%** of the sale price.

Advise the developer as to the maximum bid for the site.

1   **Flat prices are increasing at 5% per annum or 0.4% per month.**

In month 9,
5 flats will sell for £103,660 each
=   £518,300

In month 10,
5 flats will sell for £104,070 each
=   £520,350

In month 11,
5 flats will sell for £104,500 each
=   £522,500

In month 12,
5 flats will sell for £104,910 each
=   £524,550

2   **Building costs are estimated at £800 per m^2, spread evenly over 12 months, rising at 0.5% per month.**

**Total building costs for the entire block of £880,000 divided by 12 gives a cost of £73,330 in month 1 which will increase by 0.5% in month 2, etc.
This results in a building cost flow of :**

month 1:	£73,330
month 2:	£73,700
month 3:	£74,060
month 4:	£74,440
month 5:	£74,810

**in month 6 fees are payable on the costs to date at a rate of 10%
(10% of £445,490 = £44,549)**

month 6:	£75,180 + £44,549
month 7:	£75,560
month 8:	£75,940

**in month 9 the first of the sales of 5 flats is achieved adding fees @ 1% and profit @15% of the sale price to the costs
(1% of £518,300 = £5,183 *and*
15% of £518,300 = £77,745)**

month 9:	£76,320 + £5,183 + £77,745
month 10:	£76,700 + £5,204 + £78,053

(calculated as above but on month 10 sale prices)

month 11:	£77,080 + £5,225 + £78,375, (see above)
month 12:	£77,470 + £5,246 + £78,683 + £45,900 (Arch/QS fees @ 10% costs months 7–12)

Example 11.2 (cont.)

From this information a cash-flow table can be constructed incorporating the effects of interest charges at 1% per month.

Month	Benefits(£)	Costs (£)	Net (£)	Capital (£) Outstanding	Interest (£)
1	-	73,330	-73,330	-73,333	733
2	-	73,700	-73,700	-147,760[1]	1,480
3	-	74,060	-74,060	-223,301	2,233
4	-	74,440	-74,440	-299,974	3,000
5	-	74,810	-74,810	-377,784	3,778
6	-	119,729	-119,729	-501,291	5,013
7	-	75,560	-75,560	-581,863	5,819
8	-	75,940	-75,940	-663,622	6,636
9	518,300	159,248	+359,052	-311,206	3,112
10	520,350	159,957	+360,393	+46,075[2]	+ 461
11	522,500	160,680	+361,820	+408,355	+4,084
12	524,450	207,299	+317,251	+729,690[3]	

Residual = £729,690

Let site value = x,

let fees on site purchase = 3% = $0.03x$.

Then

$1.03x$ + interest for 12 months at 1% per month

= £729,690

$1.03x(1.01)\ 12$	=	£729,690
$1.03x(1.1268)$	=	£729,690
$1.1606x$	=	£729,690
x	=	£628,718

Site value = £628,718

Notes:

.   Already outstanding from month 1 is a debt of £73,330, and an interest charge of £733. Added to these is a new loan of £73,700, the total being £147,763 on which the interest charge for month 2 will be levied.

.   This figure if positive, as the total debt of £311,206 plus £3,112 interest is more than repaid by the receipt in month 10 of £360,393. Hence a surplus of £46,075 remains. This can be invested to earn interest at 1% per month.

.   This final surplus remains after paying all costs except the cost of the site itself, and fees and finance on its purchase. Calculated as before, the developer's maximum site bid is £628,718.

Example 11.3

In *example 11.2* the cash flow has been undertaken on a terminal value basis.

In this example the same development is valued using a present value approach.

Month	Benefits (£)	Costs (£)	Net (£)	PV£1 @ 1% Outstanding	PV
1	-	73,330	-73,330	0.99001	-72,604
2	-	73,700	-73,700	0.98030	-72,248
3	-	74,060	-74,060	0.97060	-71,882
4	-	74,440	-74,440	0.96098	-71,535
5	-	74,810	-74,810	0.95147	-71,179
6	-	119,729	-119,729	0.94205	-112,270
7	-	75,560	-75,560	0.93272	-70,476
8	-	75,940	-75,940	0.92348	-70,129
9	518,300	159,248	+359,052	0.91434	+328,296
10	520,350	159,957	+360,393	0.90529	+326,259
11	522,500	160,680	+361,820	0.89632	+324,308
12	524,450	207,299	+317,251	0.88745	+281,544

$$\text{NPV} = £647,563$$

Let site value $= x$,

let fees on site purchase $= 3\% = 0.03x$.

Then

$1.03x$	$=$	£647,563
x	$=$	£628,702 (variation from example 11.2 due to rounding).

Site value   =   £628,702

An important prerequisite for a cash flow approach is an accurate scheduling of construction activities. This uses network analysis, or critical path analysis whereby critical sequential events become the critical path and other non-sequential events can be scheduled to run in parallel; in turn some of the parallel costs may also be sequential.

The end result is the production of a project network with a start and finish date with all the intermediate critical dates. The actual costs can then be estimated and transferred to a cash flow. The two together will then become part of the project manager's management tools for monitoring the development programme. Such an approach, if applied to *example 11.1*, would highlight the need to reduce the construction period in order to reduce the high finance costs. The need to reduce finance costs in periods of high interest rates has played its part in developing innovative *'fast track'* construction techniques.

Cash flows and residuals can be calculated on a current cost basis, or on a future cost basis building in variations in rents as well as variations in labour and materials. None of the computerised sophistications can, however, overcome the problem that the acceptability of residual and cash flow development appraisal methods rests not with their rationale, which is irrefutable, but with the quality of the evidence used by the appraisal team to estimate costs and benefits.

Viability studies

Early in this chapter it was stated that the residual method of valuation is based upon a simple equation:

Gross development value

- development costs (including profit)

= Residual value

The aim of the residual valuation is to find the unknown in this equation, the residual value. Often, however, a prospective developer will be aware of the likely site cost and consequently of the cost of fees and finance, either because the vendor has stated an asking price, or because negotiations have revealed the minimum figure which the vendor will accept. This is particularly likely in the case of an existing building which is to be improved or replaced.

In such a case the single unknown in the equation can now become the developer's profit. The aim of viability study is to assess the profit likely to be made from a development scheme, given the cost or asking price of the subject site.

Computer packages, for example CIRCLE, allow the user to select from a drop down menu whether the system is to calculate residual land value or developer's profit. The input screens and processing are then adjusted according to the user's selection.

The cash flow approach is advocated by most software manufacturers, if not valuers, because of its greater accuracy and ability to model the payment of contractors, architects and finance charges much closer to the actual payment profile than the smoothed assumptions often contained in a traditional appraisal.

In addition a detailed cash flow approach allows the modelling of complex financial arrangements that may often underpin major property developments around the world. For example, equity sharing and joint ventures where the interest rates may differ for each project partner depending upon their risk profile.

The cash-flow table is particularly adaptable as a viability study and the authors recommend that valuers using appraisal software always utilise a cash flow approach.

Example 11.4 Using the facts of example 11.2, advise the developer of the potential profit if the total cost of the site, including fees, is £500,000

Month	Benefits(£)	Costs (£)	Net (£)	Capital (£) Outstanding	Interest (£)
1	-	573,330	-573,330	-573,333	5,733
2	-	73,700	-73,700	-652,763	6,528
3	-	74,060	-74,060	-733,351	7,334
4	-	74,440	-74,440	-815,124	8,151
5	-	74,810	-74,810	-898,086	8,981
6	-	119,729	-119,729	-1,026,796	10,013
7	-	75,560	-75,560	-1,112,623	11,126
8	-	75,940	-75,940	-1,199,690	11,997
9	518,300	81,503	+436,797	-774,890	7,749
10	520,350	81,904	+438,446	-344,193	3,442
11	522,500	82,305	+440,195	+92,561	+ 926
12	524,450	128,616	+395,934	+489,420	

£489,420 represents the developer's profit

This can be expressed as $\frac{£489,420}{£2,085,700} = 23.47\%$ of GDV; or as $\frac{£489,420}{£1,515,897} = 32.29\%$ of total costs.

The residual method has become a straightforward DCF exercise. Nevertheless, there will still be areas of variability, and the criticism that the result is sensitive to changes in inputs remains. The next stage is therefore to incorporate probability measures in the analysis *(see Chapter 13)*. Rents, costs and interest charges may be weighted according to the valuer's expectation of possible changes, such an approach being eminently suited to computer analysis.

Q **Assess the residual site value of a parcel of land suitable for 5,000m² of office space .**

The scheme will take 12 months to complete. Rents are £200 per m² (net lettable area).
Construction costs are £400 per metre².
The scheme would sell on a 7% basis and finance is available at 14%.
Promotion costs are budgeted at £40,000.
Letting fees are agreed at 15% of the first year's rent.
Purchases costs are 1.75%, site purchase costs 1.5%, stamp duty 1%.
Agents' fees are 1% of GDV.
Developer's profit required is 15% of GDV.

Summary

11

- Residual valuations or development appraisals are used to assess the value of land and buildings with latent development potential.

- The method is based upon established economic principles and the method itself is logical.

- However, the accuracy of the residual method relies on the valuer's ability to estimate all of the variables within the calculation. The costs and benefits must be carefully estimated with respect to the development market, using hard evidence where possible to support the rents, capitalisation rates and building costs adopted.

- Development appraisal is an ideal application for information technology, allowing the valuer to assess the sensitivity of the valuation to changes in the underlying variables.

- The final opinion of development value should, wherever possible, be checked against comparable market evidence. However, as each development opportunity is unique in terms of its highest and best use, market comparison will only provide the valuer with a basic 'yardstick' with which to cross reference the appraisal.

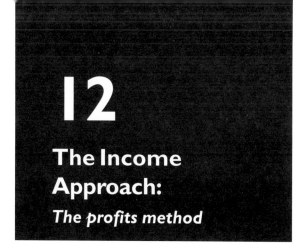

12

The Income Approach:

The profits method

Introduction

Where comparable rental transactions are not available, it may be necessary to adopt a profits method of valuation based on the audited accounts of a business. The rationale for the approach is based on the economic theory that the rental value of a property is a function of its earning capacity, productivity or profitability.

For most commercial and industrial properties comparable transactions are available and rental values can be ascertained by analysing recent market behaviour. Comparables will not normally be available when a property enjoys an element of monopoly. A monopoly may be either factual or legal. Property with an element of factual monopoly might include a seaside car park, a railway station kiosk, a racecourse and an amusement park. In these cases little, if any, competition will exist. A legal monopoly, however, may arise where a business can only operate with a licence and where perhaps only one licence is issued for a large area - this could be the case with a licence to sell alcohol.

In addition, the profits method may be used to value a business property where accounts are available and where the comparative method cannot be employed easily because of a lack of satisfactory evidence. Examples might include hotels, theatres and cinemas.

In outline, the profits (or accounts) method of valuation requires an estimate of the gross profits that can be earned by the business in the property. All normal working expenses are then deducted excluding any rent or loan interest payments on the property. The resulting figure, known as the 'divisible balance', represents the amount available for the tenant's share (or remuneration) and the landlord's share. Thus, a deduction

of the tenant's share leaves the surplus for payment to the landlord in the form of an annual rent.

Example 12.1:

A simplified model of the profits method of valuation takes the following form:

(a)	**Gross profit**		
	Estimated Gross Earnings		£220,000
	Less purchase of goods		£120,000
			£100,000

(b)	*Less*		
	Working Expenses		
	(Excluding Rent)	£70,000	
	Divisible balance		£30,000

(c)	*Less*		
	Tenant's Share:		
	Interest on Capital	£5,000	
	Remuneration	£15,000	
			£20,000

(d)	**Surplus available as rent**	=	£10,000 p.a.
	(payable to landlord)		

This rental, derived from accounts, can then be capitalised to arrive at an opinion of open market value.

Notes

(a) **Gross Profit**

The valuer will normally examine the last complete set of accounts produced, before the date of valuation, together with the preceding two or three years' accounts. The aim is to determine a level of profit that can reasonably be expected in the future, reflecting any past trends or fluctuations in the profit. The actual accounts may not always be a good indicator of the earning capacity of the property as, for example, the current business may have been operated by either a workaholic or a sloathful character lacking in business acumen. The aim should be to determine the profits which a tenant of reasonable competence could make from occupation of the property.

(b) **Working Expenses**

These will include such items as wages and insurance, heat and light, telephone, cleaning, advertising, printing, postage and stationery, insurance, accountancy charges and depreciation of fixtures, fittings and equipment. As the final balance is to represent the surplus available as rental value for the property, any rent that is actually paid is not deducted as a working expense. This includes any ground rental payment and/or any interest payable by the operator on loans.

(c)   Tenant's Share

The deduction for the tenant's share represents:

- Interest on the tenant's own capital tied up in the business; that is, capital for the purchase of fixtures and fittings, equipment furnishings, stock, cash, etc.; and

- Remuneration for the tenant's time and effort in running the business. The term *'tenant'* in this context may be the owner occupier. The deduction represents the *'opportunity cost'* of capital and labour (very simply, salary or wages).

(d)   Rent as a Surplus

The method of valuation illustrates that the rental value of all land and property is derived from earning capacity or productivity. The valuer is required to calculate rental value from the viewpoint of a potential occupier of the property. In contrast, the comparative method merely requires the valuer to study the outcome of negotiated transactions between several landlords and tenants. Nevertheless, it must be remembered that the tenants in these cases will probably have prepared a profits type of calculation to convince themselves that the rent agreed can be paid out of the surplus earnings of the proposed business.

The RICS Guidance Note 7 *'Trading Related Valuations and Goodwill'* confirms these general principles, in particular it states that:

'The valuation method adopted by the valuer should reflect the approach generally used by the market for the particular type of property. Different methods, including the profits method, the discounted cash flow (DCF), analysis of comparable transactions or a combination of these will be appropriate for different types and sizes of property.

In arriving at the valuation, the valuer should analyse and review the trading accounts for the current and previous years and projections for future years ... The accounts of a particular property will only show how that property is trading under the particular management at the time. The task of the valuer is to assess the fair maintainable level of trade and future profitability that can be achieved by an operator of the business, upon which a potential purchaser would be likely to base his offer ... it is particularly important to be able to identify closely the type of

person or entity which constitutes a potential purchaser ... The determination of the capitalisation multiplier or discount rate to be applied in arriving at the capital value of the property relies upon the experience and judgement of the valuer ...'

The **British Association of Hotel Accountants (1993)** confirms these general notes of guidance in relation to hotels, 'Hotels should be valued by reference to their recent/current performance and future trading potential. This is achieved by the "Income Capitalisation" approach which seeks to assess value by reference to projected net cash flows. It requires the application of a capitalisation factor which may be either a multiple of marketable earnings or a Discount Rate.'

There has been strong criticism of the BAHA view on the use of a full DCF approach from certain sections of the leisure industry. It is argued that DCF is a technique for assessing worth to a specific individual rather than for assessing market value and that the proper approach is the simple process of capitalising average or 'maintainable' earnings. DCF is considered to be more appropriate for appraisal or analysis of development projects rather than existing operational entities. As is often the case in discussion on valuation methods all opinions have their strengths and weaknesses.

The appropriateness of the use of the two alternatives in the specialist area of valuation of leisure and other businesses sold as operational entities might be summarised as follows:

- **Define bases of valuation, OMV, ERP, etc.**

- **Analyse the market and the behaviour of buyers and sellers in the market.**

- **Identify the most probable type/class of purchaser having regard to property size and use.**

- **Adopt the appropriate market valuation technique.**

In practice smaller properties in this category, such as small family hotels, retirement homes, pubs, might be valued by a form of direct comparison or quasi-profits approach where there is strong market evidence. Analysis of the relationship between expected maintainable earnings and **OMV**, price, **ERP** provides a realistic view of the probability of a sale being achieved at the figure obtained, simply by relating the absolute return and rate of return to the level of return a rational person would consider to be adequate from such an expenditure.

In the case of larger properties which would attract core operators in the sector the valuer will need to assess the level of maintainable profit, as previously described, and to apply a multiplier based on the valuer's knowledge and experience of the marketplace.

In the case of substantive properties or new developments, where there will be less direct evidence in the market and where purchasers and investors are driven by current and future profitability, there is a strong case for a full DCF valuation.

The strongest case for DCF seems to lie where a new enterprise is planned and where there is a need for a viability study. The crux of the problem here is that new schemes generally take a number of years to mature to their full potential. A parallel can be drawn here with, say, a large residential development or a major retail scheme where sales and/or lettings will take a number of years to complete. The result is a fluctuating cash flow which can be realistically estimated by the key players based on their experience of similar schemes in other localities. The valuer, in seeking to mirror the market behaviour, should therefore follow market practice.

The difficulty is that having accepted the argument for using a form of projected cash flow and discounting techniques for assessing **OMV/ERP** for substantive new schemes there seems to be no logical argument for rejecting its use in circumstances where such cash flows should be capable of more accurate measurement - that is, where a maintainable business is supported by current accounts.

The argument for the use of the simpler *'income capitalisation'* is that it is derived direct from the market but, as has been seen in the case of investment property, this approach is an implied approach where increasingly lenders and purchasers are seeking a more explicit assessment of the return to be achieved in the short to medium term.

'The DCF approach is more rigorous in that it requires consideration to be given to the dynamic nature of the future income of the hotel, inflation and interest rates. However, it requires skill, expertise, experience and an understanding of the approach adapted by potential operators/purchasers' (**BAHA 1993**).

The BAHA suggested that the valuer should look at future earnings and cash flow over a period of ten years with an estimate of reversionary value in the tenth year. Readers are referred to the BAHA publication: *Recommended Practice for the Valuation of Hotels,* for a more detailed discussion of the DCF approach to Hotel valuations and to the considerations of *'net free cash flows'* and *'maintainable earnings'*.

Valuers in this market segment must be experienced and will often specialise in a very narrow sub-market as detailed market knowledge of the players and the *'business activity'* are such critical elements.

(The authors are grateful to M. Green for permission to use extracts from his Sheffield Hallam University course material in this chapter.)

The Profits Method:

This method and quasi-profits methods are the preferred methods for the valuation of property bought and sold as operational entities such as hotels, public houses, petrol filling stations and most real estate used for the leisure industry.

Each segment of the leisure industry is so specialist that only a few valuers have the knowledge and experience to act in the marketplace.

The method relies on :

- specialist business knowledge and the ability to read accounts.

- an ability to assess sustainable profits and /or net benefits as a cash flow over a 5-10 year period.

- a thorough knowledge of the major operators in the specialist sector.

- an ability to convert sustainable profit or net cash flow into an expression of capital value using capitalisation techniques or discounted cash flow.

- broad comparators, such as price per bedroom, which can be used to gauge probable values in an active market should not be used as the sole method of valuation.

13

Investment analysis:

The other side of the valuation coin is the analysis of property investment opportunities. This requires careful consideration of the relationship between the known and expected returns and costs. Expected returns can only be estimated by a consideration of the future. This necessarily introduces the valuer to the concepts of risk.

Risk and uncertainty in valuation

A property investment is an exchange of capital today (current purchasing power) for future benefits. These future benefits may be in the form of income or capital growth, or a combination of both. As indicated earlier in the text, this requires the valuer to have some regard for the future and, as has so frequently been said before, the only certain thing about the future is its lack of certainty. When an investor purchases future rights he has accepted *'risk'*.

Risk and uncertainty in everyday usage are taken to be one and the same, but for our purposes there is an essential difference. Risk is used in those cases where a probability or weight can be assigned to alternative expectations' and uncertainty is used to mean that no measure of certainty (probability) can be assigned to any of the alternative expectations.

When a valuer describes a property investment as being *'risky'*, he/she is implying some relative measure, further that by such comparison:

- *The rents expected in the future may not be realised, i.e. the rental growth will be less than anticipated.*

- *Increases in rent will not occur at the time expected or the property may become vacant and take some time to re-let.*

- *The principal sum involved may not be realisable, may not increase with time or may fall with time.*

- *Some market money rates may move against the property, i.e. an increase in rates will result in a fall in value, ceteris paribus.*

- *Other property investments will out-perform the subject property.*

- *The long-term property investment may be out-performed by short-term investments.*

As previously noted these property risks may be systematic or unsystematic. Tenant risk, sector risk, planning risk, and legal risk are unsystematic and, in a portfolio context, risk reduction can be achieved through diversification. Taxation, legislation, structural risks are more systematic and cannot be actively reduced through diversification. But at an individual property level the investor is concerned in minimising risk, and in valuation respects the valuer is seeking to reflect the market's view of the risk relating to a specific property.

In terms of the valuation of a property valuers will seek to reduce riskiness through thorough analysis. Thus the more detailed the research into current tenants, the physical structure, political opinion, regional economics, etc., the more able the valuer is to express his opinion of OMV. The less certain the valuer and the market are in respect of all these factors then the more risky the property will appear to be.

For one or more reasons a valuer may wish to reflect this greater risk in the valuation. A common approach is to increase the discount rate. The use of a **Risk Adjusted Discount Factor (RADF)** is still the most popular market approach, but the objective view of the valuer is largely a subjective or intuitive adjustment based on experience; that is, upon market knowledge.

Such an adjustment is inevitably arbitrary and by adding to the discount rate one is implying that the risk itself grows over time. For example, a property producing an income of £100 **per annum** might be valued in perpetuity at **10%**, giving a total present value of **£1,000**. Assume a similar property is to be valued but certain risks suggest an increase in the rate to **20%**. The present worth is £500. Initially this may seem perfectly acceptable but the present value of any income stream can be considered to be the sum of the present values of each year's income. This means that the PV of £100 after 1 year at **10%** and **20%** is respectively £90 and £83, a reduction of 7.78%; but deferred 40 years the £100 is worth **£2.20** and **£0.06** respectively today, a reduction of **97.27%**. Thus by comparison, between the investments, it is being inferred that the risk attached to each **£100** is increasing at an increasing rate.

To overcome this problem one approach adopted is to make three estimates of the future - the best estimate, the most likely, and the worst - and to estimate the probability of each occurring. This approach, however, ignores all the other possible outcomes. In fact, estimates should be attempted for all the probable outcomes.

The following section is reprinted with amendments from an article which first appeared in the *Estates Gazette, 234:29-31*, entitled '**The investment method - an objective approach**' by **P.J. Byrne and D.H. Mackmin**[1]. (Reference in the original to square feet has been amended to square metres).

In preparing the fourth edition thought was given to deleting or amending this 20 year old reference but it has stood the test of time for it was not until the late 1980's and 1990's that this general theory was developed by *Baum and Crosby* (1988) revisited by *Dubben and Sayce* (1991) and characteristically explored by *Brown* (1991).

'You are instructed by a banking organisation to prepare a valuation for mortgage purposes of a new owner-occupied office building.

Having measured and surveyed the building and checked your findings with the architect's plans, you are satisfied that the building contains a total lettable area of 12,000 sq. m. It is your considered opinion, having regard to all the relevant factors, that the property would let at a figure between £2.50 and £3.00 per sq. metre and would sell at an investment on the basis of a **5-6.5%** rate.

After further deliberation a preliminary valuation is prepared:

Area:	12,000 sq.m.
Full rental value:	£31,000 (approx £2.60 per sq.m.)
Yield:	6%
Income	£31,000
YP perp @ 6%	16.67
	£516,770

[1] Reproduced by kind permission of the Estates Gazette Ltd., and without any updating of figures.

In time, this may be demonstrated to be a valid solution.

An experienced valuer may well be able to reduce the range of rents and yields, but in the absence of absolute levels for either of these factors any valuation must entail some consideration of the variability which is possible over the range within which the eventual selection will be made.

The ranges suggested for rents in the example is **£2.50** to **£3.00** per sq. m. and for yield **5-6.5%**. Given these limits, and taking steps of, say, **5p** and **0.25%** on the yield, *Table 13.1* shows the variations in final valuation obtained by altering these two variables within their respective ranges.

Table 13.1

Rental (£ sq.m.)	Yield (%)						
	5.0	5.25	5.50	5.75	6.0	6.25	6.50
2.50	600000	571429	545455	521739	500000	480000	461539
2.55	612000	582857	556364	532174	510000	489600	470769
2.60	624000	594286	567273	542609	520000	499200	480000
2.65	636000	605714	578182	553044	530000	598800	489231
2.70	648000	617143	589091	564378	540000	518400	498462
2.75	660000	628572	600000	573913	550000	528000	507693
2.80	672000	640000	610909	584348	560000	537600	516923
2.85	684000	651429	621819	594783	570000	547200	526154
2.90	696000	662858	632728	605218	580000	556800	535385
2.95	708000	674286	643637	615653	590000	560400	544616
3.00	720000	685715	654546	626087	600000	576000	553847

There are 77 possible '*outcomes*' in *Table 13.1*.

Which one is correct?

Are any of them correct?

Can the valuer justify his best assessment - which is clearly only one of a much larger number of possible solutions - because this selection also implies the conscious rejection of, in this case, at least 76 other values?

Is it possible to use the information at our disposal to arrive at a closer estimate of the likely value of this property?

Initially, a range of value between **£461,539** and **£720,000** may be noted. The valuer in his best assessment has subjectively and/or objectively endeavoured to reduce this range. The approach suggested here merely formalises this process.

If an analysis of file data is made it may be possible to determine the relative frequency of occurrence for the various rental levels between the minimum of £2.50 and maximum £3.00.

Let us suppose that for this example such an analysis is possible for 50 comparable transactions: the results can then be tabulated, as in *Table 13.2*. This gives a good indication of the probability of occurrence of the various possible rentals presupposing, of course, that the 50 transactions are truly comparable. If insufficient data are available it may be necessary to use other methods, as described below.

Table 13.2

Rental (£ sq.m.)	Frequency	% Occurrence	Probability
2.50	1	2.0	0.02
2.55	2	4.0	0.04
2.60	5	10.0	0.10
2.65	6	12.0	0.12
2.70	7	14.0	0.14
2.75	9	18.0	0.18
2.80	7	14.0	0.14
2.85	6	12.0	0.12
2.90	5	10.0	1.10
2.95	1	2.0	0.02
3.00	1	2.0	0.02
Total	**50**	**100.0**	**1.00**

Each rental may now be *'weighted'* by multiplying it by its probability of occurrence and summated to give one overall expected rental value, each element being included in proportion to the probability of its occurrence (i.e. the total of the individual answers to these calculations gives the rent that can be expected on the basis of the available data).

All possible rental values have been built into the result; none are actually discarded at this stage, but their importance is now related to the known frequency of occurrence of each rental level. Since the distribution of probabilities in *Table 13.2* is almost symmetric, then the expected rental will be in the centre of the distribution. In this case it is £2,746 (£2.75).

The expected rental obtained here is specific to the distribution shown in *Table 13.2*; other shapes of probability distribution can occur, and when this happens the expected value will be different. An analysis of transactions, for example, might show a different frequency and probability pattern, as in *Table 13.3*.

It is not unreasonable to argue that in each of these distributions the 'modal value' - that rental having the largest observed frequency of occurrence - could be taken as representative, since it is the most likely value. The application of this average measure would at least imply that a full analysis had been carried out.

Table 13.3

Rental (£ sq.m.)	Frequency	% Occurrence	Probability
2.50	2	4.0	0.04
2.55	5	10.0	0.10
2.60	20	40.0	0.40
2.65	10	20.0	0.20
2.70	4	8.0	0.08
2.75	2	4.0	0.04
2.80	3	6.0	0.06
2.85	2	4.0	0.04
2.90	1	2.0	0.02
2.95	1	2.0	0.02
3.00	0	0.0	0.00
Total	**50**	**100.0**	**1.00**

However, in the second case (*Table 13.3*), the relative frequency of other classes shows that some rentals are quite probable, £2.65 for example. The use of the expected value - the weighted mean - reflects the possibility that these other results might occur. The expected rental value in this case is £2.65, showing that in spite of the evidence that 40% of observed rentals are at £2.60, 46% are above £2.60, and 14% below.

The different results from these two sample distributions of rents are compared in *Table 13.4* for the seven possible yields used before. This range of values may be acceptable if the number of alternatives remains relatively small. The range of possible alternatives may be very large, however - and, more important, it may be possible to determine how likely they are to occur by means of an analysis of observed frequencies.

Table 13.4

Yield (%)	Rental (£ sq.m.)	
	£2.75	£2.65
5.00	660000	636000
5.25	628572	605714
5.50	600000	578182
5.75	573913	553044
6.00	550000	530000
6.25	528000	508800
6.50	507693	489231

There are three possible ways of dealing with this problem:

- Ignore it.

- Use a computer to calculate and display the results for all possible alternatives. (Such an exercise is called ' a simulation'.)

- Make use of available experience to determine subjective probabilities for the occurrence of 'likely' values for these variables. These probabilities can then be built into the consideration of alternatives.

The final method is usually more likely to appeal to the financial advisers of investing organisations because it is conceptually closest to the procedures currently in use. We shall therefore amplify these comments on it.

In the example above, *Tables 13.2* and *13.3*, the various yields were all suggested as equally possible. Clearly the valuer should be able to say from his knowledge that all are not equally possible, but that some are most unlikely and, more important, that some are very likely. This view is based upon the considered opinion of the valuer.

There are standard and easily learned rules to enable such considered opinions to be converted to subjective probabilities recognised to be just as valid and formalised as the objective assessments derived from long-run frequencies, as in *Tables 13.2* and *13.3*. A complete probability distribution can be built up for any variable using these methods. As has been seen earlier yields are just as likely to vary as rentals in this example, and after consideration the following subjective probabilities have been placed against the possible yields (see *Table 13.5*).

Table 13.5

Yield (%)	Probability
5.00	0.02
5.25	0.03
5.50	0.05
5.75	0.15
6.00	0.45
6.25	0.20
6.50	0.10
Total	**1.00**

The distribution of probabilities is such that only a few yields are considered likely to occur. From this distribution the expected value for the yield may be obtained by weighting each yield by its probability: in this case the value is **5.995% (6.00)**.

The implication of the subjective selection of a high probability of occurrence for a particular yield is that it is considered relatively risk free. It is also possible, therefore, to use such assessments as indicators of individuals' attitudes to risk in their investment.

The year's purchase may then be calculated, and the capital value arrived at in the usual way.

Distribution 1 (Table 13.2)
Estimated yield	6%
Estimated full rental value	
12,000 x 2.75	£33,000
YP perp. @ 6%	16.67
	£550,110

Distribution 2 (Table 13.3)
Estimated yield	6%
Estimated full rental value	
12,000 x 2.65	£31,800
YP perp. @ 6%	16.67
	£530,106

Note that these valuations are not comparable with one another, but may be compared individually with the original best estimate, or preliminary valuation.

Any solution derived in this way must be understood to be an estimate. The use of a statistical analysis of this type can only produce estimates. But - and this is more important - it produces a more consistent approach to uncertain situations, highlighting the stages in the appraisal process and pointing to any inconsistencies requiring correction or modification. As such, the method outlined is part of a more scientific approach to valuation. It must be emphasised that in this illustration many questions of market data collection, storage and analysis which are integral to the rigorous statistical consideration of the variables the valuer needs to use have been bypassed.

This approach emphasises the role of the valuer. Every input - variable or otherwise - is dependent upon the strength of the valuer's file evidence, his rental and value analysis, and his understanding and assessment of current market conditions. The approach differs in that the valuer is enjoined to consider ranges of uncertain variables much more carefully, any single *'figure'* arrived at always being recognised as an estimate based on a proper analysis of the market.

Using a method such as this, a valuer may quite reasonably derive a series of results for any valuation. In that case, great care must be taken in presenting such findings to the client. The complete findings should be incorporated into valuation reports as appendices, as they are a full summary of the valuer's views of the investment.

Naturally the method should not be applied automatically. It requires a clear understanding of the statistical methodology and its implications; it could also be inappropriate in some situations.'

Many valuers see little need for the explicit use of probability in their valuations. In this book it has been indicated that on many occasions there is a lack of certainty. One cannot be certain what the rent of a vacant building really is until it is actually let, one cannot be certain what rent will be achieved on review (indeed, it is possible to miss the review date or for legislation to be introduced freezing rents), one cannot be certain of the capitalisation rates to be used, and one cannot be certain about future costs on repairs and refurbishment. There is a risk; why not reflect it.

In the market the use of simulations has been largely restricted to Development Appraisal work. An argument for adhering to market approaches rests with the well established view that accuracy in assessment of the key variables at today's date is sufficiently problematic without adding the difficulty of estimating future rental levels and capitalisation or discount rates. Thus the further the valuer ventures away from the market the greater is the probability that one is adding human error to the already high levels of risk and uncertainty that attach to the property.

Baum and Crosby (1988) explore the use of sensitivity analysis. This they regard as *'a somewhat rudimentary risk analysis technique* which helps investors to arrive at a decision but fails to identify the chances of the possible variations becoming fact'. Recognising the popularity of the RADF approach they explore and recommend the use of *'Certainty Equivalent Cash Flow Models'* , in particular the use of the hybrid *'Sliced Income Approach'*.

These models make use of normal distribution theory which holds that some 68 per cent of all values in a normal distribution will be within ± 1 standard deviation (σ) of the mean; 95 per cent within $\pm 2\sigma$ and 99 per cent within $\pm 3\sigma$. From this a certainty cash flow can be constructed. **Baum and Crosby** apply this concept to the income stream whilst **Dubben** and **Sayce (1991)** consider both the income, the rental growth rate and the likely yield. Thus given the best estimate of rent $\pm 1\sigma$, the best estimate of growth $\pm 1\sigma$ and the best estimate of yield $\pm 1\sigma$ and a risk free discount rate, a Certainty Equivalent Cash Flow can

be constructed. Thus based on Dubben and Sayce's example of a property let at £10,000 for 2 years with an ERV of £15,000 the cash flow could be considered as:

Current Rent £10,000 p.a. for 2 years.

FRV £15,000 p.a. minus	1σ	£1,000	**CE** =	£14,000
Rental Growth 5% minus 1 σ		1%	**CE** =	4%
Cap. Rate	**6% plus** 1 σ	0.5 %	**CE** =	6.5%

It will be noted that this is a typical risk averse method as the worst scenario has been adopted. This, it is suggested, provides an 84% Certainty Equivalent Value. The problem as identified by **Dubben and Sayce** is that combining probabilities at **84%** certainty produces **59%** certain situation (**84% x 84% x 84%**). Such a view raises some doubts as to the usefulness of this technique when weighed against the best estimate of value based on market experience. The technique may, however, have benefit when seeking to choose between investments.

The Sliced Income Approach is a more logical model for the typical property investment as it accepts the fact that the current rent payable under a lease is relatively risk free. The riskiness is likely to be a function of tenant ability to pay the rent, which can be judged reasonably accurately given a thorough assessment of the tenant's credit rating. This method allows the income to be split between the current rent which is certain and the future rent which is less certain. Hence, given the underlying criteria of the model it is possible to assess the value of the certain rent at the risk free rate.

The future *'certain'* rent can be assessed at the level of certainty required **84%, 99%** and a risk averse or worst certain scenario cash flow constructed, to which it is argued that it is necessary to add the 'overage'; namely, the difference between the most likely discounted reversionary value and the certain scenario.

Whilst both approaches are advocated by **Baum and Crosby** for the purpose of guiding investors in decision taking when selecting between alternative investments, they have not gained much support in either market valuation work nor in the area of investment advice.

The next section looks at the normal practice of the property investment adviser.

Risk and uncertainty in analysis

The phenomenal growth in institutional investment in land and buildings in the 1970s turned the attention of valuers to investment analysis. The violent boom and slump of property prices in the early 1970s and again in the late 1980s would suggest that the market still has much to learn about the relationship between economic activity and the property market.

When property is purchased as an investment it is purchased for its present and future income and for capital growth. Occasionally other factors (such as prestige) enter into the decision, but for the rational investor such factors should not override decisions based on sound appraisal.

The following information may be required by investors, and is usually presented in a written report *(see Appendix B)*.

Location :
Here the valuer provides a description of the town, its geographical location in relation to other major towns and cities, details the population and road, rail and air communications, and comments upon the town's economic base. The position of the property within the town or city is then outlined.

Description of the property :
This section of the report deals with the age, design, construction and condition of the building(s) comprising the subject property. A comment may also be made concerning running costs.

Town planning :
A full report of the result of enquiries made with the local planning authority should be included.

Highways :
existing and any proposed changes or improvements.

Rating assessment :
uniform business rates payable etc.

Tenure :
freehold or leasehold, with details.

Details of occupation tenancies :
including comments on the tenants' covenants following investigation of the companies' accounts, etc.

Fire insurance :
extent of coverage required and premiums payable.

Management problems.

Terms of the transaction, including the valuer's recommendations.

Market Analysis and context.

Whilst much of a valuer's report is descriptive and capable of factual accuracy investors now require a much fuller statement of opinion on the market to be made by the valuer. This is a clear need when a valuation for purchase and investment advice is sought and when a valuation of ERP is needed.

The investor requires full details of the street, town and the region in which the property is located. This part of the report must include details of the current operating expenses, income and future rental growth prospects, the latter being substantiated with economic projections of the town and region's growth. Future rental growth will in part be influenced by the quality and/or suitability of the building for its permitted user. The tenant's covenant is relevant and it may be a crucial factor. As far as management is concerned most investors wish to see that the burden of management is minimised.

The different types of property available for investment funds can be readily sub-divided in terms of their suitability as investments into prime, secondary and other. But as more statistical information on performance becomes available traditional distinctions between, say, prime and secondary shop properties may disappear. Greenwells as long ago as their October 1976 report on property, whilst emphasising rental growth, covenant, fashion, marketability and volatility as the five main reasons for many institutions pursuing a policy of investing only in prime properties, indicated that in terms of income growth and long-term return secondary property could turn out to be a better investment.

In addition to the foregoing, investors require information on the rate of return or yield that they can expect from the investment. As indicated in *Chapter 4*, DCF techniques have been developed for analysing investments. Where a valuer is asked to advise on a specific property investment for a specific client the prospective purchase price is generally a known factor. For analysis purposes all acquisition costs such as solicitors' fees, survey and valuation fees, stamp duty, etc., must be added to the estimated purchase price before the yield is calculated.

Yields

Some reference has already been made to problems of the terminology relating to yields (**Chapter 5**). In the following paragraphs we outline the type of information required by investors and the methods of calculation used by valuers, adhering to what we consider to be currently acceptable and accurate terms. *(See also 'Mainly for Students' Estates Gazette, 4 September 1993.)*

In the case of most investments it is possible to calculate the *'initial yield'*. This is the simple relationship between the first year's income from an investment and the purchase price.

$$\frac{\text{Income or dividend}}{\text{Purchase price}} \text{ x } 100 = \textbf{Initial yield}$$

In the case of stocks this is frequently called the interest-only yield, and it may also be called the flat or running yield.

When, in the case of property, the first year's income is the full rack rental on net-of-outgoing terms this measure of return becomes the capitalisation rate for conventional valuations of comparable properties.

Another measure in the case of Government Stocks is the 'Redemption Yield' which may be gross or net after allowing for tax on income and/or capital gain. Information on stock yields appears in the financial press in the following format:

High	Low	Stock	Price	Chg	Red Yld
140 $^3/_{16}$	122	Tr 15 1/2% 98	122 $^9/_{16}$	+1/16	8.40
101 $^{21}/_{32}$	88 $^{13}/_{16}$	Tr 6%	99	90 $^{11}/_{16}$ +1/16	8.47

This translates to mean that Treasury Stock with a face value of £100 sold at a price of £122$^9/_{16}$. This was £1/16 higher than the day before and compares to the high price in the preceding 12 months of £140$^3/_{16}$ and a low of £122. The stock produces a nominal yield of 15$^1/_2$% (£15.50 per £100 face value), will be redeemed (paid back at face value) in 1998 and represents a return (on an IRR basis) of 8.40% if held until redeemed in 1988.

The initial yield is:

$$\frac{15.50}{122^9/_{16}} \text{ x } 100 = \underline{\textbf{12.65 \%}}$$

But investors are interested in the total return; that is, the IRR or, in stock terms, the Gross Redemption Yield. In these two stocks one represents a capital loss and the other a capital gain; this makes direct comparison impossible but when the relationship between price, the dividends and the

redemption value of £100 is calculated as a redemption yield then a comparison can be made. Here the yields are very close at **8.40%** and **8.47%**. These represent the rate which discounts all the benefits to equate with the purchase price.

It is not possible to check these figures exactly because certain information is missing. In particular, there is no information as to when, and how frequently, dividends are to be paid, nor precisely when the stocks will be redeemed. For the calculations to be exact one would also need to know whether they were cum- or ex-dividend.

When property is purchased the initial yield may be very low. This will be true where the property is let at less than FRV with an early reversion to FRV.

Institutional investors have long recognised this factor and have generally requested details of *'initial yield'*, *'reversionary yield'*, *'equivalent yield'* and sometimes *'equated yield'*. The latter are today relatively easy to calculate, but valuers might care to reflect upon the lengthy reiterative processes that had to be followed by the investment valuer before the age of programmable calculators and computers, in order to calculate such a yield to at least two decimal places.

Up until the mid-1960s the investment valuer would always base his yield calculations on current rental estimates. Thus a freehold property worth **£1,000** per annum producing **£500** per annum for the next **3** years and offered at **£8,500** would be analysed to give an initial yield of:

$$\frac{500}{8,500} \text{ x } 100 = 5.8\%;$$

a yield on reversion of $\frac{1,000}{8,500} \text{ x } 100 = 11.76\%$

and an equivalent yield of 10.26%.

The latter is an internal rate of return and represents the rate of interest which will discount 3 receipts of £500 and £1,000 in perpetuity starting in 3 years to equal £8,500.

Redemption yields as such cannot be calculated for property investments because, unlike Government Stock, the future benefits of income are not fixed and the redemption value is the resale value, which again is not fixed. However, there may be cases where an expected redemption yield will be calculated. To do this some assumption must be made as to future sale date or dates, following which estimates of projected rent and resale value need to be made It will then be possible to calculate the expected redemption yield either on a gross basis or net-of-tax basis.

It is a basic assumption that property is purchased for its expected rental growth as well as its current yield (initial yield) and that the expected growth in conjunction with the current yield will match long-dated gilt yields. The growth necessary in respect of a specific set of assumptions can be calculated. This is generally called the *'implied growth rate'*.

A common starting point for this type of analysis is the gross redemption yield from British Funds or the interest-only yield on undated stock. At the time of writing (1995) these were in the region of **8.5%**.

These rates represent nil growth in income, nil risk to income and nil risk to capital if held to redemption. They are viewed as risk free as they are underwritten by the Government. In reality purchasers accept the risk that if they need to resell before redemption the price may be above or below their purchase price. Any other investment can only be worthwhile if its comparable return is in excess of these yields. There is much truth in this statement; but the selection of the appropriate yield requires some care, as these vary from day to day and property is a less volatile long term investment.[2]

A stock may go up or down 10% in 24 hours but this does not imply an immediate comparable movement in property yields.

Logically an investor would not purchase equity investments at less than the safe return from Government Stock unless the expected growth income was sufficient to cover the yield gap.

Thus when ICI shares are yielding **5.3%, BP 6.7%** and **stocks 8.5%** there is an assumption or market implication *ceteris paribus* of a continuous annual or semi-annual growth expectation.

The return could be more realistically expressed by substituting in the formula for a growth stock. This formula is given as

$$D = \frac{D_0(1 + b)}{(r - b)}$$

where **b** is the per cent increase on previous year's dividends (the expected growth rate per annum), **D_0** is the last dividend paid, **D** is the current price and **r** is the redemption yield.

Here given an assumption as to dividend growth the investor can calculate the total return and/or alternatively, given a target return or expected redemption yield, it is possible to calculate the dividend growth needed. As discussed earlier the investor may wish to undertake sensitivity analysis of one form or another before making a decision but unless the expected total return is likely to exceed the stock return by an adequate margin to reflect the added risk then the price will be considered to be too high. Funds are withheld from the market until prices fall to the market perceival revised equilibrium price and purchase will again be made.

Property, on the other hand, can rarely be considered to produce a continuous annual growth in income. But if an owner-occupied freehold property was under consideration producing an imputed income of £100 per annum with annual rental growth predicted at **10%** per annum and selling for £1,250 a similar calculation would be possible.

Thus:

$$\frac{100}{1,250} \times 100 = 8\% \text{ initial yield}$$

Assuming a 10% growth in rent per annum then

$$1,250 = \frac{100(1 + 0.10)}{(r - 0.10)}$$

$$1,250r - 125 = 110$$

$$= 0.188$$

i.e. a return of 18.8%

Reconsidering the formula and rephrasing, one can state that when initial yield = **i**, growth rate = **b** and discount rate = **r**, *then*

[2] In the text the opportunity cost of capital for property investors has been taken to be 2% above the rate earned on Government Stock, but this is subject to argument. The Economic Development Institute in its *Compounding and Discounting Tables for Project Evaluation* states: 'For private enterprise the opportunity cost of capital will be a weighted average of the borrowing rate for funds and an acceptable price-earnings ratio for equity shares. For the society as a whole, the opportunity cost of capital is the return on the last (that is, marginal) investment which could be made were all the available capital fully invested in the most remunerative alternative manner' (World Bank, 1973).

$$i = \frac{1+r}{1+b} - 1$$

$$b = \frac{(1+r)}{(1+i)} - 1$$

$$r = (1+i)(1+b) - 1$$

Thus in the example given where $i = 8\%$ and $b = 10\%$

$$r = (1.08)(1.1) - 1 = 0.188 = 18.8\%$$

Property let at rack rental with rent reviews restricts the potential receipt of any increase in rent to the rent review date. Although rents may rise continuously at some long run average compound rate, for property investments to equate with yields from stocks and shares the growth between reviews must be sufficient to compensate for the contracted fixed income between reviews.

Hence the purchase of a property let at £100 per annum for 5 years with reviews assumed to be every 5 years for the sum of £1,250 must, if the discount rate is **18.8%,** reflect a rate of growth in income greater than **10%** per annum compound.

The problem can be phrased as :

$$£1,250 = £100 \times \frac{(1 - PV)}{r} + \left[x \times \frac{1}{i} \times \frac{1}{(1+r)^n} \right]$$

where $r = 18.8\%$ and $i = 8\%$ and $x =$ rent on review.

$$1,250 = 100 \times \left(\frac{1 - \frac{1}{(1 + 0.188)^5}}{0.188} \right)$$

$$+ \left[x \times \frac{1}{0.08} \times \frac{1}{(1 + 0.188)^5} \right]$$

$$1,250 - \left[100 \times \frac{1 - \frac{1}{(1 + 0.188)^5)}}{0.188} \right]$$

$$= x \times \frac{1}{0.08} \times \frac{1}{(1 + 0.188)^5}$$

$$1,250 - [100 \times 3.074] = x \times 12.5 \times \frac{1}{(2.366)}$$

$$
\begin{array}{ll}
1,250 - 307.40 & = x \times 12.5 \times 0.422 \\
942.60 & = 5.275x \\
£178.69 & = x
\end{array}
$$

Thus the rent on review in 5 years' time must be (say) **£179** in order that the investment can be considered to be as acceptable as a continuous growth income of £100 per annum compounding at **10%** per annum.

£100 x amount of £1 = £179

$$\text{Amount of £1 in 5 years} = \frac{£179}{100}$$

Amount of £1 in 5 years = 1.79

rate of growth = approx 12.5% $((1.225)^5 = 1.7821)$

Clearly, given any initial yield, cost of capital rate and rent review pattern, the growth yield can be calculated. Formulae *(see Chapter 3)* and tables have been produced for certain rates, years, etc., but most valuers will be better advised to consider the ideas rather than memorise the formulae. It is always preferable to consider the expectation (probability) of a particular income on reversion than to become lost in tables.

An alternative approach is to consider the appropriate yield gap between property investments and comparable equity shares. If equities are moving from **6%** to **7%** property should perhaps move from **6.5%** to **7.5%.** It is, after all, logical to state that if first class industrial and commercial organisations are increasing dividends by **10%** p.a., presumably they can increase their rent payments by a comparable amount; thus first class factory rents should rise in line with the performance of the leading industrialists and if retail sales are rising by **30%** p.a. then retail rents can increase by a similar percentage.

Most investors will require to know the initial yield on total acquisition costs, the reversionary yield (yield on reversion), the equivalent yield and the equated yield, i.e. the internal rate of return on specific assumptions.

All of these calculations can be carried out on a before or after tax basis, but from the point of view of a specific client or investor it is suggested that if the client is subject to tax of any form on income or capital gains from property then net of tax returns should be provided.

In *Chapter 3* the valuation of a property let at £10,000 per annum for 2 years with a current market rental value of £20,000 per annum, was considered in some depth. The relationship between the all risks yield (or market capitalisation rate) of **5%** and the expected or equated yield requirement of **10%** was examined and on a **5** year rent review pattern an implied annual rental growth of **7.6355%** was calculated. This produced an implied rent in 2 years of £23,170 and a capital value on a modified DCF basis of £386,323. These figures would be rounded in the market but are used here to indicate the kind of information that an investor might require.

Acquisition costs

The majority of investors require yield calculations to be based on total acquisition cost. Solicitor's fees, surveyor's fees and stamp duty are the usual costs that need to be added to purchase price. In special cases it may be necessary to take account of immediate capital costs such as repairs, or in the case of a vacant building, refurbishment and letting expenses. In other cases it may be sensible to take account of rental apportionment and/or outstanding arrears of rents.

e.g.
Purchasing at the valuation of	£386,323
Add for Legal fees ⎫ say 3.5%[3] Surveyor's fees ⎬ inclusive Stamp duty ⎭ of VAT	£13,521
	£399,844

Initial yield

The initial yield may mean the relationship between the before tax net rents receivable during the first 12 months of ownership and total acquisition cost; the return expected during the investor's current financial year or the relationship between current contracted rents and total acquisition cost. In the absence of specific direction from the client it would be normal to assess the relationship between current contracted rent and total acquisition costs.

e.g.
Current rents	£10,000
Less landlord's expected non-recoverable management expenses inclusive of VAT Minimum fee, say	£500
	£9,500

[3]Competition has currently reduced the cost of professional fees to an inclusive average of 2.75-3.0%.

$$\frac{9,500 \times 100}{399,844} = 2.376\%$$

This yield can be crucial to some investors. Actuarial calculations of the relationship between expected repayments or claims on a fund and that fund's current income may dictate an absolute cut-off rate. Thus a fund may be operating on a 3.5% cut-off or target rate and be forced to reject this property.

Other funds, whilst having regard to the initial yield and its implication for their whole portfolio, will be aware that a low initial property yield can be balanced by high yielding stocks to achieve a total return for the fund above the target rate.

Yield on reversion

It is normal in an investment report to include an assessment of the yield at reversion calculated on the basis of current estimates of open market rentals.

e.g.
Estimated rental value	£20,000
Less Non-recoverable management fees say	£750
	£19,250

$$\frac{19,250 \times 100}{399,844} = 4.814\%$$

Equivalent yield

The amount of additional information provided depends upon the client. Most will require advice on the internal rate of return based on current rentals and values.

e.g.
Value in 2 years' time on basis of open market rental of	£20,000
x YP perp. @ 5%[4]	20
	£400,000

Then the IRR on annual in arrears assumption is found from

0	(- £386,323 + £13,521)	- £399,884
1		+ £9,500
2		+ £409,500

and is 2.395%

[4]5% is taken to be an ARY based on gross rents.

It should be clear that further adjustments could be made for quarterly in advance and for sale fees. Such sophistication is not going to explain to an investor that this could be a good investment. The potential for the investment can only be indicated by making some assessment of the future.

Equated Yield

Not all investors will require an equated yield analysis but it is a useful measure and one which can help the investment valuer in formulating his or her investment purchase advice.

e.g. **Implied rent in 2 years**
as previously £23,170
x YP perp. @ 5% 20
———
£463,400

Here the IRR on an annual in arrears assumption is found from

0	- £399,884
1	+ £9,500
2	+£472,900

and is 8.849%.

In *Chapter 6* it was suggested that the real return might be expected to be **12%** and yet this analysis suggests **8.849%,** which may not be sufficient to persuade an investor to buy.

This variation highlights some very important but as yet unresolved issues in the professional areas of valuation and investment advice. In the *Chapter 6* valuation it was assumed that the **5%** all risks yield was accounting for the non-recoverable management costs, and no account was taken of acquisition costs.

The profession is still divided over the correct approach.

A strongly held view is that :

(a) management costs should always be deducted in all valuations other than true net situations and that

(b) acquisition costs should be deducted from the valuation figure before expressing an opinion on value.

Note the effect this has in the following amended valuation and analysis.

e.g. **Revised valuation:**
Next 2 years £10,000
Less management, say £500
———
£9,500

YP 2 years at 12% 1.6901
———
£16,056

Reversion to £23,170
Less management, say £750
———
£22,420

YP perp. @ 5% 15.944
———
£357,464

£373,520
══════

Let x = purchase price and acquisition costs at 3.5% = 0.35x

Then $x + 0.035x$ = £373,520

$1,035x$ = £373,520

x = £360,889
══════

the corrected valuation figure.

Revised equated yield analysis:

0 - £373,520 (£360,889 + 3.5%)
1 + £9,500
2 + £457,900 (£22,420 x 20 YP + £9,500)

which gives an IRR of 12%

In the property market valuations are prepared for vendors and investment advice given to buyers. The parties are different, the valuers are different and neither side actually knows why the other decided the price was acceptable and a bargain struck. It should, however, be clear that investors will be interested in the expected returns, and in the actual returns; they are not interested in the rates per cent used in the valuation.

How much information the valuer provides the investor with will depend upon the investor's requirements. The assessment of implied rental growth rates allows the valuer to compare historic growth patterns in the specific market with current market expectations with the growth needed to achieve an overall acceptable return for the investor. That detailed analysis coupled with detailed market analysis provides the valuer with the knowledge to advise if only in the general form of saying, *'Our records indicate that over the last 15 years rents in the High Street have risen on average by 12% per annum. The population of the area is rising and is expected to continue to rise. There are no plans at the moment before the planning authority for any increase in retail space. If the current growth in rentals continues then a purchase at £x should produce a return over the next n years in excess of medium term redemption yields of 10%.'*

A number of writers believe that investment advice needs to be based on a more rigorous cash flow approach. If undertaken by computer the process can be very simple as well as being very sophisticated and provides the analyst with the opportunity to test the sensitivity of the investment. The additional data that can be handled could include: adjustments for rent review costs and lease renewal costs; adjustments for voids and refurbishment; more accurate allowance for other non-recoverable service or repair costs; adjustment for sale costs; adjustment for income and capital gains tax; adjustment for depreciation. Such modelling also allows the valuer to test the effect of different rental growth factors either on an average long-term basis or by adopting different rates of growth over different time periods.

It has already been indicated that the complexities of certain geared leaseholds can only effectively be handled in this way. The complexities of current development funding schemes also suggest that the valuation and analysis of these kinds of property investments will also have to be handled by computer.

In order to calculate these yields an assumption of certainty has been made. The more sophisticated investor will wish to take the analysis a stage further, because the advice as it stands gives no indication of the probability of achieving the stated yield. Consider *Example 13.1.*

End year	Net sum	Probability	Expectation	
One	£1,000	1	£1,000	
Two	£1,000	1	£1,000	
	£30,000	0.20	£6,000	£36,500
	£37,500	0.60	£22,500	(Expected return
	£40,000	0.20	£8,000	in 2 years' time)

To assess the internal rate of return the generalised formula

$$\frac{I_1}{(1+i)} + \frac{I_2}{(1+i)^2} + \ldots \frac{I_n}{(1+i)^n}$$

must be solved for i, in this case in terms of:

$$£32,640 = \frac{1,000}{(1+i)} + \frac{1,000 + 36,500}{(1+i)^n}$$

$$i = 0.08$$

The internal rate of return is virtually 8%. If this calculation involved more inputs and more probability factors it could only be solved quickly be using a computer.

If the client's target rate is 7% the valuer would reconsider the NPV on this basis given his expectations.

Year	Sum	PV at 7%	
One	£1,000	0.9346	£934.60
Two	£37,000	0.8734	£32,752.50
			£33,687.10
	Less purchase costs		£32,640.00
	Positive NPV say		£1,047.00

The investment on this basis is worth while.

Such calculations should of course be carried out on a true net basis from the specific client's viewpoint.

Here it has been recognised that the position in 2 years' time is not certain, as there is a rent review. In this example the rent on review has been assumed to be certain at **£3,000**, but the future benefit of **£3,000** in perpetuity may have a present worth between **£30,000** and **£40,000** depending upon the analyst's assumptions as to the discount rate. The 'expected value' in 2 years' time has therefore been calculated before considering the internal rate of return on this basis. The normal analysis would have opted for the most probable figure of **£37,500** and would have ignored the other possible out-

Example 13.1

Your clients are contemplating the acquisition of a property investment. The property is fully let producing a net cash flow from contracted rents of **£1,000** per annum for the next **2** years. These rents are considered to be certain. In **2** years' time the rents are due for review. You have considered the likely level of rents in **2** years' time and expect the rent roll to be in the region of **£3,000**; expressing this in capital terms you have prepared the following table of cash flows together with a probability measure for the capital reversions in **2** years' time. The asking price plus acquisition cost gives a total purchase price of **£32,640**.

Advise your client.

comes. A certainty equivalent approach could be used.

It is essential for the prudent investor to pause and consider the other possible outcomes and the effect that a change in the reversionary value might have on expected return. In this example it has been stated that the rent will be £3,000 but that the market capitalisation rate of 8% could, under certain circumstances, fall as low as 7.5% and, under others, rise as high as 10%. These forecasts would of course be based on a reasonable interpretation of the state of the economy and the extent to which national and local economic factors might affect future capitalisation rates for this type of investment. It will therefore be desirable in some instances to consider not only the possible rates of return but also their probability, and hence the variance of the return and the standard deviation.

He can also judge whether the added return from the more speculative investment is likely to compensate for the added risk.

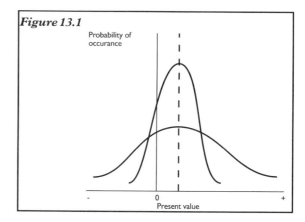

Figure 13.1

Table 13.6

Possible rate (%)	Probability of occurrence	Expected rate of return %	Deviation of possible from expected	Deviation squared	Deviation squared x probability
7.5	0.2	1.5	-0.8	0.64	0.128
8.0	0.6	4.8	-0.3	0.09	0.054
10.0	0.2	2.0	1.7	2.89	0.578
	1.0	8.3			0.760%

Table 13.6 indicates that the expected rate of return is 8.3%, this being the weighted average of all possible outcomes which, in relation to an income of £3,000, would give an expected value of £36,144 (YP x income). The variation of return in this case is 0.76%, which can be converted into a standard deviation by taking the square root, giving a standard deviation of 0.87%. These latter two measures are measures of the risk involved. The smaller the standard deviation the smaller is the probability of the actual return deviating from the expected rate of return. In certain cases such a measure is extremely useful, particularly if one has an extreme case of two projects both with an expected rate of 8.3%, but one with a standard deviation of say 0.87% and the other with a standard deviation of 3%, for it is clear, in these terms, that the former is a far less risky investment.

An alternative is to consider the probability distribution of present values for alternative investments. For example, given distributions as in **Figure 13.1** the less speculative investment is investment A. The client is therefore in a position to make a better decision between investments than he would have been if the only information he had received was the figure of present value.

Probability distributions as in **Figure 13.1** help to emphasise the possibility of a negative present value. Different investors have different attitudes towards risk and some cannot afford to make an investment if there is the slightest possibility of a loss. So to advise on the purchase of a property merely because it shows a positive NPV at the investor's target rate of discount is inadequate advice, because it again ignores the other possible outcomes which could occur with a change in income forecasts. Some indication of this possibility should be given to the investor.

A further alternative for considering uncertainties in investment decision-taking is the decision tree. Here again informed guesses as to probable outcomes need to be made.

In **example 13.1**, whilst a number of probability factors were incorporated, these were based on a specific assumption as to a future event at the end of year 2, namely that the income would be £3,000 per annum. In reality this will be uncertain. Thus at the end of year 2 the tenant could renew the lease or he could vacate the property, and in the latter case it might either be re-let immediately, or there might be some probability that it

151

would take a year to find a new tenant.

Provided probability factors can be assessed for each of the alternative outcomes a decision tree can be constructed. With this information the valuer is able to assess the present value of the entire tree.

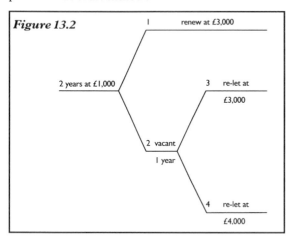

Figure 13.2

Present valuation calculations on an 8% basis

Branch 1

Fixed income for 2 years	**£1,000**
PV £1 p.a. for 2 years @ 9%	1.7833
	£1,783
Re-let at	**£3,000**
PV £1 p.a. in perp. @ 8%	
PV £1 in 2 years @ 8%	10.71674
	£32,150
	£33,933

Branch 3

Income of £1,000 for 2 years as before		**£1,783**
Re-let at	**£3,000**	
PV £1 p.a. in perp. @ 8%		
PV £1 in 3 years @ 8%	9.9229	
		£29,769
		£31,552

Branch 4

Income of £1,000 for 2 years as before		**£1,783**
Re-let at	**£4,000**	
PV £1 p.a. in perp. @ 8%		
PV £1 in 3 years @ 8%	9.9229	**£39,691**
		£41,474

Depending on the actual income, this investment has a present value at 8% of £33,933, or £31,552, or £41,474. Allowing for the probabilities and conditional probabilities we have:

£33,933 x 0.08	=	£27,146
£31,552 x 0.2 x 0.6	=	£3,786
£41,474 x 0.2 x 0.4	=	£3,317

Weighted present value: £34,249

This can be compared to the asking price of **£32,640.** This figure could also be calculated by working back down the decision tree. These techniques have long been used in business management but are still in their infancy in the valuation profession, and valuers who use such techniques will need to have a thorough knowledge of statistics.

Provided there is good market evidence, and the valuer uses that evidence with sound judgement, then the best defensible valuation is likely to be based on a best-estimate income capitalisation approach.

The problems of how to fully reflect risk in analysis increases with the complexity of the problem itself. The simplest decision is in respect of the single investment opportunity and the yes/no decision. From that one moves to the decisions which involve choices between alternative investments, after which one becomes inevitably involved in portfolio risk analysis. An investor must concern himself not only with the risks of a proposed new investment, but also he must consider the impact of that new investment on any existing investments held within a portfolio. Thus a valuer advising on a property might view it as a high risk and advise against the purchase, but in terms of the addition of that investment to an existing portfolio and in terms of the investor's overall aims it might be a perfectly acceptable risk. The subject of portfolio analysis has to be treated in a rigorous mathematical format, and for that reason it is felt to be outside the scope of this book.

However, almost all valuers are now agreed that in the property development world one cannot make any assumption as to certainty, and for long this has been held by the Lands Tribunal to be one reason for rejecting the traditional developers' or residual valuation *(see Chapter 11)*.

Future uncertainty continues to be the reason given by most valuers for restricting the amount of detail provided for investors to a minimum. However, a number of investors currently expect their investment surveyors to provide them with more information on yields and more supportive data on market rents, market analysis and market performance. This information is used by the investors in their own assessment of the probability of achieving their investment aims.

Similarly, banks requesting **Estimated Realisation Price** are now expecting valuers to provide much more detail. That is to set down explicitly their current opinion of the market. An open market valuation in accordance with the RICS definition is a snapshot of the market and provides the client with an expression of the best price the property could have been expected to sell for at the valuation date, given proper prior marketing. On its own it can be likened to a photograph of a ball in mid air. The problem is that (except with exceptional photography) the untrained eye cannot judge whether the ball is going up or coming down. The same is true of the **OMV** snapshot where investors and lenders are now concerned to discover from the valuer a considered and supported opinion as to the state of the market in rental and capital terms. In this respect any statements as to implied growth need to be supported by supported statements as to actual growth currently being experienced and currently expected.

Regression analysis

Regression analysis continues to be discussed by valuers as a potential tool for valuation and analysis. In its simplest form, the statistical technique of regression analysis enables the analyst to predict the value of one variable from the known value of another. Valuation would be an extremely simple science if, for example, the valuer could predict the sale price of a property from its total floor area. This would indicate that a linear relationship between value and size existed which, if plotted on a graph, would produce a straight line, the slope of which would be dependent upon the value of the variable factor, b. Where a is a constant, the standard formula for a linear relationship is

$$y = a + bx$$

where the simple case selected above y represents house value and x represents total floor area. For example, it might be noted that in a given locality the price of houses was always equal to **£5,000** plus the floor area multiplied by 5. Then:

$$y = £5,000 + 5x$$

It is a usual presumption that value is a function of a number of variables. Multiple linear regression enables the analyst to bring into play as many variables as may be considered to be likely to affect the value or likely selling price of the subject property, such as parking facilities, outlook, location, size, specific facilities such as central heating and garage space and other factors such as the age and condition of the building.

Though little used in the UK, linear and multiple linear regression has been extensively used and developed in appraisal work in the USA, primarily because of the greater acceptance in America of the computer. Most multiple regression computer packages are of the step-wise form. The program input consists of a list of property characteristics for the type of property under analysis, together with details of the actual sale prices or rentals achieved, or repair costs incurred. The computer correlates each feature with the known factor, sale price, selects that feature with the highest correlation, produces a regression equation and estimates the sale prices on that basis. The computer then calculates the difference between actual price and the estimated price, and then proceeds to select from the remaining features the next highest correlation and proceeds until all the features have been used.

The end result is an equation which can, with care, be used to estimate sale price, or whatever other factor is required in respect of another property. As more data becomes available these are added to the existing store and the program re-run to check for any significant changes in preferences by purchasers such as for natural gas in preference to oil-fired central heating.

Any predicted figure must not be regarded as an absolute, and the valuer requires some indication of accuracy or acceptability.

The statistical measure is generally **R (the correlation coefficient)** and **R^2 (the coefficient of determination)**.

When the data produces a value for **R** as close as possible to **1(1^2 = 1)** this would imply that the variation of the dependent variable (sale price, rental value) is explained fully by the independent variable(s). If **R** falls below **0.9** then only about 80% of the variation of the dependent variable is explained by the independent variable(s) and the smaller **R** becomes the less meaningful is the whole analysis.

The use of multiple regression analysis has been limited to mass valuation problems, particularly for land-tax purposes. Its use is fairly widespread in America, but it has also been used in Japan, Australia, Canada and South Africa, and in the UK studies have been carried out by the Inland Revenue. Currently it is being used in market building for forecasting purposes.

Users of this technique need no reminder of the old motto **'garbage in - garbage out'**, but for others the warning needs to be made. The results can only be as good as the raw data permit.

The majority of reported examples concern house prices, but it is suggested that regression and multiple regression could be used for:

- *Testing the relationship between size and price or rent (for example, the rate at which land price per hectare decreases with the increase in the size of the holding being sold, or the extent to which rents per square metre for office or industrial space decrease with the size of the letting).*

- *Time/value trend analysis.*

- *Determining the rental value of all types of premises (as rent is a function of size, location, facilities, running costs, consumer income, etc. it should be possible to produce a regression equation).*

- *Predicting gross trading income from licensed premises, theatres, restaurants, etc., from the number of persons using the premises.*

- *Predicting petrol throughput for service stations based on traffic counts and other variables.*

- *Estimating repair expenses based on property maintenance records.*

Clearly valuations and analyses of the type outlined in this chapter are only likely to be undertaken by the larger national valuation practices, government and institutional investors. For these reasons the description of the alternative techniques used has been kept to a minimum to give the average reader and student valuer a general idea of the developing techniques. Readers requiring a more detailed approach to the techniques are referred to the recommended reading at the end of the book.

We began by suggesting that valuers should keep their minds open to new techniques. A major development in appraisal techniques in the near future will be the use of statistics, and **Norman Benedict** aptly summarised our own feelings in an article published in the **Appraisal Journal** as long ago as October 1972:

'*Statistical analysis can significantly broaden the role of the appraiser and substantially increase his effectiveness, providing him with the tools to attain greater sophistication and expertise in the areas of marketability, feasibility and investment analysis.*

Correspondingly, the appraiser who clings to yesterday's tools to meet tomorrow's challenges will become progressively less effective and less involved in his work, while the appraiser who seeks constantly to acquire new skills will develop both personally and professionally. In summation, then, statistics represents a golden opportunity for an appraiser to experience both personal and professional growth.'

This statement is as apt today as it was in 1972. Its pertinence is obvious to those valuers developing econometric models and willing to tackle the critical area of property market forecasting. The issue for the investor remains the same, ideally they need to buy at the bottom of the market and sell at the top, there is thus a need to identify when the market and individual properties are over priced or under priced.

In this book we have set out the current thinking behind the use of the income approach to assessing Open Market Value and Estimated Realisation Price. It is in essence a book about techniques, it is for the practitioners to develop the proper use of these techniques in responding to their clients' needs. An opinion of value will only ever be as good as the advice that goes with it.

Q

Define :

a)   IRR

b)   gross redemption yield

c)   equivalent yield

d)   equated yield

Q A property has just been sold for £1 million freehold. It is currently producing a rent of £60,000 p.a. net. The full rental value is £110,00 p.a. The lease will be renewed in 4 years' time.

Calculate:

a) total acquisition costs with fees and stamp duties @ 4%;

b) current return based on purchase price plus acquisition costs;

c) expected return after the lease is renewed;

d) the capitalisation rate(s) used by the valuer;

e) the internal rate of return assuming rental growth @ 5% per annum and a re-sale in 4 years' time; assuming no change in the capitalisation rate;

f) the growth in rental value needed over the next 4 years:

      i) in pounds

      ii) as a rate of growth per annum in order to achieve a redemption yield or equated yield (IRR) of 12%.

appendix

A

Professional guidance and rules of engagement

In this Appendix material reproduced by permission of The Royal Institution of Chartered Surveyors, which owns the copyright of the Appraisal and Valuation Manual, is printed in bold.

On 10 July 1995 the RICS General Council approved the new *Appraisal and Valuation Manual* which became mandatory on 1 January 1996. The new practice statements do not apply to those listed in PS 1.3; namely, in brief:

· valuations prepared in connection with legal and quasi-legal proceedings for settlement of property related disputes;

· decisions and reports of arbitrators, independent experts and mediators;

· valuations by internal valuers solely for internal use;

· compensation claims, rating appeals and valuations for taxation purposes;

· valuations quoted for the purpose of or in course of negotiations;

· estate agency and marketing services including letting, but purchase and disposal reports are not excluded;

· valuation/market advice in the course of design of developments, improvements and conversion schemes;

· assumed prices or rent made in the course of calculations or opinions as to yields and forecasts as to future values;

· valuations in the course of rent reveiw and lease renewal negotiations.

The first seven Practice Statements apply to all other valuations and the remainder apply to valuations that fall within the public arena and/or to the specific class of property or valuations covered by the Practice Statement. Practice Statements from 8 onwards must be read in the context of 1-7 but take precedence over 1-7.

The coverage of the various statements is summarised in the following list:

PS1   The Application of these Practice Statements

PS2   Clarification and Agreement of Conditions of Engagement

PS3   The Purposes of Valuations and their Bases

PS4   Definitions of Bases of Valuation; Assumptions

PS5   Qualifications of Valuers and Conflicts of Interest

PS6   Inspections and Material Considerations

PS7   Valuation Reports and Published References to them

This book is concerned with the income approach to property valuation and method used for the valuation of income producing property or potentially income producing property. The method is used for many valuations which would have to be valued in accordance with the Practice Statements, and, whilst the book is primarily concerned with method rather than process, the following key points from the manual are relevant. Practising valuers must refer to the full statements contained in the Manual.

PS2   'Valuers must establish their Clients' needs and confirm the service to be provided before the valuation is reported'

This PS requires the valuer to establish and understand the client's needs and confirm the instructions with the client and/or professional advisers in writing. Conditions of engagement must as a minimum cover the following matters which are set out in greater detail in PS2:

· purpose of the valuation or appraisal;

· subject of the valuation or appraisal;

· basis or bases of valuation and any assumed sale completion period;

· assumptions appropriate to the basis;

· date of valuation;

· currency or currencies for appraising the value;

· treatment of plant and machinery;

· treatment of specialist items such as jigs, patterns etc;

- any restrictions on how or what the valuer may do;

- the requirements of consent to publication;

- limits/exclusions of liability to third parties;

- the nature of information provided and the extent to which the valuer is to rely upon such information;

- that a formal environmental assessment is not provided and either the property is to be valued on the assumption of no contamination or that the valuation is to reflect the contents of an environmental audit, or land quality statement or other report;

- arrangements in respect of the appointment of consultants;

- fees and charges where the valuer is not an employee.

The PS contains specific requirements in respect of limited inspection, revaluations, valuation reviews, level and scope of responsibility where other valuers are to be used, identification of the property to be valued. Plant and machinery issues, valuations on trading potential, bricks and mortar valuations, valuations for purposes other than originally agreed.

Professional Indemnity Insurers maintain that many cases of negligent valuations would have been avoided if both parties had entered into a formal agreement which set out the terms and conditions of engagement now required by PS2.

PS3   **'Valuations for particular purposes must be provided on specified bases'**

This PS requires the valuer to agree the appropriate basis or bases with the client at the outset. It also requires the valuer to provide a valuation on the basis of MV or OMV whenever an ERP or ERRP basis is required, and where a calculation of worth is required a clear statement must be given as to the extent to which it differs from MV or OMV. 'A calculation of worth must never be described in a report or published reference thereto as a valuation.'

The PS sets out a Table of Purposes, Properties and Bases which is reprinted overleaf.

PS3 also covers the following wide range of matters:

PS3.2	Classes and categories of fixed assets for certain valuation purposes
PS3.3	Land and buildings in the course of development
PS3.4	Land and buildings classified as a wasting asset
PS3.5	Specialised properties
PS3.6	Land and buildings for specialised development
PS3.7	Negative values
PS3.8	Damaged properties
PS3.9	Damaged plant and machinery

PS4   **'There are defined bases of valuation and related assumptions which must be used where the Practice Statements so require.'**

This PS provides at length all the definitions of value used for property valuation and for plant and machinery valuations. In this book reference has been made to the three key base definitions MV, OMV and ERP; these are reprinted here in full.

PS4.1   **Market Value (MV)**

The definition and commentary which follows is that settled by IVSC (International Valuation Standards Committee). Including the commentary, the Institution considers that its application results in the same valuation figure as the application of the OMV definition which follows it. Whenever the MV definition is reported as having been used, the fact that its interpretative commentary has been applied must always be stated as well.

PS4.1.1   *Definition*
The estimated amount for which an asset should exchange on the date of valuation between a willing buyer and a willing seller in an arm's length transaction after proper marketing wherein the parties had each acted knowledgeably, prudently and without compulsion.

PS4.1.2   *Commentary*
The term 'asset' is used because of the focus of these Standards. However, the term 'property' may be substituted for general application of the definition. Each element of the definition has its own conceptual framework:

Table of purposes, properties and bases

	Purpose of Valuation	Property Class or Category	Basis In the case of land and buildings in the course of development see also PS3.3 and in the case of land and buildings classified as a wasting asset, see also PS22)	For Title and Definition of Basis see PS
1	Valuation of property which is to be bought or sold except where 2 below applies	All	MV OMV ERP OMV (P&M) ERP (P&M)	4.1 4.2 4.5 4.13.1 4.13.3
2	Valuation of property for which a sale is contemplated subject to a defined restriction of the period for achieving the sale	All	ERRP ERRPEU ERRP(P&M)	4.6 4.7 4.13.4
3	(a) Valuation of commercial land and buildings for secured lending purposes(b) Company assets as security for mortgagedebenturesAs to specialised properties, See PS3.5.1(a)	All	MV OMV ERP ERRP ERRPEU	4.1 4.2 4.5 4.6 4.7
4	Valuation of plant and machinery for secured lending purposes	All	OMV (P&M) ERP (P&M) ERRP (P&M)	4.13.1 4.13.3 4.13.4
5	Valuations for residential mortgages	Residential property	OMV excluding incentives and (unless otherwise stated) the value of any development which has or requires planning permission (See Annex to PS9)	
6	(a) Incorporation in company accounts and other financial statements which are subject to audit*	1.1 Held as an investment	MV* OMV*	4.1 4.2
	1.2 Non-specialised and not included in 1.3 to 1.7 below		MV* OMV*	4.1 4.2
	(c) Take-overs and mergers under the City Code(d) Pension and Superannuation funds or under the Insurance Companies Acts, and for unit linked property assets of life assurance companies	1.3 Non-specialised and occupied for the purposes of the undertaking (this category can include land and buildings fully equipped as an operational entity and valued having regard to trading potential) including property, owned within United Linked Funds,	EUV but also MV/OMV where the value for purposes other than its existing use differs substantially from EUV	4.3 4.1/4.2
	(e) Unregulated Property Unit Trusts)	1.4 Housing stock owned by registered housing associations	EUV - RHA	4.4
	(f) Property Funds (Authorised Property Unit Trusts)	1.5 Held as trading stock	See PS 21	
		1.6 Land and buildings held for development	MV* OMV*	4.1 4.2
	* In the case of the valuation of insurance company assets for financial statements, Market Value is defined by an EU Directive and UK Statutory Instrument - see Annex to PS12	1.7 Non-specialised land and buildings in course of development	MV* OMV* or OMV as cleared site plus costs of development incurred by date of valuation(see PS 3.3)	4.1 4.2
		1.8 Specialised properties in the private sector, except for purposes (d), (e), (f)	DRC subject to adequate potential profitability	4.8
		1.9 Specialised properties in the public sector, except for purposes (d), (e), (f)	DRC subject to the prospect and viability of the continuance of the occupation and use.See PS 3.5.4	4.8
		1.10 Damaged properties	MV* OMV* EUV or DRC according to the classification listed in paragraphs 1.1 to 1.10 above but subject to the provisions of PS3.8	4.1 4.2 4.3 4.8
		1.11 Plant and machinery not being valued as part of land and buildings	OMV (P&M)	4.13.1, except for purposes 6(a), (b) and (c), see 4.13.2

Key	
MV	Market Value
OMV	Open Market Value
ERP	Estimated Realisation Price
ERRP	Estimated Restricted Realisation Price
ERRPEU	Estimated Restricted Realisation Price Existing Use
EUV	Existing Use Value
DRC	Depreciated Replacement Cost

PS4.1.3 **'The estimated amount'** refers to a price expressed in terms of money (normally in the local currency), payable for the asset in an arm's length market transaction. *Market Value* is measured as the most probable price reasonably obtainable in the market at the date of valuation in keeping with the *Market Value* definition. It is the best price reasonably obtainable by the seller and the most advantageous price reasonably obtainable by the buyer. This estimate specifically excludes an estimated price inflated or deflated by special terms or circumstances such as atypical financing, sale and lease-back arrangements, special considerations or concessions granted by anyone associated with the sale, or any element of *Special Value* (defined in IVSC Standard 2 in the following terms:

'*Special Value*. A term relating to an extraordinary element of value over and above *Market Value*. Special value could arise, for example by the physical, functional, or economic association of a property with some other property such as the adjoining property. It is an increment of value which could be applicable to a particular owner or user, or prospective owner or user, of the property rather than to the market at large; that is, to a purchaser with a special interest. Special value could be associated with elements of *Going Concern Value*. The Valuer must ensure that such criteria are distinguished from *Market Value*, making clear any special assumptions made.')

PS4.1.4 '*... an asset should exchange ...*' refers to the fact that the value of an asset is an estimated amount rather than a predetermined or actual sale price. It is the price at which the market expects a transaction that meets all other elements of the *Market Value* definition should be completed on the date of valuation.

PS4.1.5 '*... on the date of valuation ...*' requires that the estimated *Market Value* is time-specific as of a given date. Because markets and market conditions may change, the estimated value may be incorrect or inappropriate at another time. The valuation amount will reflect the actual market state and circumstances as of the effective valuation date, not as of either a past or future date. The definition also assumes simultaneous exchange and completion of the contract for sale without any variation in price that might otherwise be made in *Market Value* transaction.

PS4.1.6 '*... between a willing buyer ...*' refers to one who is motivated, but not compelled to buy. This buyer is neither over-eager nor determined to buy at any price. This buyer is also one who purchases in accordance with the realities of the current market, and with cur-rent market expectations, rather than an imaginary or hypothetical market which cannot be demonstrated or anticipated to exist. The assumed buyer would not pay a higher price than the market requires. The present asset owner is included among those who constitute 'the market'. A Valuer must not make unrealistic assumptions about market conditions or assume a level of *Market Value* above that which is reasonably obtainable. In some countries an explicit reference to a willing buyer is omitted from the definition of *Market Value* to emphasise this responsibility.

PS4.1.7 '*... a willing seller ...*' is neither an over-eager nor a forced seller, prepared to sell at any price, nor one prepared to hold out for a price not considered reasonable in the current market. The willing seller is motivated to sell the asset at market terms for the best price attainable in the open market after proper marketing, whatever that price may be. The factual circumstances of the actual asset owner are not a part of this consideration because the 'willing seller' is a hypothetical owner.

PS4.1.8 '*... in an arm's-length transaction ...*' is one between parties who do not have a particular or special relationship (for example, parent and subsidiary companies, or landlord and tenant) which may make the price level uncharacteristic of the market or inflated because of an element of special value. The *Market Value* transaction is presumed to be between unrelated parties, each acting independently.

PS4.1.9 ' ... *after proper marketing ..*' means that the asset would be exposed to the market in the most appropriate manner to effect its disposal at the best price reasonably obtainable in accordance with the *Market Value* definition. The length of exposure time may vary with market conditions, but must be sufficient to allow the asset to be brought to the attention of an adequate number of potential purchasers. The exposure period occurs prior to the valuation date.

PS4.1.10 ' ... *wherein the parties had each acted knowledgeably and prudently ..*' presumes that both the willing buyer and the willing seller are reasonably informed about the nature and characteristics of the asset, its actual and potential uses, and the state of the market as of the date of valuation. Each is further presumed to act for self-interest with that knowledge, and prudently to seek the best price for their respective positions in the transaction. Prudence is assessed by referring to the state of the market at the date of valuation, not with benefit of hindsight at some later date. It is not necessarily imprudent for a seller to sell property in a market with falling prices at a price which is lower than previous market levels. In such cases, as is true for other purchase and sale situations in markets with changing prices, the prudent buyer or seller will act in accordance with the best market information available at the time.

PS4.1.11 ' ... *and without compulsion ...*' establishes that each party is motivated to undertake the transaction, but neither is forced or unduly coerced to complete it.

PS4.1.12 *Market Value* is understood as the value of an asset estimated without regard to costs of sale or purchase, and without offset of any associated taxes.

PS4.2 **Open Market Value (OMV)**

PS4.2.1 *Definition*
An opinion of the best price at which the sale of an interest in property would have been completed unconditionally for cash consideration on the date of valuation, assuming:

(a) a willing seller;

(b) that, prior to the date of valuation, there had been a reasonable period (having regard to the nature of the property and the state of the market) for the proper marketing of the interest, for the agreement of the price and terms and for the completion of the sale;

(c) that the state of the market, level of values and other circumstances were, on any earlier assumed date of exchange of contracts, the same as on the date of valuation;

(d) that no account is taken of any additional bid by a prospective purchaser with a special interest; and

(e) that both parties to the transaction had acted knowledgeably, prudently and without compulsion.

PS4.2.2 *Commentary*
The use of the expression 'Open Market Value', not qualified by any reference to Existing Use or Alternative Use, implies the value for any use to the extent to which that value is reflected in the price obtainable in the open market.

PS4.2.3 The definition first requires the Valuer to assume that completion of a sale of the interest in the property took place on the valuation date and then to list further assumptions to be made in relation to that hypothetical sale.

PS4.2.4 ' .... *the best price ...*'
Open Market Value is the Valuer's opinion of the best price which would have been obtained in the market on the date of valuation (subject to the exclusion of any additional bid by a prospective purchaser with a special interest); not a 'fair' price, or an average price, or the price which the vendor thinks ought to be achieved.

PS4.2.5 *Hope Value*
Open Market Value includes such element of 'hope value' (if any) as the property may have for uses other than the existing use, (ie Alternative Uses) or for the realisation of any 'marriage value', which the property may have for merger with another property, or which an interest in the property may have for merger with another interest in the same property, but limited to the extent that the expectation of realising such 'hope value' would, in practice, be reflected in offers made in the open market by prospective purchasers (other than the additional bid of 'a prospective purchaser with a special interest').

PS4.2.6 Therefore, alternative use value should be related to definite information as to statutory and/or other consents, or the prospects thereof, (e.g. superior landlord's approval) regarding change of use or other matters. The Valuer must not make unrealistic assumptions.

PS4.2.7

(a) It is frequently necessary to value a property capable of development or redevelopment for a purpose for which no planning permission exists. In an open market valuation, planning permission should not be assumed unless the market would make such an assumption, and even then an allowance for risk would be appropriate where the market would do so.

(b) For example, prospective purchasers in the market might make an assumption that planning permission would be granted but nevertheless would make an allowance or deduction from the amount of their offers to reflect the risks involved and the likelihood of delay in obtaining an acceptable permission. In such circumstances, an open market valuation on the assumption that planning permission would be granted should only be made with the corresponding allowance for risk and delay, thus reflecting the view that would be taken in the market in practice.

(c) As a further example, in the case of an outline planning permission already granted, it might be reasonable to consider that prospective purchasers would assume a particular density

or plot ratio and value accordingly. In such a case it would be proper to make assumptions about planning permission which would be made by prospective purchasers in the market without any deduction for risk.

PS4.2.8 '... *sale ... completed ... cash consideration ... on the date of valuation ...*' The Valuer must state the date of valuation in the Report. It may be the same as the date of the Report or an earlier date, but must not be a future date. The definition contemplates that the date of valuation is contemporaneous with the completion of the hypothetical sale. 'Cash consideration' means that the price to be paid on completion is to be in money, rather than other valuable consideration such as shares or other securities, goods, materials or services. It is not to be assumed that the purchaser is one able to fund the purchase from his own resources rather than by borrowing.

PS4.2.9 '*A willing seller*' The assumption of a 'willing seller' is vital to the definition of Open Market Value because the real circumstances of the actual owner of the property must be ignored and must not be confused with the notional circumstances of the hypothetical 'willing seller'. For the purposes of the definition, the vendor of the property is a hypothetical owner with the right to dispose of the premises. The hypothetical owner is neither an eager nor a reluctant seller, or a forced seller prepared to sell at any price. Thus, the willing seller is not afflicted

by personal difficulties such as a cashflow crisis or importunate mortgagors, nor is that seller in the happy position of someone who wishes to sell only if the price he regards as satisfactory is obtained.

PS4.2.10 Whether the real owner of the property being valued actually considers himself to be a 'willing seller' is irrelevant to the definition of Open Market Value or to the amount of the valuation. One way of explaining the point is to say that a willing seller has to be assumed in the sense that the seller has a genuine intention to sell at the best price (subject to PS4.2.18 below) which can be obtained in the real market after proper marketing, whatever the price might be.

PS4.2.11 '*..a reasonable period ..*' The length of a 'reasonable period' will have varied according to the circumstances, not just of the particular property itself, but of the economy, of the state of the market and of supply and demand. The Valuer must form a judgement of what constituted a 'reasonable period' in each case, just as the Valuer must form an opinion of value, and the 'reasonable period' may have been longer in a poor market than in a good one but its length is related only to the time necessary to market the property properly, to agree price and terms and to complete the sale.

PS4.2.12 '*... proper marketing ...*' Proper marketing means that the interest must be marketed in the most appropriate manner to effect a disposal at the best price having regard to the type of property, its characteristics, locality and the state of the market at the time. The essentials of proper marketing are that the availability of the property for sale and the terms on which it is offered should be brought, by appropriate means, to the attention of an adequate number of potential purchasers and that those potential purchasers should have adequate time in which to obtain such information as they may need in order to make their offers to purchase and, if successful, to complete the transaction.

PS4.2.13 *'.. state of the market .. on the date of valuation.'*
Open Market Value equals the best price that would have been obtained in the market on the date of valuation and, thus, the amount of the valuation must reflect the state of the market and other circumstances on the date of valuation; not on any past or future date. Value is not a price which might be expected some months or years hence when the market may have changed - it is the best price which could have been obtained in the circumstances current on the date of valuation after proper marketing. In a poor or falling market, the Valuer is not entitled to assume that marketing will be delayed until the market has recovered; and, in a rising market, values must not be projected forward.

PS4.2.14 In practice, it is usually the case that the bargain is struck and the price finally fixed, not on the completion of the sale, but on an earlier date when unconditional contracts were exchanged. The Valuer must assume that circumstances, values and market conditions at the date of contract were the same as those prevailing at the date of completion (i.e. the date of valuation).

PS4.2.15 *Evidence of Open Market Transactions*
Generally, open market valuations are based on evidence of open market transactions in similar property. A valuation, however, is an exercise in judgement and should represent the Valuer's opinion of the price which would have been obtained if the property had been sold at the valuation date on the terms of the definition of Open Market Value. The Valuer is not bound to follow evidence of market transactions unquestioningly, but should take account of trends in value and the market evidence available to him, whether or not of directly comparable transactions, adjusting such evidence to reflect the OMV definition, and attaching more weight to some prices of evidence than others, according to the Valuer's judgement. It is seldom that a Valuer has evidence of contemporaneous transactions in precisely similar property to that being valued and the art of valuation often involves subjective adjustments to evidence of transactions which are not wholly comparable and interpretation of trends in value. A Valuer must exercise skill, experience and judgement in valuing and in making such adjustments and comparisons, even to the extent of making an open market valuation (of property for which it is thought there

would have been a market) in the absence of any direct transaction evidence.

PS4.2.16 In a poor or falling market, it is sometimes said that there are few 'willing sellers', that most transactions in the market are the result of 'forced sales' and that prices paid in such a market are not truly representative of Open Market Value and should be ignored by Valuers in favour of some higher level of value. There is little merit in such an argument and there are far fewer truly forced sales (within the meaning of the definition of Estimated Restricted Realisation Price in PS4.6 below) than is sometimes supposed. Valuers must not ignore the evidence of the market; they should take account of all market evidence, attaching such weight to individual transactions as they believe appropriate. In a depressed market, a significant proportion of sales may be by vendors who are obliged to sell, such as Liquidators and Receivers, but the Valuer should establish whether or not those sales took place after proper marketing for a reasonable period. Liquidators and Receivers are normally under a duty to obtain the best price and their sales should be regarded generally as open market transactions if there has been proper marketing for a reasonable period and the transactions otherwise comply with the definition of Open Market Value.

PS4.2.17 In a rapidly rising or falling market, undue weight should not be attributed to historic evidence which may have become outdated, even within a brief period.

163

PS4.2.18 *'... a prospective purchaser with a special interest...'*

(a) The definition of open market value requires the assumption 'that no account is taken of any additional bid by a prospective purchaser with a special interest'.

(b) A purchaser with a 'special interest' (sometimes referred to as a 'special purchaser') may be defined as one to whom the property (or the interest in the property) being valued has a particular attraction which it does not have for the market in general. The special purchaser is, in almost every case, the owner of either:

    (1) an interest in land which has or could have a particular relationship with the property concerned, e.g. the owner of an interest in a nearby or adjacent property; or

    (2) another interest in the property being valued, e.g. a superior landlord or an under-tenant.

(c) There is no certainty that the special purchaser will be prepared to make an offer to purchase the property or interest in the property at the date of the valuation, and it is therefore correct to exclude his additional bid from the open market value. However, if the special purchaser is in the market he can usually afford, or be willing, to pay more than any other purchaser, and if he enters the bidding, he may reasonably be expected to succeed in purchasing the property - certainly in theory - by paying 'one bid more' than any other purchaser. In practice, it is often difficult to quantify the special purchaser's additional bid, since he may not need to go to the level he could afford to bid in order to secure the property. On the other hand, in his determination to secure the property, he may overbid by a margin greater than necessary.

(d) A purchaser who is simply prepared to pay a high price is not necessarily a special purchaser. Neither is someone who is a known purchaser of the particular class of property being valued, nor someone who is an active purchaser of property in the locality. A purchaser who is only one of a class of purchasers to whom the property has particular interest, would not be regarded as a special purchaser; eg tax immune funds which purchase short leasehold investment property. Generally, for a prospective purchaser to be a special purchaser there will be an element of additional potential value which is unique to him.

(e) A superior landlord, or a sitting tenant, may be a special purchaser because the merging of the two interests might liberate 'marriage value' which would justify a higher price than any other purchaser could afford to pay. It must be remembered however that the price which a non-special purchaser would pay might include some part of that marriage value because of the hope that the non-special purchaser might eventually be able to re-sell to the special purchaser at an inflated price. Thus 'hope value' and 'marriage value' may legitimately be included in open market value to the extent that offers from non-special purchasers in the open market themselves reflect those elements of value, as in practice they often do. It is only the additional bid of the special purchaser which has to be excluded from the open market value.

(f) The definition of open market value does not require the Valuer to ignore the existence of the special purchaser, but to take no account of that special purchaser's additional bid, ie the amount by which his offer might exceed offers made by non-special purchasers. In practice, the existence of a special purchaser may affect (usually to a limited degree) the level of offers made by non-special purchasers and, to that extent, may be taken into account in arriving at Open Market Value.

PS4.2.19 *'... the parties had each acted knowledgeably, and prudently...'*

This presumes that both the buyer and the willing seller are reasonably informed about the nature and characteristics of the asset, its actual and potential uses, and the state of the market at the date of valuation. Each is further presumed to act for self-interest with that knowledge, and prudently to seek the best price for their respective positions in the transaction. Prudence is assessed by referring to the state of the market at the date of valuation, not with benefit of hindsight at some later date. It is not necessarily imprudent for a seller to sell property in a market with falling prices at a price that is lower than previous market levels. In such cases, as is true for other purchase and sale situations in markets with changing prices, the prudent buyer or seller will act in accordance with the best market information available at the time.

PS4.2.20 *'... and without compulsion.'*

This establishes that each party is motivated to undertake the transaction, but neither is forced or unduly coerced to complete it.

PS4.5 **Estimated Realisation Price (ERP)**

PS4.5.1 *Definition*

An opinion as to the amount of cash consideration before deduction of costs of sale which the Valuer considers, on the date of valuation, can reasonably be expected to be obtained on future completion of an unconditional sale of the interest in the subject property assuming:

(a) a willing seller;

(b) that completion will take place on a future date specified by the Valuer to allow a reasonable period for proper marketing, (having regard to the nature of the property and the state of the market);

(c) that no account is taken of any additional bid by a prospective purchaser with a special interest;

(d) that both parties to the transaction will act knowledgeably, prudently and without compulsion.

PS4.5.2 *Commentary*

The commentary on the definition of OMV applies equally to the definition of ERP, except for the important difference that in the latter case completion is after the date of valuation; hence the second sentence in PS4.2.8, paragraphs PS4.2.13 and PS4.2.14 do not apply to ERP and in paragraph 4.2.19 'date of valuation' is replaced by 'date of exchange of contracts'. Also PS4.2.4 does not apply.

PS4.5.3 When producing an ERP, the Valuer is required to consider how long, starting with the valuation date, would be reasonably necessary to market the property properly to achieve the best price, without extending the period in the hope of an upturn in the market. The Valuer then has to specify his assumption as to the date of completion of the sale which accommodates the marketing period he considers would be necessary.

PS4.5.4 In most cases the Valuer is likely to approach the formulation of his opinion of ERP in the same way as OMV and then, having reached an opinion of OMV, consider what further changes in the market for the property are likely during the marketing period which precedes the exchange of contracts at the resulting price, (which price should ignore the effect of the additional bid of any special purchaser). Changes during this period may be in external factors such as yields, interest rates, the quality of the location, reduction in void properties in the locality; and/or

changes in the subject property, such as the outcome of rent reviews. The Valuer must reflect in his valuation his belief as to how prospective purchasers would behave in response to the changes he believes can be expected. In summary, the aim is to answer the question, 'For how much do you think the property can be sold, starting the selling process at the date of valuation, and how long do you expect it to take?'

PS4.14 This statement deals with the assumptions to be made regarding environmental factors.

PS5 This Practice Statement sets out **'the restrictions as to when RICS, ISVA and IRRV members may undertake valuations generally and for particular purposes.'**

PS6 **'Inspections and investigations must be adequate and their limits must be clear.'**

This Practice Statement sets out those matters the valuer must consider in preparing a valuation. Not all are relevant to every valuation and their appropriateness will vary with the specifics of the property. Each is detailed in PS6 but the key headings are:

Referencing
Locality, communications, facilities, age, description, use, accommodation, construction, installations, amenities, services, dimensions and areas, repair and conditions, site stability, altitude, topography, soil type, quality, crop details (where appropriate).

Nature of Interest
Freehold, leasehold, restrictions, lease terms, easements, rights of way, wayleaves etc.

Planning and legal

Town planning, environmental, highway and other requirements like considerations.

Other factors

For example rating, plant and machinery, fixtures, fittings, presence of deleterious or hazardous materials, allowance for disrepair, development potential.

Analysis of comparable evidence.

Contamination.

Verification of information supplied to or adopted by the valuer.

PS7 **'There are minimum requirements as to what has to be covered in Valuation Reports, and minimum requirements as to the contents of published references to valuations.'**

The purpose of valuation, assumed date of valuation, basis of valuation and its definition and assumptions and caveats as agreed in the condition of engagement will normally be noted in the report.

This PS deals with the nature and content of reports and requires all reports other than **'those provided on forms provided by the client'** to refer to the following:

· Addressee

· Special instructions and assumptions

· The address(es) and identifications of the subject property/properties and their respective values

· Plant and machinery

· Sources, extent and non-disclosure of information

· Tenure

· Date and extent of inspection

· the opinion of value in words and figures

· VAT, taxation and costs of acquisition or realisation

· Any additional information available to or established by the valuer which he *[sic]* believes to be crucial to the client's ability to understand and benefit from the valuation ....

· where statements are made upon the prospect of future growth in rental and/or capital value, a statement to the effect that such growth may not occur and that values can fall as well as rise

· Third party reference

· References to the manual, either that the valuation has been made in accordance with the Practice Statements or that due to circumstances it is inappropriate (a statement of reason for departure must be given; together with a statement that the value conforms to the requirements of the Practice Statements)

· Clause prohibiting publication

· Whether valuer is internal, external or independent

· Name of the valuer or his organisation and signature

· Date of report.

PS7.5 This completes the schedule with a listing of other matters which must be included where appropriate.

The comprehensive coverage of the Manual is evidenced by the contents which cover:

PS8   Valuation and appraisal of commercial land and buildings for secured lending purposes

PS9   Valuation of residential properties for mortgage purposes

PS10   Valuation and appraisal of Housing Associations' housing stock for secured lending purposes

PS11   RICS/ISVA Home Buyers' Survey and Valuation Scheme

PS12   Valuations for Company Accounts and Financial Statements

PS13   Valuations of Land and Buildings for Incorporation or Reference in Stock Exchange Prospectuses and Circulars

PS14   Valuations under the City Code on Takeovers and Mergers

PS15   Valuations for Business Expansion Schemes

PS16   Valuations under the Insurance Companies Regulations 1994

PS17   Valuations of Unit Linked Property Assets of Life Assurance Companies

PS18   Valuations of Land and Buildings owned by Unregulated Property Unit Trusts

PS19   Valuations of Land and Buildings owned by Property Funds (Authorised Property Unit Trusts)

PS20   Valuations for Pension and Superannuation Funds

PS21   Valuations of Trading Stock and Work in Progress including

Whilst every element of the Manual is important to the practising valuer, students reading this book and undertaking coursework as part of their assessment will find a particular need to refer to PSA3 and PSA7. PSA3 covers typical paragraphs that may need to be incorporated in reports covering: hazardous materials, radon, caveats in respect of: contamination, consent to publication, limitation of liability, state of repair, whilst PSA7 contains a number of suggested examples of acceptable paragraphs to be used where reference is to be made in published documents to valuation reports.

(The Appraisal and Valuation Manual is regularly reviewed and practising valuers must refer to the most recently amended version of the manual.)

appendix

B

Illustrative investment property purchase report

Based on material provided for the third edition by Gooch and Wagstaff, Chartered Surveyors.

Contents

Pension Funds and Life funds act in a trustee capacity when they invest policyholders' moneys. It is customary for an investment purchase report to be commissioned following agreement on purchase price to protect the trustee status. These reports are very similar to full reports commissioned for loan and other purposes. Each in turn will reflect the agreed instructions and will be prepared, where applicable, in accordance with mandatory requirements and/or general guidance notes issued by the RICS. Additional caveats will be agreed at the time of instruction and included in the report if so required by the valuer's Professional Indemnity Insurance Policy.

The format of these reports is as follows and will be supported by photographs, location plans, building plans, extracts from 'Focus' and other dat bases to support opinions in the report including evidential material on rents and market capitalisation rates. All measurements used in reports should be stated to be approximate, and are now required to be in metric, or both metric and imperial.

1.0 Summary

Terms have been agreed on behalf of XYZ Limited to purchase this freehold shop investment from . . .

Purchase Price:	£450,000 (FOUR HUNDRED AND FIFTY THOUSAND POUNDS).
Tenure:	Freehold
Approximate Area:	159 sq.m.
User:	High-class retail shop.
Letting:	Let to AAA and BBB trading as ZZZ Bakers on assignment from XXXX (UK) Ltd. 25 years from 00/00/00 to 00/00/00, FRI terms at £11,750 p.a.
Reviews:	00/00/00 and every 5 years upwards only.
Estimated Rental Value:	£21,350 p.a.
Estimated Yields:	2.54% net initial rising to 4.61% on reversion in 00/00/00. Net equivalent yield 4.53%.

We conclude that the price agreed reflects the current market and we recommend the acquisition to XYZ Limited.

This summary should only be read in conjunction with the detailed comments which follow:

Address of property

2.0 Instructions

We are instructed to prepare a Report and Valuation on the freehold shop investment located at XXXX on behalf of XYZ Ltd. It should be noted that whilst we have inspected the property and briefly describe its structure, we are not instructed to report on its structural condition and we understand that you have carried out your own structural survey and are satisfied with the result.

2.1   This report is subject to the Limitations set out in the extract from the Guidance Notes on the Valuation of Assets produced by the Royal Institution of Chartered Surveyors which is attached as Appendix 1.

1.0 Reports may be written in letter style or report format. Each page should be numbered and should bear the name of the valuer's practice. Paragraph numbering may avoid the risk of sections becoming detached and not missed and helps with cross referencing.

2.0 In accordance with RICS requirements terms and conditions will have been agreed in writing prior to acceptance of the instruction. This section would refer back to the details set out in the Conditions of Engagement. Where a structural survey is part of the same instruction the valuer's report should draw on the findings of the Building Surveyor's report.

2.1 This section will refer in future to the RICS *Appraisal and Valuation Manual.*

3.0 Location

XXXX, is a historic City with a population in the region of 50,000 persons which is substantially increased by visiting tourists and by students. The estimated shopping catchment is some 120,000 persons. The City is situated close to the junction of the M4 and the A111 thus providing good access to London (100 kilometres), XXX (12.5 kilometres) and XXXX (6.25 kilometres). The A222 to Z, the A333 to B and C and the A444 to D all radiate from the Town thus providing good communications to the surrounding centres and to the M4.

A British Rail main line service connects XXXX to London Kings Cross (the fastest journey time being 2 hrs and 55 mins) and X Airport is approximately 25 miles to the North by road. A location map is attached as *Appendix 2.*

The property is located within the established shopping area in the City Centre on the South side of XXXX at the top of XXXX Street and is close to the Town's main car parks. A Street Map is attached as *Appendix 3*. The City Centre is well represented in terms of national multiples and includes such occupiers as Next, Boots, Marks & Spencer, F. W. Woolworth, Burtons and W. H. Smith. A market is held in XXXX Place on Saturdays and this is a busy pedestrian thoroughfare linking the Town's main car park with the principal shopping area of Market Place and Street. An extract from the traders' plan is attached as *Appendix 4.*

4.0 Site

The site which slopes up to the rear is roughly rectangular in shape and has a frontage to XXXX of 4.35 metres and a depth of 31.6 metres. The site extends to an area of approximately 126 square metres and is outlined in red on the attached Ordnance Survey Extract *(Appendix 5).*

5.0 Description and construction

The property is a Grade II Listed Building constructed circa 1850 comprising a ground floor shop unit with rear storage and 3 floors of disused residential space above having access from the rear yard. Access to the yard is provided via a passageway to the side of the shop. The shop has a somewhat limited internal width averaging 3.2 metres

The building is constructed of brick and sandstone quoin blocks and eaves cornice under a pitched slate roof. The windows are single glazed wooden sash.
The shop has no central heating. The upper floors are heated by a coke burning boiler in need of replacement, serving radiators.

6.0 Accommodation

We have measured the property in accordance with the **RICS Code of Measuring Practice** and the building has the following approximate floor areas and dimensions:-

3rd floor	– residential	43.2	sq.m.
2nd floor	– residential	37.5	sq.m.
1st floor	– residential	41.1	sq.m.
Ground floor– Sales		39.8	sq.m.
	– Rear Store	10.2	sq.m
Total		**171.8**	**sq.m.**

Overall frontage (including passageway)	4.32	m.
Gross frontage	3.98	m.
Net frontage	3.2	m.
Internal Width (Average)	3.2	m.
Shop Depth	22.5	m.
Built Depth	31.6	m.

7.0 Services

We understand that the property is supplied with mains water, electricity and drainage.

8.0 Rating

We have made verbal enquiries of XYZ Council and are informed that the property is included within the current Valuation List having the following description and assessments:

Description	*Rateable Value*
Shop and Premises	£11,000

9.0 Town Planning

We have made verbal enquiries of the Local Planning Authority, XYZ Council, and understand that the property is a Grade II Listed Building situated within the City Centre Conservation Area as defined by the City of XYZ Local Plan dated March 1988 but not yet adopted. The listing is recorded as:

'House now shop. Mid 19th century, circa 1900 shop front grey (yellow) brick; flemish bond, ashlar dressings. Welsh slate roof. Six panel door at right and recessed shop door at left have fan lights with glazing bars. Rounded top light to shop window with similar glazing bars. Shop door has bevelled glass in patterned glazing bars. Tuscan pilasters and bracketed cornice frame shop. Upper floors have sashes with glazing bars. Projecting stone sills cut back underneath at forty five degrees. Chamfered stone quoins support similar cutback in cornice with paved brackets and finishing in pyramidal coped blocks. Low pitched roof with tall banded chimney on left.'

Policy E18 in the Local Plan generally aims to protect and enhance the character, appearance and setting of the City's conservation areas. Policy E19 sets out a number of restrictions and guidelines relating to the City Centre Conservation Area itself, covering the visual historical and architectural importance of the buildings.

Under the section headed 'Land Use Policies' in the Local Plan it is stated that no major development or re-development for shopping will be allowed in the City Centre except in the shopping and business centre as allocated in the XYZ Zone (Policy CC1). Policies CC2 and CC3 stipulate that in the Shopping and Business Centre commercial and community purposes will take precedence over other uses except where upper floor space is to be converted to residential use. Furthermore, XXXX is included in the area in which changes of use of ground floors to office use (as covered by Class II of the Town and Country Planning (Use Classes Order) 1972), betting offices and amusement arcades will not be permitted. Elsewhere in the Shopping and Business Centre office users will be given consideration by the Local Planning Authority provided they do not exceed more than 10% of the net frontage length of ground floor properties in retail and commercial uses.

We are informed that there are no plans to review traffic management in the XXXX Place area to restrict service vehicle access during the shopping hours.

We have traced the planning history through the local planners. It has been assumed that the property has planning consent for use as a shop and we are aware of a planning consent dated 11th February 1982 permitting change of use from residential to office of the 1st, 2nd and 3rd floors which expired in 1987. We are informed that this is the only planning consent given since 1974.

A new development is planned for the site on XXXX between Boots and No. 10 XXXX which will span the slip road and the through-road off XXXX Bridge. The developers are ABC Ltd and the landowners are the City Council. We anticipate that this development will improve XXXX as a shopping location and increase the pedestrian flow past the subject property.

CDE Ltd and the City Council are planning a joint development of a scheme incorporating a hotel, 25,000 sq.m. of retail, 1,000 space carpark, an ice-rink and a swimming pool, on the site of the existing ice-rink and car park north of A Road by the river. It is anticipated that an application for planning permission will be submitted in 1989 but this proposal is very much in its early stages. However its location should serve to enhance XXXX.

In B Street XXXX Estates are currently refurbishing Nos. 68-70 and the ABC Centre on the other side of the river has recently been extended with only one remaining unit unlet. North of the City a mixed development of shops, industrial and residential units is to be constructed near XXXX. The planning consent is still subject to a Section 52 Agreement relating to infrastructure works but it is not anticipated that this should hinder the works. An application has been made on a site to the east of the City for an industrial estate incorporating bulky goods retail warehouses.

We are of the opinion that none of the developments or policies described are likely to adversely affect the subject property and we are not aware of any other relevant current policies or proposals.

10.0   Tenure

The property is freehold with a right-of-way in Fee Simple granted to the occupiers of the adjoining premises over the passageway along the side of the subject property. This gives access to the upper floors of the adjoining building.

11.0   Occupation and letting

The entire property was let to XXXX Ltd by virtue of a lease dated 00/00/00 for a term of 25 years from 00/00/00 subject to five-yearly upward only rent reviews at a current rent of £11,750 p.a. The lease is drawn on full repairing and insuring terms with the landlord effecting insurance and recovering the premium direct from the tenant.

The lease was recently assigned to .... and .... The tenant is prohibited from assigning or underletting the whole or part of the demised premises without prior written consent from the landlord which is not to be unreasonably withheld.

The tenant covenants 'not without consent in writing of the lessor first obtained to use the demised premises or any part thereof or suffer the same to be used otherwise than as a high-class retail shop only'. Although the upper floors are fitted out for residential use and such a use would be acceptable in planning terms, we have valued the upper parts as storage ancillary to the retail in accordance with the terms of the lease.

12.0   Covenant

We have no information on the covenant of the tenant and have assumed that you are satisfied with the covenant status.

We understand from your solicitors that the assignment does not appear to be documented and they should satisfy themselves as to the legal position in this regard, particularly as we understand that a schedule of repairs dated 00/00/00 is still outstanding and should have been completed within six months of the date of the licence to assign.

13.0   Rental value

XXXX is a Cathedral City with a substantial catchment area and is much sought after by national multiple retailers. The main shopping area in the City Centre is centred around A Street and XXXX with B Street being relatively secondary in terms of rental value and location.

The XXXX Centre on the other side of the river, was opened in 1976 and commands rents equating to between £4 and £4.50 per square metre Zone A. A second phase was opened in 0000 extending the original 7,000 sq. metres by a further 10,000 sq. metres where rents equating to between £3.50 and £3.75 per square metre Zone A have been achieved. A Street and XXXX command higher rental values, the highest rent achieved on review is reported as equating to £9.20 Zone A at No. 10 A Street. However we understand that this was not an armslength deal in that the landlords were reluctant to grant permission for the tenant to assign his lease until the review was settled, and the tenants consequently accepted the landlords quoting figure without further negotiation. We have therefore attached little relevance to this deal. The XXXX Shop unit at No. 20 A Street was let recently at a rent equating to £6.5 per square metre Zone A, although this is generally regarded as being underlet.

We understand that the proposed ABC Ltd's scheme on XXXX was appraised on the basis of shop rents equating to £7.20 Zone A at today's rents and that CDE's scheme is being appraised on rents in excess of £7.20 Zone A.

No. 15 A Street was reviewed in 00/00 to a rent equating to £6.40 Zone A and Nos. 4/5 A Street were reviewed to a rent equating to £5.50 Zone A in 0000. At the bottom of A Street No. 18 was reviewed in 0000 to a rent equating to over £6.30 Zone A. However it was agreed between the respective parties that the restrictive user had the effect of discounting the rent by 15%. On this basis the Zone A open market rental equates to over £7.20 Zone A. We believe similar rents are being achieved in A Street on premium deals but are unable to obtain precise information in this respect.

The current rent reserved under the lease is **£11,750 p.a.** exclusive, which equates to £3.45 Zone A.

We are of the opinion that the current open market rental value of the property is approximately **£21,350 p.a.**, equating to £6.65 Zone A.

14.0 Valuation

Terms have been agreed to purchase this freehold shop investment in the sum of **£450,000 (FOUR HUNDRED AND FIFTY THOUSAND POUNDS)**, subject to contract.

We therefore estimate that the agreed acquisition price reflects a net initial yield of 2.54%, rising to 4.61% on reversion in 00/00 to produce a net equivalent yield of 4.53%. These yields are after allowance for acquisition costs of 2.75% to cover fees and Stamp Duty.

15.0　　　Recommendation

We draw attention to the fact that at the time of valuation there was a limited amount of directly comparable rental evidence available on which to base our valuation, particularly taking account of the limited shop width. It is relevant that we were aware of other parties bidding for the investment and indeed, having submitted an offer for this property we were informed that two other offers had been received by the vendor at the same level and are subsequently informed of a further offer of £475,000.

We are of the opinion that the agreed purchase price of £450,000 (**FOUR HUNDRED AND FIFTY THOUSAND POUNDS**) for this freehold shop investment is appropriate in the current market and recommend the purchase to .... Limited.

> **15.0** This section may be split between the recommendation - to buy at - and the investment considerations. The latter would develop the valuer's opinion of the state of the market supported by direct evidence, research findings and observations based on, say, the IPD forecasts and an indication of possible growth expectations and yields given that growth.

REF/DATE

16.0　Limitations

Extracts from the RICS guidance notes on the valuation of assets - 2nd edition.

'The Valuer shall have regard to the apparent state of repair and condition of the property but shall be under no duty to carry out a structural survey of the property nor to inspect woodwork or other parts of the structure of the property which are covered, unexposed or inaccessible; neither shall he have a duty to arrange for the testing of electrical heating or other services.

Unless otherwise expressly agreed the Valuer shall, in arriving at his valuation of the property, assume that:

(a)　good freehold or leasehold title (as the case may be) can be shown that the property is not subject to any unusual or onerous restrictions, encumbrances or outgoings;

(b)　the property is unaffected by any statutory notice and that neither the property nor its use or its intended use gives rise to a contravention of any statutory requirement; and

(c)　the property is free from dry rot, woodworm and latent defects and that no deleterious materials have been used in the construction of the property.

The Valuer shall be under no duty to verify these assumptions.'

'This report is confidential to the client for the specific purpose to which it refers. It may be disclosed to other professional advisers assisting the client in respect of that purpose, but the client shall not disclose the report to any other person.'

'Neither the whole nor any part of this report or any reference thereto may be included in any published document, circular or statement nor published in any way without the Valuer's written approval of the form and context in which it may appear.'

> **16.0** Any limitations on the valuation must form part of the condition of engagement.
>
> As indicated these will draw on the **RICS** guidance both mandatory and on any P.I. policy requirement.
>
> Particular key issues which must be covered are those relating to contamination and pollution.
>
> Details of current approved *typical paragraphs* are covered in **PSA 3**.

appendix

C

Illustrative development site appraisal report

The following report is based on the standard report produced by CIRCLE Systems Development Appraisal System using the data from Example 11.1 on page 121.
The report is annotated with comments to explain the functionality of the sytem and the additional variables not analysed in the simple illustrative example in Chapter 11.

Cover page

PROJECT REPORT
DEVELOPMENT APPRAISAL
DEVELOPMENT X
FOR CLIENT Y

Report date: 07/11/1995

Contents page

CONTENTS

	Section
Timescale & Summary	1
Valuation and Appraisal	2
Areas, Capitalisation & Sales	3
Construction costs	4
General Costs & Fees	5

The Circle system allows the user considerable flexibility in the tailoring of development appraisal reports . The valuer can select from the basic appraisal to a report containing some or all of the components indicated in the contents page. In addition the sensitivity analysis and cash flows can be printed.

TIMESCALE & SUMMARY

_____ PROJECT SUMMARY_____

CONTENT

Part 1

	SqM	
	Gross	Net
Offices	7,000	6,000
Total	7,000	6,000

Net: Gross Ration = 85.71

TIMESCALE
Part 1

Commencement	Oct 1995	
Pre-Construction Void	0	months
Construction Start	Oct 1995	
Construction Duration	24	months
Void begins	Oct 1997	
Void duration	0	months
Terminating end of	Sep 1997	
Part timescale	24	months

The first part of the timescale and summary section shows the project summary.

The development may be split into a number of phases or 'parts' each of which would be described in this section.

The project summary shows the gross and net or lettable areas of each area of development and indicates the net to gross efficiency ratio.

The page then shows all of the various time periods that will be used in the calculation.

In our simple calculation there is no void period; this however is unrealistic unless the development is pre-let.

In most cases a void period, i.e. the period between completion of construction and letting, will be assumed. This period will extend the payback period of the funding required for development. It is one of the variables carefully considered when development scenarios are being modelled using this type of software.

Because the void extends the funding of the whole outstanding debt an increase in this period can have a significant impact upon the profitability of a scheme.

TIMESCALE & SUMMARY cont'd

FINANCIAL SUMMARY

Project Timescale	24 months	
INCOME		
Sales Income		0
Annual Rental Income	720,000 p.a.	
Net Cap Value		10,285,714
Other Income		0
Completed Value		10,285,714
EXPENDITURE		
Site Purchase Cost	3,516,795	
Site Purchase Fees	105,504	
Total Purchase Cost		3,622,299
Construction Costs	2,800,000	
Construction Fees	350,000	
Total Construction		3,150,000
Sale Costs/Fees		102,857
Purchaser's Costs		0
Other Costs		0
Marketing/Letting		194,000
Site Finance	1,168,191	
Constr. Finance	505,510	
Void Finance	0	
Offset Interest	0	
Total Finance		1,673,701
Net VAT		0
Total Expenditure		8,742,857
Balance		1,542,857
Profit on GDV	15.0%	
Void Interest Cover	1.16 yrs	
Void Rent Cover	2.14 yrs	
Dev. Yield on Cost	8.24%	

ASSUMPTIONS

Construction Interest Compound: Weighted 50%
Payments annually in advance
Professional Fees based on construction excluding demolition and site works
Profit measured against gross development value
Purchaser's costs based on gross capitalisation
Fees on Sales based on Sales plus NDV

This page gives a financial summary of the value of the development and lists the development expenditure.

The system can be used for capital sales (e.g. residential developement) and capitalised rental income or a mixture of the two.

The expenditure summary shows additional items not considered in the simple manual calculation on page 122. For example VAT and offset interest.

This page also shows some useful statistics for the development scheme.

The Profit on Gross Development Value (or costs) as selected by the user.
In this case the profit has been stipulated by the user at 15% in order to calculate site value. Where the system is used for development appraisal and the land value is known: it is this figure which will be calculated as the residual sum.

The void interest cover shows the period of time over which the profit would be completely eroded by continuing interest payments where the development remains unlet.

The void rent cover is calculated by dividing the residual profit by the rental value. If the developer is guaranteeing rent as part of a funding arrangement a profit will still be made providing the development is let within the period of years shown, in this case 2.14 years.

The Development Yield on cost is calculated by dividing the income by the total costs and expresses income as a percentage of total costs incurred in creating the scheme.

The assumptions of the calculation including the weighting of the interest on construction costs (in this case 50%) are clearly shown on this page of the report.

APPRAISAL

REALISATION	%		
SALES			N/A
GROSS RENT 6000 SqM @ 120.0 psm		720,000 pa	
Less Ground Rent		0 pa	
Net Rental Income		720,000 pa	

CAPITALISATION @ Yield 7.00% x 14.29 YP   10,285,714

(NDV = 10,285,714)	GDV 10,285,714
Other Revenue	0

NET REALISATION   10,285,714

OUTLAY

SITE PURCHASE PRICE		3,516,795	
Stamp Duty	1.000%	35,168	
Land Acq. Agent	1.000%	35,168	
Land Acq. Legal	1.000%	35,168	
Grd Rent Agt Fee		0	
Grd Rent Lgl Fee		0	
Town Plan/Survey		0	
Arrangement Fee		0	
			3,622,299
CONSTR. 7000 SqM @ 400.00 psm		2,800,000	
Contingency		0	
Demolition		0	
Site Works/Roads		0	
FEES			
Architect	9.000%	252,000	
Quant. Surveyor	3.5000%	98,000	
Struct Engineer		0	
Mech/Elec Eng.		0	
Misc. Fees		0	
Project Manager		0	
Statutory costs		0	
Misc Costs		0	
MARKETING		50,000	
LETTING Agt/Legal	20,000%	144,000	
			3,344,000
Purchasers Costs		0	
Sale Agent Fees	1.000%	102,857	
Sale Legal Fees		0	102,857
EXTRA COSTS		0	
Value Added Tax		0	
			0
INTEREST (site 15.00% building 15.00%)			
Site (excl. void)	24 mth	1,168,191	
Building (Comp 50%)	24 mth	505,510	
Void	0 mth	0	
Offset Interest		0	
			1,673,701
	COSTS		8,742,857
	PROFIT 15.00%		1,542,857

This one page appraisal shows clearly the key components of the appraisal. Where a development is phased the results of each phase are aggregated into the single appraisal.

The layout of the appraisal is the same whether you are using it for calculating the residual land value or residual profit.

In this case the land value is calculated and inserted as the sale purchase price in the outlay section. The appraisal is calculated at the pre-determined target profit rate of 15%.

The contingency is a figure, usually a percentage of construction costs, to reflect the difficulties of precisely estimating building costs and to cover extras in the contract that may occur for unforeseen circumstances.

The system can cope with a wide range of professional fees, VAT and extra income and expenditure which can be inserted using a number of expandable screens from within the main appraisal screens.

The difference in figures between the Circle analysis and the manual calculation on page 122 is due to the more realistic treatment of marketing costs based on a percentage of the first year's rent and a more accurate calculation of the interest charges.

SENSITIVITY ANALYSIS

Residual Land Value Table

Rent Rate	Bldg Rate				
	380.00	390.00	400.00	410.00	420.00
105.00	2,871,328	2,804,247	2,737,160	2,670,070	2,602,984
112.50	3,261,153	3,194,069	3,126,980	3,059,890	2,992,801
120.00	3,650,976	3,583,884	3,516,795	3,449,708	3,382,616
127.50	4,040,793	3,973,699	3,906,614	3,839,521	3,772,432
135.00	4,420,608	4,363,519	4,296,432	4,229,340	4,162,246

The system can be used to generate a sensitivity analysis matrix.

In this case the matrix shows the effect on the residual land value of changes in two variables: the rent and the building cost rates.

The 'worst' case scenario is therefore in the top right-hand corner of the matrix and the 'best' case scenario in the bottom left-hand corner.

When using the system for appraisals the matrix would show the amount of profit in £ (or other currency) and as a percentage of either GDV, NDV or construction costs as preselected by the user.

The sensitivity analysis can also produce a three-variable matrix by using five layers or windows which are printed separately.

Solutions to Part I questions

1. £975.33 (A £1)

2. £663.429 (PV £1)

3. £3,553.20 (Annuity x. or PV £1 p.a.)

4. £21,321.44 (A £1 p.a.)

5. £97.38 (ASF)

6. a) Lump sum or annual sinking fund
    b) £8,049.25 or £1,424.60 p.a.
    c) £25,000 x A £1 at 12% = £25,000 x 3.1058 = £77,645 x PV £1 at 12% = £25,000.
       Therefore £25,000 or £77,645 x ASF 0.05698 = £4,424.21.

7. a) £2,763 (A £1 p.a.)   b) £5,764.75   c) £8,085.36

8. £465,292 (10,000 x PV £1 p.a. @ 8% + 50,000 x PV £1 p.a. in perp @ 8% x PV £1 in 10 years @ 8%)

9. 13%

Solutions to Part II questions

Chapter 5

Q   Yields

$\dfrac{75,000}{1,250,000}$ x 100 = 6% (All Risks Yield/ARY or capitalisation (cap) rate.

Note: $\dfrac{1,250,000}{75,000}$ = 16.667 Years' Purchase = $\dfrac{100}{16.667}$ = 6%

Q   Equivalent Yield Analysis

Term Income	£30,000			
YP 2 years at x%	(1.8080)	(£54,240)		
Reversion Income	£40,000			
YP per at x%				
PV £1 in 2 years at x%	(12.477)	(£499,080)	(£553,320)	
				£553,000

By trial and error the rate percent that discounts the income to a present value of £553,000 will be found to be 7% to the nearest per cent. This is the equivalent yield, which in turn is the internal rate of return.

In both questions valuers might deduct management fees from the net rent before seeking to calculate the capitalisation rate or ARY.

Chapter 6

Q   Growth Rate

ARY (k)	= 6%
Gilts	= 8%
Target rate (e)	= 8% + 1% = 9%
Rent review (t)	= 5 years
Substituting in	

$k = e - (ASF \times P)$

$0.06 = 0.09 - (0.16709 \times P)$

0.16709P	=	0.09 - 0.06
0.16709P	=	0.03
P	=	0.03/0.16709
P	=	0.18 (18% over 5 years)

Therefore annual growth is:

$(1 + g)^5$	=	1.18
$(1 + g)$	=	$\sqrt[5]{1.18}$
or $(1 + g)$	=	$1.18^{0.2}$
$(1 + g)$	=	1.03365
g	=	1.03365 - 1
g	=	0.03365 x 100
	=	3.365% per year

Q   Freehold Warehouse   p.71

Step 1: Find the ARY from comparable:

$$\frac{£42,500}{£472,000} \times 100 = 9.0\%$$

Step 2: Find rental value from comparable:

Given as £42,500

Step 3: Equivalent Yield Valuation:

Assume no market variation from ARY

Term Income	£30,000		
YP 2 years @ 9%	1.7591	£52,773	

Reversion Income	£42,500		
YP perp. def'd 2 yrs			
@ 9%	9.3520	£397,460	
		£450,233	

Step 4: Modified DCF - Rational Method:

K =   0.09
e =   0.12
t =   5-year standard review patters

$K = e - (ASF \times P)$

0.09	=	0.12 - (0.15741P)
0.15841P	=	0.12 - 0.09
0.15741P	=	0.03
P	=	0.03/0.15741
P	=	0.19058 (say 0.19)

Therefore annual growth

$(1+g)^5$	=	0.19	(Note: A £1 formula is $(1+i)^n$ is 1 +
$(1+g)$	=	$5\sqrt{1.19}$	interest to produce £1.19 in 5 years)
or $(1+g)$	=	$1.19^{0.2}$	
$(1+g)$	=	1.0354	
g	=	0.0354×100	
	=	3.54%	

Term Income	£30,000		
YP 2 years @ 12%	1.6901	£50,703	

Reversion Income	£42,500	
A £1 in 2 years @ 3.54%	1.072	
	£45,562	

YP perp. @ 9% 11.111			
PV £1 in 2 yrs @ 12% 0.79719	8.8575	£403,571	
		£454,274	

Step 5: Real Value Approach:

Assess IRFY

$$\frac{e - g}{1 + g}$$

$$\frac{0.12 - 0.0354}{1.0354}$$

$$\frac{0.0846}{1.0354}$$

$0.0817 = 8.17\%$

Term Income	£30,000	
YP 2 years @ 12%	1.6901	£50,703
Reversion Income	£42,500	
YP perp. @ 9% 11.111		
PV £1 in 2 yrs @ 8.17% 0.8546 9.4959		£403,578
		£454,281

(Note: a number of calculations have been rounded giving rise to a marginal difference in totals between Rational and Real Value figures.)

In this example the variation in opinion of value is small and in valuation terms the opinion might be rounded in all cases to £450,000. The variation is small due to a number of factors; namely, the short period to the reversion, the relatively low implied growth rate and the fact that the term income is some 70% of the market rental value.

Chapter 7

Q   Leasehold Valuation

Profit rent	£20,000
YP 4 years @ 8% and 3% Tax 40%	2.0904
	£41,808

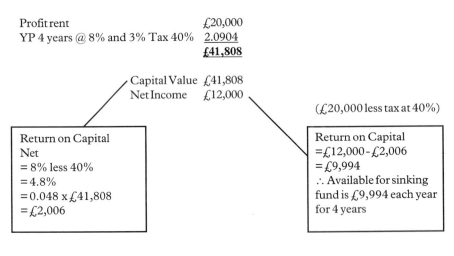

Capital Value £41,808
Net Income   £12,000

(£20,000 less tax at 40%)

Return on Capital
Net
= 8% less 40%
= 4.8%
= 0.048 x £41,808
= £2,006

Return on Capital
= £12,000 - £2,006
= £9,994
∴ Available for sinking fund is £9,994 each year for 4 years

Sinking fund	=	£9,994
A £1 p.a. for 4 years @ 3%	=	4.1836
		£41,810

Note small cumulative error flowing from YP of 2.0904 instead of 2.0903738.

Q. Shopping Centre - geared leasehold

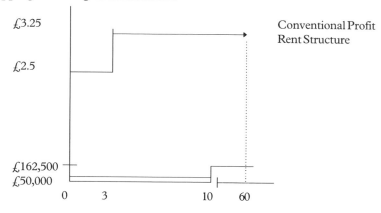

Conventional Profit Rent Structure

Conventional Valuation of 60-year lease

Current Rent Receivable	£2,500,000	
Head Rent	50,000	
Profit Rent	£2,450,000	
YP 3 years @ 8% and 3% tax 40p	1.6149	£3,956,505
Reversion to	£3,250,000	
Head Rent	50,000	
Profit Rent	£3,200,000	
YP 7 years @ 8% and 3% tax 40p 3.3612		
PV £1 in 3 years @ 8% 0.79383	2.6682	£8,538,308
Reversion to	£3,250,000	
Head Rent (5%)	162,500	
Profit Rent	£3,087,500	
YP 50 years @ 8% and 3% tax 40p 10.5512		
PV £1 in 10 years @ 8% 0.46319	4.8872	£15,089.261
		£27,584.074

Notes

- Variable profit produces 3 separate sinking funds, one for each tranche of income when only one is needed to recover capital over 60 years which is, in valuation terms, approaching perpetuity.

- Valuation should be reworked using Sinking Fund method to correct arithmetic error.

- Conventional approach fails to reflect the difference between fixed profit rents and growth profit rents.

- Conventional approach cannot adequately deal with the profit rent growth from year 10 to year 60.

- Head rent review in year 10 is taken to be 5% of today's estimate of open market rental value.

All these issues have probably resulted in an undervaluation of the leasehold interest.

DCF Valuation

Step 1: Calculate the implied growth rate. Using market yields requires the valuer to adopt freehold yields.

Given K = 0.07 (conventionally freehold is 1-2% below leasehold)
             e = 0.10
             P = unknown
             t = 5 years

Then

$$K = e - (ASF \times P)$$

0.07	=	0.10 - (0.16380P)
0.16380P	=	0.10 - 0.07
0.16380P	=	0.03
P	=	0.03/0.16380
P	=	0.18315
P	=	18.315% (over 5 years)
$\therefore P$	=	$(1+g)^t - 1$
1.18315	=	$(1+g)^5$
$^5\sqrt{1.18315}$	=	$(1+g)$ or $1.18315^{0.2}$
1.0342-1	=	g
0.0342	=	g
3.42%	=	g

Assuming income is all annual in arrears, and allowing for implied rental growth in the cash flow at 3.42% on the OMRV of £3.25m, produces the following cash flow which is discounted at a net of tax rate on net of tax income.

Period (end of year)	Shop Rents	Head Rent	Profit Rent	Net of Tax @ 40p	PV£1 pa @ 7.2%[1]	PV £1 @ 7.2%	PV
1	2,500,000	50,000	2,450,000	1,470,000	-	0.9328	1,371,216
2	2,500,000	50,000	2,450,000	1,470,000	-	0.8702	1,279,194
3	2,500,000	50,000	2,450,000	1,470,000	-	0.8117	1,193,199
4[2]	3,594,983	50,000	3,544,983	2,126,989	-	0.7572	1,610,556
5	3,594,983	50,000	3,544,983	2,126,989	-	0.7063	1,502,292
6	3,594,983	50,000	3,544,983	2,126,989	-	0.6589	1,401,473
7	3,594,983	50,000	3,544,983	2,126,989	-	0.6146	1,307,247
8	3,594,983	50,000	3,544,983	2,126,989	-	0.5734	1,219,615
9[3]	4,253,225	50,000	4,203,225	2,521,935	-	0.5348	1,348,731
10	4,253,225	50,000	4,203,225	2,521,935	-	0.4989	1,258,193
11[4]	4,253,225	212,661	4,040,564	2,424,338	-	0.4654	1,128,287
12	4,253,225	212,661	4,040,564	2,424,338	-	0.4342	1,052,647
13	4,253,225	212,661	4,040,564	2,424,338	-	0.4050	981,857
14-18[5]	5,031,991	212,661	4,819,330	2,891,598	4.078	0.4050	4,775,734
19-23	5,953,348	212,661	5,740,687	3,444,412	4.078	0.2860	4,017,245
24-28	7,043,406	212,661	6,830,745	4,098,447	4.078	0.2021	3,377,791
29-33	8,333,054	212,661	8,120,393	4,872,235	4.078	0.1427	2,835,302
34-38	9,858,837	212,661	9,646,176	5,787,705	4.078	0.1008	2,379,108
39-43	11,663,990	212,661	11,451,329	6,870,797	4.078	0.0712	1,994,961
44-48	13,799,966	212,661	13,587,305	8,152,383	4.078	0.0503	1672244
49-53	16,326,739	212,661	16,114,078	9,668,446	4.078	0.0355	1,399,695
54-58	19,316,165	212,661	19,103,504	11,462,102	4.078	0.0251	1,173,235
59-60	22,852,955	212,661	22,640,294	13,584,176	1.803	0.0177	433,513
							£40,713,331

1. 12% gross less tax @ 40p = 7.2% net.

2. £3,250,000 (ERV) x A £1 in 3 years @ 3.42% = £3,594,983.

3. Shop rents reviewed every 5 years with implied growth 3.42%.

4. Head rent reviewed at 5% of shop rents, taken here as 5% of rents collected but could in some leases be 5% of OMRV. Head rent remains fixed for 50 years.

5. Each 5-year cash flow is discounted for 5 years using the PV £1 p.a. factor. The resultant sum is the present worth at the beginning of the 5 years and which must then be discounted to point zero using the PV £1. In the period 14–18 the PV £1 p.a. has brought the cash flow back to the end of year 13 (see formula for PV £1 p.a.) and hence the use of the PV for 13 years not 14 years.

6. This opinion of value is £13m more than that arising from a conventional dual rate approach. The errors in the dual rate, if corrected would reduce this difference but the critical factor is that the conventional approach only partially allows for the profit rent growth from year 10 by using a remunerative rate of 8%. The DCF using an implied growth rate identifies this investment opportunity. The issue for the valuer is one of determining (open) market value and unless the DCF approach can be shown to be the market method then the conventional method may represent the best price one can expect in the market place.

Chapter 9

Q **Premium Calculation** P.18

| Freehold All Risks Yield | = | 5% |
| Leasehold | = | 6%/3% tax 40p |

Then:

Proposed Profit rent or rental loss is:		£75,000
less		£50,000
		£25,000
Average of YP 5 years @ 5%	4.3295	
and YP 5 years @ 6%/3% tax 40p	2.6743	3.502
Premium		£87,547

1. In theory there could be no agreement using this conventional approach. Comparing the Freehold YP of 4.3295 and the Leasehold YP of 2.6743 indicates that the freeholder needs a larger premium than the tenant can afford.

2. In practice the freeholder is likely, under normal market conditions, to insist on a sum close to £25,000 x 4.3295; that is, £108,237.

Q **Surrender and Renewal** p.103

(a) A Freeholder's Present Interest

Current Rent	£10,000	
YP 10 years @ 9%	6.4177	64,177
Reversion to OMRV	£100,000	
YP perp. def'd 10 years @ 9%	4,6935	469,350
		£533,527

Equivalent yield approach. The ARY of 8% has been revised by 1% to reflect the fixed nature of the rent for the next 10 years. A rational or real value approach should be used as a check.

B   Freeholder's Proposed Interest

| Rent to be reserved | $£x$ | |
| YP 5 years @ 8% | 3.9927 | $3.9927x$ |

Reversion to	$£100,000$	
YP perp. def'd 5 years @ 8%	8.5073	850,730
		$£850,730 + 3.9927x$

Let:

Value of Present Interest	=	Value of Proposed Interest
$£533,527$	=	$£850,730 + 3.9927x$
$£533,527 - 850,730$	=	$3.9927x$
$-317,203$	=	$3.9927x$
$-317,203/3.9927$	=	x
$-£79,445$	=	x

This transaction is sufficiently beneficial for the freeholder to be able to pay $£79,445$ a year to the tenant for the next 5 years.

C   Tenant's Present Interest

Open Market Rental Value	$£100,000$
Rent Payable	10,000
Profit rent	$£90,000$
YP 10 years @ 10%/3% tax 40p	4.0752
	$£366,768$

D   Tenant's Proposed Interest

Open Market Rental Value	$£100,000$
Rent to be reserved	x
Profit rent	$£100,000 - x$
YP 5 years @10%/3% tax 40p	2.4159
	$£241,590 - 2.4159x$

Let:

Value of Present Interest	=	Value of Proposed Interest
$£366,768$	=	$£241,590 - 2.4159x$
$£366,768 - £241,590$	=	$2.4159x$
$£125,178/2.4159$	=	x
$£51,814$	=	x

This suggests, because of the dual rate approach, that the tenant would be willing to pay $£51,814$ (say $£52,000$). On these terms a deal would be negotiated and both parties would be financially better off.

(b) A Freeholder's Present Interest as in (a) = $£533,527$.

B   Freeholder's Proposed Interest

Open Market Rental Value	$£100,000$	
YP perp. @ 8%	12.5	$£1.250,000$
Less reverse premium to tenant		x
		$£1,250,000 - x$

| Present Interest | = | Proposed Interest |
| $£533,527$ | = | $£1,250,000 - x$ |

$$x \quad = \quad £1,250,000-£533,527$$
$$x \quad = \quad £716,473$$

C   Tenant's Present Interest as in (a)   =   £366,768

D   Tenant's Proposed Interest

Open Market Rental Value   £100,000
Rent to be paid   £100,000
Profit rent   £0

Tenant's Proposed Interest = £0

Here the tenant needs £366,768 and the freeholder will pay up to £716,473 to secure the surrender; hence a negotiated settlement will be achieved.

These calculations illustrate how important it is to assess the strengths and weaknesses of both parties before commencing negotiations. It also illustrates how the use of a dual rate year's purchase places a different 'value' on what is essentially the same monetary gain or loss.

This problem could be reset as a marriage value exercise. The freehold value in possession is £1,250,000, whilst the freehold subject to the lease is £533,527 and the leasehold is £366,768. The combined value is £900,295 and hence a marriage or merger value of £349,705 exists (£1,250,000 - £900,295).

Q   **Non Standard Rent Review**

The formula approach as set out on page 103 produces a multiplier k to correct the known rent to the unknown rent thus:

$$k \quad = \quad \frac{(1+r)^n - (1+g)^n}{(1+r)^n - 1} \quad \times \quad \frac{(1+r)^t - 1}{(1+r)^t - (1+g)^t}$$

and
$$k \quad = \quad \text{multiplier}$$
$$r \quad = \quad \text{equated yield of } 10\% = 0.10$$
$$n \quad = \quad \text{number of years to review in subject lease} = 3$$
$$g \quad = \quad \text{annual rental growth} = 0.05$$
(this might have to be calculated using the implied growth rate formula)
$$t \quad = \quad \text{number of years to review normally agreed} = 5$$

hence substituting:

$$\frac{(1+0.10)^3 - (1+0.05)^3}{(1+0.10)^3 - 1} \qquad \times \qquad \frac{(1+0.10)^5 - 1}{(1+0.10)^5 - (1+0.05)^5}$$

$$\frac{1.331 - 1.1576}{1.331 - 1} \qquad \times \qquad \frac{1.6105 - 1}{1.6105 - 1.2763}$$

$$\frac{0.1734}{0.331} \qquad \times \qquad \frac{0.6105}{0.3342}$$

$$0.5238 \times 1.8267$$

$$0.9568$$

Therefore:

$$£25,000 \times 0.9568 = £23,920$$

A landlord in a 5% a year rising market will be willing to accept either £23,920, with rent reviews every 3 years, or £25,000 when rent reviews are less frequent at 5-year intervals. In theory the position is reversed in a falling market with landlords willing to accept less rent for the security of a longer term, but theory here is distorted by upward-only rent review clauses.

Chapter 10

(a)   Full rental value of the building as improved:

4th floor	$250m^2 \times 200$	=	£50,000
Ground, 1st, 2nd, 3rd floors	$4 \times 400m^2 \times 200$	=	£320,000
			£370,000

S.34 market rent disregarding improvements:

1st, 2nd, 3rd floors	$3 \times 400m^2 \times 150$	=	£180,000
Ground	$400m^2 \times 200$	=	£80,000
			£260,000

Probable S.34 rent in 3 years on current values: £260,000

(b)   The freehold interest:

Law of Property Act 1969 - 21-year rule will apply:

Landlord's present interest:

Current net income	£150,000	
YP 3 years @ 7%	2.6243	£393,645

Reversion to S.34 rent	£260,000	
YP 14 yrs @ 7% 8.7455		
PV £1 in 3 yrs @ 7% 0.81630	7.1389	£1,856,127

Reversion to ERV	£370,000	
YP perp. def'd 17 yrs @ 7%	4.5225	£1,673,325
		£3,923,097

(The courts might allow a review after 11 years to ERV but has been taken here for 14 years with the assumption of reviews after 5 and 10 years only. ARY reflects market growth expectations in rents and the probability that rent review covenants will protect the tenant with S.34 and LPA 21-year rule disregards.)

Tenant's present interest:

ERV	£370,000	
Rent reserved	£150,000	
Profit rent	£220,000	
YP 3 years @ 8%/3% 40p	1.6149	£355,278

Reversion	£370,000	
Rent reserved (S.34)	£260,000	
Profit rent	£110,000	
YP 14 year @ 8%/3% 40p 7.2188		
PV £1 in 3 yrs @ 8% 0.79383	5.7305	£630,355
		£985,633

(Variable profit rent needs to be checked with more accurate method.)

If the tenant acquires the freehold, the interests would be merged and would be worth:

<table>
<tr><td>YP perp. @ 7%</td><td>£370,000
4.2857
£5,285,709</td></tr>
</table>

A freeholder recognising the marriage value will ask for a sum in excess of the open market value of £3,923,000.

(c)   Surrender for new 20-year lease with rent review after 5 years to ERV.

Note: Surrender implies the releasing of all contractual and statutory rights by the tenant. The tenant must therefore account for the fact that in 5 years the rent will be the open-market rental value of the property as demised at the commencement of the new 20-year lease.

Landlord's present interest as (b) £3,923,097

Landlord's proposed interest
Let proposed rent for 1st 5 years = $£x$
then $£x$
YP 5 years @ 7%   4.1002 $£4.1002x$

Reversion to ERV   £370,000
YP perp def'd 5 years @ 7%   10.1855   £3,768,635
                                           $£3,768,635 + £4.1002x$

present = proposed

$£3,923,097$ = $£3,768,635 + £4.1002x$
$£154,462$ = $4.1002x$
$£37,671$ = x

Tenant's view:
Tenant's present interest: £985,633

Tenant's proposed interest
ERV   £370,0000
Rent reserved $£x$ x
Profit rent $£370,000 - x$
YP 5 years @ 8%/3% 40p   2.5386
                                  $£939,282 - £2.5386x$

$£985,633$ = $£939,282 - 2.5386x$
$2.5386x$ = $£939,282 - £985,633$
$2.5386x$ = $-£46,351$
x = $-£18,258$

When this occurs in examinations, candidates assume that they have miscalculated. This is not the case; the negative rent is correct. Here a tenant is surrendering very valuable profit rents to be enjoyed over a total of 17 years from today for a new 20-year lease with a profit rent for 5 years. This cannot be achieved unless from the tenant's point of view the landlord pays a reverse rent. Even so the extremes of -£18,258 and +£37,671 are likely to defeat the negotiators. A solution would be for the parties to agree that the rent on review after 5 years will exclude the £110,000 p.a. of tenant's improvements. This emphasises the essential differences between landlords' and tenants' rights under the 1954 Act and the specific provisions of a rent review clause. The two must not be confused.

(d)   Repossession can only be obtained on the following grounds:

     (i)   breach of repairing obligation;
     (ii)   persistent delay or failure to pay rent;
     (iii)   other substantial breaches of covenants;

(iv)   availability of suitable alternative accommodation;
(v)   uneconomic sub-letting;
(vi)   demolition or substantial reconstruction;
(vii)   required by owner for his own occupation (5-year rule).

The amount of compensation will vary depending upon grounds, but the maximum would be:

Loss of security under 1954 Act as specified in the 1990 order is 1 or in the case of 14-year occupation it becomes 2, which on £350,000 is £700,000. Plus Compensation for Improvements (1927) being the lesser of:

(i)   Net addition to value
(ii)   Reasonable cost of carrying out the improvements at the termination of the tenancy

(i)   Net addition to value

Rental value improved	£ 370,000
Unimproved	£ 260,000
	£ 110,000
YP perp. @ 7%	14.2857
	£1,571,427

(ii)

Cost 7 years ago	£300,000
Increase in costs at say 10% per annum x amount £1 for 7 years @ 10%	1.9487
	£584,610

Hence maximum compensation might be £700,000 + £584,610.

Chapter 11

GDV
5,000m² (gross) x 85% = 4,250m² net

4,250 @ £200m² p.a.	£850,000	
YP perp. @ 7%	14.29	£12,146,500
Less purchaser's costs and stamp duty @ 2.75%		£325,089
		£11,821.411

Less costs

(a) Building 5,000m² @ £400m²	£2,000,000	
(b) Fees @ 12.5%	£250,000	
Total	£2,250,000	
(c) Finance 14% for 1 year on 50% of total	£157,500	
(d) Legal fees (1%) and agent's (1%) on sale and promotion	£276,428	
(e) Profit @ 15% GDV	£1,773,211	£4,457,139
Total NDV		£7,364,271

Let site value = £x

Fees on acquisition + stamp duty	= 2.5% = 0.025x
Total debt after 1 year @ 15%	= 1.025x x (1.15)
£7,364.271	= 1.1787x
£6,247.525	= x

Site value = £6,247.525, say £6,250,000.

This short solution would form the basis for an initial assessment but would need to be checked using a cash flow approach. Kel and Circle software are recommended.

Chapter 13

(a)   IRR = Internal Rate of Return; that is, the discount rate that makes the Net Present Value of a project equal to zero.

(b)   The IRR of an investment before allowing for the incidence of taxation.

(c)   The IRR of a property investment after adjustment for acquisition costs, outgoings but not taxation taking account of current income and reversionary incomes expressed in current value terms.

(d)   The IRR of a property investment after adjustment for acquisition costs, outgoings but not taxation taking account of current income and reversionary incomes expressed in future value terms.

(a)   £1m plus, say, 4% = £1,040,000

(b)   5.77% $\dfrac{60,000}{1,040,000}$ x 100

(c)   10.58% $\dfrac{110,000}{1,040,000}$ x 100

(d)   Trial and error try 9.5%
       Term rent   £60,000
       YP 4 years @ 9.5%   3.2045   £192,270

Reversion to   £110,000
YP perp. def'd 4 years @ 9.5%   7.32183   £805,401
                                                              £997,671

Allowing for negotiations on sale price, say 9.5%; that is, an equivalent yield of 9.5% (9.15% on £1,040,000).

(e) Rental growth @ 5%
       Therefore rent on review =   £110,000
       x Amount of £1 for 4 years @ 5%   1.2155
                                            £133,705

       Value in 4 years' time @ 9.5% =   £133,705
                                             10.5263
                                          £1,407,421

Therefore possible cash flow adjusted for growth

       0 - £1,040,000
       1   +   £60,000
       2   +   £60,000
       3   +   £60,000
       4   +   £60,000
                         +   £1,407,421

IRR by calculator = 13.048%. This yield might be called an equated yield.

(f)   Requirement is an IRR or Target rate of 12%

Outlay   =   £1,040,000
Income   =   £60,000
                               £60,000
                               £60,000
                               £60,000 + £CV

Term rent   £60,000
YP 4 years @ 12%   3.0373
                              £182,238

Reversion x
YP perp. at 9.5%
x PV £1 in 4 years @ 12%   6.6896

                              £182,238 + 6.6896x

BUT   £182.238 + 6.6896x - £1,040,000 = NPV = 0
Therefore 6.6896x =   £1,040.000 - £182,238
           x =   £128,223.21

The rent in Year 4 must have risen to £128,223.
Note: For purists the sale disposal costs should be accounted for and Capital Gains Tax if purchased by a taxpayer.

(i)   £18.223
(ii) £110,000 x Amount of £1 for 4 years @ 1%   = £128,223
                     Amount of £1 for 4 years @1%   = £128,223 ÷ 110,000
                                                    = 1.1656
            (1.1656 - 1) x 100   = 16.56% over 4 years
            AND where $(1 + i)^4$ = 1.1656
            i = $(^4\sqrt{1.1656}) - 1$
                                                    = 1.0390 - 1
                                                    = 0.390 x 100
                                                    = 3.9%

Further reading

Part One Valuation mathematics

Baum, A.E. (1977) 'Discounted cash flow: the internal rate of return and the cost of borrowing', *Estates Gazette*, no.244, p.28.

Bowcock, P. (1977) 'High speed NPV', *Estates Gazette*, no.242, p.443.

Bowcock, P. (1977) 'High speed IRR', *Estates Gazette*, no.243, p.739.

Bowcock, P. (1978) 'High speed quarterly in advance', *Estates Gazette*, no.245, p.551.

Bowcock, P. (1978) *Property Valuation Tables*, London: Macmillan.

Brown, G.R. (1977) 'NPV/IR: Some qualifying comments on mutual exclusivity', *Estates Gazette*, no.244, p.533.

Compounding and Discounting Tables for Project Evaluation, World Bank, (1973) London.

Davidson, A.W. (compiler), *Parry's Valuation and Conversion Tables*, London: Estates Gazette.

Rose, J.J. (1977) *Rose's Property Valuation Tables*, Oxford: The Freeland Press.

Part Two The income approach

Baum, A. and Crosby, N. (1995) *Property Investment Appraisal*, 2nd edn, London: Routledge.

Byrne, P.J. and Mackmin, D.H. (1975) 'The investment method: an objective approach', *Estates Gazette*, no.234, p.29.

Enever, N. (1981) 'The valuation of property investments', 2nd edn, London, *Estates Gazette*.

Fraser, W.D. (1984) *Principles of Property Investment and Pricing*, London: Macmillan and 2nd edn, (1993).

Isaac, D. and Steley, T. (1991) *Property Valuation Techniques*, 2nd edn, Basingstoke and London: Macmillan Education.

Mackmin, D.H. (1975) 'Valuations or guesstimates?' *Estates Gazette*, no.233, p.663.

Mackmin, D.H. (1977) 'The appraisal process', *Estates Gazette*, no.244, p.123.

Trott, A. (1980) *Property Valuation Methods: Interim Report*, London Polytechnic of the South Bank, R.I.C.S.

Chapter 6 Freeholds

Baum, A. (1984) 'The valuation of reversionary freeholds: a review', *Journal of Valuation*, no.3, pp.157-67, pp.230-47.

Baum, A. (1984) 'The all risks yield: exposing the implicit', *Journal of Valuation*, no.2, pp.229-237.

Baum, A. and Crosby, N. (1995) *Property Investment Appraisal*, 2nd edn, London: Routledge.

Baum, A. and MacGregor, B. (1992) 'The initial yield revealed: explicit valuations and the future of property investment', *Journal of Property Valuation and Investment*, no.10, pp.709-726.

Bornand, D. (1985) 'Conveyancing of commercial property investments', *Solicitors Journal*, August 9 and 16.

Bowcock, P. (1983) 'The valuation of varying incomes', *Journal of Valuation* no.1, pp.366-371, pp.372-376.

Crosby, N. (1982) 'The investment method of valuation: a real value approach', Ryde Memorial prizewinning paper, R.I.C.S. (unpublished).

Crosby, N. (1983) 'The investment method of valuation: a real value approach', *Journal of Valuation* no.1, pp.341-50, no.2, pp.48-59.

Crosby, N. (1984) 'Investment valuation techniques: the shape of things to come?' *The Valuer* no.53/7, pp.196-197.

Crosby, N. (1985) 'The application of equated yield and real value approaches to the market valuation of commercial property investments', unpublished PhD thesis, University of Reading.

Crosby, N. (1986) 'The application of equated yield and real value approaches to market valuation', *Journal of Valuation* no.4, pp.158-69, pp.261-74.

Crosby, N. (1987) *A Critical Examination of the Rational Model*, Reading Department of Land Management and Development, University of Reading.

Crosby, N. (1991) 'The practice of property investment appraisal: reversionary freeholds in the UK', *Journal of Property Valuation and Investment* no.9, pp.109-122.

Crosby, N. (1992) 'Over-rented freehold investment property valuations', *Journal of Property Valuation and Investment* no.10, pp.517-524.

Crosby, N and Goodchild, R. (1992) 'Reversionary freeholds: problems with over-renting' *Journal of Property Valuation and Investment* no.11, pp.67-81.

Greaves, M.J. (1972) 'Discounted cash flow techniques and current methods of income valuation', *Estates Gazette* no.223, pp.2147 and 2339.

Greaves, M.J. (1985) 'The valuation of reversionary freeholds: a reply', *Journal of Valuation* no.3, pp.248-252.

Greenwell, W. & Co. (1976) 'A call for new valuation methods', *Estates Gazette* no.238, p.481.

Harker, N. (1983) 'The valuation of varying incomes: 1', *Journal of Valuation* no.1, pp.363-365.

Jones, I.G. (1983) 'Equivalent yield analysis', *Journal of Valuation* no.1, pp.246-252.

Mackmin, D.H. (1995) 'DCF discounted: further implications for the valuation surveyor arising from the over-rented property debate.' *Journal of Property Valuation and Investment* no.13, pp.5-16.

Marshall, P. (1976) 'Equated yield analysis: a valuation method of the future?', *Estates Gazette* no.239, pp.493.

Marshall, P. (1979) *Donaldsons Investment Tables*, 2nd edn, London, Donaldsons.

Sykes, S.G. (1981) 'Property valuation: a rational model', *The Investment Analyst* no.61, pp.20-26.

Sykes, S.G. and McIntosh, A.P.J. (1982) 'Towards a standard property income valuation model: rationalisation or stagnation', *Journal of Valuation* no.1, pp.117-135.

White, P. (1977) 'The two faces of Janus', *Occasional Paper in Estate Management* no.9, Reading, College of Estate Management.

Wood, E. (1972) 'Property investment - a real value approach', unpublished Ph.D. thesis, University of Reading.

Wood, E. (1973) 'Positive Valuations: a real value approach to property investment', *Estates Gazette* no.226, pp.923-5, 115-117, 1311-13.

Chapter 7 Leaseholds

Baum, A. (1982) 'The enigma of the short leasehold', *Journal of Valuation* no.1, pp.5-9.

Baum, A. and Butler, D. (1986) 'The valuation of short leasehold investments', *Journal of Valuation* no.4, pp.342-353.

Baum, A. and Crosby, N. (1995) *Property Investment Appraisal*, 2nd edn, London: Routledge.

Baum, A. and Yu, S.M. (1985) 'The valuation of leaseholds: a review', *Journal of Valuation* no.3, pp.157-167, 230-257.

Bowcock, P. (1995) 'The valuation of varying incomes', *Journal of Valuation* no.1, p.4.

Colam, M. (1983) 'The single rate valuation of leaseholds', *Journal of Valuation* no.2, pp.14-18.

Davidson, A.W. (1968) 'The deferment of terminable incomes', *Chartered Surveyor*, July.

Fraser, W.D. (1977) 'The valuation and analysis of leasehold investments in times of inflation', *Estates Gazette* no.244, pp.197.

Greaves, M.J. (1969) 'The valuation of varying profit rents', *Chartered Surveyor*, March.

Harker, N., Nanthakumaran, N. and Rogers, S. (1988) 'Double sinking fund correction methods', University of Aberdeen discussion paper.

McIntosh, A.P.J. (1983) 'Valuing leasehold interests', *Estates Gazette* no.265, pp.939-41.

McIntosh, A.P.J. (1983) 'The rational approach to reversionary leasehold property investment valuations', in *Land Management: New Directions* (Chiddick, D. and Millington, A. eds), London, Spon.

Mackmin, D.H. (1975) 'Dual rate for leaseholds?' *Estates Gazette* no.234, p.663.

Mackmin, D.H. (1976) 'The analysis of leasehold transactions', *Valuer* 48(9), p287.

Mackmin, D.H. (1978) 'A matter of amortisation', *Estates Gazette* No.245, p.289.

Mackmin, D.H. (1991) 'The negative leasehold', *Journal of Property Valuation and Investment* no.13 pp 53-70.

'Mainly for Students' (1968) *Estates Gazette* no.206, p.1166.

Trott, A (1980) *Property Valuation Methods: Interim Report*, Polytechnic of the South Bank, R.I.C.S.

Wood, E. (1974), 'Valuations in an inflationary economy', *Estatesman*, January.

Chapter 8 Taxation and valuation

Baum, A. (1985) 'Premiums on acquiring leases', *Rent Review and Lease Renewal* no.5, pp212-222.

Baum, A. and Butler, D. (1986) 'The valuation of short leasehold investments', *Journal of Valuation* no.4, pp.342-353.

Bowcock, P. (1977) 'Capital gains: the tax equation', *Estates Gazette* pp.241:823.

Davidson, A.W. (1973) 'Valuation and taxation: a question of convention', *Valuer*, January/February.

Greaves, M.J. (1967) 'The effects of taxation on the investment method of valuation -capital gains tax', *Estates Gazette* no.203, p.603.

Johnson, T.A. (1967) 'Valuation allowance for capital gains tax', *Estates Gazette* no.201, p.871.

Macleary, A. (1988) 'Irregularities in the capital taxation of "short" leaseholds', *Journal of Valuation* no.6, p.4.

Rose, J.J. (1967) 'Reversionary valuation allowing for capital gains tax', *Estates Gazette* no.202, p.873.

Chapter 9 Landlord and tenant valuations

Baum, A.E. (1980) 'Rent reviews: full rental value', *Estates Gazette* no.254, p.717.

Bowcock, P. (1973) 'Lease rents and the hypothetical tenancy', *Estates Gazette* no.227, p.1271.

Clarke, P.H. (1980) 'Rent Reviews: A Framework for Valuers', JPEL.

Crosby, N. and Murdoch, S. (1991-92), 'The legal and valuation implications of abnormal rent review patterns', *Rent Review and Lease Renewal* no.11, pp.130-146.

Crosby, N., Baum, A. and Murdoch, S. (1993), *Commercial Property Leases*, Reading: Centre for European Property Research, University of Reading.

Mackmin, D.H. (1975) 'Valuation commentary', *Rating and Valuation Reporter*, June.

Nicholls, A.D. (1975) 'Valuation Commentary', *Rating and Valuation Reporter*, March.

Rose, J.J. (1979) *Tables of the Constant Rent*, Oxford: The Freeland Press.

Rose, J.J. (1979) 'Inflation-proof rents', *Estates Gazette* no.249, p.531.

Ward, C. (1980) 'Negotiation of Rents', *Estates Gazette* no.255, p.769.

Chapter 10 The effects of legislation

Baum, A. and Sams, G. (1991) *Statutory Valuation*, 2nd edn, London: Routledge.

Mackmin, D.H. (1994) *Valuation and Sale of Residential Property*, London: Routledge.

Chapter 13 Investment Analysis

Baum, A. and Crosby, N. (1988), *Property Investment Appraisal*, 1st edn, London: Routledge; and 2nd edn (1995).

Brown, G.R. (1991) *Property Investment and the Capital Markets*, London: E. and F.N. Spon.

Byrne, P.J. and Mackmin, D.H. (1975) 'The investment method: an objective approach', *Estates Gazette* no.234, p.29.

Dubbin, N. and Sayce, S. (1991) *Property Portfolio Management*, London: Routledge.

Venmore-Rowland, P. and Lizieri, C. (1992) 'Valuation accuracy: a contribution to the debate', *Journal of Property Research* no.8, pp.115-122.

General

Britton, W., Davies, K. and Johnson, T. (1989) *Modern Methods of Valuation*, 8th edn, London: Estates Gazette.

Darlow, C. (ed) (1983) *Valuation and Investment Appraisal*, London: Estates Gazette.

Enever, N. (1995) *The Valuation of Property Investments*, 5th edn, London: Estates Gazette.

Merrett, A.J. and Sykes, A. (1973) *Capital Budgeting and Company Finance*, London: Longmans.

Millington, A.F. (1994) *An Introduction to Property Valuation*, 4th edn, London: Estates Gazette.

RICS (1995), *Appraisal and Valuation Manual*, London, The Royal Institution of Chartered Surveyors.

Rees, W. (editor) (1984) *Valuation: Principles into Practice*, 2nd edn, London: Estates Gazette.

Richmond, D. (1985) *Introduction to Valuation*, 2nd edn, London: Macmillan.

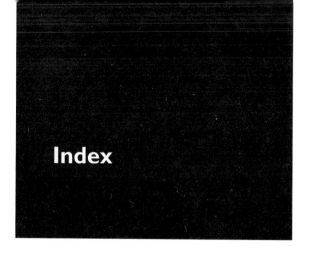

Index